PARDON US, MR. PRESIDENT!

Other books by Arthur Power Dudden

Woodrow Wilson and the World of Today (editor)
Understanding the American Republic
The Assault of Laughter
*The United States of America: a Syllabus
of American Studies*
Joseph Fels and the Single-tax Movement

Artemus Ward

Pardon Us, Mr. President!

American Humor on Politics

Edited and Introduced by

Arthur Power Dudden

South Brunswick and New York:
A. S. Barnes and Company
London: Thomas Yoseloff Ltd

A. S. Barnes and Co., Inc.
Cranbury, New Jersey 08512

Thomas Yoseloff Ltd
108 New Bond Street
London W1Y OQX, England

Library of Congress Cataloging in Publication Data

Main entry under title:
Pardon us, Mr. President!

   Revision and expansion of an earlier work published in 1962
under title: The assault of laughter.
   1.   United States—Politics and government—Anecdotes, face-
tiae, satire, etc. 2.   American wit and humor. I.   Dudden,
Arthur Power, 1921–
PN6231.P6D8   1975   817'.5'408031   74–3614
ISBN 0–498–01566–1

PRINTED IN THE UNITED STATES OF AMERICA

For my Father, who liked to laugh . . .
and my Mother, who liked to hear him.

CONTENTS

EDITOR'S NOTE TO THE READER

This book runs backward instead of forward in time and organization. Its contents are arranged in retrograde sections from the present post-Watergate epoch to George Washington, from the third quarter of the twentieth century all the way back to the middle of the eighteenth. This reversal of normal anthologies is based on the simple premise that most readers prefer topical humor about recent events with which they enjoy some familiarity. Readers will find Watergate and its aftermath at the beginning of the book, while the more historically minded and informed will hopefully not object to plowing backward into the past toward the book's end.

The reason that most people prefer recent political humor to the older outpourings is self-evident. Political humor diminishes itself with each ticking of the clock. Subtleties of merriment and malice evaporate quickly, as the audiences for whom they were intended lose their grasp on essential points of fact and then themselves sooner or later fade from the scene. Most people can relish only the least time-defined elements of humor from bygone days. Footnotes or other scholarly appendages provided by well-intentioned experts in history or literature to make the essential connections and derive inferences usually make matters worse instead of better, in that they tend to destroy the last ingredients of laughter by their seriousness.

My rule of thumb has been to follow the original texts

as closely as possible in editing the selections in this book, and to retain idiosyncrasies of spelling and grammar and punctuation. Some slight modifications have been made for clarity to support my own eccentric conviction that an important function of anthologists is to eradicate obvious typographical errors, not to perpetuate them.

A. P. D.

ACKNOWLEDGMENTS

For permissions to reprint selections from published works protected by copyright, I am indebted to the following. Selections from *The Collected Writings of Ambrose Bierce* reprinted by permission of The Citadel Press. "The Supreme Court's Decisions" and "Discusses Party Politics" from *Mr. Dooley's Opinions* by Finley Peter Dunne, copyright 1900, 1901 by Robert Howard Russell, reprinted by permission of Harper & Brothers. "The Vice-President," "Senatorial Courtesy," and "The Candidate" from *Dissertations by Mr. Dooley* by Finley Peter Dunne, copyright 1906 by Harper & Brothers, reprinted by permission. "Drink and Politics," from *Mr. Dooley on Making a Will and Other Evils* by F. P. Dunne, is reprinted with the permission of Charles Scribner's Sons, copyright 1919 Charles Scribner's Sons, renewal copyright 1947 David Leonard Dunne and Finley Peter Dunne.

The selections by H. L. Mencken are included with the permission of Mr. Charles H. Dorsey, Jr., managing editor of the Baltimore *Sun*. Excerpts from "The Democrats of 1924" and "On Prohibition," from "On Politics" in *First and Last* by Ring Lardner, are reprinted with the permission of Charles Scribner's Sons, copyright 1934 Charles Scribner's Sons. The Margot Johnson Agency has obtained permission from Mr. Donald Day and the Rogers Company for my inclusion of selections from *The Autobiography of Will Rogers*, copyright 1949 and published by

Houghton Mifflin Co., and from *How We Elect Our Presidents,* copyright 1952 and published by Little, Brown & Co.

The selections by Westbrook Pegler are included with the gracious permission of their author; they originally appeared in the New York *World-Telegram* and the Chicago *Tribune,* and were carried as syndicated columns by other newspapers; later certain of these selections appeared in *'T Ain't Right,* Doubleday, Doran & Co., 1936, and others in *The Dissenting Opinions of Mister Westbrook Pegler,* Charles Scribner's Sons, 1938. Oliver Jensen has kindly permitted use of "And Now for a Few Closing Remarks by President Eisenhower," which first appeared over his name in the Virginia City (Nevada) *Territorial Enterprise.* Art Buchwald generously granted permission for use of the pieces included herein. The four poems by Marya Mannes which appeared originally in *The Reporter* are reprinted by permission, copyright 1952 by The Fortnightly Publishing Company, Inc., copyright 1960 and 1961 by The Reporter Magazine Company.

Charles Levy graciously granted permission for the use of his article, which originally appeared in *Monocle.* "Confessions of an Ex-Anti-Communist" is reprinted by permission of Marvin Kitman, copyright 1962 by Monocle Periodicals, Inc. John Crosby generously permitted the inclusion of his column, which first appeared in the New York *Herald Tribune.* Langston Hughes, "Radioactive Red Caps," is reprinted by permission of Farrar, Straus & Giroux, Inc. and Harold Ober Associates, copyright © 1957 by Langston Hughes. "Little Cindy Ella" is reprinted by the very kind permission of "Moms" Mabley, and appeared previously in *The Book of Negro Humor,* edited by Langston Hughes and published by Dodd, Mead 1966. Barbara Garson granted permission for the inclusion of selections from *MacBird!,* Grove Press copyright 1967 by Barbara Garson, and "MacDick?", copyright 1973 by *The Village Voice*. "Let's Look at the Record" by W. C. Fields is reprinted by permission of Dodd, Mead & Company, Inc. from *Fields for President* by W. C. Fields, with an introduction and commentary by Michael M. Taylor. Copyright 1939, 1940 by Dodd, Mead & Company, Inc. Copyright renewed 1967, 1968 by W. Claude Fields, Jr. Copyright © 1971 by Michael M. Taylor. The articles by Russell Baker are reprinted by permission, © 1962–1973 by The New York Times Company; "Taxpaying" also appeared in *All Things Considered,* copyright 1965, published by J. B. Lippincott and Co. Philip Roth graciously permitted the inclusion of "The President Addresses the Nation," which appeared in *The New York Review of Books,* and "Tricky Holds a Press Conference," from *Our Gang,* Watergate edition, copyright 1973 and published by Random House (Bantam Books). The articles by Donald Kaul, Washington columnist for the Des Moines *Register,* are included by his kind permission. Judith Wax granted permission to reprint "The Pardoner's Tale," copyright 1974, which first appeared in *The New York Times* and was reprinted in *Newsweek.*

For other permissions and various direct quotations, I am indebted to many individuals and organizations: Christopher Morley is quoted from the foreword which he contributed to William Murrell, *A History of American Graphic Humor* (New York: Whitney Museum of American Art, 1933), Vol. I, p. ix. James Thurber is quoted from "State of the Nation's Humor," *The New York Times Magazine,* December 7, 1958, p. 26, and from comments on a television program cited in an editorial in the Philadelphia *Inquirer,* March 25, 1959. Malcolm Muggeridge, "America Needs a PUNCH," *Esquire,* April 1958, pp. 59–61. John Crosby is quoted in the introduction from his syndicated column "Around the Dials," July 6, 1959; Jerry Lewis from "State of the Nation's Humor," *The New York Times Magazine,* December 7, 1958, p. 27. Mort Sahl is quoted from "State of the Nation's Humor," *The New York Times Magazine,* December 7, 1958, pp. 26–27, and from Herbert Mitgang, "Anyway, Onward with Mort Sahl," *The New York Times Magazine,* February 8, 1959, pp. 32, 34, 37.

Other material is quoted from: Walter Blair, *Native American Humor: 1800–1900* (New York: American Book Company, 1937; San Francisco: Chandler, 1960), *passim.* Hennig Cohen, "Pre-Revolutionary Political Verse from the *South Carolina Gazette,*" a paper presented at the South Atlantic Modern Language Association, Miami, November 28, 1952. Bruce Ingham Granger, *Political Satire in the American Revolution, 1763–1783* (Ithaca: Cornell University Press, 1960), pp. vii–viii, 1–28, 239, 303–305, *et passim. Dictionary of American Biography* (American Council of Learned Societies), for material on Davy Crockett, Artemus Ward, Bill Arp, Bill Nye, and Will Rogers. Kenneth S. Lynn, ed., *The Comic Tradition in America: An Anthology* (New York: Doubleday, 1958), pp. 166–168. James Atkins Shackford, *David Crockett: the Man and the Legend* (Chapel Hill: University of North Carolina Press, 1956), pp. 156–164. Carey McWilliams, *Ambrose Bierce: A Biography* (New York: Albert and Charles Boni, 1929), pp. 3–12, 301–317, *et passim.* Vincent Starrett, *Ambrose Bierce: A Bibliography* (Philadelphia: The Centaur Book Shop, 1929), pp. 13–19 *et passim.* Elmer Ellis, *Mr. Dooley's America: A Life of Finley Peter Dunne* (New York: Knopf, 1941), pp. 79, 294, *et passim.* Arthur M. Schlesinger, Jr., *The Crisis of the Old Order* (Boston: Houghton Mifflin, 1957), pp. 148–149. Donald Elder, *Ring Lardner: A Biography* (New York: Doubleday, 1956), pp. 328–334. *Current Biography* (1940), for material on Westbrook Pegler. Will Stanton, "View from the Fence, or How to Tell a Democrat from a Republican," *Ladies Home Journal,* Vol. LXXIX (Nov. 1962), pp. 58–59. The engraving of George Washington from *The American Past,* by Roger Butterfield (New York: Simon and Schuster, 1947), is reprinted by permission of the author. Russell Baker, *The New York Times,* December 30, 1973. Richard Milhous Nixon, *The Presidential Transcripts,* with commentary by the staff of *The Washington Post* (New York: Dell, 1974), pp. xxxi–xxxii, 40, 95, 98, 120, and 346.

THE REBIRTH OF
AMERICAN POLITICAL HUMOR

The fate of Richard Milhous Nixon will be to dwell in Watergate forever, notwithstanding his pardon by President Ford. Yet Nixon never lived in Watergate himself, preferring the White House while in Washington.

The Watergate complex of apartment houses and enterprises on the Potomac, where rich and powerful Washingtonians dwell in splendid isolation, became the all-purpose symbol of President Nixon's vendetta against the American political process following revelations of the activities of spies and saboteurs operating in his behalf against the Democrats in 1972, which included burglarizing and wiretapping their national headquarters in the Watergate. An unprecedented eruption of political humor poured out in retaliation. Jokes, satires, parodies, and tall tales abounded, whose target or butt was the Chief Executive. Lapel buttons and bumper stickers delivered their shafts. Even "Nixon's the One," the triumphant slogan employed to reelect him in 1972, was subverted to aim accusing fingers at the falling hero. Not since the New Deal of Franklin Delano Roosevelt had so much witty malice and vulgar humor been directed at the White House and its occupants, including heaping doses of profanity and obscenity.

Americans were enjoying or enduring a renaissance of political humor, the "Watergate Watershed" to characterize the epoch. Readers of newspapers consulted Art Buchwald and Russell Baker and Donald Kaul before pundits like Reston or Alsop. Philip Roth provided the scenario for a military dictatorship to be established by the beleaguered President, though the White House staff declared it off limits for being in bad taste, while John Kenneth Galbraith was advising that "we've passed from the age of the common man to the common crook." Commuters regaled each other with epigrams such as "Behind Every Watergate Stands a Milhous," "Impeach With Honor," "Dick Nixon Before He Dicks You," and "National Security über Alles." Bookstores and novelty vendors displayed choice items, among them *The National Watergate Test,* in which one multiple-choice question asks: "Which of the following actions were most effective at disassociating the President from the Watergate conspiracy: a) Executive privilege, b) Constitutional guarantees of separation of powers, c) Hiding under his desk?" *The Watergate Cookbook* introduced its recipes with "Puree of Scoundrel" and "Watergate Vichyssoise," which began "Take a bunch of leaks. . . ." Another book, *The Watergate Follies,* applied impertinent captions to pertinent photographs, one of Queen Elizabeth saying of Nixon, "Yes, he once visited me. He took a spoon." And for smokers with twisted tongue in cheek, there was the nationally advertised *Watergate,* "a Crooked Cigar." Meanwhile, juke-boxes bouncily sang out the recorded misdeeds of presidential aides "Haldeman, Ehrlichman, Mitchell, and Dean."

Historians of the future will discover that the epoch of Watergate was best understood as a comedy, an excrudescence from a troubled nation which revealed what American political humor of that period was all about. With President Nixon's departure from the White House in August 1974, the epoch of Watergate ended except for its repercussions. The Watergate period of political humor ended as well.

What is political humor? It is simply the directing of

wit and satire against politics and politicians, political ideas
and persuasions, political parties and their proponents. With
honor gone, was there anything else to supply what John
Crosby once called "fresh slants on the human race and the
painfully funny business of being alive?"

"The art form in '73 was public comedy," Russell Baker decided, in a year's end retrospective in *The New York Times*
(December 30, 1973). "Nobody had to turn on the telly,
certainly not the radio, to enjoy the fun. It was right there
on Page One. Government after forty years of being melodrama abruptly turned into farce." Opening triumphantly
with Richard M. Nixon's second inauguration amid prospects of peace and prosperity, 1973 proceeded to dive as-
tonishingly downward like the stock market in 1929, at first
affording a convincing imitation of Warren G. Harding's
carelessly corrupt presidency, next staggering ahead from one
humiliation to another, while the energy crisis deepened
and inflation raged out of control, as if to mimic Herbert
Hoover's futile efforts to overcome economic catastrophe.
President Nixon's resignation in favor of Gerald Ford, in
August 1974, supplied the final incredible note. "As the
farce ground on," Baker had added, "the White House
ceased to be the fearsome juggernaut which used to awe us
and became close kin to Laurel and Hardy trying to get
undressed together in an upper Pullman berth with a bass
fiddle."

Not all the comedy was at the top either. Earlier there
was Vice President Spiro T. Agnew, onetime zealot for law
and order, resigning the second highest elected office in
the nation while playing out the cruel satire of incriminating
himself, and being cast out by the Maryland Bar Association as "morally abstruse." What about Congress, to which
Americans turned for help in their shock and chagrin?
"What delicious squalor!" Baker had exclaimed. "What

terror at discovering that we had all learned it was not dead after all, but only almost." People had forgotten how to laugh at politics. But Watergate and Nixon's resignation reminded them that there was precious little else left to do, except to laugh. "We were so ridiculously serious about it all," Baker had recalled. "We looked for melodrama, for significance, instead of laughing, and feeling free, free at last."

Comedy it might have been, yet laughing afforded an uneven response.

Philip Roth, in a new preface to the Watergate Edition (1973) of *Our Gang* (1971), his corrosive satire starring Trick E. Dixon and his friends, publicly apologized to the President for having portrayed him without evidence two years before "as a moral hypocrite, a lawless opportunist, a shameless liar, and a thorough-going totalitarian at heart." One's shock at Roth's savagery illuminates his own contention that "people would be surprised, not only by the imaginative richness but by the ferocity of the political satire that appeared in ordinary daily newspapers throughout the country in the nineteenth century, especially during the decades leading up to and following the Civil War."

While in gentler vein before Watergate, Will Stanton wrote a funny piece for *Ladies' Home Journal* (November 1962) entitled "How to Tell a Democrat from a Republican." The all-too numerous Democrats were offensively vulgar and liberal, while Republicans were rich snobs yet thinner in ranks. For particulars:

> Republicans tend to keep their shades drawn, although there is seldom any reason why they should. Democrats ought to, but don't.
> Republicans study the financial pages of the newspaper. Democrats put them in the bottom of the bird cage.

Democrats buy most of the books that have been banned somewhere. Republicans form censorship committees and read them as a group.

Republicans raise dahlias, Dalmatians, and eyebrows. Democrats raise Airedales, kids, and taxes.

Republican boys date Democratic girls. They plan to marry Republican girls, but feel they're entitled to a little fun first.

Republicans sleep in twin beds—some even in separate rooms. That is why there are more Democrats.

This kind of writing, Baker's, Roth's, Stanton's, and Art Buchwald's—Buchwald, who "never danced at the White House"—and the works of many, many others, is American political humor. It anticipates Watergate by two centuries at least. Thanks to Watergate, it attained its finest hour. Yet a number of critics, a majority possibly, continue to reject outright the notion that subject matter can afford important clues to literary or cultural patterns. There is insufficient realization, as one result, that the subject of politics has always supplied humorists in the United States with a comic organ of the most generous dimensions and hilarious proportions. "There is," in the self-serving words of Petroleum Vesuvius Nasby, "a vacancy in the mind uv the public for jist sich a book ez this, else it had never been published."

A great deal of humor passed over correctly enough by tastemakers as inferior, or spurned as low-level vulgarity by sophisticates preferring high-level comicality, nevertheless embodied the elemental power to bring laughter. It mattered little whether the laughter was cheerful, effervescent, and sympathetic, or skeptical, sardonic, and antagonistic. The American people have grown accustomed to laughing at political behavior, not all of the time, of course, but enough for the sources of their laughter to deposit an impressive written record. This was especially noticeable in the literature of the Republic's formative years. Politics, though vital in that period when independence and democracy were new and love of country was exuberantly youthful, was still sufficiently harmless to afford diversions and targets for merriment.

Humor by politicians themselves ought not to be included, but considered separately. Here is a category peculiar to itself, and comparisons would be odious. Will Rogers resented the label "professional joke maker," applied by a congressman who opposed the insertion of five of Rogers' newspaper articles in the *Congressional Record.* Exploded Rogers: "I am an amateur beside them. If I had that guy's unconscious humor, Ziegfeld couldn't afford to pay me I would be so funny. Of course I can understand what he was objecting to was any common sense creeping into the *Record.*" This restriction will regretfully exclude the efforts of Franklin D. Roosevelt, Adlai E. Stevenson, Jr., and John F. Kennedy, polished quipsters all of them. It will also bar such an achievement as Senator Joe McCarthy's immortal verdict: "That is the most unheard-of thing I ever heard of!"

Leaving out conscious or unconscious humor by politicians ought to offend no one. It will save us, for example, from having to relive the election of 1964 between Lyndon Johnson and Barry Goldwater, when we were repeatedly assured that the candidates were witty men with well-developed senses of humor, which, in retrospect, was the funniest commentary on the campaign. Alvin Shuster, in the Sunday magazine of *The New York Times* (September 13, 1964), characterized L.B.J. as having "forgotten more kneeslappers than most people have heard," but the term "kneeslappers" betrayed all too accurately the level of humor in Lyndon Johnson's well, a reservoir replenished from

vaudeville and county fairs attended by wearers of gal-
luses, sleeve garters, and overalls which wore like a pig's
nose, in fact, from the Congress he served so long. Nor
shall we have to reevaluate the many versions of Goldwater's purported inaugural address, winding up with his
mercifully undelivered stirring appeal to the people to follow him wherever he might lead, "Ten! Nine! Eight! Sev-
en! Six!. . . ."

Instead we can stand happily reminded of the lines
cherished by President Kennedy from *The Ramayana:*

> There are three things which are real,
> God, human folly, and laughter.
> The first two are beyond our comprehension,
> So we must do what we can with the third.

Never should we forget Will Rogers' joyful appraisal of
election season in his beloved Cuckooland. "Come pretty
near having two holidays of equal importance in the same
week," he observed. "Halloween and Election, and of the
two Election provides the most fun. On Halloween they
put pumpkins on their heads, and on Election they don't
have to." Nor that possibly apocryphal occasion when Al
Smith was making a speech, and a heckler cried out: "Tell
them all you know, Al. It won't take long!" Whereupon Al,
without hesitation, retaliated: "I'll tell them all we both
know, and it won't take any longer!"

Observers have delivered opinions at one time or another on the state of the nation's humor. Some attempted to
define its essential qualities, others its directions. Christopher Morley wrote in 1933: "There has always been something *sui generis* in the American comic spirit, though I
don't know that it has ever been recognizably defined. A

touch of brutality perhaps? Anger rather than humor? Various words rise to the mind—*sardonic, extravagant, macabre*—we reject each one, yet the mere fact that it suggests itself points to some essential hardness or sharpness of spirit." James Thurber, indicating Will Rogers as his example, decided that "as a people we have always preferred the gentle to the sharp." Yet Rogers could be as devastating as H. L. Mencken or Ambrose Bierce. "Ohio claims they are due a President," he observed in 1920, "as they haven't had one since Taft. Look at the United States, they haven't had one since Lincoln." Even poet e. e. cummings could write, "Warren Gamaliel Harding/ the only man, woman, or child/ who could make seven grammatical errors/ in a simple declarative sentence." Extravagance? A touch of brutality? Anger rather than humor?

Some light is shed by Malcolm Muggeridge's conviction that "all great humor is in bad taste." The former editor of *Punch* noted in *Esquire* magazine (April 1958) that Cervantes' *Don Quixote* and Shakespeare's Falstaff were insulting to the nobility of their times, that Gogol's *Dead Souls* infuriated the Czar, that Swift's *Gulliver's Travels* and Orwell's *Animal Farm* enjoyed a great deal of popularity because of their apparent application only to faraway places. Humor expresses the grotesque disparity between human aspiration and performance. Jokes about religion, politics, sex, or even death will never cease to amuse. "On a basis of this definition," Muggeridge continued, "it can readily be seen why humor, in its social application, is normally distasteful to those set in authority over us. When the governed laugh, the governors cannot but have an uneasy feeling that they may well be laughing at them. Power, indeed, is inherently ridiculous, and those who traffic in it are rarely, if ever, dowered with much sense of appreciation of humor. Otherwise, they would not become powerful." Further, he added: "By its nature, humor is anarchistic, and implies, when it does not state, criticism of existing institutions, beliefs, and functionaries."

Does Christopher Morley's discovery of American humor's "hardness or sharpness of spirit" establish its high quality by Muggeridge's standards? Or do Thurber's acidulous commentaries on the human species repudiate his own affadavit for the "gentle" traditions of America's humor? Is it evident that the nation's humorists have testified by their works not only to the abundance of the country's self-confident freedom, but also to the enormous disparity between American aspiration and American performance?

A retrospective historical view of American humor, in particular political humor, should help to provide the answers.

Great Britain's New World colonists matured to literary self-consciousness, as well as political independence, during the epoch of the American Revolution, and they poured out their new-found convictions and self-assuredness after 1763 in political satire on both sides of the growing struggle as well as in between. Earlier colonial satire had moved more slowly, as Hennig Cohen showed in his examination of the *South Carolina Gazette,* "from restrained criticism of concepts of government and vague denunciations of public officials to bold expressions in the cause of liberty and praise for the leaders of the opposition to the Crown." Throughout the struggle for American independence, the newspaper and pamphlet press bristled with scurrilous political commentaries, mostly in verse, with some clever attempts at parody, most of it either anonymous or pseudonymous in authorship. The "grand American rebellion," in a contemporary's judgment, was "a legitimate moment for satire," but many years were to pass before Americans would again equal the best of their revolutionary output.

With independence achieved, an uncertain period followed during which new lines of political battle and factional struggle had to define themselves. The young Republic was plagued with financial crises and growing pains, both internal and external, while existing precariously more at war than at peace until 1815 against France, Spain, Britain, and the Indians on the frontiers. The Constitution's First Amendment guaranteeing freedom of utterance vied with the Sedition Act's strictures and penalties against criticism of government officials, while the record of events came to include arrests and convictions, fines and jail terms, for editors, authors, and publishers. Not before 1820, with the triumph of popular sovereignty, did the humorous possibilities of native politics enjoy the opportunity for full literary development, but by 1830 regional styles of political humor were abundant in almanacs, newspapers, and popular melodramas which flourished thereafter. Even so, pseudonyms would be employed almost universally, at first to disguise authorship and then to enrich the effect desired by creating characters to personalize humor.

It all began in an important way with Seba Smith's immortal characterization of Major Jack Downing from Downingville, Away Down East in the State of Maine. Jack was both patriarch and prototype for generations of comic figures. Shrewdly he embodied all the humorous elements of American literature, together with an extraordinary delight in politics. He combined keen perceptiveness with stalwart audacity, a trait recognizable in Brother Jonathan and later in Uncle Sam. At the outset of his long career, Jack realized that Maine's partisan conflicts were in "such a close rub" that it would be difficult, if not dangerous, to anticipate results. Whigs and Democrats, Jack observed, were "acting jest like two boys playin see-saw on a rail. First one goes up, and then 'tother; but I reckon one of the boys is rather heaviest, for once in a while he comes down chuck, and throws the other up into the air as though he would pitch him head over heels." Two decades later Major Jack was flourishing on the national level of the political seesaw as the fictional confidant of Presidents, his ability to penetrate the fog undiminished. When news came of the Whigs' nomination of General Winfield S. Scott, the popular hero and captor of Mexico City, Maine's Democrats suffered "the cold shuggers" at their own prospects for the presidential election of 1852. Downing cleverly persuaded his Uncle Joshua "to take hold and help elect" the unknown Franklin Pierce of New Hampshire as "the hero of Mexico." Jack knew his people from long experience. Within the state of Maine, heroes were made, not born. Said he, confidently: "Downingville is wide awake, and will do her duty in November."

Artemus Ward appeared next. Ward, "the genial showman," was the creation of Charles Farrar Browne, who was plainly and openly indebted to Seba Smith's Jack Downing. Ward was a national figure, his satire unlocalized either in situation or characterization. His outrageous dialect resembled a generic semiliteracy skimmed from the prattle of America's small towns, rather than the speech pattern of any identifiable region—a cross section of rustic communication, not a faithful reproduction. His tricks and travesties of spelling, for example, his numerical renditions of *there4* and *be4,* reflected a tendency then current among humorists to employ comic verbal and typographic devices to sustain an aura of not-so-innocent merriment. In his famous "Interview with President Lincoln," Artemus Ward avowed: "I hav no politics. Nary a one. I'm not in the bizniss. . . . I'm in a far more respectful bizniss nor what pollertics is." Perhaps it was true, as Ward protested, that he was in "a far more respectful bizniss" than politics. Yet the secret of "bizniss" was the same. And showman that he was, Ward knew it well. Once, in a postscript to a letter he wrote heralding his traveling show, he put his cards on the table. "You scratch my back," he offered, "& Ile scratch your back."

Next came David Ross Locke, whose chief stock in trade was irony—caustic and corrosive irony. He marshaled his mocking pen for the Union cause during the Civil War against extremists of all persuasions, then, after Appomattox, directed it against the North's vindictive radicals, who would have beggared the victory to destroy Southern society. His nom de plume, Petroleum Vesuvius Nasby, reflected only too accurately the incendiary tempers of the times. Like Jack Downing before him, Nasby professed intimacy with Presidents. Like Artemus Ward, Nasby skated boldly over the thin ice atop the vicious undercurrents of sectional and racial bitterness. Nasby's politics were moderate, his social philosophy commonplace for his century. Like Ward also, he valued the Union and liberty over abolition, secession, and upheaval. His insights were so incisive that readers were able to gain from them some comprehension of life's impossible complexities, as was evident, for example, from his outwardly sympathetic treatment of the North's peace Democrats, or Copperheads as they were spitefully known. After the Civil War and Reconstruction, Locke's sectionalism and racism lost their appeal. He and his works faded rapidly into obscurity to join the lesser political humorists of his time—Bill Arp, Orpheus C. Kerr, and Bill Nye, while in this same period, Mark Twain's ill-controlled fury at his country's politics expressed his frustration more eloquently than his attempts at evoking laughter.

In Finley Peter Dunne's characterization of Mr. Dooley, the Irish saloonkeeper, the crackerbox tradition of literary humor reached its climax. Appropriately enough, the United States and Mr. Dooley turned the nineteenth century together. Peter Dunne recorded the excitement of the days of Cleveland, McKinley, Bryan, the war with Spain, the first Roosevelt. He wrote in a delightfully musical amalgam of Irish immigrant dialects, which the readers could recognize instantly from the patois of America's city streets. Mr. Dooley's humorous comment on political affairs and his comic accents of speech placed him in direct lineal descent from Downing, Ward, and Nasby. His early pieces for Chicago's newspaper readers were almost as regional, topically speaking, as the first efforts of Seba Smith, the sage of Downingville. Similarly, Mr. Dooley's early observations made more conspicuous use of dialect than did those belonging to his period of nationwide fame. Yet no other literary humorist in American history ever concentrated more on the subject of politics. Even when he essayed into topical problems that were primarily religious, philanthropic, or educational, such as Christian Science, Andrew Carnegie's gospel of wealth, and John Dewey's theories of learning, his viewpoints were political in their implications. Mr. Dooley's greatness still shines. The reader can chuckle today at the confusion in his friend Hennessy's mind, in "The O'Briens Forever," between presidential candidate William Jennings Bryan and William J. O'Brien, a welterweight alderman from Chicago's South Side. The consequence of meaningless oratory is captured for all time in an exchange between the defeated Dorgan and the victorious O'Brien: " 'Well,' says Dorgan, 'I can't understand it,' he says. 'I med as manny as three thousan' speeches,' he says. 'Well,' says Willum J. O'Brien, 'that was my majority,' he says. 'Have a dhrink,' he says." On the level of national affairs, if Mr. Dooley had accomplished nothing else, his fame would endure for his "book review" of Teddy Roosevelt's self-centered account of the Spanish-American War. "If I was him," said Dooley, "I'd call the book 'Alone in Cubia.'" On and on he went, discoursing merrily on candidates and issues, on "Raypublicans," "Dimmycrats," and Populists, on the relationship of marriage and drink to politics, the Supreme Court ("th' supreme coort follows th' iliction returns"), the Vice-Presidency ("it isn't a crime exactly"), and senatorial courtesy. A twinkle gleamed in Mr. Dooley's eyes. Politics was serious business, but never critical. Politics comprised a great game to drive away dull care. "It's a game iv hope, iv jolly-ye'er-neighbor, a confidence game," Mr. Dooley decided. Best of all, the sweet allure of success was always in the air. "If ye don't win fair ye may win foul," said Dooley. "If ye don't win ye may tie an' get the money in th' confusion," he added.

Ambrose Bierce was the first important American political humorist to break away from the tradition of Downing, Ward, and Nasby. His rhetoric expressed the precision and polish of a master lexicographer's luminous vocabulary. His settings and characters were neither regional nor national, but were universal and timeless. They achieved the near-surrealist effects of Jonathan Swift's *Gulliver's Travels*. Bierce represented the second and less popular strain of political humor in the United States. The framework of American political humor was now established. Jack Downing, Artemus Ward, Mr. Dooley, and Will Rogers practiced their comic art in the tradition of homespun, common-sense wisdom, and the shared, gentle laughter of second-guessers, while Ambrose Bierce and later H. L. Mencken and Philip Roth chose the thornier path of blistering iconoclasm. Bierce's revelations of mankind's follies and foibles, his puncturing of conviction and convention, achieve the nihilistic effect of an air raid upon the intellect. A satiric history of the United States can be traced from his definitions alone, which ridiculed all pretensions to progress. Revolution, specifically the American Revolution of 1776? "An abrupt change in the form of misgovernment, . . . the substitution of the rule of an Administration for that of a Ministry, whereby the welfare and happiness of the people were advanced by a full half-inch." Aristocracy? "Government by the best men. (In this sense the word is obsolete; so is that kind of government.)" Senate? "A body of elderly gentlemen charged with high crimes and misdemeanors." Washingtonian? "A Potomac tribesman who exchanged the privilege of governing himself for the advantage of good government. In justice to him it should be said that he did not want to." Many critics acquainted with Bierce's writings resist the proposition that such anarchism affords any serviceable purpose. Others who disagree respect the cleansing properties of ridicule. Why not inscribe alongside those noble words which ordinarily adorn public buildings Bierce's warning that politics affords nothing else than "the conduct of public affairs for private advantage"?

H. L. Mencken was unlike any humorist now at work. He seems almost incredible today. Lexicographer and iconoclast, he closely resembled Ambrose Bierce, whom he admired extravagantly, more than any other American writer before or since. Mencken mocked his fellow citizens with withering scorn. Yet he was rarely content with demolishing their pretensions to sense and sensibility. He tried to clear the soil of his country for new and healthier growths. One example arises from Mencken's review of President Harding's inaugural address, which he regarded with good reason as the worst piece of English literature he had ever encountered. "It reminds me of a string of wet sponges," he wrote. Turning to Harding's applauding listeners, he said that they were precisely the type of crowd Harding had been accustomed to all his life, "to wit, an audience of small town yokels, of low political serfs, or morons scarcely able to understand a word of more than two syllables, and wholly unable to pursue a logical idea for more than two centimeters." Such an audience, according to Mencken, would be wearied and exasperated by continuous thoughts. "What it wants is simply a loud burble of words, a procession of phrases that roar, a series of whoops." Mencken was certain that four more years of the same inanity would follow, unless a miracle intervened. A miracle of a tragic sort did take place. Harding died, and Calvin Coolidge succeeded to the Presidency. Coolidge, in Mencken's opinion, was no more than a political camp follower, "simply a cheap and trashy fellow, deficient in sense and almost devoid of any notion of honor—in brief, a dreadful little cad." Even so, Coolidge's followers admired him as safe. Would it matter if he were elected in 1924 in his own right? Growled Mencken: "The four years of Coolidge will be four years of puerile and putrid politics. The very worst elements in the Republican party, already corrupt beyond redemption, will be in the saddle and full of intelligent self-interest. It will be a debauch of grab. And it will be followed by a revolt that will make the cautious radicalism of Dr. LaFollette appear almost like the gospel of Rotary. Let the friends of safety paste that in their hats. They are trying to put out a fire by squirting gasoline upon it." And again: "Having pussy-footed all his life, it is highly probable that Dr. Coolidge will go on pussy-footing to the end of the chapter." Thereafter Coolidge and Mencken ran true to form, the former fading into the shadows of historical obscurity, the latter impartially harpooning Hoover and Roosevelt in turn to compile an unequaled record for audacity.

Will Rogers was the last of America's great political humorists before the epoch of Watergate. Mencken and even Finley Peter Dunne outlived him, but they reached their peak earlier than Rogers. By the time he died in an airplane crash in the middle of the 1930s, he had become the nation's jester. Rogers possessed uncommon gifts of sagacious wit and gentle satire. He spun out humorously homely observations true to the traditions of crackerbox philosophy. People laughed with him, and through him, at themselves. Both Mencken and Rogers pulled out all their stops against the national travesty of Prohibition. The difference between them reveals itself in the beguiling question asked by Rogers during the presidential campaign of 1920: "Can you imagine anything more cheerful than a party of friends gathered, opening home brew, and listening to a record, 'Voters, if I am elected, I will enforce the law to the letter?' " And on the same alcoholic theme in 1926: "The South is dry and will vote dry. That is everybody sober enough to stagger to the polls will." Rogers was irrepressible in his gibes at the major political parties. They provided him with his meat and potatoes. "You take a Democrat and a Republican and you keep them both out of office," he suggested, "and I bet they will turn out to be good friends and maybe make useful citizens." In 1924 he explained the extraordinary length of the Democratic platform very neatly: "When you straddle a thing it takes a long time to explain it." Ten years later, in a "bedtime story," he spelled out the distinctive features of the major parties. The Republicans of course had become extinct by then, but Rogers recalled them as "a thrifty race" that "controlled most of the money." "Never warlike," he went on about the G.O.P., "—in fact they would step aside and egg the Democrats on till they declared war, then afterwards say, It was you that did it." What about the Democrats? "Their greatest traits were optimism and humor," Rogers declared. "You had to have optimism to join the Democratic Party and you had to have humor to stick with 'em." Will Rogers' theory of American history was that, "while the Republicans are smart enough to make money, the Democrats are smart enough to get in office every two or three times a century and take it away from 'em." He even had an answer for the familiar question, What would Lincoln do if he were here today? Replied Rogers: "Well, in the first place he wouldn't chop any wood, he would trade his ax in on a Ford. Being a Republican he would vote the Democratic ticket. Being in sympathy for the underdog he would be classed as a Radical Progressive. Having a sense of humor he would be called eccentric." Will Rogers chose to be eccentric, dedicating himself to making people laugh, and he never forgot that a comedian could last only until he began taking himself seriously, or, worse, until his audiences did.

For two or three decades after Rogers' death in 1935, systematic wit, satire, and fun-poking at politics were conspicuously lacking. There were Mencken's twilight essays, Westbrook Pegler's mellower moments, a string of astutely sensitive views from American society's dark underside by Langston Hughes through his characterization of Jess B. Simple, Art Buchwald's beginnings, and various scatterings by part-time practitioners. Hardly any writer in the United States was regularly making merry with politics. No humorist as lustrous as Seba Smith, Charles Farrar Browne, David Ross Locke, Ambrose Bierce, Finley Peter Dunne, H. L. Mencken, or Will Rogers, jesters for the populace, came forward to lead the derision against public affairs. Whether the Second World War and the Cold War aftermath were responsible for the decay is unclear even today, but it became commonplace by the middle of the 1950s to decry the dwindling output and declining quality of humor in the United States.

Malcolm Muggeridge and James Thurber placed the blame squarely on the frightful dangers of the atomic age. The ghastly warfare of the twentieth century and the strains of the Cold War had extracted their toll from the people's sense of humor, with the specter of still worse to come. Few persons could laugh even grimly when Mort Sahl admitted he didn't know whether the unidentified aircraft approaching was going to unload a hydrogen bomb or spell out *Pepsi-Cola* in skywriting. "The enemy of humor is fear," Muggeridge wrote. "Fear requires conformism. It draws people together into a herd, whereas laughter separates them as individuals. When people are fearful, they want everyone to be the same, to accept the same values, say the same things, nourish the same hopes, to wear the same clothes, look at the same television, and ride in the same motorcars. In a conformist society, there is no place for the jester. He strikes a discordant note, and therefore must be put down." While Thurber, in noting that we live next door to total destruction, "on the Brink of Was," wrote at the end of 1958 that we were too near the witch-hunting era of Senator Joseph McCarthy to deal comically with politics or any of the shibboleths of "the American way of life." "It is not expected that we will soon recover," Thurber went on, "and contribute to a new and brave world literature of comedy." Political satire, he judged later, in words that brought anguished protests from the dairy industry and threats to investigate him from congressmen, had declined to the point where it reminded him of a drink of milk. "It won't hurt anybody, but who likes it?"

Will Rogers' sudden death in an airplane crash grew

more grievous in retrospect. He embodied the major traditions of American political humor, yet he faced forward at the same time. His mastery of the stage and newspaper syndication were augmented by his triumphs in motion pictures and radio broadcasting. Hopes for his successor concentrated in due course on television, it being asserted that televised scripts could be published, distributed, and preserved as easily as humorous lectures and radio commentaries. But the sharpest wits of the 1950s and 1960s bypassed television altogether or were jettisoned quickly by timid authorities. Others pursued the acidulous examples of Bierce and Mencken to profane or even obscene ends, their talents admired only by off-beat nightclub audiences. They failed to appeal to the majority of persons who needed sugar coatings on their dosages of irony. Vaughn Meader's parodies of the Kennedys as *The First Family* and Barbara Garson's pseudo-Shakespearean account in *MacBird!* of the Kennedy-Johnson struggles for power were stifled abruptly by the grisly succession of assassinations they unwittingly heralded. Mort Sahl with his carping vote for progress, "anyway onward," and Lenny Bruce on Vice President Nixon's sniveling relationship to General Eisenhower enjoyed only restricted audiences and narrow circulation.

Television critic John Crosby stated flatly: "Nobody has a sense of humor any more. Not about themselves anyhow." Both he and comedian Jerry Lewis blamed organized pressure groups, whose tools of the trade were spiteful and threatening letters, plus the timidity of the television and motion picture industries. Mort Sahl's allegation that, "the ultimate taboo is not against racial jokes or off-color jokes but against intellectual content," emphasized their complaints. Sahl's thought was sweetened but slightly by his cheeky query: "Are there any groups I haven't offended?"

Several explanations were offered for these dismal circumstances, in addition to the tensions of the times. Great changes were transforming book and newspaper publishing. Soaring costs plagued the book industry. New and untried authors experienced great difficulty breaking into print. This condition affected all writers, not humorists alone. Other things being equal, humorous writers would have had a fair chance. But other things were not equal. The decline of local individuality in newspapers was significant. Smith, Locke, Dunne, Bierce, and Mencken first appeared and became prominent on the pages of newspapers whose editors (themselves in some cases) had space to fill. Small-town newspapers scarcely have such problems any longer. Wherever they survive, it is by a mixture of local advertising and gossip. Feature articles are supplied by national syndicates. Humor, especially political humor, is absent. Changes in publishing were drying up fresh currents of literary humor just as the decay of burlesque comedy was eliminating the training schools for stage and screen comedians.

The onetime use of dialect brings up another point. Dialects were rural or urban, regional or class, immigrant or native-born, but always ridiculous. Dialect comedy might win sympathy from those who shared its patterns of speech, or admiration for its faithfulness from critics outside. Dialect humor was often merely grotesque, yet effective because it supplied unmistakable targets for laughter. Such humor had virtually disappeared, except in rural tent shows or Yiddish theaters—each area set somewhat apart from the central strands of American life. The waning of dialect comedy afforded a measure of the amalgamation of American speech patterns and the homogenization of society. The spreading sameness of habits and tastes rendered meaningless the idiosyncrasies of the classic stereotypes of the nineteenth century, while equalitarian democracy was making Americans increasingly loath to laugh at the "other" fellows (the shrewd Yankee, the laconic Hillbilly, the easily duped Hayseed, the oily City Slicker, the brash Paddy, the melancholy Jewish Peddler, the haughty Limey, the stupid German or Swede, the bewildered Dago) who were once gleefully manhandled by native wits. There is some resurgence of dialect comedy today, which may reflect the hard-won security achieved by ethnic groups openly proud of their dual identities as Americans and children of the uprooted and enslaved.

There are other frustrating effects of mass standards of living and uniform concepts of virtue, among them a dearth of acceptable subject matter for parody, burlesque, distortion, or ridicule. The jungle of international relations contains a rich potential, but it is seldom penetrated. Any humorist able to cope with Arabs and Jews, Chinese and Russians, Latin Americans, Africans, and Europeans, would untap the world's greatest reservoirs of the ridiculous. Fear of offending friends and foes alike leaves this wealth to be transformed only through the caricatures of cartoonists and propagandists. Americans have been contriving a life for themselves that G. B. Shaw would have viewed askance, a world which imposes taboos on all the greatest possibilities for humor—on sex, on religion, on politics.

Fear and witch-hunting were detrimental to humor, or so it is reasonable to assume. Conformism, the herdlike resistance to any deviation from group unity, had undermined the older foundations of humor. This was not alone the product of the last decade or so. Long before the Cold War and the wars in Korea and Vietnam, the traditional wellsprings of American humor were evaporating. Americans were groping for new and different paths to laughter, but many of the conditions so fruitful for political humor in the past no longer existed. It was useless to wish for their return. Americans venerated their political institutions almost defensively. They expected their leaders to be serious in the face of weighty problems, as Adlai Stevenson learned to his sorrow.

With Watergate, a new dawn of political humor brought forth rays of light. Humorous disbelief radiated in all directions. Mark Russell, Washington's Shoreham Hotel's stand-up comic commentator on public affairs, reportedly said: "I hope that Watergate never ends. If it does, I'll have to go back to writing my own material. Now I just tear it off the news service wires." Parody was back, and little of it, if any, displayed that allegedly essential note of admiration for the events or persons being parodied. Mocking satirical wit gleamed from bumper stickers and lapel buttons. "Impeachment with Honor!" or "Impeach the Cox-sacker!" were the plaintive though brave slogans of masses of ordinary men and women. Tongue-in-cheekier were the stirring cries, "Bail to the Chief!" and the unforgiving "Jail to the Chief!"

There was much more besides.

Hard to beat among the early suggestions for a statue to symbolize the Nixon administration, as passed on to us by Donald Kaul, Washington columnist for the Des Moines *Register,* would be "a treatment of a dove of peace, with a ribbon of tape in its beak, flying through a tax loop hole." Promoting President Nixon to Chairman of the Board, U.S.A., a post with purely ritualistic duties which he was able to perform with grateful zeal, was the solution for the Watergate troubles put forward by Laurence J. Peter, whose hierarchical *Peter Principle* explains why it is that things must always go wrong whenever individuals are elevated above their competence to their levels of incompetence. Art Buchwald proposes to celebrate June 17 as Watergate Day, the anniversary of the break-in: "Americans would memorialize this historic event by taping other people's doors, tapping telephones, spying on their neighbors, using aliases, wearing red wigs and making inoperative statements." In Washington the President would review CIA and FBI bands leading aging veterans of CREEP down Pennsylvania Avenue, and he would lay a wreath at the Watergate complex just under the window of the former headquarters of the Democratic National Committee. Judith Wax, Chicago's Chaucer, afforded us in "The Waterbury Tales" glimpses of that merry crew of buggers and burglars, including the Ehrlichman who looks like "he eats babys for desserte," and the FBI's Patrick Gray who burned the files and sorely sinned, "and dizzy-grow from hangyn slow, slow in the wynd."

Meanwhile in Paris, in April 1974, the newly founded Association for the Promotion of Humor in International Affairs presented its first Noble Award to Art Buchwald. Its booby prize, a repudiated Czarist government bond, went to President Nixon's press secretary Ronald Ziegler for his "unconscious humor" in defending the U.S. Chief Executive, although Libya's leader Colonel Qadhafi nearly stole the honor for his unfailingly maladroit diplomacy.

In truth, that fresh, if hauntingly familiar, sound of our times is laughter at American politics and politicians. It is bipartisan laughter aimed from all sides at targets in all directions. It is a deep and skeptical ridicule without quarter, cynical if you like, deadly in aim, yet healthy in its accuracy. It declaims unequivocally that a President of the United States was both a knave and a fool. It distrusts all the president's men who were his closest advisors and spokesmen on domestic affairs. It knows that he himself and his first Vice-President were unworthy successors to the great men and women of American history if personal integrity is the test. It was delighted by a Los Angeles firm's offering of a wristwatch for sale with Nixon's own plea, "I'm not a crook!" above his face on the dial. "Watch his eyes . . ." the advertisement screamed, "they shift back & forth 60 times a minute."

Ward, Dooley, Bierce, and Mencken would have understood these things, and so do the wits of our times who are leading the renaissance of political humor. Even Mark Twain's "Mysterious Stranger," who derided mankind for neglecting the supreme weapon of laughter against oppressors, might concede that hope emerged for us all from the popular outcry against Watergate and all that it represented and symbolized. We were reminded again that the land of absurdity lies all around us.

A.P.D.

PARDON US, MR. PRESIDENT!

"You have a mongrel perception of humor, nothing more; a multitude of you possess that. This multitude see the comic side of a thousand low-grade and trivial things —broad incongruities, mainly; grotesqueries, absurdities, evokers of the horse-laugh. The ten thousand high-grade comicalities which exist in the world are sealed from their dull vision. Will a day come when the race will detect the funniness of these juvenilities and laugh at them—and by laughing at them destroy them? For your race, in its poverty, has unquestionably one really effective weapon— laughter. Power, money, persuasion, supplication, persecution—these can lift at a colossal humbug—push it a little— weaken it a little, century by century; but only laughter can blow it to rags and atoms at a blast. Against *the assault of laughter* nothing can stand. You are always fussing and fighting with other weapons. Do you ever use that one? No; you leave it lying and rusting. As a race, do you ever use it at all? No; you lack sense and the courage."

MARK TWAIN, *The Mysterious Stranger.*

"Has the art of politics no apparent utility? Does it appear to be unqualifiedly ratty, raffish, sordid, obscene, and low down, and its salient virtuosi a gang of unmitigated scoundrels? Then let us not forget its high capacity to soothe and tickle the midriff, its incomparable services as a maker of entertainment."

H. L. MENCKEN, *A Carnival of Buncombe.*

"In other words, I have to know why you feel that we shouldn't unravel something?"

RICHARD MILHOUS NIXON, *Transcripts.*

Today and Yesterday
The Assault of Laughter

The Assault of Laughter
(1973–1975)

Watergate became a laughing matter for the American people almost as soon as its dark secrets emerged, but it was difficult for them to accept it as the national tragi-comedy it proved to be. "When they subpoenaed the President, that's not comedy," said Ken Barry, a Chicago area comic. "It's like when they killed President Kennedy." But when President Nixon spurned the subpoenas or complied grudgingly, evasively, and only partially, the people's mood grew increasingly uneasy, apprehensive, grim, while their jests directed at the White House and its machinations multiplied in self-defense. As pressures mounted to impeach the President, the country uneasily faced its greatest constitutional crisis since the Civil War. President Nixon's resignation and disgrace left Americans benumbed.

In David Frye's album, "Richard Nixon: a Fantasy," Mr. Frye had imitated the President's voice in a mock address to the nation: "Today I have regretfully been forced to accept the resignations of 1,541 of the finest public servants it has ever been my privilege to know. As the man in charge, I must accept full responsibility, but not the blame. Let me explain the difference. People who are to blame lose their jobs; people who are responsible do not." Off Broadway a show called "National Lampoon Lemmings" included a skit that wound up with a Senator asking a witness: "What did the President know, and when did he stop knowing it?" Bumper stickers emblazoned, "Honk If You Think He's Guilty," intensified the din of traffic everywhere.

For pure comedy, nothing could equal the Presidential transcripts, nor their impact. Released April 30, 1974, the 1,254 pages of edited transcripts from tape recordings of White House conversations revealed that, as Haynes Johnson of *The Washington Post* wrote, the President and his trusted advisers regarded their troubles over Watergate and related matters as primarily a public relations problem, "to be handled by seizing the initiative, by minimizing the public impact, by cutting losses, by bold and vigorous counterattacks."

"You really can't sit and worry about it all the time. The worst may happen, but it may not," had argued President Nixon, September 15, 1972. "So you just try to button it up as well as you can and hope for the best, and remember basically the damn business is unfortunately trying to cut our losses." "What I mean is we need something to answer somebody, answer things, you know they say, 'What are you basing this on,' I can say, 'Well, my counsel has advised me that'—Is that possible or not, or are—," Nixon pleaded over the telephone, March 20, 1973. The next day, March 21st, in a meeting in the Oval Room, Nixon put his finger on the problem: "It is better to fight it out. Then you see that's the other thing. It's better to fight it out and not let people testify, and so forth. And now, on the other hand, we realize that we have these weaknesses,—that we have these weaknesses—in terms of blackmail." His problem remained: "No, we, at least I think now," Nixon stated on April 14, 1973, "we pretty much know what the worst is. I don't know what the hell else they could have that is any worse. You know what I mean. Unless there is something that I don't know, unless somebody's got a piece of paper that somebody signed or some damn thing, but that I doubt."

The tapes were impossible to beat, except by a presidential pardon from his successor. These selections chart the way.

JUDITH WAX
(1931-   )

Judith Wax is a Chicago free-lance writer, a parodist and Chaucerian of note. Her pieces have appeared in *New York, Playboy, The Chicagoan, The New Republic,* and *The New York Times.* Ms. Wax contrives gems of parody out of the facts as reported by news media and her own scholarly virtuosity. She evokes splendid contemporary applications for Geoffrey Chaucer's *Canterbury Tales.*

In "The Waterbury Tales," in *The New Republic* in 1973, Judy Wax dealt unforgettably with the Watergate mess. Among her cast of characters were the *good wyf,* Martha Mitchell, of Attorney General John Mitchell, and Mitchell himself a *stout and placyd type,* sorrowing that: "The White House Horrors had not my accorde/ But all was mete to reelect Milord." Also delineated were Democratic Senator Sam J. Ervin, Jr. of North Carolina, *the Chairman* of the Senate's Special Investigating Committee; the vice-chairman, *the Baker,* Republican Senator Howard Baker of Illinois; *a Clerk of Law,* ex-White House counsel John Dean, who fingered the others, and his wife *Maureen;* G. Gordon *Liddy,* ex-F.B.I. Agent and unsuccessful politician who became general counsel to **CREEP,** the Committee to Re-Elect the President; Anthony T. Ulasewicz, a former New York City cop hired to provide undercover services for the White House including wiretaps and transfers of currency; *the Lord,* President Nixon; H. R. (Bob) *Haldeman,* White House Chief of Staff; and John D. *Ehrlichman,* one-time counsel to the President, next his chief assistant for domestic affairs. L. *Patryk* (Patrick) *Gray,* 3rd, nominated by President Nixon to succeed J. Edgar Hoover as Director of the F.B.I., who himself was quickly compromised and disgraced, brought up the end of this *merrye crew*: "Ful well I loved to serv the FBYe/ But shame, I burned the fyls and sore have synned/ And dizzy-grow from hangyn slow, slow in the wynd."

Judy Wax celebrated President Nixon's fall from office and his forgiveness by President Ford, late in the summer of 1974, in "The Pardoner's Tale." Her references are to Nelson A. Rockefeller, wealthy Vice-President designate, the Vietnam War defectors, Nixon's intimate friend Charles "Bebe" Rebozo, President Gerald Ford's Grand Rapids, Michigan, origins, and J. F. terHorst, Ford's press secretary who resigned in protest against the pardoning of Nixon. The peculiar traits of President Ford himself are unmistakably summed up, along with Lyndon B. Johnson's unsettling appraisal that Gerald Ford was not smart enough to chew gum and walk at the same time.

The Pardoner's Tale

Whan that August with his summer searings
Men alle watch Judiciayre Hearyngs
Til one Lord pilgrymage to San Clemente
And folk do get a newe Presydente.
   A GERYLD was ther with strong footbal legges,
Wel koud he cook his bacyn and his egges.
Some seyd he chew his gum and walk with trubl,

Yet still myght blow a verray good y-bubbl.
He trow to endyth tayps and tapt phone calle
And lyk it not the olde art, stonewalle.

(The KNYGHT OF ROCKYFELYR get his nodde
He maken a ful rich vyce-enchylade.)
The press, they mak the GERYLD swich good talke
For all he was a parfait gentil hawke
Since late he tel the Old Vet Compaignye
Should thynken on some modyst amnestye
For hym that years in Canyda hath spende—
GOD WOT, NOW GIV IT FUL TO BEBE'S FRIENDE!

Folks weary be from natynl insomnya.
Koud wel y-Ford some Amor vincit omnia.
Thys litel honymoon men seyd myght serv us
(Though Democratyc Lords some getten nervys)
But he that pardyn mayd on Richyrd's hed
Hath blis y-blown in thys Grand Rapyds bed.
The fyrst to lyk it not, the Earl tyrHorst,
Was also fyrst to getten hym divorsyt.
Forsooth, the good wyf U.S., ful dyspondent
Now name the Nixyn lord y-co-respondynt!

The New York Times, September 11, 1974.

DONALD KAUL
(1934-   )

For almost a decade, Don Kaul has delighted Iowans and other readers of the *Des Moines Register and Tribune* with his column, "Over the Coffee," which for the past two years or so has been written from Washington five times a week. A book of these pieces has appeared entitled *How to Light a Water Heater and Other War Stories*. Mr. Kaul is a Detroiter (West Side) by origin, who attended Wayne State University for a time before taking two degrees from the University of Michigan. An avid cyclist, he threatens to join the bicentennial's bicycling buffs on their transcontinental tour.

Watergate

Watergate is more than a scandal, you know. It is a place. To veteran Washingtonians it is a nice place on the Potomac where they give concerts.

More recently it has been known as a complex of enormous apartment houses on the Potomac where rich people can live in splendid isolation.

They have their own shops and stores right in the building, along with doctors and hairdressers, and if they want

entertainment—the Kennedy Center is right there across the street, just a few steps away.

But the amazing thing about the building—the truly amazing thing—is if you were to stage a Watergate scandal and were looking for a place to put it, you'd pick the Watergate apartments. It's as though they named the building after the scandal, rather than the other way around.

I mean, what other building have you ever seen where the balconies look like teeth?

Chance for Advancement

Albatross Ives was standing in front of the White House, watching the changing of the guard, when he spotted his

Des Moines *Register,* April 16, 1973.

good friend Sam Currier headed for the White House gate.

"Hey, Sam!" he said. "Over here. Where are you going?"

"Oh, hi Al. I heard there were some vacancies on the White House staff and I thought I'd go and apply. Nothing ventured, nothing gained; that's what I always say."

"Well, I'd certainly be the last one to discourage you, old man. The way they keep changing positions over there, you might wind up an assistant secretary."

"I don't know, Al—my shorthand's lousy."

"I mean at a sub-cabinet level, Sam. Why, Elliot Richardson has held three Cabinet posts this year, and it's only May."

"I was looking for something with more security."

"Better stay away from the White House then. I've been standing here a half-hour and I've already seen three secretaries of defense, two directors of the FBI, both secretaries of state, any number of directors of the CIA and more attorneys general than you can shake a stick at pass through those gates. I understand they're considering giving Cabinet members offices with revolving doors."

"Well, you have to give the President credit for one thing. He's living up to his campaign promise, 'More Now Than Ever.'"

"I think you've got that wrong, Sam. As I remember it, the slogan was 'Get Even Now, More Later.'"

"Whatever it was, he's living up to it. Did you happen to see him on the tube the other night explaining Watergate?"

"Yes I did and I must say I thought it was funny without being vulgar."

"Gee, you shouldn't talk that way, Al. Show some respect for the office."

"I'm sorry, Sam, but I feel that he missed Checkers badly."

"Didn't you even enjoy it when he led us in the Pledge of Allegiance?"

"Not really. I thought it would have been better theater if they'd staged it as a musical. Imagine the scene: Ed Mc-Mahon comes out to introduce the President and as he says, 'Here's Dicky . . .' Mr. Nixon comes out and sings:

Not a soul out in the West Wing,
That's a pretty certain sign,
That Watergate is breaking up
That old gang of mine."

"That's pretty catchy."

"It would have been a real grabber, Sam. Then he could have followed it up with a couple of choruses of 'I Apologize.' You know:

If I told a lie,
If I made you cry,
If I didn't say I'm sorry,
From the bottom of my heart, dears,
I apologize . . ."

"You're right, Al. That would have gone over bigger than Pat's good Republican cloth coat. Gee, maybe you should apply for a job on the White House staff."

"I don't think so, Sam. That's all inoperative now. Besides, Mr. Nixon brought in John Connally to clean up the Watergate mess."

"Honest John Connally. Lyndon Johnson's Old Buddy?"

"The very same."

"That's a good choice. He's had a lot of experience with

scandals. You know, I suppose it will take years for the real truth about Watergate to come out."

"Oh, I don't know, Sam. Things are moving pretty fast. For example, Henry Kissinger is writing a book on Watergate for publication in the fall."

"Kissinger? No kidding. What's he calling it?"

"*The Goys of Summer.* Truman Capote was going to write one called *In Cold Cash* but he couldn't decide whether it was a non-fiction novel or novel non-fiction."

"I'm glad I don't have decisions like that to make. Well, see you, Al. I'm going home and listen to my police radio. It's time for the political news."

Another Soap Opera

Sam Currier was standing on the second overlook of the George Washington Parkway, gazing at the murky waters of the Potomac below, when his reveries were interrupted by the squeal of tires as a car pulled into the area.

It was a 1957 Edsel and behind the wheel was none other than Albatros Ives. "Hi, Sam," he said, jumping out of the car. "I was just passing by and I noticed you standing here."

"Yeah, I come here sometimes to commute with nature. I see you got a new car."

"Yes, my Reo wore out. What have you been doing lately?"

"Watching television, mostly."

"Of course, the Watergate hearings. What do you think of them?"

Des Moines *Register,* May 13, 1973.

"I haven't watched them. I keep trying, but all I get is some soap opera."

"As the World Turns?"

"I don't know the name, but it's about a telephone technician who falls in with a bad crowd—politicians, retired policemen, lawyers—and how it ruins his life and the lives of his loved ones."

"Sam, does this soap opera come on once in the morning and once in the afternoon?"

"Yeah and it runs for a couple of hours each time."

"That's no soap opera, that's the Watergate hearings!"

"You know, I thought Watergate was a funny name for a baby."

"What baby?"

"Don't you ever watch soap operas, Al? There's always somebody who either wants a kid and can't have one or is single and having one."

"I'm afraid I haven't had the pleasure of . . ."

"Well, to my experienced eye, this thing I was watching on the TV looked like a paternity suit from a soap opera. I figured it was a courtroom scene and they were trying to find out who the father of the Watergate kid was."

"I can certainly see where . . ."

"Everybody in the bar was saying 'Nixon's the One' so, naturally, I put two and two together and figured out this Nixon guy was Watergate's father, but wouldn't admit it."

"That's not so terribly different from the truth of the matter, Sam. The purpose of the hearings is, in a sense, to find out whether Nixon is the father of Watergate."

"Well, is he or isn't he?"

"There are those who claim that Watergate looks just like him, but he claims he didn't do it; and if he did, he didn't mean to."

"Didn't mean to? What kind of a defense is that? What

is he, a sleepwalker? Either he did it or didn't. You can't be just a little bit burglarized."

"I can't disagree with you, Sam. I'm just relaying the President's views."

"I think if he did it, he should own up to it, marry Burglary and take responsibility for little Watergate."

"It's not that easy, Sam. Nixon's already married—to Four More Years."

"That's tough, but I think he should get a divorce and make an honest felony out of this Burglary. That would be the decent thing to do."

"A lot of people agree, Sam, but there are others to consider."

"Others?"

"The children—Peace With Honor, the New Federalism, the Great Silent Majority."

"He should have thought of them before he started messing around with Burglary. I'll tell you, Al, Nixon has got to take responsibility for Watergate. If you can't depend on soap operas for moral leadership, what *can* you depend on?"

"A lot of people are asking that very question, Sam. More or less."

Watergate Scapegoat

I don't know exactly how it happened, but I got lost in the White House the other day. I had gone over there for a press briefing and, while trying to find the restroom, took a wrong turn down some stairs.

Still thinking I was on the way to the restroom, I walked through a couple of corridors and around several

Des Moines *Register*, May 27, 1973.

corners. When it became obvious I had gone astray, I tried to retrace my steps but couldn't manage to find those stairs.

With a rising sense of panic, I began striding up and down the bleak corridors, trying to find a way out. I was obviously in a place I shouldn't be and, in the White House, that can get you in trouble.

Finally, I came to an unmarked door that was ajar. Inside the room I could see a man, pacing.

At first, I thought I recognized him. He was in his early thirties and wore a dark pinstripe suit of conservative cut, with wingtip shoes. His face reflected earnestness without candor, amiability without humor. I couldn't quite place him. I decided to ask directions.

"Pardon me . . ." I began, tapping lightly on the door.

"Sedan Chair Two?" he said, making an instinctive move out of the light. "Is that you, Ruby I? This is Scapegoat Four, come in please."

"I'm sorry. My name is O. T. Coffee and I . . ."

"I'm afraid I don't know that code."

"It's not a code. That's my real name."

"I see. You're right in not telling me. I have no need to know."

"Right, well, if you'll excuse me now, I think I'd better be going . . ."

"No, don't go. I'm glad to have someone to talk to. It's been lonesome around here lately. Hardly anyone comes around anymore."

"Pardon me for being inquisitive, but just who are you anyway?"

"I'm Sloane MacPorter Wasp III, special assistant to the President."

"A special assistant to the President, Eh? What do you do?"

"Well . . . say, you're not a reporter are you? I wouldn't want this to get out."

"Believe me, no one's ever accused me of being a reporter. You can trust me."

"I didn't think you looked like a reporter. I guess I can tell you. I am the presidential assistant in charge of taking the blame for Watergate."

"But what about Magruder, Dean, Haldeman and Ehrlichman? Haven't they already taken the blame?"

"They're just the shock troops. I'm the only one in the White House who knew ALL about Watergate. I planned it, handled all the money, and did all the covering up. I even invented Gordon Liddy."

"Invented him?"

"Yes, I thought it was a nice touch. I got an actor from New York to play the part after I wrote it. I was going to invent Howard Hunt too, but I didn't have to."

"And the President knew nothing about it."

"Absolutely nothing. I told Magruder I was giving him orders from Haldeman and I told Haldeman that Colson had passed on the President's wishes. I told Colson that my orders came straight from Ehrlichman and I told Ehrlichman that it was Haldeman's order."

"Why did you do it?"

"National security. I knew it was the only way to save the country from radicals like Abby Hoffman and Leonard Bernstein."

"But didn't you know it was illegal?"

"Sometimes you have to destroy a constitution in order to save it."

"But *didn't* you tell the President?"

"I knew he wouldn't go along with it. He's too moral, too good, too kind to do a lowdown, dirty, underhanded thing like Watergate just to save the country. I've been a

fan of his for years, ever since I was a baby in La-
guna Beach and he leaned over my baby carriage and said
'Helen Gahagan Douglas is a commie.' "

I tiptoed out of the room as he was reminiscing and
found my way back to the briefing room. The briefing was
over. It was just as well.

Who Did It?

A really terrific idea came out of the Watergate hearings
the other day. Senator Howard Baker suggested the President could have served his own cause as far back as June
17, 1972, the day of the infamous break-in, by lining up
all of his aides on the south lawn of the White House and
asking them what was going on.

He didn't, of course, and thus was plunged into an ignorance of the facts surrounding Watergate that, if reports
are to be believed, persists to this very day.

The point is, it wouldn't be too late to try a similar strat-
agem even now. Instead of lining everybody up on the
lawn, which might frighten the tourists, he could invite
all the suspects to dinner, just as they used to in the old
private-eye movies.

Think of it—all the people associated with the Watergate thriller seated at a banquet table in the East Room,
when the President strides in, wearing a trench coat and
a snap-brim hat.

"Fellow suspects," he says, "as you may or may not know,
on the morning of June 17, 1972, there was a break-in at
the headquarters of the Democratic National Committee."

"It wasn't me, Chief, honest!" shouts Richard Klein-

Des Moines *Register*, June 19, 1973.

dienst. "I was giving Tricia and Julie piggy-back rides in the Rose Garden on June 17."

"It could have been any one of you," says the President, lighting a match by scratching it on Ron Ziegler's forehead. "For instance, you, Haldeman."

"I'm Ehrlichman."

"Why don't you two wear different colored suits or something? I keep getting you mixed up. But either one of you could be guilty. You have the motive. You wanted to find out the name of Larry O'Brien's barber. Both of you are wildly jealous of his hair."

"You're right," wailed Haldeman. "It's so wavy."

"You'd have done anything to find out his secret; but, as it happens, you lacked the opportunity. Lucky for you, I kept you chained to the foot of my bed every night."

"Thanks, Boss."

"And you, Mitchell. You had the opportunity. You were the attorney general of the United States and used to consorting with a criminal element—former FBI and CIA agents—but you didn't do it either."

"I didn't?"

"You had no motive. You're bald, Mitchell. O'Brien's barber had no secrets that would help you. But you, Colson. You not only have straight hair, you've carried a grudge against the Democrats ever since your father took you to a Roosevelt rally and you got your head stepped on."

"I still get headaches."

"But a caper like this is too big for you, Colson. Your speed is hiring college boys to forge mash notes to voters. There's only one person in this room with the motive, the opportunity and the know-how to pull off an operation like this. And that man is serving your baked Alaska right now."

All eyes turn toward a black man in a tuxedo who has been in and out of the kitchen all evening.

"The butler did it?" shouts Robert Mardian.

"Yes, but he's better known to the world as Frank Wills, the night watchman who discovered the break-in. He financed the entire Watergate operation out of the Black Panther milk fund, then rigged the books to make it look like a White House job."

"Devilishly clever," says Herb Klein.

"Yeah, and he'd have gotten away with it, too, but he got too cute. He had to finger the burglars himself. When I saw that one of my butlers was moonlighting as a watchman at the Watergate, I knew it was too pat to be a coincidence, and put two and two together."

The butler bolts through a closed window with a scream.

"Don't worry," says the President. "I've got the place surrounded, as usual. He can't escape. In the meantime, Ron Ziegler's been taping this meal. Tomorrow morning take the tape around to the Ervin committee and . . . play it for Sam, Ron."

Mr. Nixon's Memorabilia

The news that President Nixon was bugging his own office for historical purposes caught the nation by surprise the other day, but it shouldn't have.

Mr. Nixon's acute sense of history is well-known and there is nothing extraordinary about his wish to preserve all of his conversations for the archives at the Nixon presidential library, when that institution is built.

The story set me to thinking about that library, though,

Des Moines *Register*, July 15, 1973.

and the other preparations for it that must be going on right now. With that in mind, I called on the curator of the Nixon presidential library collection, Sylvester J. Clandestine, and was able to arrange a tour of the artifacts gathered thus far.

The collection is currently housed in an abandoned Mexican laundry in the Watergate apartments. Mr. Clandestine ushered me into the main gallery, apologizing for the cramped quarters.

"We're hopeful of having a more prepossessing setting at the end of this administration, whenever that may be," he said. "On your right you see stacked there all the tape recordings of the important presidential conversations of recent years."

"Wow! And this is going to be available to the public?"

"Certainly. The library will be open to anyone willing to sign a loyalty oath. Would you like to hear this tape? It's a recording of Henry Kissinger giving the President a report on a meeting with Jill St. John."

"Are you sure it doesn't violate national security?"

"As it turns out, it doesn't even violate Jill St. John."

"Then I don't want to hear it."

"How about this one? It's the transcript of a White House Christmas party. There's a wonderful segment during which Jeb Stuart Magruder sings 'I Lied for You' to the President."

"I'm sure it's very touching, but I'd rather learn about some of these other exhibits. What's that big metallic container over there?"

"That's Maury Stan's little tin box. At the end of every day Mr. Stans, the finance chairman of the presidential campaign, would empty his pockets of any loose $100 bills he had and put them in the box. Before you could say Boss

Tweed, he had saved up enough to finance two burglaries, five surreptitious entries and a mugging."

"It's amazing what thrift can do for you. What's that funny shaped thing with a handle?"

"That's the plunger used by the White House plumbers unit. We're quite proud of that. It's one of a kind."

"It doesn't look like any other plunger I've ever seen."

"That's because it's for stopping up drains, rather than unstopping them. We hope to set this up as a dual exhibit with that shredder over there and allow visitors to the library to shred their guidebooks before they leave, just to give them a little flavor of life in the highest office in the land."

"Very thoughtful. What's that cloak doing on the wall over there?"

"That's the cloak of righteous indignation Ron Ziegler used to wear when denying Watergate rumors at press conferences."

"Looks about worn out."

"Well, it got some pretty rough usage. They got him a new one a few weeks ago. It's one of those new, synthetic fabrics—testy defensiveness I think they call it. I understand it's kind of hot."

"Well, this certainly is a marvelous collection. The President must be very proud."

"Are you kidding? The President doesn't know a thing about it."

"But why not?"

"If we told him, we'd have to tell everybody. It's best he doesn't know. By the way, on your way out would you spell your name into the light fixture? I'd like to get this conversation properly documented for posterity."

Des Moines *Register*, July 22, 1973.

A Colorful Dialogue of Nixons

There I was, surrounded by Richard Nixons. On my right there was a red Richard Nixon, looking like a creature from the netherworld, saying: ". . . the time has come for me to speak out. . . ." On my left, there was a bright green Richard Nixon, green as a cucumber, saying: ". . . I accept full responsibility. . . ." The room was filled with yellow Nixons and orange Nixons and Technicolor Nixons; black-and-white Nixons and Nixons of varying shades of gray.

I was, I confess, watching the latest presidential address on Watergate at a television showroom, on the advice of a friend. He had told me that one could not claim a total Nixon experience until one had been confronted by 50 Richard Nixons smiling the same 50 little smiles, glaring the same 50 little glares.

And, I was forced to admit, he had something. There is a quality at once sinister and ludicrous about the presidential image repeated wall-to-wall, as though it were a happening jointly designed by George Orwell and Andy Warhol.

But the viewing of the speech was as nothing compared to what was to come.

At the conclusion of the address, the networks flipped to their anchor men for some instant analysis but, on a group of sets in a remote corner of the store, the President's images *did not leave the screen.*

Indeed, they seemed to begin to talk to each other! Naturally, I moved closer to eavesdrop.

"Well fellows," a beautifully modulated color Nixon was saying, "how did I do?"

"Lousy," said the bright green Nixon. "You stunk out the joint."

"But I did everything they told me," the Technicolor Nixon said. "I didn't make large gestures or funny faces or make myself perfectly clear."

"You should have done the politically easy thing," said Nixon the Green.

"You always want me to do the politically easy thing."

"And you never do it. The politically easy thing to do would have been to blame Haldeman and Ehrlichman. The public wants scapegoats for this mess."

"But Haldeman and Ehrlichman are two of the finest public servants I've ever known. I couldn't blame them. They were only doing what they thought was right."

"If they're such loyal public servants, they'd understand you dumping on them. You could tell them it was a matter of national security."

"No, no, no," said Nixon the Red. "The public doesn't want scapegoats, it wants raw meat. You should have attacked. Don't apologize for Watergate, defend it. You should have said that the Watergate committee is a tool of the International Communist Conspiracy; that it's following the Party Line. What's the matter with you? In the old days I didn't have to tell you things like this."

"But I've matured in office. I'm the Leader of the Free World. I can't go around doing things like that anymore. Besides, some of my best friends are leaders of the International Communist Conspiracy."

"Red is wrong," said Nixon the Yellow. "You should have confessed your sins and thrown yourself on the mercy of the American people. There's nothing so moves the American spirit as a repentant sinner."

"But I didn't do anything wrong," said Technicolor Nixon. "I didn't know about the break-in, I didn't know about the cover-up. They all lied to me; the FBI, the CIA, Mar-

tha Mitchell, everybody. They're all against me. I didn't
know, I tell you."

"We believe you," said Nixon the Yellow.

"Thousands wouldn't," said Nixon the Green.

"I don't care what anybody says," came a voice from
the other side of the room. "I liked the speech." It was a
six-inch black-and-white set that needed more contrast.

"You did?" the other sets said as one.

"Yes. It may not have been quite so good as your fourth
Watergate explanation, but it was definitely superior to
the first three. I particularly liked the way you blamed
the peace demonstrators for everything. There's only one
thing that puzzled me."

"What's that?" said Technicolor Nixon.

"In that part where you talked about the confidential
relationship that exists between lawyer and client, priest
and supplicant, husband and wife, president and adviser . . ."

"Yes?"

"Why didn't you mention doctor and patient?"

They all started to speak at once then, and I left before
there was a scene. Weird.

New Shrines in Capital

Things were simpler in the old days. When friends came
to visit you in Washington, you knew where to take them.

You took them to the White House, the Washington
Monument, Arlington Cemetery and the Lincoln Memorial.
If it was their second trip to the city, you might steer them
toward more esoteric attractions like the gardens at Dum-

Des Moines *Register*, August 19, 1973.

barton Oaks or the reading room at the Library of Congress.

It got monotonous at times, sure. I remember there was a two-week period last spring when I visited the Lincoln Memorial six times. I learned the Second Inaugural by heart.

And I have a colleague who, having lived in Washington many years claims he has visited Mount Vernon more often than George Washington ever did.

But we never complained, we Washingtonians. Showing our out-of-town friends the city, we felt, was our responsibility and patriotic duty. Besides, it allowed us an opportunity to show off our expertise, such as it was.

We knew that the Capitol dome was 287-feet, $5\frac{1}{3}$-inches high, that the British burned the White House in 1814 and that the house on the hill in Arlington Cemetery is Robert E. Lee's old place. We could recite these facts and others at the drop of a guidebook and were glad to do so.

That was then.

Things have changed. Now you pick a visiting friend up at the airport and take the trouble to drive homeward via the Mall, so as to give him a little of the sense of history in which Washington is so rich.

You are saying:

"On your left you see the majestic Jefferson Memorial, with the Tidal Basin there in front of it. Many people prefer the Lincoln Memorial to this but, as for . . ."

"Where's the Watergate?" the friend will say.

"Pardon me?"

"The Watergate complex, where McCord and the Cubans broke in to the Democratic National Committee Headquarters. Where is it?"

"Over there behind the Kennedy Center."

"Could we go see it? I mean, are you allowed near the place?"

"Sure," you say, "There's nothing much to see, frankly. It's just a big, ostentatious building."

So you drive over and nothing will suffice but to park across the street from the monstrosity while your friend gets out.

"Which window is it?" he asks. "Which one was the Democratic Headquarters?"

"Gee, I don't know. All windows look alike to me."

"Oh wow! Look, right across the street here is the Howard Johnson's where Hunt and Liddy maintained the surveillance room. I can hardly believe I'm standing here."

"I'll pinch you if you want."

"Can you take me to the second overlook on the George Washington Parkway? I promised my kids I'd pick up some rocks from the very place where John Caulfield promised amnesty to James McCord. You know how kids are."

"Yes, I do; the thing is, I am not exactly sure which of the overlooks is the first and which is the second."

"We'll go to them both. Would it be out of the way to stop at Lafayette Park to see the bench John Dean was sitting on when he told Herb Kalmbach to make broad gestures because they might be watched?"

"If you want to go by way of the overlooks it is. I live way out in Maryland."

"In Maryland; not near Rockville?"

"Not too far. In that direction, anyway."

"Terrific. We can go see the telephone booth in front of the Blue Fountain Inn, where Tony Ulasewicz made his anonymous calls to McCord. I better get a picture of that. The guys at the office won't believe I've seen it. We can do it tomorrow."

"I kind of thought we'd go to Mount Vernon tomorrow."

"Mount Vernon? That's funny, I don't remember any Mount Vernon.

"Was that the golf course Kleindienst was on when Liddy came up to him right after the burglary?"

Before this is over, we Washingtonians will have President Nixon's Watergate explanation memorized, wait and see.

Des Moines *Register*, August 22, 1973.

ART BUCHWALD
(1925-   )

Art Buchwald's columns are syndicated in newspapers throughout the world. For several years, a decade and more ago, he was based in Paris to explain the foibles of Frenchmen to Americans and *vice versa*, which he accomplished neatly. Mr. Buchwald packs his wallop into his last line after owlishly setting up his readers more than any humorous writer before Finley Peter Dunne or since. Having been summoned home to Washington, as he saw it, to discover what had prompted President Kennedy to cancel his subscription to *The New York Herald Tribune* which carried his columns, Art Buchwald was ready and waiting for Watergate long before the story broke.

Sinking of SS Watergate

The Naval Court of Inquiry into the sinking of the SS Watergate was held in executive session here last week.

On the stand was Capt. Richard M. Nixon, who commanded the ship at the time it went down.

Here is a partial transcript of the hearings, which do not violate national security.

"Capt. Nixon, the SS Watergate sprang a leak on the morning of June 17, 1972. What did you do about it at the time?"

"I didn't think much of it. I was told by my executive officer that seven men had been fooling around in the shower room and the nozzle broke off."

"Did you order an investigation of the incident?"

"Yes, I did, and it was the most thorough investigation ever held on the high seas. I told my officers I wanted to know if anyone on my staff had anything to do with the leak. They reported back to me categorically that no one in the crew except for the seven men was involved in the incident. I accepted this as fact."

"Did you try to repair the damage at the time?"

"There was nothing to repair as far as I was concerned. The seven men were court-martialed and that was the end of it."

"But isn't it true that during the court-martial of the seven, there were hints that other people were involved in the leak?"

"It was only hearsay. A captain has many enemies on a ship, and I was not about to put credence in a lot of gossip and rumor."

"Now, Capt. Nixon, since the leak was not repaired, the lower compartments of the ship began to flood. Didn't you feel at that time you should take some action?"

"I sent my people down to inspect the damage and they said the ship was completely dry below decks."

"You didn't go down to inspect the damage yourself?"

"I had to stay on the bridge. It is a mistake for a captain to know too much about what is going on in the crew's quarters. Besides, I had great faith in my officers and their ability to judge whether the ship was in jeopardy or not."

"Is it true that your communications officer, Lt. Ronald Ziegler, kept announcing over the loudspeaker that there was nothing wrong with the ship?"

"Yes, he did it on my orders."

"Then Lt. Ziegler hadn't gone below to inspect the damage either?"

"Not to my knowledge. We were getting continual reports from our legal officer, Lt. John Dean III, and he assured us that we were safe and our crew was clean."

"But didn't you get suspicious when the water rose to the main deck?"

"I didn't like it, but I didn't consider it my problem. I've been in storms before, six to be exact, and I've always been able to weather them. Besides, my staff told me not to pay any attention because the ship was built to withstand any kind of pressure."

"When did you decide that you were really in danger?"

"On March 21, 1973, I received some startling information from my officers that the leak did not come from a shower, but that we had really hit an iceberg."

"Then you decided to take action?"

"Yes, I went on the loudspeaker myself and said that anyone responsible for hitting the iceberg would be immediately removed from the crew."

"And when did you decide to abandon ship?"

"When the water got up to my hips and I noticed all my officers starting to take to the lifeboats."

"How did you feel about losing so many of your crew?"

"I felt bad about it, but by that time it was every man for himself."

Nixon Goes to the Mountain

Last weekend President Richard Nixon went to Camp

Philadelphia *Evening Bulletin*, April 26, 1973, syndicated from Washington *Post*.

David alone, without family or aides. Press Secretary Ron Ziegler denies it, but it has been reliably reported that the President went up the top of the mountain to speak with God.

"God, God, why are You doing this to me?"

"Doing what, Richard?"

"The Watergate, the coverup, the grand jury hearings, the Senate investigations. Why me, God?"

"Don't blame me, Richard. I gave you my blessing to win the election, but I didn't tell you to steal it."

"God, I've done everything You told me to do. I ended the war. I defeated poverty. I cleaned the air and the water. I defeated crime in the streets. Surely I deserve a break."

"Richard, I tried to warn you that you had sinful people working for you."

"When, God?"

"Just after the Committee to Re-Elect the President was formed. When I saw the people you had selected to head up the committee, I was shocked. We've got a long file on them up here."

"Why didn't You tell me, God?"

"I tried to, but Ehrlichman and Haldeman wouldn't let Me talk to you on the phone. They said they'd give you the message I called."

"They never told me, God."

"It figures. Then I sent you a telegram saying it was urgent that you contact me."

"The only telegrams I read during that period were those in support of my bombing North Vietnam."

"Finally, Richard, I made one last effort. I showed up at a prayer meeting one Sunday at the White House and after the sermon I came up to you and said there were men among you who would betray you. Do you know what you did, Richard? You introduced me to Pat and then you gave Me a ballpoint pen."

"I didn't know it was you, God. So many people show up at these prayer meetings. Is that why You're punishing me—because I snubbed You?"

"I'm not punishing you, Richard. But even I can do just so much. If it were merely a simple case of bugging at the Watergate, I could probably fix it. But your Administration is involved in the obstruction of justice, the bribing of witnesses, the forging of papers, wiretapping, perjury and using the mails to defraud."

"Good God, nobody's perfect!"

"I guess that's what the grand jury is saying."

"Look, I've got less than four years in which to go down as the greatest President in the history of the United States. Give me a break."

"You've got to clean house, Richard. Get rid of everyone who has any connection with the scandal. You must make it perfectly clear you were hoodwinked by everyone on your staff. You must show the American people that when it comes to the Presidency, no one is too big to be sacrificed on the altar of expediency."

"God are You asking for a human sacrifice?"

"It would show your good faith, Richard."

"All right, I'll do it. Will You take Jeb Magruder, Richard Kleindienst and John Dean III?"

"What kind of sacrifice is that?"

"John Mitchell?"

"Keep going."

"Haldeman and Ehrlichman?"

"That's more like it."

"And then, God, if I sacrifice them, will You keep me out of it?"

"Richard, I can't work miracles."

Philadelphia *Evening Bulletin,* May 3, 1973, syndicated from Washington *Post.*

Operator, Take a Telegram!

It's been revealed that the Committee for the Re-Election of the President sent thousands of telegrams to the White House supporting President Nixon's mining of Haiphong Harbor. The White House was then able to claim that the American people were in favor of the action by more than five to one.

"Hello, Operator. I wish to send a telegram to the President of the United States at the White House."

"Yessir. Is this to be charged to the Committee for the Re-Election of the President?"

"No, dammit, I want it charged to my own telephone number."

"Just a minute, I'm not sure we can do that. If you charge it to the Committee for the Re-Election of the President we can give you a group rate."

"I'm not interested in a group rate. I want to pay for this telegram in full."

"Well, here's the problem, sir. If you charge it through the committee, we can assure delivery. But if you send it on your own, it might take several days to get there."

"How's that?"

"The committee picks up the telegrams it sends and delivers them in its own truck. Of course, in order to qualify for this service, you would have to send a telegram *favorable* to the President."

"This telegram does not happen to be *favorable* to the President."

"Just a minute, sir. May I read you several form telegrams? You can send any one of them for 75 cents."

"No, I don't want to send a form telegram. Can't I just say what I want to?"

"The Committee for the Re-Election of the President won't like that."

"I don't give a hoot about the Committee for the Re-Election of the President."

"Well, we do. They're our best customers. They send 1000 telegrams to the White House every day. And they get very annoyed if someone sends one on his own."

"Don't you ever get telegrams from people who don't support the President?"

"Oh, once in a while someone calls in and takes issue with a particular presidential decision."

"What do you do about it?"

"We take his number and report it to the Justice Department."

"What do they do with it?"

"They tap his telephone."

"Maybe I'd better not send this telegram after all."

"That's up to you, sir. After all, it's a free country."

The Voice from the Empty House

I was walking by the White House the other night when I heard an anguished cry from inside. "Alger Hiss. Where were you when I needed you?"

I thought nothing of it and walked a few more steps. Then I heard the same voice again. "Where were those college bums when I needed them?"

A guard standing by the gate asked, "Can I help you, sir?"

"That voice coming from inside. It's so eerie."

Philadelphia *Sunday Bulletin*, May 20, 1973, syndicated from Washington *Post*.

"Aye," he said, "it's been going on for weeks now. It does give you the willies."

"Who's in there?" I asked.

"Nobody. The house is empty."

"Empty?"

"Aye, they all moved out. There's nobody there."

"But the voice. I heard a voice."

"That you did. They say the place is haunted, and full of ghosts."

I heard the voice again. "Ehrlichman. Haldeman, Kleindienst, Gesundheit."

"Do you believe in ghosts?" I asked the man.

"After what's been happening around here for the last two months, I don't know what to believe any more. I reported the voice to my superiors, and they told me to forget it. They said if anyone asked me, I heard nothing."

"You mean it's another coverup?" I asked.

"I just follow orders. They say it's a matter of executive privilege, and I can't talk about anything I've heard here, even if it's a ghost who has done the talking."

"It must be lonely work."

"Aye, that it is. Sometimes when the fog rolls in over the Rose Garden, I think I hear the U.S. Marine Band playing 'Hail to the Chief.' Once, I saw the White House guards marching in their old uniforms."

The voice came out loud and clear again. "Martha Martha, why have you deserted me?"

"The voice sounds so familiar," I told the guard.

"That it does. It's somebody I know, but can't make out who."

"I'm sure it isn't Lincoln."

"And it isn't FDR," the guard said.

"Lyndon Baines Johnson had more of a twang in his voice."

The guard scratched his head. "It beats me."

"When did they board up the house?"

"About three weeks ago. It seems after all the trouble, they couldn't get anyone to work here. The secretaries were frightened, and after the big shots left, no one would take their place. So they closed it down and moved to Camp David."

The voice again: "In our own lives let each of us ask —not just what Government will do for me, but what can I do for myself?"

"You don't have any grass on you?" the guard asked.

"No, I'm sorry I don't. Why do you ask?"

"I don't know. You hang around here for a little while, and pot kind of makes you forget what's going on. Tell you the truth, mister, I really got the shakes."

"Why don't you go to a psychiatrist?"

"Not on your life. If I did, somebody would break in his office and steal my records."

The Anniversary of Watergate

In just a few days—on June 17—the United States will celebrate the first anniversary of the breaking in of the Watergate. A group of patriotic citizens under the leadership of a friend of mine, Julian Stein, are urging President Nixon to declare it a national holiday.

He told me, "The one thing England has that we don't is Guy Fawkes Day. For more than 365 years the British have indulged in all sorts of shenanigans in memory of the man who tried to blow up Parliament in the Gunpowder Plot of 1605. Among other things, they burn Guy

Philadelphia *Evening Bulletin*, May 24, 1973, syndicated from Washington *Post*.

Fawkes in effigy, make huge bonfires and set off firecrackers. In further commemoration of 'the Plot,' a formal and ritualistic search of the vaults beneath the houses of Parliament is made each year at the opening of their sessions."

"We think that June 17 should be duly celebrated in this country as 'Watergate Day.' "

"It sounds great," I said. "What would people do to observe it?"

"On 'Watergate Day' Americans would memorialize this historic event by taping other people's doors, tapping telephones, spying on their neighbors, using aliases, wearing red wigs and making inoperative statements."

"You mean people could lie to each other?" I asked.

"Of course. Parents would not have to tell the truth to their children, bosses would not have to level with their employees, and husbands would be permitted to make up stories to tell their wives."

"June 17 would be like April Fools' Day," I said.

"It would be much wilder. Anyone breaking into a doctor's office would be granted immunity. People could raise money for phony causes, and only cash would be accepted as legal tender."

"Would you have parades?" I asked Mr. Stein.

"You bet we would. We would have plumbers' parades all over the country, honoring the plumbers in the White House who were supposed to turn off all the leaks.

"In Washington, the President would review CIA and FBI bands as they marched down Pennsylvania Avenue leading the loyal members of the Committee for the Re-Election of the President.

"In the afternoon, the President would lay a wreath at the Watergate complex just under the window of the former headquarters of the Democratic National Committee."

"That would be nice," I said.

"In the evening, there would be a fireworks display in every town to remind us all of the fireworks the Watergate has caused in this country."

"I get chills just thinking about it," I admitted.

"If the President declares June 17 a national holiday, you could have 'Watergate Day' sales in the department stores with giant savings on burglary tools, shredding machines and lie detectors. And grand juries would only have to work a half-day."

"Of course," added Mr. Stein, "the churches would remain open for people who wanted to pray for their country."

"I don't see anything wrong with it," I said. "There's only one question. In England on Guy Fawkes Day, they burn Guy Fawkes in effigy. Who would Americans burn in effigy on 'Watergate Day?'"

"We may have to wait until June 17, 1974, before we figure that one out."

Red Flags Over Washington

I was walking down Pennsylvania Avenue the other day when I ran into an old man. His hair was white and his beard was gray and he was muttering to himself.

"Oh, my God. Oh, my God."

"What's the trouble, sir?" I asked.

"I never thought I'd see the day when the hammer and sickle would be flying from the Executive Office Building next to the White House."

"Don't get upset," I said. "It's just to honor Leonid Brezhnev's visit to the United States. He's the general secretary of the Communist Party in the Soviet Union and

Philadelphia *Evening Bulletin,* June 5, 1973, syndicated from Washington *Post.*

he's visiting the President. Don't you read the newspapers?"

"I've been asleep for 20 years," the old man said. "Oh, my God, Richard Nixon warned us this would happen."

"You don't understand, old man. Nixon *is* the President and he's the one who is entertaining Leonid Brezhnev."

"It couldn't be the same Nixon," the old man said adamantly. "The Nixon I knew sent Alger Hiss to jail for playing footsie with the Communists. In every political campaign he warned of the Red menace. He fought the Communists while everyone was being duped by them. Nixon would never entertain one in his home."

"Times have changed, sir."

"The name's Rip," the old man said.

"Well, since you've been asleep, a lot of things have happened. The President has even visited the People's Republic of China."

"Oh? How's Chiang Kai-shek?"

"Not *that* China, Rip. The other one—mainland Communist China."

"The President of the United States went to Communist China?"

"Yes, and then he went to Moscow. And he's sworn friendship to the Socialist People's Republic of the Soviet Union on Russian television."

"Oh, my God," Rip said. "Didn't Sen. Joe McCarthy try to stop him?"

"McCarthy is dead."

"No wonder Nixon could get away with it," Rip said.

"Listen, Rip, I think I'd better clue you in on a few things. There is no such thing as a 'Red menace' any more. The President of the United States has made his peace with the two major Communist powers in the world. Communism is no longer a threat to the security of the

Free World except in Indochina."

"Indochina?"

"Yes, we've been fighting a war in Indochina for ten years to keep the North Vietnamese Communists from spreading their insidious ideology over the globe. The President is committed to keeping them from achieving their goals."

Rip seemed confused. "That's the only threat of communism there is in the world?"

"Exactly. All other forms of communism, as far as President Nixon is concerned, are inoperative."

"Can my ears deceive me?" Rip said. "Is that the 'Internationale' I hear being played by the U.S. Marine Band on the White House lawn?"

"Yup," I replied. "They're playing *our* song."

"Oh, my God," Rip said. "Why did I ever wake up?"

"Don't worry, Rip, the detente with the Communist countries has been the greatest thing to happen in the last 20 years. It could mean a generation of peace for all mankind, except for those rotten Commies in Cambodia. If it hadn't been for Watergate, President Nixon might have gone down as one of the greatest Presidents in the history of our country."

"What's Watergate?"

"Rip, I think you better sit down. It's a long story. . . ."

An Honest Presidential Election to Mark 1976!

The United States is having a very difficult time trying to figure out how to celebrate its 200th anniversary. Many

Philadelphia *Evening Bulletin,* June 21, 1973, syndicated from Washington *Post.*

ideas have been suggested for the Bicentennial but few have grabbed the American people. The President's commission on the anniversary is bogged down in red tape and no one is certain we will have a celebration at all.

The other day a man walked into my office and said he had a revolutionary plan for Americans to celebrate their country's 200th birthday.

I tried to be polite, but it was difficult because I have people like this coming in to see me all the time.

"Make it brief," I said.

"Well," he said hesitatingly, "I have this idea to celebrate 200 years of independence and it won't cost the country a cent."

"You're out of your mind," I said.

"Get to it," I said impatiently.

"Why don't we, in 1976, hold the *first* honest presidential election in the history of the country."

"I've got it worked out here on paper. There would be only one fund-raising committee in each party, and no one would be allowed to contribute more than $25 to a presidential candidate."

"Impossible," I said. "What would happen to your $1,000-a-plate dinners? What about people who want to buy ambassadorships and jobs in the Government?"

"I know it's a wild idea," the man said, "but it could work. No one would be permitted to give any donations in cash. Every gift would have to be by check or money order. All moneys would have to be accounted for, and if there is any hanky-panky committed by the finance committee of either party, the presidential candidate of that party would automatically forfeit the election."

"Have you lost your senses?" I said, trying to hold my temper. "Do you know what it costs to run a presidential campaign? Do you have any idea of the payroll, printing bills, television fees and national security costs that it takes to elect a President of the United States?"

"Well, if it costs too much," the man said, "then let's eliminate a lot of it. Why should money be the decisive factor in electing a President of the United States?"

"Because money is the mother's milk of politics!" I shouted. "Do you think Richard Nixon would be President of the United States today if people were allowed to contribute only $25 to his election?"

"I'm not talking about President Nixon," the man said. "I'm talking about 1976. Look, I'm not saying we would have to continue with my plan. But I thought for just *one* presidential election we could do it."

"You've got to be kidding. This country is not ready for an honest presidential election and you know it. We've been brought up on the principle that in politics anything goes. Everyone knows the only reason one party resorts to dirty tricks is that if they don't, the other party will. Do you expect us to change our lifestyle just because we're celebrating our 200th anniversary?"

"That's what everyone tells me," he said sadly, and he got up to leave.

After his departure, my secretary asked me what it was all about.

"He's some crackpot who wants to hold an honest presidential election. They shouldn't allow guys like that to wander around loose."

Sitting on the Tapes

"Ron, have you seen my tapes?"

Philadelphia *Sunday Bulletin,* July 15, 1973, syndicated from Washington *Post.*

"You're sitting on them, Mr. President."

"Oh yes, I forgot. No one is going to get these tapes, Ron. I want to make that perfectly clear."

"I know that, Mr. President. But you've been sitting on them for three days. Don't you think you ought to get some sleep? We could put the tapes in a safe."

"I'm not going to let them out of my sight. They would love to have me go to bed and leave my tapes in my safe."

"They?"

"All of *them* out there who are trying to get me, Ron. Do you know they're trying to hang me with my own tapes?

"Well, I have a big surprise for them.

"I've heard these tapes and I'm innocent. But they'll never hear them. For the rest of their lives, they'll always wonder what was on them."

"That's true, sir. But you can't keep sitting on the tapes for the rest of your Administration. Why don't you give them to someone you trust to safeguard them for you?"

"Ron, I learned a long, long time ago that you can't trust *anybody*. That's why I made all these tapes. Now they can't say they told me one thing when they told me another. I've got them, Ron, and they know I've got them."

"But most of the people you bugged, Mr. President, were those who worked for you."

"What about the March of Dimes child? The Maid of Cotton? What about the Boy Scouts of America when they came to the White House? I'm sitting on it all, Ron. That's what's driving *them* nuts."

"Aren't you uncomfortable sitting on them day and night?"

"No, Ron, and do you know why? Because I'm sitting on history. When future Presidents sit on these tapes they're going to say, 'God bless Richard Nixon for not giving them to the Watergate Senate committee.' "

"All the same, sir, the Secret Service has assured me any time you want to give up the tapes, they will make certain that no one gets them."

"Ron, I have only 903 days as President of the United States, and do you know what I'm going to do with that time?"

"No, sir."

"I'm going to sit on these tapes."

"That's wonderful, Mr. President."

"They can threaten me. They can subpoena me. They can even impeach me, but they're not going to get one spool."

"You're a real profile in courage, Mr. President."

"Now I know there are some people who are going to say, 'Tricky Dick is up to his dirty tricks.' And I know there are some people who are going to ask, 'If he's innocent, why doesn't he turn the tapes over to Cox?' And I know others are going to say I doctored the tapes.

"But when I took this office in 1968, I vowed I would never do the easy thing, the popular thing, the political thing. Ron, the toughest decision I ever had to make was whether I would tape some of the people all of the time, or all of the people some of the time. It was only when I talked with Butterfield that I found out I could tape all of the people all of the time. It was probably the greatest day of my life."

Out of Work, No Money—Is That All?

One of the reasons for having a holiday season is to

Philadelphia *Evening Bulletin,* July 31, 1973, syndicated from Washington *Post.*

give congressmen and senators a chance to go home and find out what the American voter is thinking. In the past, our lawmakers have gone through the motions of talking to their constituents, but this year they've traveled home with a certain amount of trepidation.

"Hi, there, Mr. Coleslaw. I'm Congressman Upchuck and I'd like to have a few words with you."

"Don't want any."

"I'm not selling anything, Mr. Coleslaw. I just want to find out how you feel about the great issues of the day so I can do my job better in Washington. Now, how's everything been working for you?"

"Ain't been working."

"Well, we'll have to do something about that, won't we?"

"What can you do about me not working?"

"Congress can do a lot of things. Pass a law, offer a resolution, filibuster if we have to.

"That's what makes America great. Give us a shortage and we'll make money on it."

"Upchuck, will you get the hell out of here."

"Now, wait a minute, Mr. Coleslaw. I want to know everything that's bothering you. I would not be serving my district if I didn't know your doubts, your fears, your hopes. Tell me, Coleslaw, besides being out of work and having no money, what else irritates you?"

"Too many crooks in Washington, starting with that guy who keeps saying he ain't one."

"I'm glad you brought that up, Coleslaw. Would you be for or against impeachment?"

"I'd settle if he just paid his income tax."

"I would like for you to see a speech I made on that

very subject, printed, of course, in the Congressional Record."

"Didn't I see you in the last election with his arm around your shoulders?"

"That was before Watergate. Coleslaw, I wasn't the only one who had his picture taken with you-know-who."

"Only congressman in my district who did."

"Do you mind if I ask why you're not working?"

"Place I worked at made shoelaces for shoes made in another place. Other place couldn't make shoes because they couldn't get leather from the leather company. The leather company couldn't get leather because there was no diesel fuel to get the cows to market. Truck drivers wouldn't deliver diesel fuel to diesel filling stations because they were losing money driving 55 miles an hour. That's why I ain't making shoe laces."

"By God, Mr. Coleslaw, you're a victim of the energy crisis! Do you know I warned the country about the energy crisis three years ago? Here is a speech I made on the floor of the House in 1970. I said unless we tightened our belts and put our shoulders to the wheel that sometime in the next 50 years we might have gas rationing? Well, how do you like that for on-the-nose predicting?"

"What did you do about energy besides predict?"

"Well, I introduced a bill a year ago giving the oil companies a special tax discount as an incentive for finding us more oil."

"Heard the oil companies have done pretty good since the crisis."

"Well, I have to be going now. I hope in the next election you'll remember that I did come to see you about your problems."

"Yup. Say, you got any other speeches I can have?"

"I certainly do. Here, help yourself. I'm very flattered you want to read them."

"Read them? Heck, I'm goin' to burn 'em to help save on firewood."

Philadelphia *Evening Bulletin,* December 27, 1973 syndicated from Washington *Post.*

PHILIP ROTH
(1933-   )

Philip Roth ranks high among the nation's literary artists. His short stories are regularly reprinted among the year's best. Two of his novels became sensational successes. *Goodbye Columbus* won a National Book Award, and was made into a motion picture bonanza. *Portnoy's Complaint* entered at once into middle-class folklore to serve as a convenient umbrella-like term for multiple household afflictions, and for precisely that reason could never be a great movie. *Our Gang* was a satirical sledgehammer aimed directly at President Nixon's foundations, which tried, in Roth's terms, "to yank him out from behind all that unearned augustness," with no quarter given and none asked. Mr. Roth is both wildly witty and fiercely courageous.

The President Addresses the Nation

My fellow Americans:
I have an announcement to make to you tonight of the greatest national importance. As you know, the Senate has

voted this afternoon to remove me from the Office of the Presidency. That, of course, is their right under the Constitution of the United States of America, and as you know, I have not interfered in any way with their deliberations on this matter, as I did not interfere some weeks ago when the House of Representatives arrived at their decision after their own deliberations. They have a right to express their opinion, as does any American, without Presidential interference or pressure of any kind from the Executive branch. That is what is known as the separation of powers. You probably know by now that there were even members of my own political party among those in the Legislative branch who voted to remove me from the Presidency. I consider that to be a vigorous and reassuring sign of their independence of mind, and of their personal integrity. I applaud them for their actions, which can only strengthen the democratic processes here at home, and enhance the image of American democracy abroad.

However, according to the doctrine of the separation of powers, the Executive branch has an equal voice in the management of government, along with the Legislative and the Judicial branches. That, after all, is only fair. It is what is meant by "The American Way." Moreover, the President, which I am, has the sole responsibility for safeguarding the security of the nation. That responsibility is spelled out in the oath of office, which, as you all know, every President takes on Inauguration Day. President Washington, whose picture you see here, took that oath. So did President Lincoln, pictured here. And so did our great President Dwight David Eisenhower, whose grandson has just completed serving his country in the United States Navy and is married to my daughter Julie, whom you see pictured here. My other daughter, Tricia, is pictured here, in her wedding dress. And of course standing beside Tricia is my wife Pat. My fellow Americans, I owe it not only to these great American Presidents who preceded me in this high office, but to my family, and to you and your families, to respect and honor that oath to which I swore on the Holy Bible on my Inauguration Day. To speak personally, I just couldn't live with myself if I went ahead and shirked my duty to safeguard the security of the nation.

And that is why I have decided tonight to remain in this Office. My fellow Americans, though I respect the sincerity and the integrity of those Senators who voted earlier in the day for my removal, I find, after careful study and grave reflection, that to accept their decision would be to betray the trust placed in me by the American people, and to endanger the security and the well-being of this nation.

As you all know, there has never been an American President yet who has stepped down in the middle of his term of office because of Congressional pressure of any kind. That is something for which there is just no precedent in American history—and, let me tell you, straight from the shoulder, I don't intend to break the record my predecessors have established of standing up under fire.

You know, no one, I don't care which party he belongs to, expects this Office to be a bed of roses. If he does he shouldn't run for the Presidency to begin with. As the late President Truman put it—and you remember, Harry Truman didn't always see eye to eye on everything with us Republicans—"If you can't take the heat, you shouldn't be in the kitchen." Well, I happen to pride myself on the amount of heat I've taken over the years—some of it, as you older folks may remember, in a kitchen in the Soviet Union with Premier Khrushchev. But in the name of the American people, I stood up to Premier Khrushchev in that kitchen; and in the name of the American people, I am standing up to the Congress tonight.

Richard Nixon is not going to be the first President in American history to be removed from office by the Legislative branch. I am sure that is not the kind of President that the American people elected me to be. Frankly, if I were to give in to this Congressional pressure to remove me from Office, if I were to come on television tonight to tell you, yes, President Nixon is quitting because he can't take the heat, well, that to my mind would constitute a direct violation of my oath of office, and I would in fact *voluntarily* step down from the Presidency, out of a sense of having profoundly failed you, the American people, whose decision it was to place me in office in the first place.

My fellow Americans, during my years as President, I have as you know devoted myself to one goal above and beyond all others: the goal of world peace. As I talk to you here tonight, negotiations and discussions are being conducted around the globe by Dr. Kissinger, Secretary Rogers, and key members of the Department of State to bring peace with honor to America, and to all of mankind. These negotiations are taking place at the highest diplomatic level and necessarily in secret—but I am pleased to report to you tonight that we are pursuing them with every hope of success.

Now I am sure that no one in Congress would willingly or knowingly want to endanger the chances of world peace, for us, for our children, and for generations to come. And yet, by calling upon the President to pack up and quit just because the going is a little rough, that is precisely what they are doing. And that is precisely why I will *not* quit. I happen to care more about world peace now and for generations to come than about making myself popular with a few of my critics in the Congress. Oh, I am sure that the easier choice would be to retire to San Clemente and bask there in the honors and tributes that we Americans lavish upon our former Presidents. But I prefer to take the hard road, the high road, if that is the road that leads to the end of warfare and to world peace for our children and our children's children. My fellow Americans, I was raised to be a Quaker, not a quitter.

Now I have to say some things to you that you may not care to hear, especially those of you who try to think the best of our country, as I do myself. But tonight I must speak the truth, unpleasant as it may be; you deserve no less. My fellow Americans, I understand there are going to be those in Congress who will not respect the decision I have announced here tonight, as I respected theirs, arrived at earlier in the day. We have reason to believe that there are those who are going to try to make political capital out of what I have said to you tonight from the bottom of my heart. There are even going to be some who will use my words to attempt to create a national crisis in order to reap political gain for themselves or their party. And, most dangerous of all, there are some elements in the country, given to violence and lawlessness as a way of life, who may attempt to use force to remove me from Office.

Let me quickly reassure you that this administration will not tolerate lawlessness of any kind. This administration will not permit the time-honored constitutional principle of the separation of powers to be subverted by a disgruntled, ambitious, or radical minority. This administration intends to maintain and defend that great American tradition that has come down to us unbroken from the days of the Founding Fathers—the great tradition of a President of the United States, duly elected by the people of the United States, serving out his term in office without violent interference by those who disagree with his policies. Disagreement and dissent are, of course, in the great tradition of a democracy like our own; but the violent overthrow of the elected government is something that is repugnant to me, as it is to every American, and so long as I am President, I promise you that I will deal promptly and efficiently with those who advocate or engage in violence as a means of bringing about political change.

In order to discourage those who would resort to violence of any kind, in order to maintain law and order in the nation and to safeguard the welfare and well-being of law-abiding American citizens, I have tonight, in my constitutional role as Commander-in-Chief, ordered the Joint Chiefs of Staff to place the Armed Forces on a standby alert around the nation. The Department of Justice and the Federal Bureau of Investigation have also been advised to take all necessary steps to ensure domestic tranquility. The National Guard has already been notified and throughout the fifty states units are being mobilized for duty. Furthermore, state and local police have been encouraged to request whatever assistance they may require, in the way of personnel or equipment, in order to maintain law and order in your communities.

My fellow Americans, I swore upon taking this office to safeguard this nation and its citizens, and I intend to stand on my word. No one—and that includes Congressmen and Senators, just as it does the armed revolutionary —is going to tell the American people that they cannot have sitting in the White House the President they have chosen in a free and open election. And I don't care whether that President happens to be myself, President Washington, President Lincoln, or President Eisenhower. I give you every assurance tonight that the President you, the American people, elected for a second four-year term will not permit the votes you cast so overwhelmingly in his favor to have been cast in vain.

God bless each and every one of you.

Good night.

New York Review of Books, Volume XX, No. 10 (June 14, 1973).

RUSSELL BAKER
[Observer]
(1925-   )

A Virginian by birth and Baltimorean by education and experience, at The Johns Hopkins University and the *Baltimore Sun,* Mr. Baker moved on to the Washington Bureau of *The New York Times* in 1954, where since 1962 he has published regular columns of lighthearted commentary and wit on a wide assortment of topics, a great many of them political and increasingly skeptical of the leaders of national affairs.

Much Ado About Tapping

The papers have made a big fuss about the wiretapping which Henry Kissinger and the President had the F.B.I. do on some of their top foreign-policy people. It is typical of the way the press is blowing things all out of proportion these days.

The fact is there was every reason to wiretap those men. National security was involved. Somebody had just leaked a military secret to the newspapers. Publication of that secret—that the United States was bombing Cambodia —could have alerted people all over Cambodia to what was going on.

Obviously, somebody on the inside could not be trusted.

In fact, nobody on the inside could be trusted, as we now know. It must have been a little like the Kremlin in the late Stalin epoch. What more natural than that Henry Kissinger should have sat down with J. Edgar Hoover and discussed the necessity for catching unloyal gabblers?

One of Mr. Kissinger's closest advisers, the papers announce with scandalous prominence, was singled out for special F.B.I. eavesdropping attention so the police apparatus could assure itself that he was clean, that he could be trusted.

It is hard to see why the papers make so much of this. In the atmosphere of distrust which suffused the White House, men were begging the F.B.I. to tap their phones and bug their bedrooms so they could prove themselves clean.

At that time, if you were a Washington reporter, it was not uncommon to pick up a ringing phone and find yourself talking to some White House man so eminent that humanity scarce dared breathe his name.

Typically, these conversations went something like this:

"Hello. Stanley of The Times speaking."

"Oh, it's you, is it Stanley, you fink! This is Preston Partridge of the National Secrets Conservation Cabal at the White House. That's spelled P-A-R-T-R-I-D-G-E. Only rats leak!"

Followed by a noisy hanging up. Partridge was not talking to Stanley, of course, but to the bug and wiretap police.

It is no secret that Mr. Kissinger himself gladly submitted to total wiretapping and always had F.B.I. bugs in his necktie knot, toothbrush and pajama-pants cord. Under round-the-clock surveillance, he was able not only to maintain his reputation for being totally clean of leaks to the press, but also to keep his enemies in the White House on the defensive, since the people who were bugging and tapping Mr. Kissinger naturally overheard Mr. Kissinger receiving his own bugging-tapping reports on rival White House giants.

I'M THE WATERGATE

Nobody, obviously, could risk saying anything anytime except what was conventional and orthodox.

And yet, somehow, certain people still managed to leak.

Harsh measures were justified and, indeed, taken. The papers do not know—and what a to-do about it they would make if they did!—that President Nixon had the F.B.I. put taps on Mrs. Nixon.

Regrettably, it was a sloppy piece of tapmanship. Wires became crossed, Mrs. Nixon's phone began performing oddly. It rang at 12:30 in the morning on one occasion, and she found herself listening to Henry Kissinger's teeth being brushed. Once she dialed Tricia's number only to find herself listening to three prominent Congressmen in a Capitol Hill hideout arguing about the best place in town to get a shoeshine.

One night at bedtime Mrs. Nixon complained. The President had to confess. He had ordered her tapped.

Mrs. Nixon was distraught until the President explained that he had done it only to let the police find out for themselves that she was clean and never leaked to the press.

Mrs. Nixon saw that it was a deed done out of love. This made her feel so splendid that she suggested that the President have a bottle of champagne sent up from the White House wine cellar.

The President picked up his phone and dialed the wine cellar. The surprise on his face startled Mrs. Nixon. "Dick," she cried, "what is it?"

"It's Kissinger," he said. "He is snoring."

Ron Ziegler's Diary

The following are excerpts from Ronald Ziegler's diary, which were leaked by sources close to the source of the Nile. Mr. Ziegler's diary entries are undated. This is because Mr. Ziegler apparently distrusts his diary. Consider the following entry:

"Dear Diary: No, no, no. I have thought about it all week, and it seems manifestly indicative of the present state of—. Oh, Diary, why do I talk that way to you? Can it be that I am now so terrified of saying something when I speak that I cannot even talk straight from the shoulder to my good old faithful Diary?

"And yet, how do I know you won't leak? Everybody is leaking these days. Nobody is safe. Even safes have begun to leak. That's why I have decided not to put dates on these entries. I am not authorized to tell anybody what day of the week it is. Why should I tell diaries?"

New York *Times*, May 19, 1973.

In the following entry, which is typical of many, Mr. Ziegler faces his diary at the end of a busy day:

"Dear Diary: Certain events of a public character eventuated in connection with two separate branches of a certain large government today. As I have indicated in multiple previous entries, I am not at liberty to disclose the identity of that particular government, nor of the two separate branches involved in the eventuation to which my opening statement alluded, and I will stand on that statement in regard to nondisclosure."

In another entry Mr. Ziegler debates how much to tell his diary about a butter pecan ice cream cone which he has eaten during the day at a drugstore:

"Dear Diary: I have a statement for you at this time in regard to a pleasurable incident involving the alimentary process in which White House personnel participated in a public place within the previous 24-hour time period. The incident referred to involved an unheated edible substance containing three elements, the whole sited atop a conical sugar module. I can neither confirm nor deny at this point in time any potential allegations in regard to unsubstantiated implications that the pleasurable incident occurred, alimentary-wise, while the White House personnel in question was riffling through a magazine rack copy of Penthouse."

Mr. Ziegler's work requires him to listen to White House correspondents' questions twice a day. In the following rare and exuberant entry he tells his diary that he has answered one of these incessant questions:

"Diary, Diary! What a day! Forgive my silly boyish lapse into monosyllabics; I know it should be 'the present diurnal cycle has been most gratifying.' Nevertheless, Diary, there are times when I feel so wonderful, spirit-wise, about a particularly good piece of work that I cannot stop myself from lapsing into English.

"The present diurnal cycle in which we are now situated has witnessed such an event. It would be constitutionally ineluctable for me to disclose the details, and as a consequence of this assertion of the doctrine of the ineluctability of excessive disclosure, I shall have nothing more to say about that at this time except that—well, Diary, I was really good in there today."

With the start of the Watergate leaks, Mr. Ziegler began to be more careful about what he told his Diary.

"Dear Diary" begins a typical entry from this period, "I'd like to tell you who I am, but in the absence of positive evidence of your absolute loyalty to the historic doctrine of the ineffability of powers, I can only caution you not to assume that I am the same person you used to think I might be. Everything that has gone before is now inappropriate."

In the following entry Mr. Ziegler tells his Diary that he has been promoted and is now the Nixon Administration's director of information:

"Dear Diary: In view of the present situation as it exists at this moment in time, it has been decided by me that excessive information supply to diary-type media must be subjected to discreet curbings. For this reason, I will have nothing to tell you today, and may not tomorrow, or thereafter, in actual point of inauspicious fact."

New York *Times*, June 12, 1973.

The Day before Yesterday
Recent Incandescents

Recent Incandescents
(1935–1973)

The sustained writing of political humor by topnotch practitioners in the United States decayed into a suspended, if not vanished, popular art for almost twenty years after Will Rogers' death in 1935. Whether the Second World War and the Cold War aftermath, including the Korean and Indochinese conflicts, were responsible for this disintegration is unclear even today. Yet it grew commonplace by the middle of the 1950s to decry the dwindling output and declining quality of humor in the land.

Of course, there were radio, motion picture, and nightclub comedians, most of whom tried television at one time or another during the medium's infancy, who made merry about politics and politicians, among other things. Bob Hope on weekly radio was the nation's favorite quipster on public events. His stock-in-trade was the polished one-liner deftly delivered. Audiences loved his predictable routines, in which only the names of persons and details of current happenings had to be revised to keep his gags up to the minute. Today almost nothing remains but our memories of Hope's performances, shallow, ephemeral, and fleeting, yet lighthearted and providing their moments of joy. They resembled nothing so much as the latest round of inspirations for office jokes and barroom guffaws.

Eventually political humor began to revive, resurrected by Art Buchwald, Russell Baker, and Philip Roth, though with no superstar to date. Until Watergate, progress was slow Vaughan Meader's parodies of the Kennedys as *The First Family* and Barbara Garson's pseudo-Shakespearean account in *MacBird!* of the Kennedy-Johnson struggles for power became tasteless after the assassinations. Mort Sahl, Lenny Bruce, and Bob Newhart enjoyed only limited appeal, except when their recordings carried their words beyond their customary audiences in night clubs, coffee houses, and universities, while the Smothers Brothers came to grief on television. Langston Hughes, among the greatest of America's black artists, created the character of Jess B. Simple, who bore a dark and close resemblance to Mr. Dooley through his underdog's wisdom and gently delivered though lingering bite. Hughes was joined by "Moms" Mabley, Alfred A. Duckett, and Dudley Randall, in attempting to humanize us all, while Dick Gregory gave his views from the back of the bus.

Scattered beacons dispelled the darkness, as these selections remind us.

Anonymous

Rejected

A stranger stood at the Gates of Hell
And the Devil himself had answered the bell
He glanced at him from head to toe,
And said "My Friend, I'd like to know
What have you done in the line of sin
To entitle you to come within,"
Then Franklin D. said with his usual guile
As he gave the Devil his winning smile,
"When I took charge in '33
A Nation's faith was mine you see
So I promised this and promised that
And calmed them down with a Fireside chat.
I put the padlocks on their banks
And called the Congress a bunch of cranks.
I spent their money on fishing trips
Fishing from decks of their battle-ships.
I gave men money with W.P.A.
Then raised their taxes and took it away.
I killed their pigs and burned their crops,
Would raise their wages then close their shops
And double-crossed both old and young
And still the fools my praises sung.
I brought back beer, then what do you think,
I taxed it so high they couldn't drink.
I gave them money with government loans,

Source unknown.

119

When they missed a payment I'd take their homes.
When I wanted to punish the folks you know,
I'd put my wife on the radio.
I paid them to let their farms lie still
And imported foodstuffs from Brazil.
I curtailed crops when I felt real mean,
And shipped in corn from 'Argentine'.
Now when they'd worry, stew or fret
I'd get them chanting the alphabet.
With the A.A.A. and N.R.L.B. the W.P.A. and C.C.C.
With all these units I got their goats
And still I crammed it down their throats.
When organizers needed dough
I closed the plants for the C.I.O.
I ruined jobs and ruined health
And put the screws on the rich man's wealth
And some who couldn't stand the gaff
Would call on me and how I'd laugh.
I ruined the country, its homes and then,
Placed the blame on Nine Old Men."
Now Franklin talked both long and loud
The Devil stood and his head was bowed.
At last he said, "Let's make this clear,
You'll have to look elsewhere, you can't come here.
For once you mingle with this mob.
I'll have to hunt myself a job."

WESTBROOK PEGLER
(1894-1969)

Westbrook Pegler distinguished himself by his propensity for irritating people. A scornfully derisive news commentator (a "fantastic fogshape" of a profession, he once described it), Mr. Pegler's fame rested on his ability to denounce and expose. His talent originated in the revolving assumption that all sides were generally in the wrong. Siding with the "common man," especially against taxes, politicians, bureaucrats, and union leaders, Pegler pitted himself *agin* many of the leaders of the selfsame people he sought to defend. During the 1930s he became notorious, an object of controversy and denunciation, for his attacks against both Fascism and Communism, against labor organizations in general and the C.I.O. in particular, which he claimed were either Communist fronts or rackets or both, and against the New Deal.

Pegler was not a humorist by profession, but he penned a good many funny pieces. He could be cruel and in bad taste, as many persons thought, as in his unforgettable labeling of President Franklin D. Roosevelt as "mama's boy," and his common scolding of Mrs. Eleanor Roosevelt.

That Man Is Here Again

Poundridge, N. Y.—That man from the government has been

around again in our neighborhood, away from it all up the country, insisting that we need a farm-to-market road, and our citizens are up in arms about the matter. He was around a couple of years ago, and we chased him off, but he curled his lips in a sinister leer as he went and said:—"You haven't heard the last of this, my fine friends. Nobody can defy the United States Government."

We all thought the matter had just been allowed to drop, but apparently some one has been going over some old papers in Washington, and that man is here again.

We haven't got any farms up here away from it all, and Ernest Schelling, the grocer at the center, buys all his tomatoes and parsley and such things from the big market in New York. But the man claims we have got to have a farm-to-market road, even if he has to import a farmer from Kansas and build a market himself.

The neighbors don't want the road, because it would draw traffic to their seclusion, which is what they came to the country for, and the supervisors are playing the chill for the proposition, because the town would have to pay for the land, which would run up the taxes and get them in wrong with the voters.

Some of the neighbors knowing that I go down to Washington pretty often have called around to ask if I can't use a little pull to get that man called off and sent to South Dakota with his farm-to-market road. But you can just imagine what drag I have after needling Mr. Big [Pres. Franklin D. Roosevelt] about his income-tax exemptions and Jim Farley about the political poor-box robbers stuck away in soft jobs.

I used to get an occasional friendly letter from Harold

Westbrook Pegler, *The Dissenting Opinions* of Mr. . . . . , New York, (1938) , pp. 90–93.

Ickes, but the last time I saw him at the Gridiron Dinner he pulled a sour puss on me and walked away, so I guess he must be sore, too. So, probably, if I should go around trying to get them to call off that man and drop his farm-to-market road into some state that has a farm and a market they would call a huddle and build another Golden Gate Bridge in front of my place.

This farm-to-market road is going to cost $100,000 or so, as near as we can figure, and we are fixing to build a new school which would cost just that, so I said to one of the boys on the town board, "Why don't you ask the guy to skip the road and build the school instead?"

But he said, "No, I asked him about that, but he says it has got to be a road, and it has got to have a farm at one end and a market at the other. So I told him we didn't have any farm or any market, and he said, 'One radish is a farm, if it comes to that, and one road-side stand is a market, if it buys the radish, so don't be trying to evade the law with technicalities having the color of legality. That is the way with you lousy rich all the time. You haven't got the first instinct of good citizenship, trying to sabotage our beloved President.' "

The last time the man was around, a couple of years ago, there was quite a lot of excitement in our neighborhood, because he went sneaking around disguised as a college boy selling magazines and poking his nose into backyards for evidence of farming.

He found several places where they were growing a tomato or a corn and claimed these were all farms, but our people got a lawyer and made affidavits that these were pets, and there was a ruling of the Supreme Court that pet vegetables do not constitute farming in the meaning of the law. But just to play it safe everybody has refrained from growing any suspicious vegetation ever since, and still here the guy is here again with his road, and now the neighbors all look on one another with suspicion in fear that some traitor has planted a mess of greens constituting a farm.

I suppose there is a lot in the way you treat these people, and maybe it was a mistake to run him off so abruptly the other time, arousing his personal spite, but, after all, his approach wasn't any too tactful either.

He just came and said, "Where do you want the farm-to-market road built?"

Citizenship and government are getting terribly complicated, anyway. About that school, the way I understand it, we were going to build a nice school for $40,000, but somebody discovered that the State won't share the burden unless you spend at least $100,000 for the school. So I suppose we are going to build a $100,000 school instead of the $40,000 one and load the poor kids down with two and a half times as much education as they need, and probably give them brain fever.

It's always something, isn't it?

Hugo Bloh's Job-Trust

I have been having a good laugh over the plight of Hugo Bloh, that smart operator who moved in quietly and started buying up jobs back in 1937, when Labor finally put over the proposition that a job is property. Hugo had a little money at the time, and he began with a couple of itinerants working in a paper box factory in Jersey City who were fixing to quit, anyway, and go somewhere else. They didn't know that they had any property right in their jobs, so naturally, when Hugo offered them three dollars each they took it and thought he was crazy.

But Hugo drew up bills of sale, and next day when the boss of the plant was about to pick two new men out of the line at the gate Hugo showed up with the documents and said, "Just a minute, Brother. Those jobs are my property."

The boss was half-crazy, anyway, from people with government badges coming around and telling him what he couldn't do, so he backed away, and Hugo rented the jobs to a couple of hungry workmen at the rate of a dollar a week each. The boss had to hire them. Operating around factory gates, Hugo soon had several hundred jobs in hand, and business was growing so fast that he opened an office and hired a lawyer, although before doing that he made the attorney sign over the job to him.

Then the attorney got looking through the new laws from Washington and decided that Hugo ought to register his property in the county seat wherever the jobs were situated.

From that point on business just pyramided. Hugo hired scouts who could tip him off whenever some man or woman was about to quit or had been fired or laid off for any reason. The people had heard that jobs were property, but they didn't put much stock in the idea, because they weren't used to it.

Hugo would offer a dollar or two, and to a person who was about to quit or lose out, anyway, that was just so much velvet. In no time he had ten thousand jobs rented out from one to three dollars a week, and from that he went on to a hundred thousand, and eventually to more than two million jobs, scattered all over the country. He had offices in all the big cities, and, owing to a peculiarity of the labor laws supporting the property right of a man who owned a job, he had the government on his side.

The Department of Labor didn't like the idea, but Hugo's

lawyer went down to Washington and showed them in the book where the jobs were the property of the one who owned them, no matter how many jobs he had. The government was bound to protect this property right, so the Department of Labor had to establish a check-off system in thousands of plants to collect the job rent every pay day from the lessees of Hugo's jobs and turn the money over to Hugo.

In 1942 Hugo paid the greatest income tax in history and bought the old Rockefeller place at Tarrytown for a country home. He bought a yacht so big that even the lifeboats carried lifeboats, and got married and divorced three times a year. And when he went to the races he would bet so much in the mutuels that the odds would just vanish, and he would take down less than his own taw, even when he won, owing to the deduction of the percentage.

Then it happened. Some little counter hopper working in one of Hugo's rented jobs was reading law at night school, and one night he happened to wonder if Hugo paid any property tax on all those jobs. Hugo had paid his income taxes all right, but the counter hopper discovered that the property tax had never been paid. Hugo tried to bluff him, then buy him in, but the counter hopper was sore and wouldn't do business. So all over the country the assessors and collectors moved in on Hugo, and now he is indicted in fifty different places, and sure to get plenty of years, because it never occurred to him that private property has to pay taxes, even if it's jobs.

And, funniest part of it all, the government moved in, paid all these local taxes and took over the jobs. So here we are now in Mr. Roosevelt's fourth term, with practically all the private jobs in the country turned over to the Job Department, under Jim Farley, at a rental of from 50 cents to $20 a week.

You don't own a job now. You rent it from the U.S.A., and, my God, the money rolls in!

W. C. FIELDS
(1880-1946)

Claude W. Dukinfield, his name theatricalized to W. C. Fields, was born in Philadelphia, which he preferred to a cemetery. He became celebrated as a juggler (cigar boxes!) in vaudeville and a comedian in Broadway musicals and motion pictures. He became famous as a master buffoon all over again after his death, as his films were revived for television and film festivals. He made the best of life as a bad business. "He moved through the world," Alan P. Twyman wrote, "with a feeling of wariness for his surroundings and a hastily assumed air of nonchalance, confident that he would in the end prevail." Children, dogs, inanimate objects, and respectable citizens were his sworn enemies.

Let's Look at the Record

No doubt most of my gentle readers were both amazed and delighted when the news of my candidacy for the chief office of this fair land blazed forth on the front pages from coast to coast. I remember one particularly colorful account in an important California daily:

LOS ANGELES MAN HELD IN
CRULLER-FACTORY BREAK

Los Angeles, March 25 (AP) —Responding to an automatic alarm signal, police apprehended an unarmed marauder in Schmackpfeiffer's Cruller Works tonight. The accused claimed that he had attended an Episcopal strawberry festival earlier in the evening and had lost his way home, ending up in the cruller factory by some strange twist. He gave his name as W. C. Fields, a comedian and a candidate for the Presidency in 1940. Officials expressed the belief that he might well be a Presidential candidate, since half the crackpots in the country were running, but they had serious doubts that he was a comedian.

It was one of the nicest police stations I've ever been in, too . . . but there! I must not digress into sweet memories. The matter at hand is this: Right off the bat I wish to dispel some of the vile rumors built up around me by my political adversaries. In the first place, I never stated that Buzzie Dall was a sarsparilla-drinking, cribbage-playing, evil old man. Nor did I ever declare that America's frontier was in France—though I know of a little hostel on the Boulevard Raspail that would make a delightful place for a frontier. And thirdly, never at any time have I promised the voters of America two chickens in every garage. The men who have spread these preposterous calumnies are merely my terrified political opponents.

The purpose of this modest little volume is to make clear to my future constituents what my moral and political background has been, and exactly how I stand on the issues of the day. So just pull up a fireside and lend an ear to your old Uncle Will, the white hope of the Bull Moose Party in 1940.

In the first place, many of you have asked why I am running for President when I already have a promising future as a veterinary (I've been studying nights). To this question I merely reply: "There's a reason for everything."

The reason Columbus discovered America was that he wished to find India. Abraham Lincoln liberated the slaves because he wanted to make all men free and equal. My cousin Haverstraw married a tattooed lady for art's sake alone.

However, the reason I am running for President is somewhat more complicated. It dates back to that fateful day when my first spark of interest in politics was fanned to a glowing ember. I was exactly nine years old, and I can remember clearly how Boss Tweed's brother, Harris Tweed, took me on his knee and said:

"Will, whatever you do in the years to come, always remember one thing: Never give a sucker an even break."

At the time, my youthful mind did not grasp the whole significance of this great precept. In fact, not until I was in my late twenties did the truth of it burst forth upon me in all its glory.

At that time I made a tour of the Southwestern states selling an amazing preparation called Raro Hair Restorer. I had obtained the formula from a beautiful Indian princess—Weeping Sinew, I believe was her name. One hot July day I sold a bottle to a baldheaded gentleman in Cowcatcher, New Mexico.

"Will this really work?" he asked.

"Squire," I returned in my inimitable manner, "this colossal medication will grow hair in a bathtub!"

The next day he returned and wanted his money back.

"What's the trouble?" I demanded. "Doesn't it do everything I said it would?"

"Oh, yes, it works all right," he said, "but I've decided

I don't like hair in my bathtub—it tickles hell out of me."

From that day on "Never give a sucker an even break" has been my watchword, and my ideal has been to rise to the one great position in the nation where I may exercise it to the fullest.

Ideals have always been a strong consideration with me, anyway. Just this past January I risked catching my death of pneumonia for an ideal. I was dining with a few political colleagues at the Mayflower in Washington. If memory serves me correctly, among the guests were Franklin and Eleanor Roosevelt, Cordell Hull, Harry Hopkins, Miss Frances Perkins, Chief Justice Hughes and Gypsy Rose Lee.

During the baked-flounder course, Secretary Hull leaned over to me and purred in a guileless tone: "Fields, would you care for the Worcestershire sauce?"

It was no more than a clumsy attempt to trick me into revealing my stand on naval appropriations.

"Sirrah!" I snapped, "my seconds will call in the morning!"

Whereupon I stalked from the dining room in high dudgeon, and it was not until I was out on the icy street that I realized I had no shoes on (I had slipped them off under the table before putting my feet in Miss Perkins's lap).

As a result I spent two weeks at the Ellin Speyer Memorial Hospital, but I did not rue my action. It proves what a man of my caliber will do for his principles.

I am truly a candidate with both feet on the ground. I take no fol-de-rol from any man, much less any fiddle-faddle. And when, on next November fifth, I am elected chief executive of this fair land, amidst thunderous cheering and shouting and throwing of babies out the window, I shall, my fellow citizens, offer no such empty panaceas as a New Deal, or an Old Deal, or even a Re-Deal. No, my friends, the reliable old False Shuffle was good enough for my father and it's good enough for me.

Furthermore, I shall not mince words in my first message to Congress. Though full many a solon's cheek may flush with embarrassment, I shall point out these trenchant and oft-evaded issues:

1. Political baby-kissing must come to an end—unless the size and age of the babies be materially increased.
2. Sentiment or no entiment, Dolly Madison's wash *must* be removed from the East Room.
3. What actually *did* become of that folding umbrella I left in the Congressional Library three summers ago?

When, on the fourteenth of February last, I outlined my plan of action in a speech at Des Moines (the night some scoundrel Tory sneaked a snapping turtle into my water pitcher) political circles were set agog. "Who is this person who proposes to revolutionize our government?" they demanded. "Merely a presumptuous dark horse!" Some even went so far as to call me a certain part of a dark horse.

To refute these charges, right here I should like to review briefly the major incidents of my amazing career, for the benefit of any benighted reader who, like my Des Moines opponents, is not acquainted with the Fields Saga.

I was born in a humble log cabin a scant stone's throw from Grant's Tomb, the second son of a lowly cordwainer. (Father was one of the lowliest men I ever knew, measuring less than twelve feet on a pair of seven-foot stilts.

He could stand on his head under the kitchen sink, but seldom did so, arguing that there was not much point to it in the first place.)

When Father was not busy waining cords, he worked as a substitute horse-car driver. One of my most vivid recollections is driving with him on the day of the blizzard of '88. He had his horses frozen stiff right in front of Mr. Terrence O'Flanagan's saloon on Eighth Street. The conductor, a very dear friend of Dad's, succumbed to the subzero weather on the rear platform, his hands frozen tight to the change box. If it had not been for Father's miraculous presence of mind, there might have been dire tragedy that day. However, he immediately jumped from the car, ran up to O'Flanagan's saloon and opened the swinging doors wide. The fumes that poured out revived the horses in a trice. Snorting with excitement, they pulled the car right off the tracks and galloped into the barroom. The conductor thawed out, finished ringing up his fare and stepped over to the bar. Everyone had a Rock 'n Rye on Dad—except the two valiant steeds, who, obviously, were already supplied with horse's necks.

Of course, I have other early recollections—but perhaps my dear readers would obtain a more colorful idea of my youth by a few peeps into my "memory basket." As other men have kept diaries all their lives, I have always kept a memory basket, in which, from earliest childhood, I have packed away all the touching little souvenirs of my everyday life. Each August 18th—in commemoration of the day I smoked my first marihuana cigarette—I run through this precious memory basket item by item, bedewing each with a nostalgic tear. Let me share a few of my keepsakes with you, my friends—in chronological order, of course.

First there is that dear baby tooth, with a small tag attached reading: "The first bicuspid that Little Willie lost. Extracted from Daddy's wrist on April 5, 1887." What a shining pearl it is, too—not a trace of a filling in it!

Next I find a fond note from my first-grade teacher to my mother, reporting my prodigious scholastic progress:

Dear Mrs. Fields:
   Unless you can dissuade your son William from blowing his nose on the pen-wipers, I shall have to request you to keep him at home.

Sympathetically
Esther N. Pertwee

The next important memento affords a revealing glimpse into my adolescent character, which seems to have been of a serious, almost brooding, nature. It is a page ripped from the autograph book of the girl who sat next to me in Algebra-1. I remember her name was Rena, though I cannot recall for the nonce the square on her hypotenuse. This is what it says:

Name: W. C. Fields
Address: 1312 Grub Terrace
Favorite Flower: Coriopsis
Favorite Book: "113 Bird Calls—and How to Simulate Them"
What Color Do You Wear Most?—Size 14½
Favorite Hobby: Crocheting Antimacassars
If you were alone on a desert island with me, what would you do?—I would rub two sticks together to induce flame.

Here the fragment ends. But I am glad to say that the next keepsake is proof that my hobbyistic leanings, at least, soon become more virile. That keepsake—one of my most precious treasures—is an exquisite pair of loaded dice, bearing the date of my graduation from high school.

Incidentally, it is of interest to note that I have remained true to the hobby of crap-shooting ever since, and on this I rely for a great many votes. For nothing will elect a President quicker than a hobby (unless it is the ability to wear an Indian hat becomingly). Just for instance, take the following Prexies:

Grover Cleveland . . . Fishing

Calvin Coolidge . . . Mechanical horseback riding

Franklin D. Roosevelt . . . Stamp collecting, in collaboration with James A. Farley

Ulysses S. Grant . . . Well, of all the Presidents' hobbies, I think General Grant's came nearer to my ideas and ideals—excepting that I was never a great cigar smoker.

But let us drop the matter for the present and continue with the story of my early life. Upon being graduated from high school I was at a loss to know what profession to turn to. I knew little of law, and medicine had always been distasteful to me. I might have made a fine pianist except that a revolving stool always made me dizzy. So, perforce, there was only one profession left—juggling.

I proved a born genius in my chosen work, and between the years 1905 and 1908 I performed before most of the crowned heads of Europe. Then came a tragic interlude of enforced retirement—during the spring of 1909 when my hand was caught in a pickle jar.

Of course, from 1910 on, my meteoric march to the pinnacle of success has been immortalized in the songs and literature of our day, so it would seem needless to repeat the tale here.

Suffice it to say, because of the length and breadth of my experience, I have been showered with countless honorary degrees from our foremost universities. Many are the scholars who have sat at my feet. I particularly remember Nicholas Murray Butler and William Lyon Phelps, sitting cross-legged before the great open fireplace and staring up at me in awe. "Tell us more," they would beg. Fine fellows, Nick and Bill.

Naturally, in the last twenty or thirty years I have become the supreme authority on a good many matters that directly affect the everyday life of all people. Indeed, they are the very matters in which the chief executive of a great nation should of necessity be well-versed. Allow me to enumerate:

1. *Marriage:* Since approximately half the population of the United States is made up of the fairer sex, any President worthy of the name should be familiar with the intricacies of the matrimonial problem—unless he wants to change his residence from the White House to the *château de la chien* (doghouse).

2. *Income Tax:* The major responsibility of a President is to squeeze the last possible cent out of the taxpayer; thus he should be at least familiar with the intricacies of the ransom notes that the Internal Revenue Department sends out each spring.

3. *Resolutions:* If the chief executive is not an expert in the art of making resolutions, how can he hope to break his campaign promises gracefully?

4. *Etiquette:* At a state dinner, should the Nazi ambassador be served *Châteaubriand à la Marseillaise?* Failure to understand this delicate question might well plunge our nation into war.

5. *Physical Fitness:* There is no room in the White House for a man who is afflicted with barber's itch, spots before the eyes, hangnails or housemaid's knee. A President must know how to keep himself fit—else who would

throw out the first ball at the Washington Senators' opening game?

6. *The Care of Babies:* Shall didies be folded square or triangular? This is the burning question of the day, and the better the candidate understands the little darlings, the more competently he can decide the issue.

7. *Business Success:* If he knows nothing else, a President should at least understand the secret of success in the business world. For, after all, what is the Presidency but a glorified business—or, at least, a fine racket?

Because of my broad understanding of these seven vital subjects, I commend myself to the great American public as the one and only logical choice for President in 1940. And in the succeeding chapters of this modest volume, I shall attempt to clarify my stand on every phase of each of the seven issues in question—as well as drop a few invaluable hints that will benefit each and every one of my readers.

And now, before we proceed further, let us all repair to the bar—the votes are on me.

W. C. Fields, *Fields for President,* introduction and commentary by Michael M. Taylor, New York (1971), pp. 4–23.

JACKIE "MOMS" MABLEY
(1897—1975)

Effervescent and ageless, "Moms" Mabley, North Carolina-born comedienne and actress, was invariably a smash hit as guest celebrity on television shows. Her Broadway performances include *Swinging the Dream* and *Blackbirds*. She was heard in the radio version of "Swingtime at the Savoy," and seen in the film *Emperor Jones*. In 1974 she appeared as Grace Teasdale Grimes, "Amazing Grace" in Matt Robinson's movie of that name, a Baltimore row-house dweller whose suspicions and political activity are aroused when she sees a white political boss making night-time visits to her neighbor, a black candidate for mayor.

Little Cindy Ella

I want to read you one about Little Cindy Ella. You-all call her Cinderella in that book you-all got. Anyhow, way down South lived a little girl. She had long black hair, pretty brown eyes, pretty brown skin. Well, let's face it—she was colored! Little Cindy Ella dressed very shabby because she had to use her money to pay the notes on her boy friend's Cadillac.

She worked for a mean, mean, mean old woman with her two ugly daughters. Ugly—UG-U-G-L-Y! They were so ugly until they had a dishonorable discharge from *The White Citizen's Council.* One day the mean old woman and her ugly daughters got an invitation to a prom dance. It was the biggest dance of the season. That was the time that they usually picked "Miss Ku Klux Klan."

The mean old woman and her two daughters left for the dance. Little Cindy Ella wanted to go but she knew it was impossible. So she sat down and started crying. Just about that time a knock came on the door. And guess who it was? Her friend Bobby Kennedy! He had two magic wands in his hand—the Constitution and the Civil Rights Bill before it was passed.

He said, "Little girl, why are you crying so hard?"

She said, "Because I want to go to the prom dance at the University of Mississippi because my boy friend James Meredith goes to school there."

One wave of his magic wand and her raggedy dress had turned into a beautiful white lace dress. On her pretty black hair she had a pretty blue ribbon. She looked down at her feet and her shoes had turned to golden glass slippers. She went over to the mirror, and to her surprise she had turned as white as snowy bleach.

She said, "Mirror, mirror on the wall, who's the fairest of them all?"

The mirror said, "Snow White and don't you forget it!"

Another wave of the magic wand and she looked out the window and there was a gold coach with a white horse and a white chauffeur. Little Cindy Ella started out the door and Bobby said, "Be sure and be back by twelve o'clock."

Little Cindy Ella was having such a good time at the dance. All the men wanted to dance with Little Cindy Ella. And all at once she forgot what time it was. The clock struck twelve. Her beautiful white dress had turned to rags. The bow on her head had turned to a stocking cap. She looked down and her gold slippers had turned to sneakers. She looked out the window and her coach had turned to a wagon. And the beautiful white horse to an old nag. And her chauffeur had turned to Pigmeat.

Everybody on the floor was gazing at poor Little Cindy Ella, the little colored girl, dancing with the president of the Ku Klux Klan.

This story is to be continued. Her trial comes up next month!

Langston Hughes, ed., *The Book of Negro Humor*, New York (1966) , pp. 1–2.

LANGSTON HUGHES
[Jess B. Simple]
(1902-1967)

Poet, essayist, columnist, autobiographer, musical lyricist
and librettist, Langston Hughes was among the greatest
of America's black artists. He edited numerous anthologies
during the nineteen sixties to popularize talented though
unsung black writers. His character, Jess B. Simple, bears
a dark and close recsemblance to Mr. Dooley in his underdog's wisdom and his gently delivered though lingering
bite.

Radioactive Red Caps

"How wonderful," I said, "that Negroes today are being
rapidly integrated into every phase of American life from
the Army and Navy to schools to industries—advancing,
advancing!"

"I have not advanced one step," said Simple. "Still the
same old job, same old salary, same old kitchenette, same
old Harlem and the same old color."

"You are just one individual," I said. "I am speaking of
our race in general. Look how many colleges have opened
up to Negroes in the last ten years. Look at the change in
restrictive covenants. You can live anywhere."

"You mean *try* to live anywhere."

"Look at the way you can ride unsegregated in inter-state travel."

"And get throwed off the bus."

"Look at the ever greater number of Negroes in high places."

"Name me one making an atom bomb."

"That would be top-secret information," I said, "even if I knew. Anyway, you are arguing from supposition, not knowledge. How do you know what our top Negro scientists are doing?"

"I don't," said Simple. "But I bet if one was making an atom bomb, they would have his picture on the cover of *Jet* every other week like Eartha Kitt, just to make Negroes think the atom bomb is an integrated bomb. Then, next thing you know, some old Southern senator would up and move to have that Negro investigated for being subversive, beause he would be mad that a Negro ever got anywhere near an atom bomb. Then that Negro would be removed from his job like Miss Annie Lee Moss, and have to hire a lawyer to get halfway back. Then they would put that whitewashed Negro to making plain little old-time ordinary bombs that can only kill a few folks at a time. You know and I know, they don't want no Negroes nowhere near no bomb that can kill a whole state full of folks like an atom bomb can. Just think what would happen to Mississippi. Wow!"

"Your thinking borders on the subversive," I warned. "Do you want to fight the Civil War over again?"

"Not without an atom bomb," said Simple. "If I was in Mississippi, I would be Jim Crowed out of bomb shelters, so I would need some kind of protection. By the time I got the N.A.A.C.P. to take my case to the Supreme Court, the war would be over, else I would be atomized."

"Absurd!" I said. "Bomb shelters will be for everybody."

"Not in Mississippi," said Simple. "Down there they will have some kind of voting test, else loyalty test, in which they will find some way of flunking Negroes out. You can't tell me them Dixiecrats are going to give Negroes free rein of bomb shelters. On the other hand, come to think of it, they might *have* to let us in to save their own skins, beause I hear tell in the next war everything that ain't sheltered will be so charged with atoms a human can't touch it. Even the garbage is going to get radioactive when the bombs start falling. I read last week in the *News* that, in case of a bombing, it will be a problem as to where to put our garbage, because it will be radioactive up to a million years. So you sure can't keep garbage around. If you dump it in the sea, it will make the fish radioactive, too, like them Japanese tunas nobody could eat. I am wondering what the alley cats will eat—because if all the garbage is full of atomic rays, and the cats eat the garbage, and my wife pets a strange cat, Joyce will be radioactive, too. Then if I pet my wife, what will happen to me?"

"You are stretching the long arm of coincidence mighty far," I said. "What is more likely to happen is, if the bombs fall, you will be radioactive long before the garbage will."

"That will worry white folks," said Simple. "Just suppose all the Negroes down South got atomized, charged up like hot garbage, who would serve the white folks' tables, nurse their children, Red Cap their bags, and make up their Pullman berths? Just think! Suppose all the colored Red Caps carrying bags on the Southern Railroad was atom-charged! Suitcases would get atomized, too, and all that is packed in them. Every time a white man took out his toothbrush to wash his teeth on the train, his teeth would get atom-charged. How could he kiss his wife when he got home?"

"I believe you are charged now," I said.

"No," said Simple, "I am only thinking how awful this atom bomb can be! If one fell up North in Harlem and charged me, then I went downtown and punched that time clock where I work, the clock would be charged. Then a white fellow would come along behind me and punch the time clock, and he would be charged. Then both of us would be so full of atoms for the next million years, that at any time we would be liable to explode like firecrackers on the Fourth of July. And from us, everybody else in the plant would get charged. Atoms, they tell me, is catching. What I read in the *News* said that if you even look at an atom bomb going off, the rays are so strong your eyes will water the rest of your life, your blood will turn white, your hair turn gray, and your children will be born backwards. Your breakfast eggs will no longer be sunny-side up, but scrambled, giving off sparks—and people will give off sparks, too. If you walk down the street, every doorbell you pass will ring without your touching it. If you pick up a phone, whoever answers it will be atomized. So if you know somebody you don't like, for example, just phone them—and you can really fix them up! That's what they call a chain reaction. I am getting my chain ready now—the first person I am going to telephone is my former landlady! When she picks up the phone, I hope to atomize her like a Japanese tuna! She will drive a Geiger counter crazy after I say, 'Hello!' "

"My dear boy," I said, "what makes you think you, of all people, would be able to go around transferring atomic radiation to others? You would probably be annihilated yourself by the very first bomb blast."

"Me? Oh, no," said Simple. "Negroes are very hard to annihilate. I am a Negro—so I figure I would live to radiate and, believe me, once charged, I will take charge."

"In other words, come what may, you expect to survive the atom bomb?"

"If Negroes can survive white folks in Mississippi," said Simple, "we can survive anything."

The Best of Simple, New York (1961), pp. 53–57. Reprinted by permission of Farrar, Straus & Giroux, Inc., and Harold Ober Associates Incorporated.

OLIVER JENSEN
(1914-   )

Editor and writer, Oliver Jensen served on *Judge,* the humor magazine, and *Life,* the newsmagazine, both now defunct, before he joined in founding *American Heritage.* He has since served in editorial positions. He is an ardent historical preservationist and railroad buff. Among his books are *Carrier War* and *The Revolt of American Women.*

The Gettysburg Address
by President Eisenhower

Gettysburg, Pennsylvania
November 19, 1863

I haven't checked these figures but eighty-seven years ago, I think it was, a number of individuals organized a governmental setup here in this country, I believe it covered certain eastern areas, with this idea they were following up based on a sort of national-independence arrangement and the program that every individual is just as good as every other individual. Well, now, of course, we are dealing with this big difference of opinion, civil disturbance you might say, although I don't like to ap-

pear to take sides or name any individuals, and the point
is naturally to check up, by actual experience in the field,
to see whether any governmental setup with a basis like
the one I was mentioning has any validity, whether that
dedication, you might say, by those early individuals will
pay off in lasting values.

Well, here we are, you might put it that way, all together at the scene where one of these disturbances between different sides got going. We want to pay our tribute to those loved ones, those departed individuals who
made the supreme sacrifice here on the basis of their opinions about how this setup ought to be handled. It is absolutely in order and one hundred per cent okay to do this.

But if you look at the over-all picture of this, we
can't pay any tribute—we can't sanctify this area—we
can't hallow according to whatever individuals' creeds or
faiths or sort of religious outlooks are involved—like I
said about this very particular area. It was those individuals themselves, including the enlisted men, very brave
individuals, who have given this religious character to the
area. The way I see it, the rest of the world will not
remember any statements issued here but it will never
forget how these men put their shoulders to the wheel and
carried this idea down the fairway.

Our job, the living individuals' job here, is to pick up
the burden and sink the putt they made these big efforts
here for. It is our job to get on with the assignment—
and from these deceased fine individuals to take extra in-
spiration, you could call it, for the same theories about
the setup for which they did such a lot. We have to make
up our minds right here and now, as I see it, that they
didn't put out all that blood, perspiration and—well—that
they didn't just make a dry run here, and that all of us
here, under God, that is, the God of our choice, shall

beef up this idea about freedom and liberty and those kind of arrangements, and that government of all individuals, by all individuals, and for the individuals, shall not pass out of the world-picture.

Virginia City (Nevada) *Territorial Enterprise*, June 14, 1957.

MARYA MANNES
[Sec]
(1904-   )

Marya Mannes is an author and journalist who has made numerous TV network appearances. She was a feature editor for *Vogue* and *Glamour* in turn, a staff writer for *Reporter* magazine, and, during World War II, an intelligence analyst for the government. She has published several collections of essays and a novel, *Message from a Stranger*. Her latest book, *Last Rights,* is an eloquent plea for the care of the dying and dignified death. She once gathered her satiric verses together under the rubric of "Subverse."

McCarran Act

The blood that made this nation great
Will now be tested at the gate
To see if it deserves to be
Admitted to democracy,
Or rather to that small elite
Whose hemoglobin counts can meet
Requirements of purity
Consistent with security

And with that small and rabid mind
That thinks itself above mankind.

Sales Campaign

Hail to B.B.D. & O.
It told the nation how to go;
It managed by advertisement
To sell us a new President.

> EISENHOWER HITS THE SPOT,
> ONE FULL GENERAL, THAT'S A LOT.

> FEELING SLUGGISH, FEELING SICK?
> TAKE A DOSE OF IKE AND DICK.

> PHILIP MORRIS, LUCKY STRIKE,
> ALKA-SELTZER, I LIKE IKE.

Birdland Revisited

Thinner and fewer the flatulent flock,
    In vain do we watch for Leftwingers,
The Pinktinted Pundits have gone out of stock,
    Along with the Redthroated Ringers.

"McCarran Act," *The Reporter*, July 22, 1952; "Sales Campaign," *The Reporter*, November 25, 1952.

The Balancing Budget is heard in the land,
    The Stockmarket chirps in the branches.
The Bankerbirds come and eat out of your hand
    And roost in your split-level ranches.

O hark to the trilling in every tree
    As the Fatbellies nest in the nation!
Who cares if their concert is slightly off key
    When their public is under sedation?

Grand Old Coalition

For us Democrats, South, and Republicans, West,
    The Congressional future is bright:
We will stalk every bill and come in for the kill
    With a hay-making blow from the Right.

Let the White House propose, we close in and oppose,
    It's as simple and easy as that—
If they're moving ahead, we'll be stopping them dead,
    For our permanent posture is pat.

For Democrats, South, and Republicans, West,
    Our policy's clear as can be:
Whatever is planned for the needs of our land
    Is bad for the future of we.

"Birdland Revisited," *The Reporter*, February 4, 1960; "Grand Old Coalition," *The Reporter*, March 2, 1961.

CHARLES J. LEVY
(1935-   )

A sociologist with his doctorate from Brandeis University, Mr. Levy recently published *Spoils of War*, a book about the readjustment problems of America's Vietnam War veterans. "Statute of Liberty" expresses a sense of exasperation earlier in his career, while he was at Yale's Law School. He wrote it at the insistence of Victor S. Navasky, *Monocle*'s guiding spirit, after he aired his feelings in the form of an idea.

Statute of Liberty*

Give me your tired unless they are aliens who are polyg-
    amists or who practice polygamy or advocate the prac-
    tice of polygamy,
Your poor unless they are aliens who are paupers, pro-
    fessional beggars, or vagrants,
Your huddled masses yearning to breathe free unless they
    are aliens who are afflicted with tuberculosis in any
    form,

---

* The italicized portion of "Statute of Liberty" is from the poem by Emma Lazarus inscribed at the base of the Statue of Liberty; the balance is from the McCarran-Walter Immigration and Nationality Act of 1952.

The wretched refuse of your teeming shore unless they
are aliens who the consular officer or the Attorney General knows, or has reason to believe, seek to enter the
United States solely, principally, or incidentally to engage in activities which would be prejudicial to the
public interest,

Send these unless the President finds that the entry of
any aliens or of any class of aliens into the United
States would be detrimental to the interests of the
United States,

The homeless unless the employment of such aliens will
adversely affect the wages and working conditions of the
workers in the United States similarly employed,

Tempest-tost to me unless they are aliens who have been
convicted of two or more offenses,

I lift my lamp beside the golden door unless they are
aliens who write or publish, or cause to be written or
published, or who knowingly circulate, distribute, print,
or display, or knowingly cause to be circulated, distributed, printed, published, or displayed, or who knowingly have in their possession for the purpose of circulation,
publication, distribution, or display, any written or printed matter, advocating or teaching opposition to all organized government.

Monocle, Vol. 2, No. 1 (1958).

ART BUCHWALD
(1925—   )

P.S. from NATO

Paris—The NATO Conference is covered by 1,700 top-flight, highly-paid journalists from every corner of the globe. Every detail of the conference is being given careful and thorough coverage. The star of the show is President Eisenhower and every facet of the President's stay in Paris is reported to the public in detail.

In order to keep the press up on the President's activities, briefings are held at the Hotel Crillon in the morning, at noon, in the early evening, and there was even a special one held late at night for reporters who couldn't sleep.

We happened to attend one with several correspondents of early morning newspapers. To give you an idea of what takes place at one of these briefings we took down a transcript.

The man behind the microphone arrived at 12:30 A.M.

"I'm sorry I'm late, gentlemen, but I thought the show at the Lido would end at 11:30.

I have a few things to report. The President went to bed at 11:06 tonight."

Q. Jim, have Premier Gaillard and Prime Minister Macmillan also retired?

New York *Herald Tribune*, December 17, 1957.

A. To my knowledge they have.

Q. Then are we to assume they will not meet with the President until morning?

A. Yes, you could assume that.

Q. Then does that mean he's going to meet with Adenauer during the night?

A. I didn't say that. As far as I know, he's asleep until morning.

Q. Jim, whose idea was it for the President to go to sleep?

A. It was the President's idea. He was tired and decided to go to sleep.

Q. Did Sherman Adams or Dr. Snyder or the President's son suggest he go to sleep?

A. As far as I know, the President suggested the idea himself.

Q. Jim, did the President speak to anyone before retiring?

A. He spoke to the Secretary of State.

Q. And what did he say to the Secretary of State, Jim?

A. He said, "Good night, Foster!"

Q. And what did the Secretary say to the President?

A. He said, "Good night Mr. President."

Q. The Secretary didn't say "Pleasant Dreams"?

A. Not to my knowledge.

Q. Jim, do you have any idea what the President is dreaming of this very moment?

A. No, the President has never revealed to me any of his dreams.

Q. Are we to assume from that the President doesn't dream?

A. I'm not saying he does or he doesn't. I just said I don't know.

Q. Jim, when the President went to sleep last night, how did he feel?

A. He was feeling chipper and in good spirits.

Q. How many blankets were on the bed?

A. I'm not sure. Maybe two or three. But certainly no more than he uses in Washington.

Q. Could we say three?

A. I better check that. I know three blankets were made available, but it's possible he didn't use all of them.

Q. One could have been kicked off during the night?

A. Yes, that could be possible, but it's unlikely.

Q. Was there a glass of water by the bed?

A. There was a glass of water and a pitcher.

Q. Jim, could we have another briefing before morning?

A. I don't see what would be accomplished by that.

Q. It might tend to clarify the situation.

A. I think the best thing would be to have the briefing after the President gets up.

Q. What about breakfast, Jim?

A. I think we better have another briefing about breakfast, after it's over.

Q. Thank you, Jim.

A. Okay. See you later.

Let's See Who Salutes

Paris—Have you ever wondered what would have happened if the people who are in charge of television today were passing on the draft of the Declaration of Independence?

The scene is Philadelphia at WJULY-TV. Several men in

Philadelphia *Evening Bulletin*, December 10, 1959, syndicated from New York *Herald Tribune*.

gray flannel waistcoats are sitting around holding copies of the declaration.

Thomas Jefferson comes in nervously.

"Tommy," says the producer, "it's just great. I would say it was a masterpiece."

"We love it, Tommy Boy," the advertising agency man says, "It sings. Lots of drama and it holds your interest. There are a few things that have to be changed, but otherwise it stays intact."

"What's wrong with it?" Mr. Jefferson asks.

There's a pause. Everyone looks at the man from the network.

"Well, frankly, Tommy, it smacks of being a little anti-British. I mean, we've got quite a few British listeners and something like this might bring in a lot of mail."

"Now don't get sore, Tommy Boy," the agency man says. "You're the best Declaration of Independence writer in the business. That's why we hired you. But our sponsor, the Boston Tea Company, is interested in selling tea, not independence. Mr. Cornwallis, the sponsor's representative, is here and I think he has a few thoughts on the matter. Go ahead, Corney. Let's hear what you think."

Mr. Cornwallis stands up.

"Mr. Jefferson, all of us in this room want this to be a whale of a document. I think we'll agree on that."

Everyone in the room nods his head.

"At the same time we feel—I think I can speak for every-body—that we don't want to go over the heads of the mass of people who we hope will buy our product. You use words like despotism, annihilation, migrations and tenure. Those are all egghead words and don't mean a thing to the public.

"Now I like your stuff about life, liberty and the pursuit of happiness. They all tie in great with tea, particularly pursuit of happiness. But it's the feeling of all of us that you're really getting into controversial waters when you start attacking the King of Britain."

Mr. Jefferson says: "But every word of it is true. I've got documentary proof."

"Let me take a crack at it, Corney," the agency man says. "Look, Tommy Boy. It isn't a question of whether it's true or not. All of us here know what a louse George can be. But I don't think the people want to be reminded of it all the time. They have enough worries. They want escape."

"This thing has to be upbeat. If you remind people of all those taxes George has laid on us, they're not going to go out and buy tea. They're not going to go out and buy anything."

"Frankly," says the network man, "I have some strong objections on different grounds. I know you didn't mean it this way but the script strikes me as pretty Left-wing. I may have read the last paragraph wrong, but it seems to me that you're calling for the overthrow of the present government by force. The network could never allow anything like that."

"I'm sure Tommy didn't mean anything subversive," the producer says. "Tommy's just a strong writer. Maybe he got a little carried away with himself."

"Suppose Tommy took out all references to the British and the King. Suppose we said in a special preamble this Declaration of Independence had nothing to do with persons living or dead and the whole thing is fictitious. Wouldn't that solve it?"

Mr. Jefferson says: "Gentlemen, I was told to write a Declaration of Independence. I discussed it with many people before I did the actual writing. I've worked hard on this declaration—harder than I've worked on anything in my life. You either take it or leave it as it is."

"We're sorry you feel that way about it, Tommy," the agency man says. "We owe a responsibility to the country, but we owe a bigger responsibility to the sponsor. He's paying for it.

"We're not in the business of offending people. British people or any other kind of people. The truth is, the English are the biggest tea drinkers of anyone in the colonies.

"We're not going to antagonize them with a document like this. Isn't that so, Corney?"

"Check. Unless Mr. Jefferson changes it the way we want him to."

Mr. Jefferson grabs the declaration and says: "Not for all the tea in China," and exits.

The producer shakes his head. "I don't know, fellows. Maybe we've made a mistake. We could at least have run it up a flagpole to see who saluted."

"As far as I'm concerned," Mr. Cornwallis said, "the subject is closed. Let's talk about an hour Western on the French and Indian War."

Constitution Class at Ole Miss

One can't help wondering what they're teaching down at "Ole Miss" during all the trouble there. We can only speculate as to what is going on in the classrooms. How, for example, do they teach the United States Constitution? Maybe something like this:

The professor speaks. "Now, class, today we're going to discuss the American Constitution, a very unique document, which, while it has nothing to do with us, should be stud-

Philadelphia *Evening Bulletin,* October 4, 1962, syndicated from New York *Herald Tribune.*

ied anyway to show how other people govern themselves."

"The most interesting part of the Constitution is the preamble, which begins, 'They, the people of the United States, in order to form a more perfect union—' "

A student stands up. "Sir do the people of the United States really believe in the Constitution?"

"Now, let's not be too harsh on them. It is a primitive document with many flaws in it; but there are also some good things in it, and even we in Mississippi have taken some things from the American Constitution to govern ourselves. For example, there is the freedom of speech amendment. Now, this is a very good thing. We also believe in freedom of speech and we have never stopped anyone in Mississippi from yelling 'Help!' if so desired.

"Freedom of religion is another thing we've taken from the United States Constitution. We not only encourage them to pray—we make them. We encourage prayer as a way of solving problems that other states solve in the law courts.

"As a matter of fact, if a sociological problem can't be solved by prayer, then we believe there is no reason to solve it.

"The Second Amendment of the United States Constitution also has some merit—the right to keep and bear arms. As our greatest constitutional expert, Major General Edwin A. Walker, has pointed out, every citizen has the right to bear arms against the United States. Otherwise what kind of a government could you possibly have?"

A student raises his hand. "Do we go along with the Sixth Amendment which provides the right to a speedy trial?"

"Yes, we do," the professor replies. "If anyone in Mississippi whom we don't like tries to register to vote, he is entitled to a speedy trial."

Another student raises his hand. "What about the right to petition and the right to peacefully assemble?"

The professor replies, "We believe in them and proof of it is that we have permitted people to petition and to assemble to prevent Mr. Meredith from enrolling in our university."

A student raises his hand. "The Americans have an amendment which says that excessive bail shall not be required, nor excessive fines imposed, nor cruel and unusual punishments inflicted. Is this a good thing?"

"Well, that's what they believe in and who is to say under their system whether it's wrong or right? You must understand that what is constitutional in one part of the country doesn't necessarily make it constitutional in another. Otherwise our governor would be in court all the time."

A student stands. "Amendment Fifteen says the right of citizens to vote shall not be denied or abridged by the United States or any state on account of race, color, or previous condition of servitude. How are we to take this amendment?"

The professor says, "I didn't understand the question."

Informing on the Communists

According to a recent story in *The Nation,* an ex-FBI agent named Jack Levine let some top secrets out of the bag.

Mr. Levine said that one-fifth or 1,700 of the 8,500 members of the registered Communists in the United States were FBI informers.

Mr. Levine said these 1,700 were dues-paying members,

who gave the party its financial support. He also predicted that as Communist membership continues to decline and the percentage of informants increases, the day will soon come when FBI informants, who are rising rapidly to the top, will capture complete control of the party.

This is something that we're sure Mr. J. Edgar Hoover never planned on and, if what Mr. Levine says is true, he will have to revise his whole book on Communist infiltration in the United States.

It isn't too far-fetched to assume that in a couple of years the entire Communist Party will be made up of FBI informants. The reason for this is that the Communists are very bad about paying their dues and the FBI informants are the only ones who have the money (provided, of course, by the FBI) to keep up their memberships.

Because they haven't paid their dues, the real Communists will be forced to leave the party, and the only ones left will be the FBI informants.

Now one informant doesn't know who another informant is, so all the informants will assume the other informants are Communists. Yet in order to make his job pay off, the informant will have to justify his job and will, therefore, have to invent things to warrant his staying on the FBI payroll.

The informants will be in severe competition with each other and, as time goes on, their reports will become more dramatic as each one has to outdo the other.

As these reports pour into the FBI, each one more harrowing than the last, the Justice Department will have to take some action. What they'll probably do is hire more informants to keep tabs on the party.

The new informants will increase the Communist Party membership by 10,000, then 20,000, then 30,000 members, and pretty soon the party, which had been dying out, will get a new lease on life.

The trouble is that as the membership increases, the FBI will have to increase its vigilance and hire new informants to infiltrate the party.

These new members, all dues-paying members, will, in order to keep it a secret that they are informants, have to prove they are Communists, and will have to get involved in subversive activities so they won't arouse suspicion.

Once these subversive activities are exposed, there will be a public outcry and the FBI will have to send in more informants to show it is in control of the situation. Requests will be made for more funds from Congress and hearings will be held, at which time several of the informants with paper bags over their faces will testify to the danger of the increasing membership of the Communist Party.

Congress will authorize the money, urging the FBI to keep them informed as to the dangers involved. In order to keep them informed, new informants will have to be recruited. In no time at all a million registered party members will be on the rolls, all paid for by the Department of Justice.

With so many informants the competition between them will get fierce. Informants will be forced to hand in longer and more complete reports. Evaluation teams will have to be set up all over the country. Each report will require new informants to check out the facts.

In no time at all the Communists could become the leading political party in the country, and to show their strength would have to put up a candidate for the presidency of the United States.

And the name of the candidate? J. Edgar Hoover, of course. Who else?

Philadelphia *Evening Bulletin,* October 30, 1962, syndicated from New York *Herald Tribune.*

Why We Remained Calm

A lot of people have been amazed at how calmly the American people took last week's crisis. There was little panic in spite of the fact we were on the verge of nuclear war, and people, at least in Washington, kept their *sang froid* to the bitter end.

We have a theory as to why no one went off the deep end or headed for the hills. We owe it all to the television commercials which were interspersed in the news programs and bulletins, and made us realize that, no matter how near we came to obliteration, the real menace to Americans was not Soviet supply ships or Cuban missile bases, but acid indigestion, halitosis, headaches, and under arm perspiration.

This is how it went as we sat glued to our television sets, hanging onto every word from our nation's army of commentators.

"Good evening, ladies and gentlemen. President Kennedy has just announced that the United States will set up a quarantine around the island of Cuba and will fire on any ship, Russian or otherwise, which tries to break through. But before that story, here is some good news for sufferers from sinus headaches."

A turning of the dial found us face to face with a grim-faced Pentagon reporter who said, "War or peace. That is the big question in the Pentagon tonight. The armed services are ready for all-out nuclear attacks, and we'll tell you more about it as soon as we bring you a message from someone who knows something about athlete's foot."

Since we didn't have athlete's foot, we turned the dial again and saw a man, standing by a map ringed with battleships.

"This is the situation tonight," he said, pointing to Cuba.

"Missile bases with offensive weapons are being built. We'll tell you where in just a moment, after an important announcement from the Glug Drug Co." A woman came on the screen screaming at her child.

"Why are you so nervous?" her friendly friend asked her.

"It's my head," the screaming mother said, holding it in both hands.

"I have just the thing for it," the friend said. "Six-way relief with twelve acting ingredients."

We switched to a fourth channel and heard the announcer say, "And from Moscow we have just received Premier Krushchev's reaction to President Kennedy's quarantine order. We'll tell you about it in a minute, after this warning for motorists who can't believe that cold weather has arrived."

You can imagine our dilemma. Washington has only four channels, and we still couldn't find out what was going on, so we tuned to the first channel again, only we were too late. The commentator said, "And that's all civil defense experts would say about the shelters. Now, let's talk about overeating and what you're doing about it."

Furiously we switched again only to hear, "Marines to Florida where an invasion was impending. Are you smoking more but enjoying it less? Maybe it's time you changed."

We started holding our head in our hands just like the woman in the commercial did. Our wife walked in and said, "What's the latest?"

"Give me a cigarette," we screamed. "I've got a headache and I have to change my oil before there's a summit meeting and we're all blown up."

"You shouldn't watch the news if it gets you so nervous," she said.

"Who's nervous? Just because I perspire and I use greasy kid stuff on my hair and I suffer from acid indigestion, is that any reason they won't tell me what's going on?"

"You're exaggerating," she said, flipping the dial.

A face came on the screen and a man was saying, "A thermonuclear war so devastating that President Kennedy said victory would be ashes in our mouth. And now let's hear a friendly message about loose dental plates."

Political Poll—1776

The political pollster has become such an important part of the American scene that it's hard to imagine how this country was ever able to function without him.

What would have happened, for example, if there were political pollsters in the early days of this country?

This is how the results might have turned out.

When asked if they thought the British were doing a good job in administrating the Colonies, this is how a cross section of the people responded:

British doing good job	*63%*
Not doing good job	*22%*
Don't know	*15%*

The next question, "Do you think the dumping of tea in the Boston Harbor by militants helped or hurt the taxation laws in the New World?

Hurt the cause of taxation	*79%*

Philadelphia *Evening Bulletin*, November 1, 1962, syndicated from New York *Herald Tribune*.

Helped the cause   *12%*
Didn't think it would make any difference   *9%*

"What do you think our image is in England after the Minute Men attacked the British at Lexington?"

Minute men hurt our image in England   *83%*
Gave British new respect for Colonies   *10%*
Undecided   *7%*

"Which of these two Georges can do more for the Colonies—George III or George Washington?"

George III   *76%*
George Washington   *14%*
Others   *10%*

It is interesting to note that 80 percent of the people questioned had never heard of George Washington before.

The next question was, "Do you think the Declaration of Independence as it is written is a good document or a bad one?"

Bad document   *14%*
Good document   *12%*
No opinion   *84%*

A group of those polled felt that the Declaration of Independence had been written by a bunch of radicals and the publishing of it at this time would only bring harsher measures from the British.

When asked whether the best way to bring about reforms was through terrorism or redress to the Crown an overwhelming proportion of Colonists felt appeals should be made to the King.

Reforms through petition	*24%*
Reforms through act of terrorism	*8%*
Don't know	*66%*

The pollsters then asked what the public thought was the most crucial issue of the time.

Trade with foreign nations	*65%*
War with Indians	*20%*
The independence issue	*15%*

The survey also went into the question of Patrick Henry. "Do you think Patrick Henry did the right thing in demanding liberty or death?"

Did a foolhardy thing and was a trouble maker	*53%*
Did a brave thing and made his point	*23%*
Should have gone through the courts	*6%*
Don't know	*8%*

On the basis of the results of the poll the militant Colonials decided they did not have enough popular support to foment a revolution and gave up the idea of creating a United States of America.

Philadelphia *Evening Bulletin*, June 18, 1964, syndicated from New York *Herald Tribune*.

MARVIN KITMAN
(1929-   )

Mr. Kitman is a popular television critic for *Newsday* and the *Los Angeles Times* syndicate. At various times he has served as columnist for the *Armstrong Daily*, staff writer for the dying *Saturday Evening Post*, and consultant to Al Capp Enterprises. His opportunity for writing humor approached its peak during his career with *Monocle* magazine, which dedicated itself to political humor. He has brightened our lives with *George Washington's Expense Account* and other books.

Confessions of an Ex-Anti-Communist

Like most members of my generation, I became an anti-communist in college. I was immature and didn't know what I was doing by falling under the spell of the anti-communists at my alma mater, City College of New York. Most outsiders knew that 20 percent of the student body and faculty at CCNY were communists. But what they didn't know was that 80 percent were anti-communists. The college was riddled with anti-communists.

During my undergraduate years 1947–53 in this hot-bed of anti-communism, being an anti-communist was "in." All my close friends were anti-communists. The best fraternities on campus were all undercover anti-communist cells. I was weak and I didn't feel that I wanted to save the world as a member of an out-group.

It made so much sense to be an anti-communist in those days. There was an economic boom on, and I was told I never had it so good because of the anti-communists. On my way to school every morning, I could see those long lines of employed men, walking to the subways and buses.

The anti-communists in the bull-sessions in the City College cafeteria warned me that I would never get a job in the communications industry unless I was a known anti-communist. Personnel departments at newspapers, magazines, TV networks, ad agencies, and Hollywood studios were all under the control of anti-communists, and they were only hiring their own people. I wanted to be a writer so much, I didn't care what I believed as long as I got a job.

On my way home from school every afternoon, I read the *Journal-American,* and somebody always seemed to be turning anti-communist: people like Harvey Matusow, Louis Budenz and Herbert Philbrick. I felt that I was joining the wave of the future.

Gradually I drifted into the Party.

I should have realized that I was being manipulated by the inner circle of the Republican Party. At the time, they were trying to inject new blood into the Party, hoping to win an election for a change. The Eastern industrialists and bankers who controlled the Party nominating apparatus sought to seduce young minds of all ages by drafting a national hero to head the ticket. I fell for the Eisenhower pitch.

The Party had other card-carrying members whose names I saw on letterheads and respected: Irving Berlin, Irene Dunne, and Jackie Robinson. Before I knew what was happening, I found myself attending meetings of anti-communist front organizations hoping to meet people like them. The only people I met seemed to be girls.

To make myself more attractive as a man, I started reading obscure anti-communist journals, like the *Herald Tribune.* I'm ashamed to admit it now, but I was influenced by the Republican press.

The Republican Party was definitely hard on communism. I really believed the Russians were our enemies in those first cold war years. Keep in mind that during the cold war, the Russians were on the other side.

I was such an innocent dupe that I even thought the Republicans were the party of the common stockholder— the little guys, widows, and orphans, none of whom owned more than half of AT&T and GM. I didn't question the party's claim, either, that they pioneered in the fight for Negro civil rights. No party would be willing to lose the South for a hundred years unless it was sincere.

Still I didn't actually join the Party. A friend sent me a gift membership. When a well-meaning relative introduced me to the *Wall Street Journal* with a gift subscription, I was finished. I wound up on every anti-communist mailing list in the nation.

I realize now that not getting out of the Party was an error in judgment. In my defense, I can only say that I was never an active member of the Party. Not wanting to be out of step with our candidates, I didn't even take the Party's platform seriously.

The Outsider's Newsletter, 1962.

JOHN CROSBY
(1912-   )

John Crosby began his career for the *Milwaukee Sentinel* and moved to the *New York Herald Tribune* to contribute columns on broadcasting and television programming which were nationally syndicated for about twenty years. Since 1965 he has lived in England as a columnist for *The Observer*.

The Pangs of Utopia

London

I was reading a letter from home to my cockney friend, Alfie, who is perennially fascinated by the golden American way of life in the golden United States. "It's going to be a slim Christmas," the lady wrote. "I'm still paying off for my broken leg."

"Payin' off," said Alfie, "Y'mean the guv'mint don't pye fer 'er broken leg?"

"We're a free country," I told him proudly. "We pay for our own broken legs."

"Coo," said Alfie. "We're 'obbled with socialism over 'ere. The guv'mint robs us of the pleasure of pyin' our medical bills. It must be wonderful to be free of all that

New York *Herald Tribune*, 1963.

guv'mint interference. How long will it tyke the poor woman to pye for 'er broken leg?"

"About 18 months, I think," I said. "Of course, she's broke—but free. That's the spirit of 1776."

"Certainly hain't the spirit of 1963," said Alfie cheerfully. "I hunnerstan' you Americans 'ave one of the 'ighest tax rates in the 'ole world. Wot do you get fer yer 'igh taxes?"

"Oh," I told him, "we get many of the good things of life. The moon probe."

"What's 'at?"

"We're preparing to land a man on the moon in 1970 —or some such thing. It'll cost between $40 and $50 billion. I don't think any one really knows."

"Blimey," said Alfie. "If 'e breaks 'is leg landin' on the moon, will 'e 'ave to pye for it?"

"No," I explained. "The government will pay for his broken leg because he's on government service. It's only the taxpayers who pay for their own broken legs."

Alfie looked quizzical. "Wut uvver good things of life do you get fer them 'igh taxes?"

"Well—" I thought a bit. "The American taxpayer gets a lot of things. The Venus probe, for example, we found out that the other side of Venus is just as hot as this side."

"That must be a grite comfort to the lady wif the broken leg," said Alfie. "She c'n warm 'er broken leg on the uvver side of Venus."

"We have private medical insurance plans. That's the democratic way," I said.

"Why didn't it pay this poor woman's bills then?"

I explained that she probably couldn't afford private medical insurance after paying her taxes. And anyhow, private medical plans only paid part of the bills. "My daughter had an eye operation that cost about $700. Blue

Cross paid about $150 of it. My daughter also had a tonsils and adenoids operation that cost $200. The Blue Cross paid $39."

"Oi don't think Oi could afford ter live in so free a country," said Alfie. "Oi'd much rather 'ave the guv'mint enslave me an' pye me bills."

"But we're free!" I cried. "Free! Free!"

"Free to pye the bills," said Alfie cheerfully. "Tell me, guv'nor, are there any other countries as gloriously free to pye its medical expenses as America?"

"Well, of course, there's Afghanistan, there's the Congo and Outer Mongolia. They're free too."

Alfie sniffed. "We calls 'em backward."

RUSSELL BAKER
[Observer]

Taxpaying

February is the time when conscientious citizens start training for the income-tax season. Such a citizen is Al Brown, thrice winner of the Internal Revenue Service's citation as Taxpayer of the Year.

Brown was interviewed recently shortly before departure for tax-training camp in Florida. He had already filed his estimated income tax form and was purring with confidence. "If I can get my eye on the old loopholes early," he said, "I ought to hit another sixty deductions with no trouble."

The new changes in the Code, he said, will make the game more wide open than ever this year. "But it just means you've got to think taxation more than ever if you want to stay out of court," he added.

At Internal Revenue, Brown is known as "The Taxpayer's Taxpayer," and no wonder. Like Rogers Hornsby, Brown refuses to read on a moving train, lest the vibration weaken the visual acuity which he brings to the depreciation table and the capital gains clause. As the tax writers say, "He came to pay—but not very much."

What explains Brown's success? Since 1937, he has habitually read the Internal Revenue Code for two hours nightly before bed. Now near the halfway point in that fantastic instrument, he expects to finish as much as three-fourths of it before his death duties become payable.

Twice weekly, in season and out, he meets with his board of tax lawyers for lengthy speculations about the meaning of the latest Tax Court rulings. He never leaves home unaccompanied by a tax consultant to advise him how much income and what sort he can afford to accept from one hour to the next.

"It's these people who accept any income you shove at them who give the Code a bad name," Brown says. "First thing they know, they're taking salary and they have to pay up, so they go around poor-mouthing the Code.

"Or they make a lot of high-surtax money writing a best-seller or winning the heavyweight championship, and the Government wants it all back. Look at Joe Louis. If he'd read his Code, he'd have gone into oil wells or bought and sold skyscrapers instead of fooling around with boxing gloves."

The secret of Brown's success is thoroughness. The upper floor of his modest two-story home is filled with filing cabinets in which every receipt he has acquired in the past three tax years is meticulously awaiting the auditor's summons.

He works there three hours each night filing the day's receipts which he collects in a large Gladstone bag as he moves about the city. "Some people say me and Alma (Mrs. Brown) have carried this thing too far," he says. "There was a lot of that talk after we had to set the bed up in the living room to make room for the gas-tax vouchers. But I tell them, 'The Code is a hard mistress.' "

Nothing irritates Brown more than modern critics who argue that the Code is hopelessly antediluvian and so complicated that nobody can understand it. These reformers argue that unless the Code is streamlined it can never hope to compete with football as a TV attraction.

"Taxpaying is the only real national pastime," says Brown. "Look at Y. A. Tittle. He's totally depleted at thirty-nine, but still has thirty or forty years of good taxpaying ahead of him. If he'd gone into taxpaying twenty years ago he would have realized there's no allowance for muscle depletion and spent his time cultivating some fast-depreciation factory machines."

"Al Brown's fidelity to the Code is a model of citizenship," comments an Internal Revenue spokesman. "Fortunately for the country, he has few imitators outside the upper brackets."

Russell Baker, *All Things Considered,* Philadelphia and New York (1965), pp. 92–93. This book is a collection by the author of some of his best pieces covering President Lyndon B. Johnson's Great Society, as syndicated through *The New York Times.*

BARBARA GARSON
(1942-   )

Playwright and satirist Barbara Garson's *MacBird!* was first performed at the Village Gate in New York City in 1967. Her acidic rendering of political combat between the Kennedy brothers and Lyndon Johnson brought down editorial castigation from many newspapers including *The New York Times*. Yet Philip Roth has praised *MacBird!* as "the closest thing" by an American writer to political satire in the crushing style of Aristophanes.

MacBird!
ACT ONE
SCENE ONE

Hotel corridor at Democratic convention. THREE WITCHES *slink in. The* 1ST WITCH *is dressed as a student demonstrator, beatnik stereotype. The* 2ND WITCH *is a Negro with the impeccable grooming and attire of a* Muhammad Speaks *salesman. The* 3RD WITCH *is an old leftist, wearing a worker's cap and overalls. He carries a lunch pail and a lantern.*

1ST WITCH:
    When shall we three meet again?

2ND WITCH:
   In riot!

3RD WITCH:
      Strike!

1ST WITCH:
         Or stopping train?

2ND WITCH:
   When the hurly-burly's done,
   When the race is lost or won.

3RD WITCH:
   Out on the convention floor.
   Or in some hotel corridor.

1ST WITCH:
   Where cheering throngs can still be heard,
   There to meet with . . . MacBird!

   A cry off-stage.

2ND WITCH:
   I come, soul brothers!

3RD WITCH:
      Comrades call!

1ST WITCH:
         Away!

   WITCHES *move off, chanting.*

THREE WITCHES:

>Fair is foul and foul is fair.
>Hover through stale and smoke-filled air.

SCENE TWO

Hotel room at Democratic Convention. The walls are covered with charts and maps showing current tally of votes, areas of strength, etc. In an armchair at one corner sits TED *playing solitaire.* JOHN *and* ROBERT *enter. They move and look alike, except that* JOHN *is bigger and more self-assured.*

JOHN:

>Like? Dislike? What foolishness is that?
>Our cause demands suppressing sentiment.

ROBERT:

>But, Jack, you know it isn't merely scruples.
>He has a fat, yet hungry look. Such men are dangerous.

JOHN:

>Good God, this womanly whimpering just when I need your manly immorality!

ROBERT:

>But John—but Jack—you know it isn't that—

JOHN:

>Enough is said! At least we have to ask.
>He won't accept and, even if he does,
>His name will just stand second on the ticket.
>You, Bob, are still the second in succession.
>And Ted is next . . . and princes yet unborn . . .

And for this land, this crownèd continent,
This earth of majesty, this seat of Mars,
This forceful breed of men, this mighty world,
I see a . . . *New Frontier* beyond her seas.
She shall o'erflow her shores and burst her banks,
Eastward extend till East does meet with West,
And West until the West does touch the East
And o'er this hot and plaguèd earth descend
The Pox Americana, a sweet haze,
Shelt'ring all the world in its deep shade.
And our descendants, locking link to link,
Shall lay a lofty line of lovèd kings
To serve the faithful, laying low the foe;
Guiding, guarding, governing this folk.

TED:

> Gee, that's keen! (*Counting on his fingers.*)
> So let's see . . . That means Jack in '60 and '64,
> then Bobby in '68 and '72, then me in . . . what
> would that make it . . . '76 and '80 and then in
> 1984 it could be . . .

ROBERT:

> Shut up, Teddy! Can't you see we're busy?

JOHN:

> There's much that must be seen and done and heard.
> Let's first bestow the title on Macbird.
> *Exit* JOHN, ROBERT *and* TED. *Enter* WITCHES.

3RD WITCH:
Where have *you* been, brother?

2ND WITCH:
In L. A.

1st witch:

How's the weather there?

2nd witch:

It's wondrous warm,
And all the world's abroad, out laughin', boppin'.
A joyful throng comes pouring out of doors
A brick in either hand—they're goin' shoppin'.
O blessèd, blessèd blaze, the land's alight!
And I have never seen so sweet a sight.

3rd witch:

And sister, where were you?

1st witch:

A troop train taking men to Viet Land
Came chugging, chugging, chugging through our town.
"Halt ho!" quoth I, and stood upon the track,
Then, tossing leaflets, leaped up to the troops:
"Turn back, turn back and stop this train.
Why fight for them and die in vain?"
But we were few and so did fail:
Shoved off the train, we went to jail.
Yet trouble stirred is always for the good.

3rd witch:

Quite right, young witch. Constant agitation
Has been assigned as our historic task.
Some precepts from the past, herein entombed
    . . . (*Lifts lantern.*)

2nd witch:

That same old torch . . .

3RD WITCH:

> At least it casts some light.
Young witch, it's time you learned these lasting lessons.
Be thou militant but by no means adventurist.
The working class and their objective interests
Grapple to our cause with hoops of steel.
But never water down the party's program
For petty bourgeois students and the like.
Neither a burrower from within nor a leader be,
But stone by stone construct a conscious cadre.
And this above all—to thine own class be true
And it must follow, as the very next depression,
Thou canst not then be false to revolution.

2ND WITCH:
Yeah, pops, yeah.

1ST WITCH:

> We really understand.

3RD WITCH:
Tell us more about L.A.

Loud footsteps, door slams off-stage.

1ST WITCH (*whisper*):

> Who's there?

2ND WITCH:
Here comes MacBird. Quick! Hide behind the chair.

The WITCHES *scurry away, concealing themselves insufficiently. In the meantime* MAC BIRD *enters, a large heavy-jowled figure, followed by his* CRONY, *a thin sharpy.*

MAC BIRD:

So foul, unfair a day I've never seen.
(He notes figures behind the chair.)
Some delegates, I guess, or shy supporters.
(Toward chair:) Why howdy there!
(To CRONY:*)* Let's give them folks a thrill.
The name's MacBird! I'm mighty proud to meet ya!

Extends hand toward chair. WITCHES *rise up slowly from behind.*

Why, it's a nigra and a filthy beatnik.

CRONY:

And there's a bum done up in worker's duds.

MAC BIRD:

God damn! Those beatnik picketers all over!

CRONY:

Perhaps I better run and call the cops.

MAC BIRD:

Now just calm down. I know how to deal with people.
I'll handle this.
(To WITCHES:*)* OK, let's hear your story.

WITCHES *move eerily out from behind chair.*

Come on, speak up, now what in thunder are you?

1ST WITCH:

All hail MacBird! All hail the Senate's leader!

2ND WITCH:
All hail MacBird, Vice-President thou art!

3RD WITCH:
All hail MacBird, that shall be President!

ALL WITCHES:
All hail MacBird, that shall be President!

CRONY:
Hey boss, how come you gulp and seem to fear?
It has a kind of pretty sound I think.
(*To* WITCHES:) If you can look into your crystal ball
And say who'll get ahead and who'll go down,
Speak then to me. When he becomes the chief
What will I be?

1ST WITCH:
You'll be his leading hack.

2ND WITCH:
It's not so high, but so much less to fall;
For you shall share the fate of his career.
MacBird shall be the mightiest of all,
But Ken O'Dunc alone shall leave an heir.

3RD WITCH:
An heir who'll play a king, like other kings.
He too shall be an extra on our set.
He'll strut and fret his hour on the boards
And be applauded wildly from the pit.
But if you skip and read a later page,
We take the final bow upon this stage.

MAC BIRD (*who has been absorbed in his thoughts*):
    The Senate leader, that I *know* I am.
    But how Vice-President, when Ken O'Dunc
    Despises me like dirt? And to be chief—
    Unthinkable while Ken O'Dunc holds sway!

WITCHES *start to slither off the stage.*

    Stay, you lying varmints! Tell me more!
    Where'd you learn this hogwash that you tell?
    And why the devil did you come to me?
    Come on! Speak out!

CRONY:

                        They're gliding off the stage.

WITCHES (*continuing to move off, and chanting together*) :
    The bosses shall be booted in the bin,
    The kings unkinged. We have a world to win!

MAC BIRD:
    Vice-President—and President to be!

CRONY:
    It's not the *natural* path to reach the top.

Enter BOBBY.

ROBERT:
    Hail MacBird, Vice-President thou art—
    That is, if you'll accept the second place.
    My brother Jack has picked you for the job
    And hopes that you'll agree to grace his slate.

MAC BIRD *(aside)*:
    Vice-President—and President to be!

ROBERT:
    I know of course it's not what you had hoped.
    It's really just an honorary post.
    And so I'm sure you must want time to think.
    Perhaps we'll get together late tonight.

MAC BIRD:
    I thank your brother. Let him know for me
    I do accept with deep humility.

ROBERT *(faltering)* :
    Well . . . That's just fine . . . I guess that means that
        we . . .
    Should go and meet together some time . . . soon.

MAC BIRD *(firmly)*:
    We've got a lot to do. Today. But when?

ROBERT:
    At ten o'clock?

MAC BIRD:
              OK, I'll see you then.

SCENE THREE

Ken O'Dunc's hotel room. On stage are JOHN *and* ROBERT *surrounded by a group of their advisors. In a chair in the corner sits* TED.

ROBERT (*gossiping with circle*):
>And just like that, he took it on the spot.

Group gasps, showing surprise and dismay.

JOHN:
>Unity required that we ask him.

ROBERT:
>The party must be made to speak as one.

JOHN:
>Consensus, lords, consensus is the thing!

ROBERT:
>The jewel upon the crown that marks the king.

JOHN:
>So gentlemen, that's now the way it stands.

Enter MAC BIRD. *Conversation stops short but* MAC BIRD
proceeds heartily.

MAC BIRD:
>Howdy, folks. (*Pause with no response.*)
>I want to thank you all. (*Earnestly.*)
>I know you all conferred in choosing me.
>I wonder if you know just what this means
>To me, a boy who nearly dropped from school?
>Vice-President of these United States!
>Why, it's an inspiration to *all* boys
>Who daily toil, and sometimes feel despair,
>To know that in the White House—or quite near—

There dwells a man who had to work like them,
Who knew the struggles, knew the ups and downs.
It gives a boy a faith in this, our land.

JOHN:

And we in turn thank *you,* your quick response.

MAC BIRD:

Why thanks.

JOHN:

Thank *you.* (*More formally.*)
Friends, brothers, lords,
All you who are nearest to us, know
We will establish our estate upon
The eldest, Robert, whom we now do name
The Lord of Laws, henceforth our closest counsel.
In all affairs of state we are as one.
To him entrust your thoughts as though to me.
And now to plan the tone of our campaign.

(*Turning to an aide:*) Have you the calculations I
requested?

AIDE:

Aye, here my liege, the output's based upon
A partial computation of the data.

AIDE *holds out IBM output sheets to* JOHN, *but* MAC
BIRD *gets hold of them.*

MAC BIRD:

A powerful mess o'numbers. Pray, what's that?

AIDE:

>A psychosexual index of the symbols
>We use in predetermining his image
>With variables projected . . . if you please!
>(*At "if you please" he takes it rudely from* MAC BIRD
>*and gives it to* JOHN.)
>The final print-out can't be made till morning.

JOHN:

>These findings, sir, we shall peruse withal.

>JOHN, ROBERT *and* FOLLOWERS *go over to desk where
>they are poring over the figures.*

MAC BIRD:

>Why stay we now? What use is here for me?

CRONY:

>Dare they presume to scorn you in this manner?

MAC BIRD:

>With forty years campaigning 'neath my belt,
>They turn from me to mind a damn machine.

CRONY:

>If they could come to know your worship's worth . . .

MAC BIRD:

>And did you hear that snippet! . . . "if you please"?

CRONY:

>I heard. I said not much, yet think the more.

MAC BIRD:

>I am a sorry second in this slate.

CRONY:

>Up here you're disadvantaged in their sight.
>A very sorry second, as you say.
>But yon, you are the pinnacle of power;
>What vast domains where you are best beloved!
>Were it not wise to bring them to your kingdom
>By such invention as we can devise
>So they can feel the force of your supporters,
>Hear it, sense it, see it with their eyes?

MAC BIRD:

>Aye, there'll be some to stand up for me there.
>(*To* JOHN:) Say, how about conferring on my ranch?

ROBERT:

>We're all engaged until the coronation.

MAC BIRD:

>And after that?

ROBERT:

>Why then we'll have to see.

MAC BIRD:

>The wife and I would gladly organize
>A welcome worthy of our honored guest.
>We'll have a grand procession through the streets
>For you to greet the people of my state.

JOHN:

>When all the coronation plans are through,
>We'll surely visit then.

ROBERT:

>For now, adieu.

JOHN:

Adieu, MacBird. We'll see you by the by.

ROBERT:

Adieu.

MAC BIRD:

Adieu my lords, adieu.

Exit all except MAC BIRD.

This Lord of Laws be blasted, there's the rub
For in my way it lies. Stars, hide thy fires.
Let no light see my black and deep desires.

MacDick?

PROLOGUE, spoken by a wily hunchback henchman to King Richard

Now is the winter of our discontent
Made glorious summer by that son of—heaven
And all the clouds they lowered on our house
In the deep bosom of the back pages buried.
Now are our brows pre-bound with victory wreaths:
The issue of the coming battle certain:
Our champion. Richard, once maligned and wretched
Shall rise from King to Twice-elected King.
Now do we launch our last and best campaign
'Gainst enemies that dare not raise again
Against a king their mewling, mean attacks.

Barbara Garson, *MacBird!*, New York (1967), pp. 3-18.

Nor post this time derisive advertisements
Showing Richard's jaw to undulate
Black and swarthy—thus they showed him once—
With scurrilous script demanding of the townsmen
"Would you buy a used vehicle
From this disfigured and dissembling creature?"
Deformed they showed him and so lamely finished
That dogs would bark if he but halted by them.
And now that same black jowled and swarthy visage,
That shell encasing his misshapen soul,
That same gray clam-shelled face shall be elected—
Anointed, overwhelmingly acclaimed!
Yet even so he shall not be beloved
But eaten without relish, coldly swallowed.
Yea millions shall be forced to pull a lever
For one they sense unwholesome and unwhole.
And yet they must perforce prefer his banner
To that which has been snatched and dragged and snarled
From hand to hand among our warring rivals.
For plots have I laid, inductions dangerous
By libels, lying letter, and false agents
To set the lords and leaders of the enemy
In deadly hate, the one against the other.
And by a subtle tipping of the balance,
As first to favor one and then the other,
Contrived to see the gentle George ascendant.
—An honest plot to see "the best man win"—
For George is of a free and open nature
Whose vanity methinks will let us lead him
As nicely by the nose as we do asses.
And if McGovern be as true and just
As Richard subtle, false and treacherous
This fall shall see the fall of all our foes,
As low they sink—so high, base Richard goes.

The Village *Voice*, November 29, 1973.

PHILIP ROTH

Our Gang
Chapter 2
Tricky Holds a Press Conference

MR. ASSLICK: Sir, as regards your San Dementia statement of April 3, the discussion it provoked seems now to have centered on your unequivocal declaration that you are a firm believer in the rights of the unborn. Many seem to believe that you are destined to be to the unborn what Martin Luther King was to the black people of America, and the late Robert F. Charisma to the disadvantaged chicanos and Puerto Ricans of the country. There are those who say that your San Dementia statement will go down in the history books alongside Dr. King's famous "I have a dream" address. Do you find these comparisons apt?

TRICKY: Well, of course, Mr. Asslick, Martin Luther King was a very great man, as we all must surely recognize now that he is dead. He was a great leader in the struggle for equal rights for his people, and yes, I do believe he'll find a place in history. But of course we must not forget he was not the President of the United States, as I am, empowered by the Constitution, as I am; and this is an important distinction to bear in mind. Working *within* the Constitution I think I will be able to accomplish far more for the unborn of this *entire* nation than did Dr. King working *outside* the Constitution for the born of a *single race*. This is meant to be no criticism of Dr. King, but just a simple statement of fact.

Now, of course I am well aware that Dr. King died a martyr's tragic death—so let me then make one thing very clear to my enemies and the enemies of the unborn: let there be no mistake about it, what they did to Martin Luther King, what they did to Robert F. Charisma and to John F. Charisma before him, great Americans all, is not for a moment going to deter me from engaging in the struggle that lies ahead. I will not be intimidated by extremists or militants or violent fanatics from bringing justice and equality to those who live in the womb. And let me make one thing more perfectly clear: I am not just talking about the rights of the fetus. I am talking about the microscopic embryos as well. If ever there was a group in this country that was "disadvantaged," in the sense that they are utterly without representation or a voice in our national government, it is not the blacks or the Puerto Ricans or the hippies or what-have-you, all of whom have their spokesmen, but these infinitesimal creatures up there on the placenta.

You know, we all watch our TV and we see the demonstrators and we see the violence, because, unfortunately, that is the kind of thing that makes the news. But how many of us realize that throughout this great land of ours, there are millions upon millions of embryos going through the most complex and difficult changes in form and structure, and all this they accomplish without waving signs for the camera and disrupting traffic and throwing paint and using foul language and dressing in outlandish clothes. Yes, Mr. Daring.

MR. DARING: But what about those fetuses, sir, that the Vice President has labeled "troublemakers"? I believe he was referring specifically to those who start in kicking around the fifth month. Do you agree that they are "malcontents" and "ingrates"? And if so, what measures do you intend to take to control them?

TRICKY: Well, first off, Mr. Daring, I believe we are dealing here with some very fine distinctions of a legal kind. Now, fortunately *(impish endearing smile)* I happen to be a lawyer and have the kind of training that enables me to make these fine distinctions. *(Back to serious business)* I think we have to be very very careful here—and I am sure the Vice President would agree with me—to distinguish between two kinds of activity: *kicking* in the womb, to which the Vice Preisdent was specifically referring, and *moving* in the womb. You see, the Vice President did not say, despite what you may have heard on television, that *all* fetuses who are active in the womb are troublemakers. Nobody in this Administration believes that. In fact, I have just today spoken with both Attorney General Malicious and Mr. Heehaw at the FBI, and we are all in agreement that a certain amount of movement in the womb, after the fifth month, is not only inevitable but *desirable* in a normal pregnancy.

But as for this other matter, I assure you, this administration does not intend to sit idly by and do nothing while American women are being kicked in the stomach by a bunch of violent five-month-olds. Now by and large, and I cannot emphasize this enough, our American unborn are as wonderful a group of unborn as you can find anywhere. But there are these violent few that the Vice President has characterized, and I don't think unjustly, in his own impassioned rhetoric, as "troublemakers" and "malcontents"—and the Attorney General has been instructed by me to take the appropriate action against them.

MR. DARING: If I may, sir, what sort of action will that

be? Will there be arrests made of violent fetuses? And if
so, how exactly will this be carried out?

TRICKY: I think I can safely say, Mr. Daring, that we
have the finest law enforcement agencies in the world.
I am quite sure that Attorney General Malicious can solve
whatever procedural problems may arise. Mr. Respectful.

MR. RESPECTFUL: Mr. President, with all the grave national and international problems that press continually upon
you, can you tell us why you have decided to devote yourself to this previously neglected issue of fetal rights? You
seem pretty fired up on this issue, sir—why is that?

TRICKY: Because, Mr. Respectful, I will not tolerate injustice in any area of our national life. Because ours is a just
society, not merely for the rich and the privileged, but
for the most powerless among us as well. You know, you
hear a lot these days about Black Power and Female Power, Power this and Power that. But what about Prenatal
Power? Don't they have rights too, membranes though
they may be? I for one think they do, and I intend to
fight for them. Mr. Shrewd.

MR. SHREWD: As you must know, Mr. President, there are
those who contend that you are guided in this matter solely by political considerations. Can you comment on that?

TRICKY: Well, Mr. Shrewd, I suppose that is their cynical way of describing my plan to introduce a proposed
constitutional amendment that would extend the vote to
the unborn in time for the '72 elections.

MR. SHREWD: I believe that is what they have in mind,
sir. They contend that by extending the vote to the unborn you will neutralize the gains that may accrue to the
Democratic Party by the voting age having been lowered
to eighteen. They say your strategists have concluded
that even if you should lose the eighteen-to-twenty-
one-year-old vote, you can still win a second term if you

are able to carry the South, the state of California, and the embryos and fetuses from coats to coast. Is there any truth to this "political" analysis of your sudden interest in Prenatal Power?

TRICKY: Mr. Shrewd, I'd like to leave that to you—and to our television viewers—to judge, by answering your question in a somewhat personal manner. I assure you I am conversant with the opinions of the experts. Many of them are men whom I respect, and surely they have the right to say whatever they like, though of course one always hopes it will be in the national interest. . . . But let me remind you, and all Americans, because this is a fact that seems somehow to have been overlooked in this whole debate: I am no Johnny-come-lately to the problem of the rights of the unborn. The simple fact of the matter, and it is in the record for all to see, is that I myself was once unborn, in the great state of California. Of course, you wouldn't always know this from what you see on television or read in the papers *(impish endearing smile)* that some of you gentlemen write for, but it happens nonetheless to be the truth. *(Back to serious business)* I was an unborn Quaker, as a matter of fact.

And let me remind you—since it seems necessary to do so, in the face of the vicious and mindless attacks upon him—Vice President What's-his-name was also unborn once, an unborn Greek-American, and proud to have been one. We were just talking about that this morning, how he was once an unborn Greek-American, and all that has meant to him. And so too was Secretary Lard unborn and so was Secretary Codger unborn, and the Attorney General—why, I could go right on down through my cabinet and point out to you one fine man after another who was once unborn. Even Secretary Fickle, with whom as you know I had my differences of opinion, was unborn when he was here with us on the team.

And if you look among the leadership of the Republican Party in the House and the Senate, you will find men who long before their election to public office were unborn in just about every region of this country, on farms, in industrial cities, in small towns the length and breadth of this great republic. My own wife was once unborn. As you may recall, my children were both unborn.

So when they say that Dixon has turned to the issue of the unborn just for the sake of the votes . . . well, I ask only that you consider this list of the previously unborn with whom I am associated in both public and private life, and decide for yourself. In fact, I think you are going to find, Mr. Shrewd, with each passing day, people around this country coming to realize that in this administration the fetuses and embryos of America have at last found their voice. Miss Charmin', I believe you had your eyebrows raised.

MISS CHARMIN': I was just going to say, sir, that of course President Lyin' B. Johnson was unborn, too, before he came to the White House—and he was a Democrat. Could you comment on that?

TRICKY: Miss Charmin', I would be the first to applaud my predecessor in this high office for having been unborn. I have no doubt that he was an outstanding fetus down there in Texas before he came into public life. I am not claiming that my administration is the first in history to be cognizant of the issue of fetal rights. I am saying that we intend to do something about them. Mr. Practical.

MR. PRACTICAL: Mr. President, I'd like to ask you to comment upon the scientific problems entailed in bringing the vote to the unborn.

TRICKY: Well, of course, Mr. Practical, you have hit the nail right on the head with the word "scientific." This is a scientific problem of staggering proportions—let's make no mistake about it. Moreover, I fully expect there are those who are going to say in tomorrow's papers that it is impossible, unfeasible, a utopian dream, and so on. But as you remember, when President Charisma came before the Congress in 1961, and announced that this country would put a man on the moon before the end of the decade, there were many who were ready to label him an impossible dreamer, too. But we did it. With American know-how and American teamwork, we did it. And so too do I have every confidence that our scientific and technological people are going to dedicate themselves to bringing the vote to the unborn—and not before the decade is out either, but before November of 1972.

MR. PRACTICAL: Can you give us some idea, sir, how much a crash program like this will cost?

TRICKY: Mr. Practical, I will be submitting a proposed budget to the Congress within the next ten days, but let me say this: you cannot achieve greatness without sacrifice. The program of research and development such as my scientific advisers have outlined cannot be bought "cheap." After all, what we are talking about here is nothing less than the fundamental principle of democracy: the vote. I cannot believe that the members of the Congress of the United States are going to play party politics when it comes to taking a step like this, which will be an advance not only for our nation, but for all mankind.

You just cannot imagine, for instance, the impact that this is going to have on the people in the underdeveloped countries. There are the Russians and the Chinese, who don't even allow adults to vote, and here we are in America, investing billions and billions of the taxpayers' dollars in a scientific project designed to extend the franchise to people who cannot see or talk or hear or even think, in the ordinary sense of the word. It would be a tragic irony indeed, and as telling a sign as I can imagine of national confusion and even hypocrisy, if we were willing to send our boys to fight and die in far-off lands so that defenseless peoples might have the right to choose the kinds of government they want in free elections, and then we were to turn around here at home and continue to deny that very same right to an entire segment of our population, just because they happen to live on the placenta or in the uterus, instead of New York City. Mr. Catch-Me-in-a-Contradiction.

MR. CATCH-ME-IN-A-CONTRADICTION: Mr. President, what startles me is that up until today you have been characterized, and not unwillingly, I think, as someone who, if he is not completely out of touch with the styles and ideas of the young, has certainly been skeptical of their wisdom. Doesn't this constitute, if I may use the word, a radical about-face, coming out now for the rights of those who are not simply "young" but actually in the gestation period?

TRICKY: Well, I am glad you raised that point, because I think it shows once and for all just how flexible I am, and how I am always willing to listen and respond to an appeal from *any* minority group, no matter how powerless, just so long as it is reasonable, and is not accompanied by violence and foul language and throwing paint. If ever there was proof that you don't have to camp on the White House lawn to get the President's attention away from a football game, I think it is in the example of these little organisms. I tell you, they have really impressed me with their silent dignity and politeness. I only hope that all Americans will come to be as proud of our unborn as I am.

MR. FASCINATED: Mr. President, I am fascinated by the technological aspect. Can you give us just an inkling of how exactly the unborn will go about casting their ballots? I'm particularly fascinated by these embryos on the placenta, who haven't even developed nervous systems yet, let alone limbs such as we use in an ordinary voting machine.

TRICKY: Well, first off, let me remind you that nothing in our Constitution denies a man the right to vote just because he is physically handicapped. That isn't the kind of country we have here. We have many wonderful handicapped people in this country, but of course, they're not "news" the way the demonstrators are.

MR. FASCINATED: I wasn't suggesting, sir, that just because these embryos don't have central nervous systems they should be denied the right to vote—I was thinking again of the fantastic *mechanics* of it. How, for instance, will the embryos be able to weigh the issues and make intelligent choices from among the candidates, if they are not able to read the newspapers or watch the news on television?

TRICKY: Well, it seems to me that you have actually touched upon the very strongest claim that the unborn have for enfranchisement, and why it is such a crime they have been denied the vote for so long. Here, at long last, we have a great bloc of voters who simply are not going to be taken in by the lopsided and distorted versions of the truth that are presented to the American public through the various media. Mr. Reasonable.

MR. REASONABLE: But how then will they make up their minds, or their yolks, or their nuclei, or whatever it is they have in there, Mr. President? It might seem to some that they are going to be absolutely innocent of whatever may be at stake in the election.

TRICKY: Innocent they will be, Mr. Reasonable—but now let me ask you, and all our television viewers, too, a question: what's *wrong* with a little innocence? We've had the foul language, we've had the cynicism, we've had the masochism and the breast-beating—maybe a big dose of innocence is just what this country needs to be great again.

MR. REASONABLE: *More* innocence, Mr. President?

TRICKY: Mr. Reasonable, if I have to choose between the rioting and the upheaval and the strife and the discontent on the one hand, and more innocence on the other, I think I will choose the innocence. Mr. Hardnose.

MR. HARDNOSE: In the event, Mr. President, that all this does come to pass by the '72 elections, what gives you reason to believe that the enfranchised embryos and fetuses will vote for you over your Democratic opponent? And what about Governor Wallow? Do you think that if he should run again, he would significantly cut into your share of the fetuses, particularly in the South?

TRICKY: Let me put it this way, Mr. Hardnose: I have the utmost respect for Governor George Wallow of Alabama, as I do for Senator Hubert Hollow of Minnesota. They are both able men, and they speak with great conviction, I am sure, in behalf of the extreme right and the extreme left. But the fact is that I never heard either of these gentlemen, for all their extremism, raise their voices in behalf of America's most disadvantaged group of all, the unborn.

Consequently, I would be less than candid if I didn't say that when election time rolls around, of course the embryos and fetuses of this country are likely to remember just who it was that struggled in their behalf, while others were addressing themselves to the more popular and fashionable issues of the day. I think they will remember who it was that devoted himself, in the midst of a war abroad and racial crisis at home, to making this country a fit place for the unborn to dwell in pride.

My only hope is that whatever I am able to accomplish in their behalf while I hold this office will someday contribute to a world in which *everbody*, regardless of race, creed, or color, will be unborn. I guess if *I* have a dream, that is it. Thank you, ladies and gentlemen.

MR. ASSLICK: Thank you, Mr. President.

Philip Roth, *Our Gang*, Watergate edition, New York (1973), pp. 10–23.

The Golden Years
Giants of Mirth

Giants of Mirth
(1885–1935)

Native literary political humor having been firmly established in its tradition of homespun, commonsense wisdom and the shared, more or less gentle laughter of second-guessers, there remained only for Ambrose Bierce and H. L. Mencken to develop its minor or acerbic theme. The major strain would continue meanwhile through Mr. Dooley, Ring Lardner, and Will Rogers.

Mark Twain and Petroleum Vesuvius Nasby had unwittingly illustrated the dilemma confronting political humorists in confiding their nagging uncertainty that politics is, or even can be, seriously funny. Mark Twain, America's greatest humorist, was never at his best on politics. He could castigate legislators, flay justices and administrators, or ridicule governmental agencies as energetically as any writer. Yet political subjects elicited more of his sense of righteous indignation than merry satire, at the expense of his sense of humor. Poor Nasby! In cracker-barrel style, he wanted only to be an elastic Democrat in high-tension times. He admired his party's historic capacity to spread itself. "We kin accommodate the prejudices uv the people uv all the various localities," he said once, in recalling happier days when the sharing of loaves and fishes was a politician's primary problem. The Nasbys of the nation could be had on easy terms, but they required ammunition to fight their battles. The proper question for politics, after all, to which all others were subordinate, was, who will get the offices? If we reflect on the bitter fruits of his ne-grophobia, however, as reflect we must, the creator of Petroleum Vesuvius Nasby fully lived up to his incendiary pseudonym, to the detriment of his evocation of laughter.

Ambrose Bierce and Henry L. Mencken, who admired Bierce extravagantly, spurned the cracker-barrel tradition of Seba Smith and Artemus Ward, choosing instead the thorny path of blistering iconoclasm. Each subscribed unwaveringly to the axiom that politics consisted of conducting public affairs for private advantage. With their efforts, the framework of American political humor was to be fully erected at last.

AMBROSE GWINNETT BIERCE
(1842-1914?)

Ambrose Bierce was the most eccentric of all the writers brought together in this book. Characterized mostly as bitter, cynical, morose, sadistic, misanthropic, or even perverted, he has only occasionally been described, by a few close friends, as idealistic, romantic, or kind.

Bierce was the author of *The Devil's Dictionary* and *Fantastic Fables,* both of which were compiled largely from his contributions to periodicals. He also wrote Poe-like tales of horror and the supernatural, essays, poems,

Ambrose Gwinnett Bierce

autobiographical pieces, and short stories. Many of his stories deal with the Civil War, some evoking unforgettable sequences of dream and memory.

Bierce was born in Ohio, one of a large family, and was raised on an impoverished Indiana farm in an oppressively stern and puritanical atmosphere which he remembered and hated all his life. He was twice wounded by Confederate gunfire, and thereafter was successively an Indian fighter, journalist and editor, writer of humorous sketches in London, mining company employee in the Black Hills, resident of San Francisco and Washington, D.C., and editorial columnist for the Hearst papers. The place and date of his death are unknown; he was lost somewhere amid Pancho Villa's uprising in Mexico.

Some men seem fated to be misunderstood, and Ambrose Bierce was such a man. Partly to blame were his frequent and erratic changes of residence or employment, and so many abrupt interruptions of his career (Clifton Fadiman remarked that some of Bierce's publishers "possessed a natural talent for bankruptcy") that contemporary critics disputed whether he was one man or several. Mainly responsible, however, were Bierce himself and his small but worshipful company of disciples. Bierce, wrote Carey McWilliams, was "a master of gestures," who, with twisted and sardonic pleasure, left tangled and confused the webs of half-truth built around him. His admirers jostled one another jealously for his favor, while each glimpsed a different façade of the master. To cap it all, Bierce, who specialized in inexplicable disappearances, contrived an exit from life so dramatic as to precipitate a minor international incident followed by recurring conjectures whether he was dead or alive. Thereafter his name was to be linked with the names of Theodosia Burr, Charlie Ross, and other notorious persons whose final whereabouts remain unknown.

Although it is extravagant praise to admit him to the company of Lucretius, Juvenal, Cervantes, Swift, and Voltaire, as Belknap Long and others have done, Bierce at his best could write of human frailties and follies with the perceptiveness of Defoe and the corrosive acid of Wilde and Shaw. Many of his fables, such as "The Reform School Board," embody timeless satiric wisdom in a few lines. His satanic definitions, that of a Populist, for example, as "a fossil patriot of the early agricultural period," are incisive wit of exalted caliber. Vincent Starrett once explained the strength and limitations of Bierce's appeal: "It requires a very special sort of sanity, I think, genuinely to appreciate the bitter satire and irony of Ambrose Bierce. Certainly he was not *caviare* to the general. Where he was anything, he was gall and wormwood, and it was seldom his intention to be anything else." Less precious and more to the point is Ambrose Bierce's own definition for the adjective *good:* "Sensible, madam, to the worth of this present writer. Alive, sir, to the advantages of letting him alone."

These selections from Bierce validate both points of view.

Selections from *The Devil's Dictionary*

ADMINISTRATION, *n*. An ingenious abstraction in politics, designed to receive the kicks and cuffs due to the premier or president. A man of straw, proof against bad-egging and dead-catting.

AGITATOR, *n*. A statesman who shakes the fruit trees of his neighbors—to dislodge the worms.

ALDERMAN, *n*. An ingenious criminal who covers his secret thieving with a pretence of open marauding.

ALLIANCE, *n*. In international politics, the union of two thieves who have their hands so deeply inserted in each other's pocket that they cannot separately plunder a third.

ARISTOCRACY, *n*. Government by the best men. (In this sense the word is obsolete; so is that kind of government.) Fellows that wear downy hats and clean shirts—guilty of education and suspected of bank accounts.

BIGOT, *n*. One who is obstinately and zealously attached to an opinion that you do not entertain.

COMMONWEALTH, *n*. An administrative entity operated by an incalculable multitude of political parasites, logically active but fortuitously efficient.

Ambrose Bierce, *The Collected Writings* . . . , New York (1946), pp. 187–392.

212

This commonwealth's capitol's corridors view,
So thronged with a hungry and indolent crew
Of clerks, pages, porters and all attachés
Whom rascals appoint and the populace pays
That a cat cannot slip through the thicket of shins
Nor hear its own shriek for the noise of their chins.
On clerks and on pages, and porters, and all,
Misfortune attend and disaster befall!
May life be to them a succession of hurts;
May fleas by the bushel inhabit their shirts;
May aches and diseases encamp in their bones,
Their lungs full of tubercles, bladders of stones;
May microbes, bacilli, their tissues infest,
And tapeworms securely their bowels digest;
May corn-cobs be snared without hope in their hair,
And frequent impalement their pleasure impair.
Disturbed be their dreams by the awful discourse
Of audible sofas sepulchrally hoarse,
By chairs acrobatic and wavering floors—
The mattress that kicks and the pillow that snores!
Sons of cupidity, cradled in sin!
Your criminal ranks may the death angel thin,
Avenging the friend whom I couldn't work in.

K.Q.

CONSERVATIVE, *n.* A statesman who is enamored of existing evils, as distinguished from the Liberal, who wishes to replace them with others.

CONSUL, *n.* In American politics, a person who having failed to secure an office from the people is given one by the Administration on condition that he leave the country.

CONTROVERSY, *n.* A battle in which spittle or ink replaces the injurious cannon-ball and the inconsiderate bayonet.

In controversy with the facile tongue—
That bloodless warfare of the old and young—
So seek your adversary to engage
That on himself he shall exhaust his rage,
And, like a snake that's fastened to the ground,
With his own fangs inflict the fatal wound.
You ask me how this miracle is done?
Adopt his own opinions, one by one,
And taunt him to refute them; in his wrath
He'll sweep them pitilessly from his path.
Advance them gently all you wish to prove,
Each proposition prefaced with, "As you've
So well remarked," or, "As you wisely say,
And I cannot dispute," or, "By the way,
This view of it which, better far expressed,
Runs through your argument." Then leave the rest
To him, secure that he'll perform his trust
And prove your views intelligent and just.

Conmore Apel Brune.

DEGRADATION, *n.* One of the stages of moral and social progress from private station to political preferment.

DELEGATION, *n.* In American politics, an article of merchandise that comes in sets.

DELIBERATION, *n.* The act of examining one's bread to determine which side it is buttered on.

DIPLOMACY, *n.* The patriotic art of lying for one's country.

EGOTIST, *n.* A person of low taste, more interested in himself than in me.

Megaceph, chosen to serve the State
In the halls of legislative debate,

One day with all his credentials came
To the capitol's door and announced his name.
The doorkeeper looked, with a comical twist
Of the face, at the eminent egotist,
And said: "Go away, for we settle here
All manner of questions, knotty and queer,
And we cannot have, when the speaker demands
To be told how every member stands,
A man who to all things under the sky
Assents by eternally voting 'I'."

ELECTOR, *n.* One who enjoys the sacred privilege of voting for the man of another man's choice.

EXECUTIVE, *n.* An officer of the Government, whose duty it is to enforce the wishes of the legislative power until such time as the judicial department shall be pleased to pronounce them invalid and of no effect. Following is an extract from an old book entitled, *The Lunarian Astonished*—Pfeiffer & Co., Boston, 1803:

LUNARIAN: Then when your Congress has passed a law it goes directly to the Supreme Court in order that it may at once be known whether it is constitutional?

TERRESTRIAN: O no; it does not require the approval of the Supreme Court until having perhaps been enforced for many years somebody objects to its operation against himself— I mean his client. The President, if he approves it, begins to execute it at once.

LUNARIAN: Ah, the executive power is a part of the legislative. Do your policemen also have to approve the local ordinances that they enforce?

TERRESTRIAN: Not yet—at least not in their character of constables. Generally speaking, though, all laws require the approval of those whom they are intended to restrain.

LUNARIAN: I see. The death warrant is not valid until signed by the murderer.

TERRESTRIAN: My friend, you put it too strongly; we are not so consistent.

LUNARIAN: But this system of maintaining an expensive judicial machinery to pass upon the validity of laws only after they have long been executed, and then only when brought before the court by some private person—does it not cause great confusion?

TERRESTRIAN: It does.

LUNARIAN: Why then should not your laws, previously to being executed, be validated, not by the signature of your President, but by that of the Chief Justice of the Supreme Court?

TERRESTRIAN: There is no precedent for any such course.

LUNARIAN: Precedent. What is that?

TERRESTRIAN: It has been defined by five hundred lawyers in three volumes each. So how can any one know?

EXILE, *n.* One who serves his country by residing abroad, yet is not an ambassador.

An English sea-captain being asked if he had read "The Exile of Erin," replied: "No, sir, but I should like to anchor on it." Years afterwards, when he had been hanged as a pirate after a career of unparalleled atrocities, the following memorandum was found in the ship's log that he had kept at the time of his reply:

Aug 3d, 1842. Made a joke on the ex-Isle of Erin. Coldly received. War with the whole world!

FLOP, *v.* Suddenly to change one's opinions and go over to another party. The most notable flop on record was that of Saul of Tarsus, who has been severely criticised as a turn-coat by some of our partisan journals.

FREEDOM, *n*. Exemption from the stress of authority in a beggarly half dozen of restraint's infinite multitude of methods. A political condition that every nation supposes itself to enjoy in virtual monopoly. Liberty. The distinction between freedom and liberty is not accurately known; naturalists have never been able to find a living specimen of either.

> Freedom, as every schoolboy knows,
>   Once shrieked as Kosciusko fell;
> On every wind, indeed, that blows
>   I hear her yell.
>
> She screams whenever monarchs meet,
>   And parliaments as well,
> To bind the chains about her feet
>   And toll her knell.
>
> And when the sovereign people cast
>   The votes they cannot spell,
> Upon the pestilential blast
>   Her clamors swell.
>
> For all to whom the power's given
>   To sway or to compel,
> Among themselves apportion Heaven
>   And give her Hell.
>   *Blary O'Gary.*

HARANGUE, *n*. A speech by an opponent, who is known as an harangue-outang.

HONORABLE, *adj*. Afflicted with an impediment in one's reach. In legislative bodies it is customary to mention all members as honorable; as "the honorable gentleman is a scurvy cur."

IMPARTIAL, *adj.* Unable to perceive any promise of personal advantage from espousing either side of a controversy or adopting either of two conflicting opinions.

IMPOSTOR, *n.* A rival aspirant to public honors.

INFLUENCE, *n.* In politics, a visionary *quo* given in exchange for a substantial *quid.*

MACHINATION, *n.* The method employed by one's opponents in baffling one's open and honorable efforts to do the right thing.

> So plain the advantages of machination
> It constitutes a moral obligation,
> And honest wolves who think upon't with loathing
> Feel bound to don the sheep's deceptive clothing.
> So prospers still the diplomatic art,
> And Satan bows, with hand upon his heart.
>
> R. S. K.

MILLENNIUM, *n.* The period of a thousand years when the lid is to be screwed down, with all reformers on the under side.

MINISTER, *n.* An agent of a higher power with a lower responsibility. In diplomacy an officer sent into a foreign country as the visible embodiment of his sovereign's hostility. His principal qualification is a degree of plausible inveracity next below that of an ambassador.

MUGWUMP, *n.* In politics one afflicted with self-respect and addicted to the vice of independence. A term of contempt.

MULTITUDE, *n.* A crowd; the source of political wisdom and virtue. In a republic, the object of the statesman's adoration. "In a multitude of counsellors there is wisdom," saith the proverb. If many men of equal individual wisdom are wiser than any one of them, it must be that they acquire the excess of wisdom by the mere act of getting together. Whence comes it? Obviously from nowhere—as well say that a range of mountains is higher than the single mountains composing it. A multitude is as wise as its wisest member if it obey him; if not, it is no wiser than its most foolish.

NEPOTISM, *n.* Appointing your grandmother to office for the good of the party.

NOMINATE, *v.* To designate for the heaviest political assessment. To put forward a suitable person to incur the mudgobbing and dead-catting of the opposition.

NOMINEE, *n.* A modest gentleman shrinking from the distinction of private life and diligently seeking the honorable obscurity of public office.

OPPOSITION, *n.* In politics the party that prevents the Government from running amuck by hamstringing it.

The King of Ghargaroo, who had been abroad to study the science of government, appointed one hundred of his fattest subjects as members of a parliament to make laws for the collection of revenue. Forty of these he named the Party of Opposition and had his Prime Minister carefully instruct them in their duty of opposing every royal measure. Nevertheless, the first one that was submitted passed unanimously. Greatly displeased, the King vetoed it, informing the Opposition that if they did that again they would pay for their obstinacy with their heads. The entire forty promptly disemboweled themselves.

"What shall we do now?" the King asked. "Liberal institutions cannot be maintained without a party of Opposition."

"Splendor of the universe," replied the Prime Minister, "it is true these dogs of darkness have no longer their credentials, but all is not lost. Leave the matter to this worm of the dust."

So the Minister had the bodies of his Majesty's Opposition embalmed and stuffed with straw, put back into the seats of power and nailed there. Forty votes were recorded against every bill and the nation prospered. But one day a bill imposing a tax on warts was defeated—the members of the Government party had not been nailed to their seats! This so enraged the King that the Prime Minister was put to death, the parliament was dissolved with a battery of artillery, and government of the people, by the people, for the people perished from Ghargaroo.

ORATORY, *n.* A conspiracy between speech and action to cheat the understanding. A tyranny tempered by stenography.

OVERWORK, *n.* A dangerous disorder affecting high public functionaries who want to go fishing.

PATRIOT, *n.* One to whom the interests of a part seem superior to those of the whole. The dupe of statesmen and the tool of conquerors.

PATRIOTISM, *n.* Combustible rubbish ready to the torch of any one ambitious to illuminate his name.

In Dr. Johnson's famous dictionary patriotism is defined as the last resort of a scoundrel. With all due respect
to an enlightened but inferior lexicographer I beg to submit that it is the first.

PLEBISCITE, *n*. A popular vote to ascertain the will of the
sovereign.

PLENIPOTENTIARY, *adj*. Having full power. A Minister Plenipotentiary is a diplomatist possessing absolute authority
on condition that he never exert it.

POLITICS, *n*. A strife of interests masquerading as a contest of
principles. The conduct of public affairs for private advantage.

POLITICIAN, *n*. An eel in the fundamental mud upon which
the superstructure of organized society is reared. When he
wriggles he mistakes the agitation of his tail for the trembling of the edifice. As compared with the statesman, he
suffers the disadvantage of being alive.

POPULIST, *n*. A fossil patriot of the early agricultural period,
found in the old red soapstone underlying Kansas; characterized by an uncommon spread of ear, which some
naturalists contend gave him the power of flight, though
Professors Morse and Whitney, pursuing independent lines
of thought, have ingeniously pointed out that had he possessed it he would have gone elsewhere. In the picturesque
speech of his period, some fragments of which have come
down to us, he was known as "The Matter with Kansas."

POVERTY, *n*. A file provided for the teeth of the rats of reform.
The number of plans for its abolition equals that of the

reformers who suffer from it, plus that of the philosophers who know nothing about it. Its victims are distinguished by possession of all the virtues and by their faith in leaders seeking to conduct them into a prosperity where they believe these to be unknown.

PREROGATIVE, *n.* A sovereign's right to do wrong.

PRESIDENCY, *n.* The greased pig in the field game of American politics.

PRESIDENT, *n.* The leading figure in a small group of men of whom—and of whom only—it is positively known that immense numbers of their countrymen did not want any of them for President.

> If that's an honor surely 'tis a greater
> To have been a simple and undamned spectator.
> Behold in me a man of mark and note
> Whom no elector e'er denied a vote!—
> An undiscredited, unhooted gent
> Who might, for all we know, be President
> By acclamation. Cheer, ye varlets, cheer—
> I'm passing with a wide and open ear!
> *Jonathan Fomry.*

PUSH, *n.* One of the two things mainly conducive to success, especially in politics. The other is Pull.

QUEEN, *n.* A woman by whom the realm is ruled when there is a king, and through whom it is ruled when there is not.

QUORUM, *n.* A sufficient number of members of a deliberative body to have their own way and their own way of having it. In the United States Senate a quorum consists of the chairman of the Committee on Finance and a messenger from the White House; in the House of Representatives, of the Speaker and the devil.

RABBLE, *n*. In a republic, those who exercise a supreme authority tempered by fraudulent elections. The rabble is like the sacred Simurgh, of Arabian fable—omnipotent on condition that it do nothing. (The word is Aristocratese, but has no exact equivalent in our tongue, but means, as nearly as may be, "soaring swine.")

RADICALISM, *n*. The conservatism of to-morrow injected into the affairs of to-day.

RAMSHACKLE, *adj*. Pertaining to a certain order of architecture, otherwise known as the Normal American. Most of the public buildings of the United States are of the Ramshackle order, though some of our earlier architects preferred the Ironic. Recent additions to the White House in Washington are Theo-Doric, the ecclesiastic order of the Dorians. They are exceedingly fine and cost one hundred dollars a brick.

REAR, *n*. In American military matters, that exposed part of the army that is nearest to Congress.

REBEL, *n*. A proponent of a new misrule who has failed to establish it.

RECOUNT, *n*. In American politics, another throw of the dice, accorded to the player against whom they are loaded.

REDUNDANT, *adj*. Superfluous; needless; *de trop*.

The Sultan said: "There's evidence abundant
To prove this unbelieving dog redundant."
To whom the Grand Vizier, with mien impressive,
Replied: "His head, at least, appears excessive."
                                    Habeeb Suleiman.

Mr. Debs is a redundant citizen.—*Theodore Roosevelt.*

REFERENDUM, *n.* A law for submission of proposed legislation to a popular vote to learn the nonsensus of public opinion.

REFORM, *n.* A thing that mostly satisfies reformers opposed to reformation.

REPRESENTATIVE, *n.* In national politics, a member of the Lower House in this world, and without discernible hope of promotion in the next.

REPUBLIC, *n.* A nation in which, the thing governing and the thing governed being the same, there is only a permitted authority to enforce an optional obedience. In a republic the foundation of public order is the ever lessening habit of submission inherited from ancestors who, being truly governed, submitted because they had to. There are as many kinds of republics as there are gradations between the despotism whence they came and the anarchy whither they lead.

RESIGN, *v.t.* To renounce an honor for an advantage. To renounce an advantage for a greater advantage.

'Twas rumored Leonard Wood had signed
    A true renunciation
Of title, rank and every kind

Of military station—
Each honorable station.

By his example fired—inclined
To noble emulation,
The country humbly was resigned
To Leonard's resignation—
His Christian resignation.
Politian Greame.

RESPITE, *n.* A suspension of hostilities against a sentenced
assassin, to enable the Executive to determine whether the
murder may not have been done by the prosecuting attorney. Any break in the continuity of a disagreeable ex-
pectation.

Altgeld upon his incandescent bed
Lay, an attendant demon at his head.

"O cruel cook, pray grant me some relief—
Some respite from the roast, however brief.

"Remember how on earth I pardoned all
Your friends in Illinois when held in thrall."

"Unhappy soul! for that alone you squirm
O'er fire unquenched, a never-dying worm.

"Yet, for I pity your uneasy state,
Your doom I'll mollify and pains abate.

"Naught, for a season, shall your comfort mar,
Not even the memory of who you are."

Throughout eternal space dread silence fell;
Heaven trembled as Compassion entered Hell.

"As long, sweet demon, let my respite be
As, governing down here, I'd respite thee."

"As long, poor soul, as any of the pack
You thrust from jail consumed in getting back."

A genial chill affected Altgeld's hide
While they were turning him on t'other side.
                                        Joel Spate Woop.

REVOLUTION, *n.* In politics, an abrupt change in the form of
misgovernment. Specifically, in American history, the substitution of the rule of an Administration for that of a
Ministry, whereby the welfare and happiness of the people
were advanced a full half-inch. Revolutions are usually accompanied by a considerable effusion of blood, but are
accounted worth it—this appraisement being made by
beneficiaries whose blood had not the mischance to be
shed. The French revolution is of incalculable value to
the Socialist of to-day; when he pulls the string actuating
its bones its gestures are inexpressibly terrifying to gory
tyrants suspected of fomenting law and order.

RICHES, *n.*

A gift from Heaven signifying, "This is my beloved son, in
whom I am well pleased."—*John D. Rockefeller.*
The reward of toil and virtue.—*J. P. Morgan.*
The savings of many in the hands of one.—*Eugene Debs.*

   To these excellent definitions the inspired lexicographer
feels that he can add nothing of value.

RIGHT, *n.* Legitimate authority to be, to do or to have; as the
right to be a king, the right to do one's neighbor, the right
to have measles, and the like. The first of these rights was
once universally believed to be derived directly from the

will of God; and this is still sometimes affirmed *in partibus
infidelium* outside the enlightened realms of Democracy;
as the well known lines of Sir Abednego Bink, following:

> By what right, then, do royal rulers rule?
> > Whose is the sanction of their state and pow'r?
> He surely were as stubborn as a mule
> > Who, God unwilling, could maintain an hour
> His uninvited session on the throne, or air
> His pride securely in the Presidential chair.
>
> Whatever is is so by Right Divine;
> > Whate'er occurs, God wills it so. Good Land!
> It were a wondrous thing if His design
> > A fool could baffle or a rogue withstand!
> If so, then God, I say (intending no offence)
> Is guilty of contributory negligence.

SENATE, *n.* A body of elderly gentlemen charged with high
duties and misdemeanors.

SHERIFF, *n.* In America the chief executive officer of a county,
whose most characteristic duties, in some of the Western
and Southern States, are catching and hanging of rogues.

> John Elmer Pettibone Cajee
> (I write of him with little glee)
> Was just as bad as he could be.
>
> 'Twas frequently remarked: "I swon!
> The sun has never looked upon
> So bad a man as Neighbor John."
>
> A sinner through and through, he had
> This added fault: it made him mad
> To know another man was bad.

In such a case he thought it right
To rise at any hour of night
And quench that wicked person's light.

Despite the town's entreaties, he
Would hale him to the nearest tree
And leave him swinging wide and free.

Or sometimes, if the humor came,
A luckless wight's reluctant frame
Was given to the cheerful flame.

While it was turning nice and brown,
All unconcerned John met the frown
Of that austere and righteous town.

"How sad," his neighbors said, "that he
So scornful of the law should be—
An anar c, h, i, s, t."

(That is the way they preferred
To utter the abhorrent word,
So strong the aversion that is stirred.)

"Resolved," they said, continuing,
"That Badman John must cease this thing
Of having his unlawful fling.

"Now, by these sacred relics"—here
Each man had out a souvenir
Got at a lynching yesteryear—

"By these we swear he shall forsake
His ways, nor cause our hearts to ache
By sins of rope and torch and stake.

"We'll tie his red right hand until
He'll have small freedom to fulfil
The mandates of his lawless will."

So, in convention then and there,
They named him Sheriff. The affair
Was opened, it is said, with prayer.
                    J. Milton Sloluck.

SUFFRAGE, *n.* Expression of opinion by means of a ballot. The
right of suffrage (which is held to be both a privilege and
a duty) means, as commonly interpreted, the right to vote
for the man of another man's choice, and is highly prized.
Refusal to do so has the bad name of "incivism." The in-
civilian, however, cannot be properly arraigned for his
crime, for there is no legitimate accuser. If the accuser is
himself guilty he has no standing in the court of opinion;
if not, he profits by the crime, for A's abstention from voting gives greater weight to the vote of B. By female suffrage
is meant the right of a woman to vote as some man tells
her to. It is based on female responsibility, which is somewhat limited. The woman most eager to jump out of her
petticoat to assert her rights is first to jump back into it
when threatened with a switching for misusing them.

TARIFF, *n.* A scale of taxes on imports, designed to protect
the domestic producer against the greed of his consumer.

> The Enemy of Human Souls
> Sat grieving at the cost of coals;
> For Hell had been annexed of late,
> And was a sovereign Southern State.
>
> "It were no more than right," said he,
> "That I should get my fuel free.
> The duty, neither just nor wise,
> Compels me to economize—
> Whereby my broilers, every one,

Are execrably underdone.
What would they have?—although I yearn
To do them nicely to a turn,
I can't afford an honest heat.
This tariff makes even devils cheat!
I'm ruined, and my humble trade
All rascals may at will invade:
Beneath my nose the public press
Outdoes me in sulphureousness;
The bar ingeniously applies
To my undoing my own lies;
My medicines the doctors use
(Albeit vainly) to refuse
To me my fair and rightful prey
And keep their own in shape to pay;
The preachers by example teach
What, scorning to perform, I preach;
And statesmen, aping me, all make
More promises than they can break.
Against such competition I
Lift up a disregarded cry.
Since all ignore my just complaint,
By Hokey-Pokey! I'll turn saint!"

Now, the Republicans, who all
Are saints, began at once to bawl
Against *his* competition; so
There was a devil of a go!
They locked horns with him, tête-à-tête
In acrimonious debate,
Till Democrats, forlorn and lone,
Had hopes of coming by their own.
That evil to avert, in haste
The two belligerents embraced;
But since 'twere wicked to relax
A title of the Sacred Tax,

'Twas finally agreed to grant
The bold Insurgent-protestant
A bounty on each soul that fell
Into his ineffectual Hell.
                              Edam Smith.

TRUST, *n.* In American politics, a large corporation composed
in greater part of thrifty working men, widows of small
means, orphans in the care of guardians and the courts,
with many similar malefactors and public enemies.

UN-AMERICAN, *adj.* Wicked, intolerable, heathenish.

WASHINGTONIAN, *n.* A Potomac tribesman who exchanged the
privilege of governing himself for the advantage of good
government. In justice to him it should be said that he did
not want to.

They took away his vote and gave instead
The right, when he had earned, to *eat* his bread.
In vain—he clamors for his "boss," poor soul,
To come again and part him from his roll.
                              Offenbach Stutz.

WHANGDEPOOTENAWAH, *n.* In the Ojibwa tongue, disaster;
an unexpected affliction that strikes hard.

Should you ask me whence this laughter,
Whence this audible big-smiling,
With its labial extension,
With its maxillar distortion
And its diaphragmic rhythmus
Like the billowing of ocean,
Like the shaking of a carpet,

I should answer, I should tell you:
From the great deeps of the spirit,
From the unplummeted abysmus
Of the soul this laughter welleth
As the fountain, the gug-guggle,
Like the river from the cañon,
To entoken and give warning
That my present mood is sunny.
Should you ask me further question—
Why the great deeps of the spirit,
Why the unplummeted abysmus
Of the soul extrudes this laughter,
This all audible big-smiling,
I should answer, I should tell you
With a white heart, tumpitumpy,
With a true tongue, honest Injun:
William Bryan, he has Caught It,
Caught the Whangdepootenawah!
Is't the sandhill crane, the shankank,
Standing in the marsh, the kneedeep,
Standing silent in the kneedeep
With his wing-tips crossed behind him
And his neck close-reefed before him,
With his bill, his william, buried
In the down upon his bosom,
With his head retracted inly,
While his shoulders overlook it?
Does the sandhill crane, the shankank,
Shiver grayly in the north wind,
Wishing he had died when little,
As the sparrow, the chipchip, does?
No 'tis not the Shankank standing,
Standing in the gray and dismal
Marsh, the gray and dismal kneedeep.
No, 'tis peerless William Bryan

Realizing that he's Caught It,
Caught the Whangdepootenawah!

YANKEE, *n.* In Europe, an American. In the Northern States of our Union, a New Englander. In the Southern States the word is unknown. (See DAMYANK.)

ZEUS, *n.* The chief of Grecian gods, adored by the Romans as Jupiter and by the modern Americans as God, Gold, Mob, and Dog. Some explorers who have touched upon the shores of America, and one who professes to have penetrated a considerable distance into the interior, have thought that these four names stand for as many distinct deities, but in his monumental work on Surviving Faiths, Frumpp insists that the natives are monotheists, each having no other god than himself, whom he worships under many sacred names.

ZIGZAG, *v.t.* To move forward uncertainly, from side to side, as one carrying the white man's burden. (From *zed, z* and *jag,* an Icelandic word of unknown meaning.)

He zedjagged so uncomen wyde
Thet non coude pas on eyder syde;
So, to com saufly thruh, I been
Constreynet for to doodge betwene.
Munwele.

Selections from *Fantastic Fables*

Treasury and Arms

A Public Treasury, feeling Two Arms lifting out its contents, exclaimed:

"Mr. Shareman, I move for a division."

"You seem to know something about parliamentary forms of speech," said the Two Arms.

"Yes," replied the Public Treasury, "I am familiar with the hauls of legislation."

The Politicians

An Old Politician and a Young Politician were traveling through a beautiful country, by the dusty highway which leads to the City of Prosperous Obscurity. Lured by the flowers and the shade and charmed by the songs of birds which invited to woodland paths and green fields, his imagination fired by glimpses of golden domes and glittering palaces in the distance on either hand, the Young Politician said:

"Let us, I beseech thee, turn aside from this comfortless road, leading, thou knowest whither, but not I. Let us turn our backs upon duty and abandon ourselves to the delights and advantages beckoning from every grove and calling to us from every shining hill. Let us, if so thou wilt, follow this

Ambrose Bierce, *The Collected Writings* . . . pp. 541–659.

beautiful path, which, as thou seest, hath a guide-board saying, 'Turn in here all ye who seek the Palace of Popular Attention.'"

"It is a beautiful path, my son," said the Old Politician, without either slackening his pace or turning his head, "and it leadeth among pleasant scenes. But the search for the Palace of Popular Attention is beset with one mighty peril."

"What is that?" said the Young Politician.

"The peril of finding it," the Old Politician replied, pushing on.

Legislator and Soap

A member of the Kansas Legislature meeting a Cake of Soap was passing it by without recognition, but the Cake of Soap insisted on stopping and shaking hands. Thinking it might possibly be in the enjoyment of the elective franchise, he gave it a cordial and earnest grasp. On letting it go he observed that a part of it adhered to his fingers, and running to a brook in great alarm, proceeded to wash it off. In doing so he necessarily got some on the other hand, and when he had finished washing both were so white that he went to bed and sent for a physician.

The Reform School Board

The members of the School Board in Doosnoswair being suspected of appointing female teachers for an improper consideration, the people elected a Board composed wholly of women. In a few years the scandal was at an end; there were no female teachers in the Department.

Alderman and Raccoon

"I see quite a number of rings on your tail," said an Alderman to a Raccoon that he met in a zoological garden.

"Yes," replied the Racoon, "and I hear quite a number of tales on your ring."

The Alderman, being of a sensitive, retiring disposition, shrank from further comparison, and strolling to another part of the garden stole the camel.

Two Politicians

Two Politicians were exchanging ideas regarding the rewards for public service.

"The reward that I most desire," said the First Politician, "is the gratitude of my fellow citizens."

"That would be very gratifying, no doubt," said the Second Politician, "but, alas! in order to obtain it one has to retire from politics."

For an instant they gazed upon each other with inexpressible tenderness; then the First Politician murmured, "God's will be done! Since we cannot hope for reward let us be content with what we have."

And lifting their right hands for a moment from the public treasury they swore to be content.

The Divided Delegation

A Delegation at Washington went to a New President, and said:

"Your Excellency, we are unable to agree upon a Favorite Son to represent us in your Cabinet."

"Then," said the New President, "I shall have to lock you up until you do agree."

So the Delegation was cast into the deepest dungeon beneath the moat, where it maintained a divided mind for many weeks, but finally reconciled its differences and asked to be taken before the New President.

"My children," said he, "nothing is so beautiful as harmony. My Cabinet selections were all made before our former interview, but you have supplied a noble instance of patriotism in subordinating your personal preferences to the general good. Go now to your beautiful homes and be happy."

Mine-Owner and Jackass

While the Owner of a Silver Mine was on his way to attend a convention of his species he was accosted by a Jackass, who said:

"By an unjust discrimination against quadrupeds I am made ineligible to a seat in your convention; so I am compelled to seek representation through you."

"It will give me great pleasure, sir," said the Owner of a Silver Mine, "to serve one so closely allied to me in—in—well, you know," he added, with a significant gesture of his two hands upward from the sides of his head. "What do you want?"

"Oh, nothing—nothing at all for myself individually," replied the Donkey; "but his country's welfare should be a patriot's supreme care. If Americans are to retain the sacred liberties for which their fathers strove Congress must declare our independence of European dictation by maintaining the price of mules."

Legislator and Citizen

A Former Legislator asked a Most Respectable Citizen for a letter to the Governor, recommending him for appointment as Commissioner of Shrimps and Crabs.

"Sir," said the Most Respectable Citizen, austerely, "were you not once in the State Senate?"

"Not so bad as that, sir, I assure you," was the reply. "I was a member of the Slower House. I was expelled for selling my influence."

"And you dare to ask for mine!" shouted the Most Respectable Citizen. "You have the impudence? A man who will accept bribes will probably offer them. Do you mean to——"

"I should not think of making a corrupt proposal to you, sir; but if I were Commissioner of Shrimps and Crabs I might have some influence with the waterfront population, and be able to help you make your fight for Coroner."

"In that case I do not feel justified in denying you the letter."

Citizen and Snakes

A Public-spirited Citizen who had failed miserably in trying to secure a National political convention for his city suffered acutely from dejection. While in that frame of mind he leaned thoughtlessly against a druggist's show-window, wherein were one hundered and fifty kinds of assorted snakes. The glass breaking, the reptiles all escaped into the street.

"When you can't do what you wish," said the Public-spirited Citizen, "it is worth while to do what you can."

Six and One

The Committee on Gerrymander worked late into the

night drawing intricate lines on a map of the State, and being weary sought repose in a game of poker. At the close of the game the six Republican members were bankrupt and the single Democrat had all the money. On the next day, when the Committee was called to order for business, one of the luckless six mounted his legs, and said:

"Mr. Chairman, before we bend to our noble task of purifying politics in the interest of good government I wish to say a word of the untoward events of last evening. If my memory serves me the disasters which overtook the Majority of this honorable body always befell when it was the Minority's deal. It is my solemn conviction, Mr. Chairman, and to its affirmation I pledge my life, my sacred fortune and my honor, that that wicked and unscrupulous Minority redistricted the cards!"

The Honest Citizen

A Political Preferment, labeled with its price, was canvassing the State to find a purchaser. One day it offered itself to a Truly Good Man who after examining the label and finding that the price was twice as great as he was willing to pay spurned the Political Preferment from his door. Then the People said: "Behold, this is an honest citizen!" And the Truly Good Man humbly confessed that it was true.

The Honorable Member

A Member of a Legislature who had pledged himself to his Constituents not to steal brought him at the end of the session a large part of the dome of the Capitol. Thereupon the Constituents held an indignation meeting and passed a resolution of tar and feathers.

"You are most unjust," said the Member of the Legislature. "It is true I promised you that I would not steal; but had I ever promised you that I would not lie?"

The Constituents said he was an honorable man and elected him to the United States Congress, unpledged and unfledged.

The Expatriated Boss

A Boss who had gone to Canada was taunted by a Citizen of Montreal with having fled to avoid prosecution.

"You do me a grave injustice," said the Boss, parting with a pair of tears. "I came to Canada solely because of its political attractions; its Government is said to be the most corrupt in the world."

"Pray forgive me," said the Citizen of Montreal.

They fell upon each other's neck, and at the conclusion of that touching rite the Boss had two watches.

A Statesman

A Statesman who attended a meeting of a Chamber of Commerce rose to speak, but was objected to on the ground that he had nothing to do with commerce.

"Mr. Chairman," said an Aged Member, rising, "I conceive that the objection is not well taken; the gentleman's connection with commerce is close and intimate. He is a commodity."

Return of the Representative

Hearing that the Legislature had adjourned, the People of an Assembly District held a mass-meeting to devise a suitable punishment for their Dishonorable Representative.

By one speaker it was proposed that he be disembowelled, by another that he be made to run the gauntlet. Some favored hanging, some thought that it would do him good to appear in a suit of tar and feathers. An Old Man famous for his wisdom and his habit of drooling on his shirt-front suggested that they first catch their hare. So the Chairman appointed a committee to watch for the victim at midnight and take him as he should attempt to sneak into town across-lots from the tamarack swamp. At this point in the proceedings they were interrupted by the sound of a brass band. Their Dishonorable Representative was driving up from the railway station in a coach-and-four, with music and a banner. A few moments later he entered the hall, went upon the platform and said it was the proudest moment of his life. (Cheers.)

Congress and People

Successive Congresses have greatly impoverished the People, they were discouraged and wept copiously.

"Why do you weep?" inquired an Angel who had perched upon a tree near by.

"They have taken all we have," replied the People—"excepting," they added, noting the suggestive visitant—"excepting our hope in Heaven. Thank God they cannot deprive us of that!"

But at last came the Congress of 1889!

Statesman and Horse

A Statesman who had saved his country was returning from Washington on foot, when he met a Race Horse going at full speed, and stopped him.

"Turn about and travel the other way," said the Statesman, "and I will keep you company as far as my home. The advantages of traveling together are obvious."

"I cannot do that," said the Race Horse; "I am following my master to Washington. I did not go fast enough to suit him, and he has gone on ahead."

"Who is your master?" inquired the Statesman.

"He is a Statesman who saved his country," answered the Race Horse.

"There appears to be some mistake," the other said. "Why did he wish to travel so fast?"

"So as to be there in time to get the country that he saved."

"I guess he got it," said the other, and limped along, sighing.

The Good Government

"What a happy land you are!" said a Republican Form of Government to a Sovereign State. "Be good enough to lie still while I walk upon you, singing the praises of universal suffrage and descanting upon the blessings of civil and religious liberty. In the meantime you can relieve your feelings by cursing one-man power and the effete monarchies of Europe."

"My public servants have been fools and rogues from the date of your accession to power," replied the State; "my legislative bodies, both State and municipal, are bands of thieves; my taxes are insupportable; my courts are corrupt; my cities are a disgrace to civilization; my corporations have their hands at the throat of every private interest—all my affairs are in disorder and criminal confusion."

"That is all very true," said the Republican Form of Government, putting on its hobnail shoes; "but consider how I thrill you every Fourth of July."

The Appropriate Memorial

A High Public Functionary having died, the citizens of his town held a meeting to consider how to honor his memory, and Another High Public Functionary rose and addressed the meeting.

"Mr. Chairman and Gintlemen," said the Other, "it sames to me, and I'm hopin' yez wull approve the suggistion, that an appropriet way to honor the mimory of the decaised would be to erect an emolument sootably inscribed wid his vartues."

The soul of the great man looked down from Heaven and wept.

FINLEY PETER DUNNE
[Mr. Dooley]
(1867-1936)

Mr. Martin Dooley, Finley Peter Dunne's immortal saloon-keeper and public oracle, was a national institution at the turn of the century. He belonged to the great crackerbox tradition of Downing, Biglow, and Ward, yet contributed an urban and immigrant flavor all his own. With stinging accuracy, Peter Dunne uncovered hollowness, sham, and inhumanity in the high and mighty, sharing his discoveries with his readers through the conversations of Mr. Dooley and his friends McKenna and Hennessy. "Imperialism, militarism, smug corruption in government and business, pretentious nonsense in education or religion, the protective tariff, fake reformers, self-deified aristocrats, and dishonest journalists—all of these," said Elmer Ellis, "he could and did satirize in masterly fashion."

Mr. Dooley's Irishness was all-important. It supplied an insider's insight into machine politics in America's raucous cities, together with an outsider's or underdog's perspective of American society, with all its democratic pretensions and nativistic contradictions. Mr. Dooley's Irish dialect accounted for his original popular success, but erects a barrier for today's readers. Fortunately Mr. Dooley's observations on life and politics lose none of their humor when translated into commonplace, everyday English. His humor transcends its own medium.

Peter Dunne, twenty-five years old and an editorial writer for the Chicago *Evening Post,* was given free rein to turn out commentaries on the affairs of the day. He possessed a rich, natural vein of satirical, jocose, and waggish humor, together with a keen ear and a facile pen for transposing an impossible brogue compounded of all the dialects of Ireland modified by the effects of many years living and working in Chicago. Beginning in 1893 Mr. Dooley emerged over a period of many months from more than one real-life prototype. Included somewhere in Dooley's ancestry was one James McGarry who ran a saloon on Chicago's Dearborn Street; but there were others, including Dunne himself.

Perhaps Mr. Dooley's greatest gift, as Mark Sullivan recognized, was to supply "the softening solvent of humor to the American atmosphere in times of acute controversy." Dooley's strength lay in an intuitive acceptance of the inevitable and a wise rejection of futile protestation. Dunne's characterization of Martin Dooley recalls McGarry's example: "His bartender, Mike Casey, stuck his head in the door to the back room and asked, 'Is George Babbitt good for a drink?'

" 'Has he had it?' asked McGarry.

" 'He has,' said the barkeeper apologetically.

" 'He is,' answered McGarry resignedly."

Was the sage of Archey Street no more than a cynic? He wrote: "A man that'd expict to thrain lobsters to fly in a year is called a loonytic; but a man that thinks men can be turned into angels be an iliction is called a rayformer— an' remains at large." Finley Peter Dunne did have his hopes for mankind, but they were simply founded and well within reach. "We do make progress," observed Mr. Dooley, "but it's the same kind Julyus Caesar made an' ivry wan has made befure or since, an' in this age iv macheenery we're still burrid be hand."

How Mr. Dooley would have relished the "iliction" of John Fitzgerald Kennedy in 1960 over Richard Nixon by the barest of margins, particularly since Chicago's Cook County votes were so efficiently tabulated to carry Illinois for JFK!

The O'Briens Forever

"I think, by dad," said Mr. Dooley, "that Hinnissy's crazy."

"I always thought so," said Mr. McKenna, amiably. "But what's he been doin' of late?"

"Well, I took him down to see th' good la-ads havin' fun with th' opprissors iv th' people at th' Colliseem," said Mr. Dooley. "I had no ticket, an' he had none. Th' frinds iv honest money had give thim all to Jawn P. Hopkins's la-ads. They're frinds iv honest money whin they'se no other in sight. But I'd like to see anny goold-bug or opprissor iv th' people keep th' likes iv me an' Hinnissy out iv a convintion. We braced up to wan iv th' dures, an' a man stopped Hinnissy. 'Who ar-re ye?' he says. 'I am a Dimmycrat,' says Hinnissy. 'Is ye'er name Hill?' says th' la-ad. 'It is not,' says Hinnissy. 'I tol' ye I'm a Dimmycrat; an',' he says, 'I'll have no man call me out iv me name.' Hinnissy was f'r rollin' him on th' flure there an' thin f'r an insult, but I flagged a polisman. 'Is ye'er name Sullivan?' says I. 'It is,' says he. 'Roscommon?' says I, fr'm th' way he spoke. 'Sure ye're right,' he says. 'Me name's Dooley,' I says. 'Here,' says he to th' durekeeper, 'don't stand in th' way iv th' sinitor iv th' State iv Mitchigan,' he says. 'Lave him an' his frind go in,' he says. I minded afther I was good to him whin Simon O'Donnell was chief iv polis, may he rest in peace!

"Hinnissy an' me got a seat be some dhroll ol' boys fr'm out in Iaway. Afther a man be th' name iv Martin, a sergeant-iv-arms, had addhressed th' meetin' twinty or thirty times,—

Finley Peter Dunne, *Mr. Dooley In the Hearts of His Countrymen*, Boston (1899), pp. 101–106.

I kep no count iv him,—th' chairman inthrojooced th' dilly-gates to nommynate th' big men. It wint all right with Hinnissy for a little while till a man got up an' shook his fist at th' chairman. 'What's that? what's that?' says Hinnissy. 'What's that?' he says. 'Hurroo, hurroo,' he says, lammin' th' man fr'm Iaway with his goold-headed cane. 'What ails ye, man alive?' says I. 'Why,' he says, 'they've nommynated Billy,' he says. 'Billy who?' says I. 'Why, Willum J. O'Brien,' he says.*

" 'A sthrong man,' says he addhressin' th' man fr'm Iaway. 'I shud say he was,' says th' man. 'Th' sthrongest man that iver come down th' road,' says Hinnissy. 'Why,' he says, 'I see that man put up an' eight iv beer with wan hand,' he says. 'None sthronger,' he says. 'But will he carry Illinye?' says th' lad fr'm Iaway. 'Will he carry Illinye? says Hinnissy. 'Why, man alive,' he says, 'I've see him carry a prim'ry in th' sixth precinct,' he says. 'Is that enough f'r ye?' he says. 'He's a good speaker,' says th' Iaway man. 'He is that,' says Hinnissy; 'an' he was wan iv th' best waltzers that flung a foot at th' County Dimocracy picnic,' he says. 'But will he make a good fight?' says th' man. 'Will he?' says Hinnissy. 'Will he make a good fight?' he says. 'Dooley,' he says, 'this here Dimmycrat wants to know if Bill 'll make a good fight. Why,' he says, 'if he iver gets to Washington an' wan iv th' op-prissors iv th' people goes again him, give him Jackson Park or a clothes closet, gun or soord, ice-pick or billyard cue, chair or stove leg, an' Bill 'll make him climb a tree,' he says. 'I'd like to see wan iv thim supreme justices again Bill O'Brien on an income tax or anny other ord-nance,' he says. 'He'd go in an' lame thim with th' Revised Statutes.' 'I

---

* Hennessy confused William Jennings Bryan, Democratic presidential nominee, with William J. O'Brien, a welterweight alderman from Chicago's South Side.

presume,' says th' lad, 'that ye'er fr'm Omaha.' 'I'll tear ye'er
hair out,' says Hinnissy.

" 'Ye idjit,' says I, whin I had him in th' sthreet, 'it wasn't
Bill O'Brien was nommynated,' says I. 'What ar-re ye talkin'
about?' says he. 'I seen him on th' flure,' he says. 'He had
th' sinitor iv Missoury be th' throat whin ye took me away,'
he says.

"I left him there; but he come into th' place at six o'clock,
an' borrid a paper an' pencil. Thin he wint back an' sat down
an' wrote. 'What ar-re ye doin' there?' says I. 'I've wrote a
sketch iv th' nominee f'r th' Stock-yards Sun,' he says. 'Listen
to it. Willum J. O'Brien,' he says, 'was born in th' County iv
Mayo forty years ago,' he says. 'He received a limited education, his parents even thin designin' him f'r th' Prisidency.
Bein' unable to complete a coorse at th' rayform school, he
wint to wurruk; but soon, tired iv this, he started a saloon.
Fr'm thince he dhrifted into politics, an' become noted as
th' boy welterweight iv th' South Branch. He was ilicted
aldherman at a time whin comparatively nawthin' was doin'
in th' council. Subsequent he become a sinitor, an' later
enthered into partnership with th' Hon. Jawn Powers in th'
retail liquor traffic. Mr. O'Brien is a fine built man, an' can
lick anny wan iv his age west iv th' river, give 'r take tin
pounds, color no bar. His heart bets up close to th' ribs iv
th' common people, an' he would make opprissors iv th' poor
wish they'd died early if ye give him a chance with a beer
bottle. How's that?' says Hinnissy.

" 'Worse,' says I. 'Foolish man,' says I. 'Don't ye know that
it ain't our Bill that's been nommynated?' I says. 'This is a
Nebraska man,' I says. 'Well,' he says, 'if 'tis Bill O'Brien,
he'd win easy. But,' he says, 'if 'tis not,' he says ' 'tis wan iv
th' fam'ly,' he says. 'I'll change this here novel an' make it

a sketch iv th' cousin iv th' candydate,' he says. An' he wint on with his wurruk.''

A Candidate's Pillory

"What's this counthry comin' to annyhow, that a man that's out f'r to be Prisident has to set up on a high chair an' be questioned on his record be a lot iv la-ads that hasn't had annything to do since th' carpetbeatin' season's ended?" said Mr. Dooley. "Ye'd think Big Bill was r-runnin' f'r chief ex-icutive iv th' Clan-na-Gael. First along comes a comity iv th' Sons iv Rest. 'Major,' says they, 'we're insthructed be th' organization to ascertain ye'er views on th' important, we may say all-important, question iv havin' wire matthresses put on th' benches in th' parks. Are we,' they says, 'goin' f'r to have to wear lumps on our backs into all eternity,' they says, 'an' have our slumbers broke be th' hot fut iv th' polis-man?' they says. 'We demand an answer,' they says, 'or, be this an' be that, we won't do a thing to ye.' Well, maybe Bill has been down to th' corner playin' a game iv spoil-five with his old frind Coalsack, an' has paid no attintion to th' Sons iv Rest. 'Well,' he says, 'gintlemen, I'm in favor iv doin' ivrything in reason f'r th' hoboes,' he says. 'Th' protection iv th' home hobo again th' pauper can trade iv Europe,' he says, 'has been wan iv th' principal wurruks iv me life,' he says; an' he gives thim each a hand out, an' bows thim to th' dure.

"In comes a dillygation fr'm th' Union iv Amalgamated

Mr. Dooley in the Hearts of His Countrymen, pp. 107–112.

Pantsmakers; an' says th' chairman, 'Major,' he says, 'we have a complaint to make again thim pants iv ye'ers,' he says. 'What's th' matter with th' pants?' says th' future Prisident. 'I thought they looked all right,' he says. 'I paid four dollars f'r thim in Bucyrus las' year,' he says. 'They have no union label on thim,' says th' chairman. 'Do you know, sir,' he says, 'that thim pants riprisints th' oppression iv women an' childher?' he says. 'D'ye know that ivry thread in thim seams means a tear an' sigh?' says he. 'D'ye know that ivry time ye put on thim pants ye take a pair off some down-throdden workman?' he says. 'Glory be!' says Big Bill: 'is that thrue? Thin what am I to do?' he says in alarm. 'Do?' says th' chairman. 'Wear pants that riprisints honest toil fairly compinsated,' he says. 'Wear pants that'll say to th' wurruld that Bill McKinley's legs are fair legs,' he says, 'that they may bow at th' knees, but they niver bow to th' opprissor,' he says; 'that niver did they wrap thimsilves in bags that bore th' curse iv monno-poly an' greed,' he says. 'An' where can I get thim?' says th' major. 'Fr'm me,' says th' frind iv labor, pullin' out a tape. 'Will ye have wan or two hip pockets?' he says.

"An' so it goes. Ivry day a rayporther comes to th' house with a list iv questions. 'What are ye'er views on th' issue iv eatin' custard pie with a sponge? Do ye believe in side-combs? If called upon to veto a bill f'r all mimbers iv th' Supreme Coort to wear hoop-skirts, wud ye veto it or wudden't ye? If so, why? If not, why not? If a batted ball goes out iv th' line afther strikin' th' player's hands, it is fair or who? Have ye that tired feelin'? What is your opinion iv a hereafther? Where did ye get that hat? If a man has eight dollars an' spends twelve iv it, what will th' poor man do? An' why an' where an' how much?'

"Thin, if he don't answer, ivry wan says he's a thrimmer, an' ought to be runnin' a sthreet-car an' not thryin' to poke his ondecided face into th' White House. I mind wanst, whin me frind O'Brien was a candydate f'r aldherman, a comity iv tax-payers waited on him f'r to get his views on th' issues iv th' day. Big Casey, th' housemover, was th' chairman; an' he says, says he, 'Misther O'Brien,' he says, 'we are desirous,' he says, 'iv larnin' where ye stand on th' tariff, th' currency question, pensions, an' th' intherstate commerce act,' he says, with a wave iv his hand. 'Well,' says O'Brien, he says, 'th' issue on which I'm appealin' to th' free an' intilligent suffrages of Ar-rchey Road an' th' assistance iv Deerin' Sthreet Station,' he says, 'is whether little Mike Kelly will have th' bridge or not,' he says. 'On that I stand,' he says. 'As f'r th' minor issues,' he says, 'I may have me opinions on thim an' I may not. Anny information I possess I'll keep tucked away in this large an commodjous mind cage, an' not be dealin' it out to th' likes iv ye, as though I was a comity iv th' Civic Featheration,' he says. 'Moreover,' he says, 'I'd like to know, you, Casey, what business have you got comin' roun' to my house and pryin' into my domestic affairs,' he says. ' 'Tis th' intherstate commerce act now, but th' nex' thing'll be where I got th' pianny,' he says; 'an', f'r fear ye may not stop where ye are, here goes to mount ye.' An' he climbed th' big man, an' rolled him. Well, sir, will ye believe me, ivry man on th' comity but wan voted f'r him. Casey was still in bed iliction day.

"I met Tom Dorsey afther th' comity called. 'Well,' says I, 'I heerd ye was up to O'Brien's questionin' him on th' issues iv th' day,' I says. 'We was,' says he. 'Was his answers satisfacthry?' says I. 'Perfectly so,' he says. 'Whin th' comity left, we were all convinced that he was th' strongest man that cud be nommynated,' he says."

On the Hero in Politics

" 'Tis as much as a man's life is worth these days," said Mr. Dooley, "to have a vote. Look here," he continued, diving under the bar and producing a roll of paper. "Here's th' pitchers iv candydates I pulled down fr'm th' windy, an' jus' knowin' they're here makes me that nervous f'r th' contints iv th' cash dhrawer I'm afraid to tur-rn me back f'r a minyit. I'm goin' to throw thim out in th' back yard.

"All heroes, too, Hinnissy. They'se Mike O'Toole, th hero iv Sandago, that near lost his life be dhrink on his way to th' arm'ry, an' had to be sint home without lavin' th' city. There's Turror Teddy Mangan, th' night man at Flaher-ty's that loaded th' men that loaded th' guns that kilt th' mules at Matoonzas. There's Hero O'Brien, that wud've inlisted if he hadn't been too old, an' th' contractin' business in such good shape. There's Bill Cory, that come near losin' his life at a cinematograph iv th' battle iv Manila. They're all here, bedad, r-ready to sarve their country to th' bitter end, an' to r-rush, voucher in hand, to th' city threasurer's office at a minyit's notice.

"I wint to a hero meetin' th' other night, Hinnissy, an' that's sthrange f'r me. Whin a man gets to be my age, he laves th' shoutin' f'r th' youth iv th' land onless he has a pol-itical job. I niver had a job but wanst. That was whin I was precin't cap'n; an' a good wan I was, too. None betther. I'd been on th' cinthral co-mity to-day, but f'r me losin' ambition whin they r-run a man be th' name iv Eckstein f'r

Finley Peter Dunne, *Mr. Dooley n Peace and in War*, Boston (1899), pp. 87–91.

aldherman. I was sayin', Hinnissy, whin a man gets to be my age, he ducks pol-itical meetin's, an' r-reads th' papers an' weighs th' ividence an' th' argymints,—pro-argymints an' con-argymints,—an' makes up his mind ca'mly, an' votes th' Dimmycratic ticket. But young Dorsey he med me go with him to th' hero's meetin' in Finucane's hall.

"Well, sir, there was O'Toole an' all th' rest on th' platform in unyform, with flags over thim, an' the bands playin' 'They'll be a hot time in th' ol' town to-night again'; an' th' chairman was Plunkett. Ye know Plunkett: a good man if they was no gr-rand juries. He was makin' a speech. 'Whin th' battle r-raged,' he says, 'an' th' bullets fr'm th' haughty Spanyards' raypeatin' Mouser r-rifles,' he says, 'where was Cassidy?' he says. 'In his saloon,' says I, 'in I'mrald Av'noo,' says I. 'Thrue f'r ye,' says Plunkett. 'An' where,' he says, 'wus our candydate?' he says. 'In somebody else's saloon,' says I. 'No,' says he. 'Whin th' Prisidint,' he says, 'called th' nation to ar-rms,' he says, 'an' Congress voted fifty million good bucks f'r th' naytional definse,' he says, 'Thomas Francis Dorgan,' he says, 'in that minyit iv naytional pearl,' says he, 'left his good job in the pipe-yard,' he says, 'an' wint down to th' raycruitin' office, an' says, "How manny calls f'r volunteers is out?" he says. "Wan," says th' officer. "Put me down," says Dorgan, "f'r th' tenth call," he says. 'This, gintlemen iv th' foorth precin't,' he says, 'is Thomas Francis Dorgan, a man who, if ilicted,' he says, 'victhry'll perch,' he says, 'upon our banners,' he says; 'an',' he says, 'th' naytional honor will be maintained,' he says, 'in th' county boord,' he says.

"I wint out to take th' air, an' I met me frind Clohessy, th' little tailor fr'm Halsted Sthreet. Him an' me had a shell iv beer together at th' German's; an' says I, 'What d'ye think iv th' heroes?' I says. 'Well,' says he, 'I make no doubt 'twas brave iv Dorgan,' he says, 'f'r to put his name in f'r th' tenth call,' he says; 'but,' he says, 'I don't like Plunkett, an' it seems to me a man'd have to be a hell iv a sthrong man, even if he was a hero, to be Plunkett's man, an' keep his hands out iv ye'er pockets,' he says. 'I'm with Clancy's candydate,' he says. 'He niver offered to enlist for th' war,' he says, 'but 'twas Clancy put Terence on th' polis foorce an' got th' school f'r Aggie,' he says.

"That's the way I feel," said Mr. Hennessy. "I wudden't thrust Plunkett as far as I cud throw a cow be th' tail. If Dorgan was Clancy's war hero, I'd be with him."

"Annyhow," said Mr. Dooley, "mighty few iv th' rale heroes iv th' war is r-runnin' f'r office. Most iv thim put on their blue overalls whin they was mustered out an' wint up an' ast f'r their ol' jobs back—an' sometimes got thim. Ye can see as manny as tin iv thim at the rollin'-mills defindin' th' nation's honor with wheelbahr's an' a slag shovel."

On Reform Candidates

"That frind iv ye'ers, Dugan, is an intilligent man," said Mr. Dooley. "All he needs is an index an' a few illusthrations to make him a bicyclopedja iv useless information."

"Well," said Mr. Hennessy, judiciously, "he ain't no Socrates an' he ain't no answers-to-questions colum; but he's a good man that goes to his jooty, an' as handy with a pick as some people are with a cocktail spoon. What's he been doin' again ye?"

"Nawthin'," said Mr. Dooley, "but he was in here Choosday. 'Did ye vote?' says I. 'I did,' says he. 'Which wan iv th' distinguished bunko steerers got ye'er invalu'ble suffrage?' says I. 'I didn't have none with me,' says he, 'but I voted f'r Charter Haitch,' says he. 'I've been with him in six ilictions,' says he, 'an' he's a good man,' he says. 'D'ye think ye're votin' f'r th' best?' says I. 'Why, man alive,' I says, 'Charter Haitch was assassinated three years ago,' I says. 'Was he?' says Dugan. 'Ah, well, he's lived that down be this time. He was a good man,' he says.

"Ye see, that's what thim rayform lads wint up again. If I liked rayformers, Hinnissy, an' wanted f'r to see thim win out wanst in their lifetime, I'd buy thim each a suit iv chilled steel, ar-rm thim with raypeatin' rifles, an' take thim east iv State Sthreet an' south iv Jackson Bullyvard. At prisint th' opinion that prevails in th' ranks iv th' gloryous ar-rmy iv ray-form is that there ain't annything worth seein' in this lar-rge an' commodyous desert but th' pest-house an' the bridewell. Me frind Willum J. O'Brien is no rayformer. But Willum J. undherstands that there's a few hundherds iv thousands iv people livin' in a part iv th' town that looks like nawthin' but smoke fr'm th' roof iv th' Onion League Club that have on'y two pleasures in life, to wur-ruk an' to vote, both iv which they do at th' uniform rate iv wan dollar an' a half a day. That's why Willum J. O'Brien is now a sinitor an' will be an aldherman afther next Thursdah, an' it's why other people are sinding him flowers.

"This is th' way a rayform candydate is ilicted. Th' boys down town has heerd that things ain't goin' r-right somehow. Franchises is bein' handed out to none iv thim; an' wanst in a while a mimber iv th' club, comin' home a little late an' thryin' to riconcile a pair iv r-round feet with an embroidered sidewalk, meets a sthrong ar-rm boy that pushes in his face an' takes away all his marbles. It begins to be talked that th' time has come f'r good citizens f'r to brace up an' do somethin', an' they agree to nomynate a candydate f'r aldherman. 'Who'll we put up?' says they. 'How's Clarence Doolittle?' says wan. 'He's laid up with a coupon thumb, an' can't r-run.' 'An' how about Arthur Doheny?' 'I swore an oath whin I came out iv colledge I'd niver vote f'r a man that wore a made tie.' 'Well, thin, let's thry Willie Boye.' 'Good,' says th' comity. 'He's jus' th' man f'r our money.' An' Willie Boye, after thinkin' it over, goes to his tailor an' ordhers three dozen pairs iv pants, an' decides f'r to be th' sthandard-bearer iv th' people. Musin' over his fried eyesthers an' asparagus an' his champagne, he bets a polo pony again a box of golf-balls he'll be ilicted unanimous; an' all th' good citizens make a vow f'r to set th' alar-rm clock f'r half-past three on th' afther noon iv iliction day, so's to be up in time to vote f'r th' riprisintitive iv pure gover'mint.

" 'Tis some time befure they comprehind that there ar-re

other candydates in th' field. But th' other candydates know it. Th' sthrongest iv thim—his name is Flannigan, an' he's a re-tail dealer in wines an' liquors, an' he lives over his establishment. Flannigan was nomynated enthusyastically at a prim'ry held in his bar-rn; an' befure Willie Boye had picked out pants that wud match th' color iv th' Austhreelyan ballot this here Flannigan had put a man on th' day watch, tol' him to speak gently to anny raygistered voter that wint to sleep behind th' sthove, an' was out that night visitin' his frinds. Who was it judged th' cake walk? Flannigan. Who was it carrid th' pall? Flannigan. Who was it sthud up at th' christening? Flannigan. Whose ca-ards did th' grievin' widow, th' blushin' bridegroom, or th' happy father find in th' hack? Flannigan's. Ye bet ye'er life. Ye see Flannigan wasn't out f'r th' good iv th' community. Flannigan was out f'r Flannigan an' th' stuff.

"Well, iliction day come around; an' all th' imminent frinds iv good gover'mint had special wires sthrung into th' club, an' waited f'r th' returns. Th' first precin't showed 28 votes f'r Willie Boye to 14 f'r Flannigan. 'That's my precin't,' says Willie. 'I wondher who voted thim fourteen?' 'Coach-men,' says Clarence Doolittle. 'There are thirty-five precin'ts in this ward,' says th' leader iv th' rayform ilimint. 'At this rate, I'm sure iv 440 meejority. Gossoon,' he says, 'put a keg iv sherry wine on th' ice,' he says. 'Well,' he says, 'at last th' community is relieved fr'm misrule,' he says. 'To-morrah I will start in arrangin' amindmints to th' tariff schedool an' th' ar-bitration threety,' he says. 'We must be up an' doin',' he says. 'Hol' on there,' says wan iv th' comity. 'There must be some mistake in this fr'm th' sixth precin't,' he says. 'Where's the sixth precin't?' says Clarence. 'Over be th' dumps,' says Willie. 'I told me futman to see to that. He lives at th' cor-ner iv Desplaines an Bloo Island Av'noo on Goose's Island,' he

says. 'What does it show?' 'Flannigan, three hundherd an'
eighty-five; Hansen, forty-eight; Schwartz, twinty; O'Malley,
sivinteen; Casey, ten; O'Day, eight; Larsen, five; O'Rourke,
three; Mulcahy, two; Schmitt, two; Moloney, two; Riordon,
two; O'Malley, two; Willie Boye, wan.' 'Gintlemin,' says
Willie Boye, arisin' with a stern look in his eyes, 'th' rascal
has bethrayed me. Waither, take th' sherry wine off th' ice.
They'se no hope f'r sound financial legislation this year. I'm
goin' home.'

"An, as he goes down th' sthreet, he hears a band play an'
sees a procission headed be a calceem light; an', in a carredge,
with his plug hat in his hand an' his di'mond makin' th'
calceem look like a piece iv punk in a smoke-house, is Flannigan, payin' his first visit this side iv th' thracks."

On a Populist Convention

"Keep ye'er eye on th' Pops, Jawn. They're gr-reat people an'
a gr-reat pa-arty. What is their principles? Anny ol' thing
that th' other pa-arties has rijected. Some iv thim is in favor
iv coining money out iv baled hay an' dhried apples at a
ratio iv sixteen to wan, an' some is in favor iv coinin' on'y
th' apples. Thim are th' inflationists. Others want th' gover'-
mint to divide up the rivinues equally among all la-ads that's
too sthrong to wurruk. Th' Pops is again th' banks an' again
the supreme court an' again havin' gas that can be blowed
out be th' human lungs. A sthrong section is devoted to th'
principal iv separatin' Mark Hanna fr'm his money.

"A ma-an be th' name iv Cassidy, that thravels f'r a liquor-

Mr. Dooley in Peace and in War, pp. 197–201.

house, was in to see me this mornin'; an' he come fr'm Saint Looey. He said it beat all he iver see or heerd tell of. Whin th' con-vintion came to ordher, th' chairman says, 'La-ads, we'll open proceedin's be havin th' Hon'rable Rube Spike, fr'm th' imperyal Territ'ry iv Okalahoma, cough up his famous song, "Pa-pa Cleveland's Teeth are filled with Goold." ' 'Mr. Chairman,' says a delegate fr'm New Mexico, risin' an' wavin' his boots in th' air, 'if th' skate fr'm Okalahoma is allowed f'r to belch anny in this here as-simblage, th' diligates fr'm th' imperyal Territ'ry iv New Mexico'll lave th' hall. We have,' he says, 'in our mist th' Hon'rable Lafayette Hadley, whose notes,' he says, 'falls as sweetly on th' ear,' he says, 'as th' plunk iv hivin's rain in a bar'l,' he says. 'If annywan has a hemorrhage iv anthems in this hall, it'll be Lafe Hadley, th' Guthrie batsoon,' he says. 'Ye shall not,' he says, 'press down upon our bleedin' brows,' he says, 'this cross iv thorns,' he says. 'Ye shall not crucify th' diligates fr'm th' imperyal Territ'ry iv New Mexico on this cross iv a Mississippi nigger an' Crow Injun fr'm Okala-homa,' he says. Thereupon, says me frind Cassidy, th' New Mexico diligation left th' hall, pursued be th' diligation from Okalahoma.

"Th' chairman knowed his business. 'In ordher,' he says, 'that there may be no disordher,' he says, 'I will call upon th' imperyal States,' he says, 'an Territ'ries,' he says, 'beginnin' with th' imperyal State iv Alabama,' he says, 'to each sind wan singer to th' platform,' he says, 'f'r to wring our hear-rts with melodies,' he says. 'Meantime,' says he, 'pathrites who have diff'rences iv opinyon on anny questions can pro-cure ex-helves be applyin' to th' sergeant-at arms,' he says. 'Now,' he says, 'if th' gintleman fr'm th' imperyal State of Mizzoury'll hand me up a cheek full iv his eatin' tobacco,' he says, 'we'll listen to Willyum G. Rannycaboo, th' boy melodjun iv th' imperyal State iv Alabama,' he says, 'who'll discoorse his well-known ballad, "Th' Supreme Court is Full iv Standard Ile," ' he says.

"Whin th' singin' had con-cluded, so me frind Cassidy says, th' chair announced that speakin' would be in ordher, an' th' con-vintion rose as wan man. Afther ordher had been enforced be th' sergeant-at-arms movin' round, an' lammin' diligates with a hoe, a tall man was seen standin' on a chair. F'r some moments th' chairman was onable to call his name, but he fin'lly found a place to spill; an' in a clear voice he says, 'F'r what purpose does th' gintleman fr'm the imperyal State iv Texas arise?' 'I arise,' says th' ma-an, 'f'r th' purpose iv warnin' this con-vintion that we have a goold-bug in our mist,' he says. Cries iv 'Throw him out!' 'Search him!' 'Hang him!' arose. 'In wandhrin' through th' hall, I just seen a man with a coat on,' he says. Great excitement ensood, says me frind Cassidy; an' th' thremblin' victim was brought down th' aisle. 'What have ye to say f'r ye'ersilf?' demands th' chair-man in thundhrin' tones. 'On'y this,' says th' goold-bug. 'I wandhered in here, lookin' f'r frinds,' he says. 'I am not a goold-bug,' he says. 'I wear me coat,' he says, 'because I have no shirt,' he says. 'Gintlemen,' says th' chairman, 'a mistake has been made,' he says. 'This here person, who bears th' ap-pearance iv a plutocrat, is all right underneath,' he says. 'He's a diligate to th' silver convintion,' he says. 'Go in peace,' he says.

"Be this time 'twas gr-rowin' late, an' th' convintion ad-journed. 'Befure ye lave,' says th' chairman, 'I have to an-nounce that on account iv th' chairman of the comity havin' been imprisoned in a foldin'-bed an' th' sicrity havin' mis-took th' fire extinguisher f'r a shower bath, they'll be no meeting' iv th' comity on rules till to-morrow night. Durin' th' interval,' he says, 'th' convintion'll continue ketch-as-ketch can,' he says."

"Well," said Mr. McKenna, "to think of taking this here country out of the hands of William C. Whitney and Grover Cleveland and J. Pierpont Morgan and Ickleheimer Thalmann, and putting it in the hands of such men. What do you think about it?"

"I think," said Mr. Dooley, "that Cassidy lied."

On Oratory in Politics

"I mind th' first time Willum J. O'Brien r-run f'r office, th' Raypublicans an' th' Indypindants an' th' Socialists an' th' Prohybitionist (he's dead now, his name was Larkin) nommynated a young man be th' name iv Dorgan that was in th' law business in Halsted Sthreet, near Cologne, to r-run again' him. Smith O'Brien Dorgan was his name, an' he was wan iv th' most iloquint young la-ads that iver made a speakin' thrumpet iv his face. He cud holler like th' impire iv a base-ball game; an', whin he delivered th' sintimints iv his hear-rt, ye'd think he was thryin' to confide thim to a man on top iv a high buildin'. He was prisidint iv th' lithry club at th' church; an' Father Kelly tol' me that, th' day afther he won th' debate on th' pen an' th' soord in favor iv th' pen, they had to hire a carpenter to mend th' windows, they'd sagged so. They called him th' boy or-rator iv Healey's slough.

"He planned th' campaign himsilf. 'I'll not re-sort,' says he, 'to th' ordin'ry methods,' he says. 'Th' thing to do,' he

Mr. Dooley in Peace and in War, pp. 218–222.

says, 'is to prisint th' issues iv th' day to th' voters,' he says.
'I'll burn up ivry precin't in th' ward with me iloquince,' he
says. An' he bought a long black coat, an' wint out to spread
th' light.

"He talked ivrywhere. Th' people jammed Finucane's Hall,
an' he tol' thim th' time had come f'r th' masses to r-rise.
'Raymimber,' says he, 'th' idees iv Novimb'r,' he says. 'Raymimber Demosthens an' Cicero an' Oak Park,' he says. 'Raymimber th' thraditions iv ye'er fathers, iv Washin'ton an'
Jefferson an' Andhrew Jackson an' John L. Sullivan,' he says.
'Ye shall not, Billy O'Brien,' he says, 'crucify th' votes iv th'
Sixth Ward on th' double cross,' he says. He spoke to a
meetin' in Deerin' Sthreet in th' same wuruds. He had th'
sthreet-car stopped while he coughed up reemarks about th'
Constitution until th' bar-rn boss sint down an' threatened
to discharge Mike Dwyer that was dhrivin' wan hundherd
an' eight in thim days, though thransferred to Wintworth
Avnoo later on. He made speeches to polismin in th' squad-
room an' to good la-ads hoistin' mud out iv th' dhraw at th'
red bridge. People'd' be settin' quite in th' back room playin'
forty-fives whin Smith O'Brien Dorgan'd burst in, an' ad-
dhress thim on th' issues iv th' day.

"Now all this time Bill O'Brien was campaignin' in his
own way. He niver med wan speech. No wan knew whether
he was f'r a tariff or again wan, or whether he sthud be
Jefferson or was knockin' him or whether he had th' inthrests
iv th' toilin' masses at hear-rt or whether he wint to mass at
all, at all. But he got th' superintindint iv th' rollin'-mills
with him; an' he put three or four good faml'ies to wurruk in
th' gas-house, where he knew th' main guy, an' he made
reg'lar calls on th' bar-rn boss iv th' sthreet-ca-ars. He wint
to th' picnics, an' hired th' or-chesthry f'r th' dances, an' voted
himsilf th' most pop'lar man at th' church fair at an expinse

iv at laste five hundherd dollars. No wan that come near him wanted f'r money. He had headquarthers in ivry saloon fr'm wan end iv th' ward to th' other. All th' pa-apers printed his pitcher, an' sthud by him as th' frind iv th' poor.

"Well, people liked to hear Dorgan at first, but afther a few months they got onaisy. He had a way iv breakin' into festive gatherin's that was enough to thry a saint. He delayed wan prize fight two hours, encouragin' th' voters prisint to stand be their principles, while th' principles sat shiverin' in their cor-rners until th' polis r-run him out. It got so that men'd bound into alleys whin he come up th' sthreet. People in th' liquor business rayfused to let him come into their places. His fam'ly et in th' coal-shed f'r fear iv his speeches at supper. He wint on talkin', and Willum J. O'Brien wint on handin' out th' dough that he got fr'm th' gas company an' con-ciliatin' th' masses; an', whin iliction day come, th' judges an' clerks was all f'r O'Brien, an' Dorgan didn't get votes enough to wad a gun. He sat up near all night in his long coat, makin' speeches to himsilf; but tord mornin' he come over to my place where O'Brien sat with his la-ads. 'Well,' says O'Brien, 'how does it suit ye?' he says. 'It's sthrange,' says Dorgan. 'Not sthrange at all,' says Willum J. O'Brien. 'Whin ye've been in politics as long as I have, ye'll know,' he says, 'that th' rolyboly is th' gr-reatest or-rator on earth,' he says. 'Th' American nation in th' Sixth Ward is a fine people,' he says. 'They love th' eagle,' he says, 'on th' back iv a dollar,' he says. 'Well,' says Dorgan, 'I can't undherstand it,' he says. 'I med as manny as three thousan' speeches,' he says. 'Well,' says Willum J. O'Brien, 'that was my majority,' he says. 'Have a dhrink,' he says."

A Book Review

"Well sir," said Mr. Dooley, "I jus' got hold iv a book, Hinnissy, that suits me up to th' handle, a gran' book, th' grandest iver seen. Ye know I'm not much throubled be lithrachoor, havin' manny worries iv me own, but I'm not prejudiced again' books. I am not. Whin a rale good book comes along I'm as quick as anny wan to say it isn't so bad, an' this here book is fine. I tell ye 'tis fine."

"What is it?" Mr. Hennessy asked languidly.

" 'Tis 'Th' Biography iv a Hero be Wan who Knows.' ' 'Tis 'Th' Darin' Exploits iv a Brave Man be an Actual Eye Witness.' 'Tis 'Th' Account iv th' Desthruction iv Spanish Power in th' Ant Hills,' as it fell fr'm th' lips iv Tiddy Rosenfelt an' was took down be his own hands. Ye see 'twas this way, Hinnissy, as I r-read th' book. Whin Tiddy was blowed up in th' harbor iv Havana he instantly concluded they must be war. He debated th' question long an' earnestly an' fin'lly passed a jint resolution declarin' war. So far so good. But there was no wan to carry it on. What shud he do? I will lave th' janial author tell th' story in his own wurruds.

" 'Th' sicrety iv war had offered me,' he says, 'th' command of a rig'mint,' he says, 'but I cud not consint to remain in Tampa while perhaps less audacious heroes was at the front,' he says. 'Besides,' he says, 'I felt I was incompetent f'r to command a rig'mint raised be another,' he says. 'I detarmined to raise wan iv me own,' he says. 'I selected fr'm me

Finley Peter Dunne, *Mr. Dooley's Philosophy,* New York and London (1900), pp. 13–18.

acquaintances in th' West,' he says, 'men that had thravelled with me acrost th' desert an' th' storm-wreathed mountain,' he says, 'sharin' me burdens an' at times confrontin' perils almost as gr-reat as anny that beset me path,' he says. 'Together we had faced th' turrors iv th' large but vilent West,' he says, 'an' these brave men had seen me with me trusty rifle shootin' down th' buffalo, th' elk, th' moose, th' grizzly bear, th' mountain goat,' he says, 'th' silver man, an' other ferocious beasts iv thim parts,' he says. 'An' they niver flinched,' he says. 'In a few days I had thim perfectly tamed,' he says, 'an' ready to go annywhere I led,' he says. 'On th' thransport goin' to Cubia,' he says, 'I wud stand beside wan iv these r-rough men threatin' him as a akel, which he was in ivrything but birth, education, rank an' courage, an' together we wud look up at th' admirable stars iv that tolerable southern sky an' quote th' bible fr'm Walt Whitman,' he says. 'Honest, loyal, thrue-hearted la-ads, how kind I was to thim,' he says.

" 'We had no sooner landed in Cubia than it become nicessry f'r me to take command iv th' ar-rmy which I did at wanst. A number of days was spint be me in reconnoitring, attinded on'y be me brave an' fluent body guard, Richard Harding Davis. I discovered that th' inimy was heavily inthrenched on th' top iv San Joon hill immejiately in front iv me. At this time it become apparent that I was handicapped be th' prisence iv th' ar-rmy,' he says. 'Wan day whin I was about to charge a block house sturdily definded be an ar-rmy corps undher Gin'ral Tamale, th' brave Castile that I afthwards killed with a small ink-eraser that I always carry, I r-ran into th' entire military force iv th' United States lying on its stomach. 'If ye won't fight,' says I, 'let me go through,' I says. 'Who ar-re ye?' says they. 'Colonel Rosenfelt,' says I. 'Oh, excuse me,' says the gin'ral in command (if me mimry serves me thrue it was Miles) r-risin' to his knees an' salutin'. This showed me 'twud be impossible f'r to carry th' war to a successful con-clusion unless I was free, so I sint th' ar-rmy home an' attackted San Joon hill. Ar-rmed on'y with a small thirty-two which I used in th' West to shoot th' fleet prairie dog, I climbed that precipitous ascent in th' face iv th' most gallin' fire I iver knew or heerd iv. But I had a few r-rounds iv gall mesilf an' what cared I? I dashed madly on cheerin' as I wint. Th' Spanish throops was dhrawn up in a long line in th' formation known among military men as a long line. I fired at th' man nearest to me an' I knew be th' expression iv his face that th' trusty bullet wint home. It passed through his frame, he fell, an' wan little home in far-off Catalonia was made happy be th' thought that their riprisintative had been kilt be th' future governor iv New York. Th' bullet sped on its mad flight an' passed through th' intire line fin'lly imbeddin' itself in th' abdomen iv th' Ar-rchbishop iv Santiago eight miles away. This ended th' war.'

" 'They had been some discussion as to who was th' first man to r-reach th' summit iv San Joon hill. I will not attempt to dispute th' merits iv th' manny gallant sojers, statesmen, corryspondints an' kinetoscope men who claim th' distinction. They ar-re all brave men an' if they wish to wear my laurels they may. I have so manny annyhow that it keeps me broke havin' thim blocked an' irned. But I will say f'r th' binifit iv Posterity that I was th' on'y man I see. An' I had a tilly-scope.'

"I have thried, Hinnissy," Mr. Dooley continued, "to give you a fair idee iv th' contints iv this remarkable book, but what I've tol' ye is on'y what Hogan calls an outline iv th' principal pints. Ye'll have to r-read th' book ye'ersilf to get a thrue conciption. I haven't time f'r to tell ye th' wurruk

Tiddy did in ar-rmind' an' equippin' himself, how he fed himsilf, how he steadied himsilf in battle an' encouraged himsilf with a few well-chosen wurruds whin th' sky was darkest. Ye'll have to take a squint into th' book ye'ersilf to l'arn thim things."

"I won't do it," said Mr. Hennessy. "I think Tiddy Rosenfelt is all r-right an' if he wants to blow his hor-rn lave him do it."

"Thrue f'r ye," said Mr. Dooley, "an' if his valliant deeds didn't get into this book 'twud be a long time befure they appeared in Shafter's histhry iv th' war. No man that bears a gredge again' himsilf 'll iver be governor iv a state. An' if Tiddy done it all he ought to say so an' relieve th' suspinse. But if I was him I'd call th' book 'Alone in Cubia.' "

Platform Making

"That sthrikes me as a gran' platform," said Mr. Hennessy. "I'm with it fr'm start to finish."

"Sure ye are," said Mr. Dooley, "an' so ye'd be if it begun: 'We denounce Terence Hinnissy iv th' Sixth Ward iv Chicago as a thraitor to his country, an inimy iv civilization, an' a poor thing.' Ye'd say: 'While there are wan or two things that might be omitted, th' platform as a whole is a statesmanlike docymint, an' wan that appeals to th' intelligince iv American manhood.' That's what ye'd say, an' that's what all th' likes iv ye'd say. An' whin iliction day comes 'round th' on'y question ye'll ast ye'ersilf is: 'Am I with Mack [William

Mr. Dooley's Philosophy, pp. 97–102.

McKinley] or am I with Billy Bryan?' An' accordin'ly ye'll vote.

" 'Tis always th' same way, an' all platforms is alike. I mind wanst whin I was an alter-nate to th' county con-vin-tion—'twas whin I was a power in pollytics an' th' on'y man that cud do annything with th' Bohemian vote—I was settin' here wan night with a pen an' a pot iv ink befure me, thryin' to compose th' platform f'r th' nex' day, f'r I was a lithry man in a way, d'ye mind, an' I knew th' la-ads'd want a few crimps put in th' raypublicans in a ginteel style, an' 'd be sure to call on me f'r to do it. Well, I'd got as far down as th' tariff an' was thryin' f'r to express me opinyon without swearin', whin who shud come in but Lafferty, that was sicrety iv McMahon, that was th' Main Guy in thim days, but aftherward thrun down on account iv him mixin' up between th' Rorkes an' th' Dorseys. Th' Main Guy Down Town said he wudden't have no throuble in th' ward, an' he declared McMahon out. McMahon had too much money annyhow. If he'd kept on, dollar bills'd have been extinct outside iv his house. But he was a sthrong man in thim days an' much liked.

"Anyhow, Lafferty, that was his sicrety, come in, an' says he: 'What are ye doin' there?' says he. 'Step soft,' says I; 'I am at wurruk,' I says. 'Ye shudden't do lithry wurruk on an empty stomach,' says he. 'I do nawthin' on an empty stomach but eat,' says I. 'I've had me supper,' I says. 'Go 'way,' says I, 'till I finish th' platform,' I says. 'What's th' platform?' says he. 'F'r th' county con-vintion,' says I.

"Well, sir, he set down on a chair, an' I thought th' man was goin' to die right there on the premises with laughter. 'Whin ye get through with ye'er barkin',' says I, 'I'll throuble ye to tell me what ye may be doin' it f'r,' I says. 'I see nawthin' amusin' here but ye'er prisince,' I says, 'an' that's not a divvle iv a lot funnier than a wooden leg,' I says, f'r I was mad. Afther awhile he come to, an' says he: 'Ye don't raally think,' says he, 'that ye'll get a chanct to spring that platform,' he says. 'I do,' says I. 'Why,' he says, 'th platform has been adopted,' he says. 'Whin?' says I. 'Befure ye were born,' says he. 'In th' reign iv Bildad th' first,' says he—he was a larned man, was Lafferty, though a dhrinkin' man. All sicreties iv pollyticians not in office is dhrinkin' men, Hinnissy. 'I've got th' copy iv it here in me pocket,' he says. 'Th' boss give it to me to bring it up to date,' he says. 'They was no sthrike last year an' we've got to put a sthrike plank in th' platform or put th' prisident iv th' Lumber Shovers' union on th' county board, an',' he says, 'they ain't room,' he says.

" 'Why,' says Lafferty, 'ye ought to know th' histhry iv platforms,' he says. An' he give it to me, an' I'll give it to ye. Years ago, Hinnissy, manny years ago, they was a race between th' dimmycrats an' th' raypublicans f'r to see which shud have a choice iv principles. Th' dimmycrats lost. I dinnaw why. Mebbe they stopped to take a dhrink. Annyhow, they lost. Th' raypublicans come up an' they choose th' 'we commind' principles, an' they was nawthin' left f'r the dimmycrats but th' 'we denounce an' deplores.' I dinnaw how it come about, but th' dimmycrats didn't like th' way th' thing shtud, an' so they fixed it up between thim that whichiver won at th' iliction shud commind an' congratulate, an' thim that lost shud denounce an' deplore. An' so it's been, on'y the dimmycrats has had so little chanct f'r to do annything but denounce an' deplore that they've almost lost th' use iv th' other wurruds.

"Mack sets back in Wash'nton an' writes a platform f'r th' comity on risolutions to compose th' week afther. He's got a good job—forty-nine ninety-two, sixty-six a month—an' 'tis up to him to feel good. 'I—I mean we,' he says, 'congratulate th' counthry on th' matchless statesmanship, onshrinkin' courage, steady devotion to duty an' principle iv that gallant an' hon'rable leader, mesilf,' he says to his sicrety. 'Take that,' he says, 'an' elaborate it,' he says. 'Ye'll find a ditchnry on th' shelf near th' dure,' he says, 'if ye don't think I've put what I give ye sthrong enough,' he says. 'I always was,' he says, 'too retirin' f'r me own good,' he says. 'Spin out th' r-rest,' he says, 'to make about six thousan' wurruds,' he says, 'but be sure don't write annything too hot about th' Boer war or th' Ph'lippeens or Chiny, or th' tariff, or th' goold question, or our relations with England, or th' civil sarvice,' he says. ' 'Tis a foolish man,' he says, 'that throws a hunk iv coal fr'm his own window at th' dhriver iv a brick wagon,' he says.

"But with Billy Bryan 'tis diff'rent. He's out in Lincoln, Neebrasky, far fr'm home, an' he says to himsilf: 'Me throat is hoarse, an' I'll exercise me other fac'lties,' he says. 'I'll write a platform,' he says. An' he sets down to a typewriter, an' denounces an' deplores till th' hired man blows th' dinner horn. Whin he can denounce an' deplore no longer he views with alarm an' declares with indignation. An' he sinds it down to Kansas City, where th' cot beds come fr'm."

"Oh, ye're always pitchin' into some wan,' said Mr. Hennessy. "I bet ye Willum Jennings Bryan niver see th' platform befure it wint in. He's too good a man."

"He is all iv that," said Mr. Dooley. "But ye bet he knows th' rale platform f'r him is: 'Look at th' bad breaks Mack's made,' an' Mack's platform is: 'Ye'd get worse if ye had Billy Bryan.' An' it depinds on whether most iv th' voters ar-re tired out or on'y a little tired who's ilicted. All excipt you, Hinnissy. Ye'll vote f'r Bryan?"

"I will," said Mr. Hennessy.

"Well," said Mr. Dooley, "d'ye know, I suspicted ye might."

Mr. Dooley

Marriage and Politics

"I see," said Mr. Hennessy, "that wan iv thim New York joods says a man in pollytics oughtn't to be marrid."

"Oh, does he?" said Mr. Dooley. "Well, 'tis little he knows about it. A man in pollytics has got to be marrid. If he ain't marrid where'll he go f'r another kind iv throuble? An' where'll he find people to support? An unmarrid man don't get along in pollytics because he don't need th' money. Whin he's in th' middle iv a prim'ry, with maybe twinty or thirty iv th' opposite party on top iv him, thinks he to himsilf: 'What's th' good iv fightin' f'r a job? They'se no wan depindant on me f'r support,' an' he surrinders. But a marrid man says: 'What'll happen to me wife an' twelve childher if I don't win out here today?' an' he bites his way to th' top iv th' pile an' breaks open th' ballot box f'r home and fireside. That's th' thruth iv it, Hinnissy. Ye'll find all th' big jobs held be marrid men an' all th' timpry clerkships be bachelors.

"Th' reason th' New York jood thinks marrid men oughtn't to be in pollytics is because he thinks pollytics is spoort. An' so it is. But it ain't amachoor spoort, Hinnissy. They don't give ye a pewter mug with ye'er name on it f'r takin' a chanst on bein' kilt. 'Tis a profissional sport, like playin' base-ball f'r a livin' or wheelin' a thruck. Ye niver see an amachoor at annything that was as good as a profissional. Th' best amachoor ball team is beat be a bad profissional team; a profissional boxer that thrains on bock beer an' Swiss cheese

Mr. Dooley's Philosophy, pp. 141–147.

can lam the head off a goold medal amachoor champeen that's
been atin' moldy bread an' dhrinkin' wather f'r six months,
an' th' Dago that blows th' cornet on th' sthreet f'r what
annywan 'll throw him can cut the figure eight around
Dinnis Finn, that's been takin' lessons f'r twenty year. No,
sir, pollytics ain't dhroppin' into tea, an' it ain't wurrukin'
a scroll saw, or makin' a garden in a back yard. 'Tis gettin'
up at six o'clock in th' mornin' an' r-rushin' off to wurruk, **an'**
comin' home at night tired an' dusty. Double wages f'r over-
time an' Sundahs.

"So a man's got to be married to do it well. He's got to have
a wife at home to make him oncomfortable if he comes in
dhrunk, he's got to have little prattlin' childher that he
can't sind to th' Young Ladies' academy onless he stuffs a
ballotbox properly, an' he's got to have a sthrong desire f'r
to live in th' av'noo an' be seen dhrivin' downtown in an
open carredge with his wife settin' beside him undher a r-red
parasol. If he hasn't these things he won't succeed in pollytics
—or packin' pork. Ye niver see a big man in pollytics that
dhrank hard, did ye? Ye never will. An' that's because they're
all marrid. Th' timptation's sthrong, but fear is sthronger.

"Th' most domestic men in th' wurruld ar-re pollyticians,
an' they always marry early. An' thats th' sad part iv it, Hinnissy. A pollytician always marries above his own station.
That's wan sign that he'll be a successful pollytician. Th'
throuble is, th' good woman stays planted just where she
was, an' he goes by like a fast thrain by a whistlin' station.
D'ye mind O'Leary, him that's a retired capitalist now, him
that was aldherman, an' dhrainage thrustee, an' state sinitor
f'r wan term? Well, whin I first knew O'Leary he wurruked
down on a railroad section tampin' th' thrack at wan-fifty a
day. He was a sthrong, willin' young fellow, with a stiff right-
hand punch an' a schamin' brain, an' anny wan cud see that

he was intinded to go to th' fr-ront. Th' aristocracy iv th'
camp was Mrs. Cassidy, th' widdy lady that kept th' boordin'-
house. Aristocracy, Hinnissy, is like rale estate, a matther iv
location. I'm aristocracy to th' poor O'Briens back in th'
alley, th' brewery agent's aristocracy to me, his boss is aristocracy to him, an' so it goes, up to the czar of Rooshia. He's
th' pick iv th' bunch, th' high man iv all, th' Pope not goin'
in society. Well, Mrs. Cassidy was aristocracy to O'Leary. He
niver see such a stylish woman as she was whin she turned
out iv a Sundah afthernoon in her horse an' buggy. He'd think
to himsilf, 'If I iver can win that I'm settled f'r life,' an' iv
coorse he did. 'Twas a gran' weddin'; manny iv th' guests
didn't show up at wurruk f'r weeks.

"O'Leary done well, an' she was a good wife to him. She
made money an' kept him sthraight an' started him for constable. He won out, bein' a sthrong man. Thin she got him to
r-run f'r aldherman, an' ye shud've seen her th' night he was
inaugurated! Be hivins, Hinnissy, she looked like a fire in
a pawnshop, fair covered with dimons an' goold watches an'
chains. She was cut out to be an aldherman's wife, and it was
worth goin' miles to watch her leadin' th' gran' march at th'
Ar-rchy Road Dimmycratic Fife an' Dhrum Corps ball.

"But there she stopped. A good woman an' a kind wan, she
cudden't go th' distance. She had th' house an' th' childher
to care f'r an' her eddycation was through with. They isn't
much a woman can learn afther she begins to raise a fam'ly.
But with O'Leary 'twas diff'rent. I say 'twas diff'rent with
O'Leary. Ye talk about ye'er colleges, Hinnissy, but pollytics is th' poor man's college. A la-ad without enough book
larnin' to r-read a meal-ticket, if ye give him tin years iv
polly-tical life, has th' air iv a statesman an' th' manner iv a
jook, an' cud take anny job fr'm dalin' faro bank to r-runnin'
th' threasury iv th' United States. His business brings him

up again' th' best men iv th' com-munity, an' their customs an' ways iv speakin' an' thinkin' an' robbin' sticks to him. Th' good woman is at home all day. Th' on'y people she sees is th' childher an' th' neighbors. While th' good man in a swallow-tail coat is addhressin' th' Commercial club on what we shud do f'r to reform pollytics, she's discussin' th' price iv groceries with th' plumber's wife an' talkin' over th' back fince to the milkman. Thin O'Leary moves up on th' boolyvard. He knows she'll get along all r-right on th' boolyvard. Th' men'll say: 'They'se a good deal of rugged common sinse in that O'Leary. He may be a robber, but they's mighty little that escapes him.' But not wan speaks to Mrs. O'Leary. No wan asts her opinion about our foreign policy. She sets day in an' day out behind th' dhrawn curtains iv her three-story brownstone risidence prayin' that somewan'll come in an' see her, an' if annywan comes she's frozen with fear. An' 'tis on'y whin she slips out to Ar-rchey r-road an' finds th' plumber's wife, an' sets in th' kitchen over a cup iv tay, that peace comes to her. By an' by they offer O'Leary th' nommynation f'r congress. He knows he's fit for it. He's sthronger thin th' young lawyer they have now. People'll listen to him in Wash'nton as they do in Chicago. He says: 'I'll take it.' An' thin he thinks iv th' wife an' they's no Wash'nton f'r him. His pollytical career is over. He wud niver have been constable if he hadn't married, but he might have been sinitor if he was a widower.

"Mrs. O'Leary was in to see th' Dargans th' other day. 'Ye mus'be very happy in ye'er gran' house, with Mr. O'Leary doin' so well,' says Mrs. Dargan. An' th' on'y answer th' foolish woman give was to break down an' weep on Mrs. Dargan's neck."

"Yet ye say a pollytician oughtn't to get marrid," said Mr. Hennessy.

"Up to a certain point," said Mr. Dooley, "he must be marrid. Afther that—well, I on'y say that, though pollytics is a gran' career f'r a man, 'tis a tough wan f'r his wife."

The Admiral's Candidacy

"I see," said Mr. Hennessy, "that Dewey is a candydate f'r prisidint."

"Well, sir," said Mr. Dooley, "I hope to hiven he won't get it. No rilitive iv mine iver held a pollytical job barrin' mesilf. I was precint captain, an' wan iv th' best they was in thim days, if I do say so that shudden't. I was called Cap f'r manny years aftherward, an' I'd've joined th' Gr-rand Army iv th' Raypublic if it hadn't been f'r me poor feet. Manny iv me rilitives has been candydates, but they niver cud win out again th' r-rest iv th' fam'ly. 'Tis so with Cousin George. I'm again him. I've been a rayspictable saloon-keeper f'r forty years in this ward, an' I'll not have th' name dhragged into pollytics.

"Iv coorse, I don't blame Cousin George. I'm with him f'r annything else in th' gift iv th' people, fr'm a lovin'-cup to a house an' lot. He don't mean annything be it. Did ye iver see a sailor thryin' to ride a horse? 'Tis a comical sight. Th' reason a sailor thries to ride a horse is because he niver r-rode wan befure. If he knew annything about it he wouldn't do it. So be Cousin George. Afther he'd been over here awhile an' got so 'twas safe f'r him to go out without bein' torn to pieces f'r soovenirs or lynched be a mob, he took a look ar-round him an' says he to a polisman: 'What's th' governmint iv this

Mr. Dooley's Philosophy, pp. 175–180.

counthry?' ' 'Tis a raypublic,' says the polisman. 'What's th' main guy called?' says George. 'He's called prisidint,' says th' polisman. 'Is it a good job?' says Cousin George. ' 'Tis betther thin thravelin' beat,' says th' bull. 'What's th' la-ad's name that's holdin' it now?' says Cousin George. 'Mack,' says th' cop. 'Irish?' says George. 'Cross,' says th' elbow. 'Where fr'm?' says George. 'Ohio,' says the peeler. 'Where's that?' says George. 'I dinnaw,' says th' bull. An' they parted th' best iv frinds.

" 'Well,' says George to himsilf, 'I guess I'll have to go up an' have a look at this la-ad's place,' he says, 'an' if it looks good,' he says, 'p'raps I cud nail it,' he says. An' he goes up an' sees Mack dictatin' his Porther Rickyan policy to a kinetoscope, an' it looks like a nice employmint f'r a spry man, an' he goes back home an' sinds f'r a rayporther, an' says he: 'I always believe since I got home in dealin' frankly with th' press. I haven't seen manny papers since I've been at sea, but whin I was a boy me father used to take the Montpelier Paleejum. 'Twas r-run be a man be th' name iv Horse Clamback. He was quite a man whin sober. Ye've heerd iv him, no doubt. But what I ast ye up here f'r was to give ye a item that ye can write up in ye'er own way an' hand to th' r-rest iv th' boys. I'm goin' to be prisidint. I like th' looks iv the job an' nobody seems to care f'r it, an' I've got so blame tired since I left th' ship that if I don't have somethin' to do I'll go crazy," he says. 'I wisht ye'd make a note iv it an' give it to th' other papers,' he says. 'Ar-re ye a raypublican or a dimmycrat?' says the rayporter. 'What's that?' says Cousin George. 'D'ye belong to th' raypublican or th' dimmycrat party?' 'What ar-re they like?' says Cousin George. 'Th' raypublicans ar-re in favor iv expansion.' 'Thin I'm a raypublican.' 'Th' dimmycrats ar-re in favor iv free thrade.' 'Thin I'm a dimmycrat.' 'Th' raypublicans ar-re f'r upholdin' th' goold standard.' 'So'm I. I'm a raypublican there.' 'An' they're opposed to an income tax.' 'On that,' says Cousin George, 'I'm a dimmycrat. I tell ye, put me down as a dim- mycrat. Divvle th' bit I care. Just say I'm a dimmycrat with sthrong raypublican leanings. Put it this way: I'm a dim- mycrat, be a point raypublican, dimmycrat. Anny sailor man'll undherstand that.' 'What'll I say ye'er platform is?' 'Platform?' 'Ye have to stand on a platform.' 'I do, do I? Well, I don't. I'll stand on no platform, an' I'll hang on no sthrap. What d'ye think th' prisidincy is—a throlley car? No, sir, whin ye peek in th' dure to sell ye'er paper ye'll see ye'er Uncle George settin' down comfortable with his legs crossed, thrippin' up annywan that thries to pass him. Go out now an' write ye'er little item, f'r 'tis late an' all hands ar-re piped to bed,' he says.

"An' there ye ar-re. Well, sir, 'tis a hard year Cousin George has in store f'r him. Th' first thing he knows he'll have to pay f'r havin' his pitchers in th' pa-aper. Thin he'll larn iv siv'ral prevyous convictions in Vermont. Thin he'll discover that they was no union label on th' goods he de- livered at Manila. 'Twill be pointed out be careful observers that he was ilicted prisidint iv th' A.P.A. be th' Jesuits.* Thin somewan'll dig up that story about his not feelin' anny too well th' mornin' iv th' fight, an' ye can imajine th' pitchers they'll print, an' th' jokes that'll be made, an' th' songs: 'Dewey Lost His Appetite at th' Battle iv Manila. Did McKinley Iver Lose His?' An' George'll wake up th' mornin' afther iliction an' he'll have a sore head an' a sorer heart, an' he'll find that th' on'y support he got was fr'm th' goold dimmycratic party, an' th' chances ar-re he caught cold fr'm goin' out without his shawl an' cudden't vote. He'll find that

---

* A.P.A. was the American Protective Association, a secret society formed in 1887 to rally bigots against Roman Catholic influence in labor and politics.

a man can be r-right an' be prisidint, but he can't be both at th' same time. An' he'll go down to breakfast an' issue Gin'ral Ordher Number Wan, 'To All Superyor Officers Commandin' Admirals iv th' United States navy at home or on foreign service: If anny man mintions an admiral f'r prisidint, hit him in th' eye an' charge same to me.' An' thin he'll go to his office an' prepare a plan f'r to capture Dublin, th' capital iv England, whin th' nex' war begins. An' he'll spind th' r-rest iv his life thryin' to live down th' time he was a candydate."

"Well, be hivins, I think if Dewey says he's a dimmycrat an' Joyce is with him, I'll give him a vote," said Mr. Hennessy. "It's no sin to be a candydate f'r prisidint."

"No," said Mr. Dooley. " 'Tis sometimes a misfortune an' sometimes a joke. But I hope ye won't vote f'r him. He might be ilicted if ye did. I'd like to raymimber him, an' it might be I cudden't if he got th' job. Who was th' prisidint befure Mack? Oh, tubby sure!"

Voices from the Tomb

"I don't think," said Mr. Dooley, "that me frind Willum Jennings Bryan is as good an orator as he was four years ago."

"He's th' grandest talker that's lived since Dan'l O'Connell," said Mr. Hennessy.

"Ye've heerd thim all an' ye know," said Mr. Dooley. "But I tell ye he's gone back. D'ye mind th' time we wint down to th' Coleesyum an' he come out in a black alapaac coat an'

Mr. Dooley's Philosophy, pp. 209–215.

pushed into th' air th' finest wurruds ye iver heerd spoke in all ye'er bor-rn days? 'Twas a balloon ascinsion an' th' las' days iv Pompey an' a blast on th' canal all in wan. I had to hold on to me chair to keep fr'm goin' up in th' air, an' I mind that if it hadn't been f'r a crack on th' head ye got fr'm a dillygate fr'm Westconsin ye'd 've been in th' hair iv Gin'-ral Bragg. Dear me, will ye iver f'rget it, th' way he pumped it into th' pluthocrats? 'I tell ye here an' now,' he says, 'they'se as good business men in th' quite counthry graveyards iv Kansas as ye can find in the palathial lunch-counthers iv Wall street,' he says. 'Whin I see th' face iv that man who looks like a two-dollar pitcher iv Napolyeon at Saint Heleena,' he says, 'I say to mesilf, ye shall not—ye shall not'—what th' divvle is it ye shall not do, Hinnissy?"

"Ye shall not crucify mankind upon a crown iv thorns," said Mr. Hennessy.

"Right ye ar-re, I forgot," Mr. Dooley went on. "Well, thim were his own wurruds. He was young an' he wanted something an' he spoke up. He'd been a rayporther on a newspaper an' he'd rather be prisidint thin write anny longer f'r th' pa-aper, an' he made th' whole iv th' piece out iv his own head.

"But nowadays he has tin wurruds f'r Thomas Jefferson an' th' rest iv th' sage crop to wan f'r himsilf. 'Fellow-dimmy-crats,' he says, 'befure goin' anny farther, an' maybe farin' worse, I reluctantly accipt th' nommynation f'r prisidint that I have caused ye to offer me,' he says, 'an' good luck to me,' he says. 'Seein' th' counthry in th' condition it is,' he says, 'I cannot rayfuse,' he says. 'I will now lave a subject that must be disagreeable to manny iv ye an' speak a few wurruds fr'm th' fathers iv th' party, iv whom there ar-re manny,' he says, 'though no shame to th' party, f'r all iv that,' he says. 'Thomas Jefferson, th' sage iv Monticello, says: "Ye can't make a silk purse out iv a sow's ear," a remark that will at wanst recall th' sayin' iv Binjamin Franklin, th' sage iv Camden, that "th' fartherest way ar-round is th' shortest way acrost." Nawthin' cud be thruer thin that onliss it is th' ipygram iv Andhrew Jackson, th' sage iv Syr-acuse, that "a bur-rd in th' hand is worth two in th' bush." What gran' wurruds thim ar-re, an' how they must torture th' prisint leaders in th' raypublican party. Sam'l Adams, th' sage iv Salem, says: "Laugh an' the wurruld laughs with ye," while Pathrick Hinnery, th' sage iv Jarsey City, put it that "ye shud always bet aces befure th' dhraw." Turnin' farther back into histhry we find that Brian Boru, th' sage iv Munsther, said: "Cead mille failthé," an' Joolyus Caesar, th' sage iv Waukeesha, says, "Whin ye're in Rome, do th' Romans." Nebuchedneezar—there's a name f'r ye—th' sage iv I-dinnaw-where, says: "Ye can't ate ye'er hay an' have it." Solomon, th' sage iv Sageville, said, "Whin a man's marrid his throubles begins," an' Adam, th' sage iv Eden, put it that "A snake in th' grass is worth two in th' boots." Ye'll see be this, me good an' thrue frins, that th' voices fr'm th' tombs is united in wan gran' chorus f'r th' ticket ye have nommynated. I will say no more, but on a future occasion, whin I've been down in southern Injyanny, I'll tell ye what th' sages an' fathers iv th' party in th' Ancient an' Hon'rable Association iv Mound-Builders had to say about th' prisint crisis.'

" 'Tisn't Bryan alone, Mack's th' same way." They're both ancesther worshippers, like th' Chinese, Hinnissy. An' what I'd like to know is what Thomas Jefferson knew about th' throubles iv ye an' me? Divvle a wurrud have I to say again' Thomas. He was a good man in his day, though I don't know that his battin' av'rage 'd be high again' th' pitchin' iv these times. I have a gr-reat rayspict f'r the sages an' I believe in namin' sthreets an' public schools afther thim. But suppose

Thomas Jefferson was to come back here now an' say to him-silf: 'They'se a good dimmycrat up in Ar-rchy road an' I think I'll dhrop in on him an' talk over th' issues iv th' day.' Well, maybe he cud r-ride his old gray mare up an' not be kilt be the throlley cars, an' maybe th' la-ads'd think he was crazy an' not murdher him f'r his clothes. An' maybe they wudden't. But annyhow, suppose he got here, an' afther he'd fumbled ar-round at th' latch—f'r they had sthrings on th' dure in thim days,—I let him in. Well, whin I've injooced him to take a bowl iv red liquor—f'r in his time th' dhrink was white—an' explained how th' seltzer comes out an' th' cash raygisther wurruks, an' wather is dhrawn fr'm th' fassit, an' gas is lighted fr'm th' burner, an' got him so he wud not bump his head again' th' ceilin' ivry time th' beer pump threw a fit—afther that we'd talk iv the pollytical situation.

" 'How does it go?' says Thomas. 'Well,' says I, 'it looks as though Ioway was sure raypublican,' says I. 'Ioway?' says he. 'What's that?' says he. 'Ioway,' says I, 'is a state,' says I. 'I niver heerd iv it,' says he. 'Faith ye did not,' says I. 'But it's a state just th' same, an' full iv corn an' people.' I says. 'An' why is it raypublican?' says he. 'Because,' says I, 'th' people out there is f'r holdin' th' Ph'lippeens,' says I. 'What th' divvle ar-re th' Ph'lippeens?' says he. 'Is it a festival,' says he, 'or a dhrink?' he says. 'Faith, 'tis small wondher ye dont know,' says I, 'f'r 'tis mesilf was weak on it a year ago,' I says. 'Th' Ph'lippeens is an issue,' says I, 'an' islands,' says I, 'an' a public nuisance,' I says. 'But,' I says, 'befure we go anny further on th' subject,' I says 'd'ye know where Minnysota is, or Westconsin, or Utah, or Californya, or Texas, or Neebrasky?' says I. 'I do not,' says he. 'D'ye know that since ye'er death there has growed up on th' shore iv Lake Mitchigan a city that wud make Rome look like a whistlin' station—a city that has a popylation iv eight million people till th' census rayport comes out?' I says. 'I niver heerd iv it,' he says. 'D'ye know that I can cross th' ocean in six days, an' won't; that if annything doesn't happen in Chiny I can larn about it in twinty-four hours if I care to know; that if ye was in Wash'nton I cud call ye up be tilly-phone an' ye'er wire'd be busy?' I says. 'I do not,' says Thomas Jefferson. 'Thin,' says I, 'don't presume to advise me,' I says, 'that knows these things an' manny more,' I says. 'An' whin ye go back where ye come fr'm an' set down with th' rest iv th' sages to wondher whether a man cud possibly go fr'm Richmond to Boston in a week, tell thim,' I says, 'that in their day they r-run a corner grocery an' to-day,' says I, 'we're op'ratin' a sixteen-story department store an' puttin' in irvrything fr'm an electhric lightin' plant to a set iv false teeth,' I says. An' I hist him on his horse an' ask a polisman to show him th' way home.

"Be hivins, Hinnissy, I want me advice up-to-date, an' whin Mack an' Willum Jennings tells me what George Wash'nton an' Thomas Jefferson said, I says to thim: 'Gintle-men, they larned their thrade befure th' days iv open plumbin',' " I says. 'Tell us what is wanted ye'ersilf or call in a journeyman who's wurrukin' card is dated this cinchry,' I says. 'An' I'm r-right too, Hinnissy."

"Well," said Mr. Hennessy, slowly, "those ol' la-ads was level-headed."

"Thrue f'r ye," said Mr. Dooley. "But undher th' new iliction laws ye can't vote th' cimitries."

The Supreme Court's Decisions

"I see," said Mr. Dooley, "Th' supreme coort has decided th' constitution don't follow th' flag."

"Who said it did?" asked Mr. Hennessy.

"Some wan," said Mr. Dooley. "It happened a long time ago an' I don't raymimber clearly how it come up, but some fellow said that ivrywhere th' constitution wint, th' flag was sure to go. 'I don't believe wan wurrud iv it,' says th' other fellow. 'Ye can't make me think th' constitution is goin' thrapezin' around ivrywhere a young liftnant in th' ar-rmy takes it into his head to stick a flag pole. It's too old. It's a home-stayin' constitution with a blue coat with brass buttons onto it, an' it walks with a goold-headed cane. It's old an' it's feeble an' it prefers to set on th' front stoop an' amuse th' childher. It wudden't last a minyit in thim thropical climes. T'wud get a pain in th' fourteenth amindmint an' die befure th' doctors cud get ar-round to cut it out. No, sir, we'll keep it with us, an' threat it tenderly without too much hard wurruk, an' whin it plays out entirely we'll give it dacint buryal an' incorp'rate oursilves under th' laws iv Noo Jarsey. That's what we'll do,' says he. 'But,' says th' other, 'if it wants to thravel, why not lave it?' 'But it don't want to.' 'I say it does.' 'How'll we find out?' 'We'll ask th' supreme coort. They'll know what's good f'r it.' "

"So it wint up to th' supreme coort. They'se wan thing about th' supreme coort, if ye lave annything to thim, ye

Finley Peter Dunne, *Mr. Dooley's Opinions*, New York and London (1906), pp. 21–26.

lave it to thim. Ye don't get a check that entitles ye to call f'r it in an hour. The supreme coort iv th' United States ain't in anny hurry about catchin' th' mails. It don't have to make th' las' car. I'd back th' Aujitoroom again it anny day f'r a foot race. If ye're lookin' f'r a game iv quick decisions an' base hits, ye've got to hire another empire. It niver gives a decision till th' crowd has dispersed an' th' players have packed their bats in th' bags an' started f'r home.

"F'r awhile ivrybody watched to see what th' supreme coort wud do. I knew mesilf I felt I cudden't make another move in th' game till I heerd fr'm thim. Buildin' op'rations was suspinded an' we sthud wringin' our hands outside th' dure waitin' f'r information fr'm th' bedside. 'What're they doin' now?' 'They just put th' argymints iv larned counsel in th' ice box an' th' chief justice is in a corner writin' a pome. Brown J. an' Harlan J. is discussin' th' condition iv th' Roman Empire befure th' fire. Th' r-rest iv th' coort is considherin' th' question iv whether they ought or ought not to wear ruchin' on their skirts an' hopin' crinoline won't come in again. No decision to-day?' An' so it wint f'r days, an' weeks an' months. Th' men that had argyied that th' constitution ought to shadow th' flag to all th' tough resorts on th' Passyfic coast an' th' men that argyied that th' flag was so lively that no constitution cud follow it an' survive, they died or lost their jobs or wint back to Salem an' were f'rgotten. Expansionists contracted an' anti-expansionists blew up an' little childher was born into th' wurruld an' grew to manhood an' niver heerd iv Porther Ricky except whin some won get a job there. I'd about made up me mind to thry an' put t' thing out iv me thoughts an' go back to wurruk when I woke up wan mornin' an' see be th' pa-aper that th' Supreme Coort had warned th' constitution to lave th' flag alone an' tind to its own business.

"That's what th' pa-aper says, but I've r-read over th' decision an' I don't see annything iv th' kind there. They'se not a wurrud about th' flag an' not enough to tire ye about th' constitution. 'Tis a matther iv limons, Hinnissy, that th' Supreme Coort has been settin' on f'r this gineration—a cargo iv limons sint fr'm Porther Ricky to some Eyetalian in Philydlphy. Th' decision was r-read be Brown J., him bein' th' las' justice to make up his mind, an' ex-officio, as Hogan says, th' first to speak, afther a crool an' bitther contest. Says Brown J.: 'Th' question here is wan iv such gr-reat importance that we've been sthrugglin' over it iver since ye see us las' an' on'y come to a decision (Fuller C. J., Gray J., Harlan J., Shiras J., McKenna J., White J., Brewer J., an' Peckham J. dissentin' fr'm me an' each other) because iv th' hot weather comin' on. Wash'n'ton is a dhreadful place in summer (Fuller C. J. dissentin'). Th' whole fabric iv our government is threatened, th' lives iv our people an' th' progress iv civilization put to th' bad. Men ar-re excited. But why? We ar-re not. (Harlan J., "I am." Fuller C. J. dissentin', but not f'r th' same reason.) This thing must be settled wan way or th' other undher that dear ol' constitution be varchue iv which we are here an' ye ar-re there an' Congress is out West practicin' law. Now what does th' constitution say? We'll look it up thoroughly whin we get through with this case (th' rest iv th' coort dissentin'). In th' manetime we must be governed be th' ordnances iv th' Khan iv Beloochistan, th' laws iv Hinnery th' Eighth, th' opinyon iv Justice iv th' Peace Oscar Larson in th' case iv th' township iv Red Wing varsus Petersen, an' th' Dhred Scott decision. What do they say about limons? Nawthin' at all. Again we take th' Dhred Scott decision. This is wan iv th' worst I iver r-read. If I cudden't write a betther wan with blindhers on, I'd leap off th' bench. This horrible fluke iv a decision throws a gr-reat, an almost dazzlin' light on th' case. I will turn it off. (McKenna J. concurs, but thinks it ought to be blowed out.) But where was I? I must put on me specs. Oh, about th' limons. Well, th' decision iv th' Coort (th' others dissentin') is as follows: First, that th' Disthrict iv Columbya is a state; second, that it is not; third, that New York is a state; fourth, that it is a crown colony; fifth, that all states ar-re states an' all territories ar-re territories in th' eyes iv other powers, but Gawd knows what they ar-re at home. In th' case iv Hogan varsus Mullins, th' decision is he must paper th' barn. (Hinnery VIII, sixteen, six, four, eleven.) In Wiggins varsus et al. th' cow belonged. (Louis XIV, 90 in rem.) In E. P. Vigore varsus Ad Lib., the custody iv th' childher. I'll now fall back a furlong or two in me chair, while me larned but misguided collagues r-read th' Histhry iv Iceland to show ye how wrong I am. But mind ye, what I've said goes. I let thim talk because it exercises their throats, but ye've heard all th' decision on this limon case that'll get into th' fourth reader.' A voice fr'm th' audjeence, 'Do I get me money back?' Brown J.: 'Who ar-re ye?' Th' Voice: 'Th' man that ownded th' limons.' Brown J.: 'I don't know.' (Gray J., White J., dissentin' an' th' r-rest iv th' birds concurrin' but f'r entirely diff'rent reasons.)

"An' there ye have th' decision, Hinnissy, that's shaken th' intellicts iv th' nation to their very foundations, or will if they thry to read it. 'Tis all r-right. Look it over some time. 'Tis fine spoort if ye don't care f'r checkers. Some say it laves th' flag up in th' air an' some say that's where it laves th' constitution. Annyhow, something's in th' air. But there's wan thing I'm sure about."

"What's that?" asked Mr. Hennessy.

"That is," said Mr. Dooley, "no matther whether th'

constitution follows th' flag or not, th' supreme coort follows th' iliction returns."

Discusses Party Politics

"I wondher," said Mr. Hennessy, "if us dimmycrats will iver ilict a prisidint again."

"We wud," said Mr. Dooley, "if we cud but get an illegible candydate."

"What's that?" asked Mr. Hennessy.

"An illegible candydate," said Mr. Dooley, "is a candydate that can't be read out iv th' party. 'Tis a joke I med up. Me frind Willum J. Bryan read th' Commoner to thim an' they pack up their bags an' lave. They'se as manny dimmycrats out iv th' party as they are in, waitin' on th' durestep to read thimsilves back an' th' other la-ads out. Th' loudest r-reader wins.

"No, sir, th' dimmycratic party ain't on speakin' terms with itsilf. Whin ye see two men with white neckties go into a sthreet car an' set in opposite corners while wan mutthers 'Thraiter' an' th' other hisses 'Miscreent' ye can bet they're two dimmycratic leaders thryin' to reunite th' gran' ol' party. 'Tis on'y th' part iv th' party that can't r-read that's thrue to th' principals iv Jefferson an' Jackson.

"Me frind Willum J. is not a candydate. He's illegible as an editor but not as a candydate. Annyhow, he don't want it or at laste he don't want to want it an' not get it. All he asks is some good man, some thried an' thrusty dimmycrat

Mr. Dooley's Opinions, pp. 93–98.

that can lead th' party on to gloryous victhry. But he can't find him. Ye say Hill? Well, me frind Willum J. was ast to ask me frind David Binnitt to go out f'r to make a speech at a dimmycratic bankit on th' thraditions iv th' dimmycratic party, Hill bein' wan iv thim an' wan iv th' worst. 'Gintlemen,' says Willum Jennings, 'I admire David Binnitt Hill. No wan,' he says. 'is a second to me in affection f'r that gr-reat an' good man,' he says. 'I shall niver fail in me devotion to him till,' he says, 'th' place heals up where he sunk th' axe into me in ninety-six. But,' he says, 'I cannot ask him to speak at ye'er bankit. I cannot bear to hear him talk. Ivry time he opens his mouth I want to put me fut into it,' he says. 'Moreover,' he says, 'if ye ask him I'll take me meal at home,' he says, 'f'r th' sight of that gallant dimmycrat turns me fr'm food,' he says. So that ends Hill. We can't go with anny wan that our sainted leader can't ate an egg with without sin.

"Well, thin, who've we got? They'se me frind Bill Whitney. He won't do because th' bookmakers niver get up on iliction day in time to vote. A thousan' to wan again Whitney, his opponent to carry th' audjiotoroom on his back. They'se me frind Charlie Towne, th' unsalted orator iv th' zenith city——"

"Thraitor," said Mr. Dooley.

"He *has* got some money," said Mr. Dooley reflectively. "I see in th' pa-apers he says they'se now enough to go ar-round —enough f'r him to go ar-round, Hinnissy. He's a thraitor. I wisht I cud afford to be wan. Well, what d' ye say to Gorman? They'se a fine, sthraightforward, honest, clane, incorruptible man. Ye put him alone in a room with th' rayturns an' ye can go out an' gather bar'ls f'r th' bonefire. Ye won't have him, eh? Oh, he knifed th' ticket, did he? Secretly? Oh, my, oh, my! Th' villain. Down goes Gorman. Well, let me

see, let me see; who've we got? I cud think iv a good manny
that cud captain a ball team, but whin I come to silictin' a
candydate f'r prisidint ivry man I think iv is ayther a
thraitor or wan that th' thraitors wudden't vote f'r. If we
don't get th' thraitor vote we're lost. They'se me frind
Sinitor Jim Jones. A good man. He won't do, ye say? Nigger
counthry? Oh, aye. We can't take a candydate fr'm th' same
part iv th' counthry that th' votes come fr'm. Ye're r-right.
There's Altgeld? Prooshen? Thrue. Aggynal—? Iv coorse
not. Schley? He may be doin' time f'r disorderly conduct an'
assault with a deadly weepin be that time. Charter Haitch?
What wud a man that's been mayor iv Chicago do with an
infeeryor job like th' prisidincy? Tom Johnson? A sthreet
car platform ain't broad enough f'r th' party. Dockery? It
sound too much like th' endin' iv a comic song. An fr'm
Missoury too. Fuller? Another thraitor, an' what's worse, a
judge. Well, there's Cleve—. Hol' on there, don't ye throw
it. Put down that chair, I tell ye.

"Ye're hard to suit, Hinnissy. I've named thim all over
an' taken me life in me hand with half iv thim an' lost me
repytation f'r common sinse be mintionin' th' others. Whin
I lead a man in through wan dure ye read him out iv another
an' throw th' book afther him. I'm thryin' to find a man to
uphold th' banner so that ye can march shouldher to
shouldher an' heart to heart, to mimrable victhry an' ivry
time I mention th' name iv wan iv ye'er fellow dimmycrats
ye make a face. What ar-re ye goin' to do? Ye might thry
advertisin' in th' pa-apers. 'Wanted: A good, active, inergetic
dimmycrat, sthrong iv lung an' limb; must be in favor iv
sound money, but not too sound, an' anti-impeeryalist but
f'r holdin' onto what we've got, an inimy iv thrusts but a
frind iv organized capital, a sympathizer with th' crushed an'
downthrodden people but not be anny means hostile to

vested inthrests; must advocate sthrikes, gover'mint be injunction, free silver, sound money, greenbacks, a single tax, a tariff f'r rivinoo, th' constitootion to follow th' flag as far as it can an' no farther, civil service rayform iv th' la-ads in office an' all th' gr-reat an' gloryous principles iv our gr-reat an' gloryous party or anny gr-reat an' gloryous parts thereof. He must be akelly at home in Wall sthreet an' th' stock yards, in th' parlors iv th' r-rich an' th' kitchens iv th' poor. Such a man be applyin' to Malachi Hinnissy, Ar-rchey r-road, an' prisintin' rif'rences fr'm his last party, can get good emplyment as a candydate f'r prisidint, with a certainty aftherward iv a conganial place as public r-reader an' party bouncer.' Ye might get an answer."

"Oh, well, we'll find some wan," said Mr. Hennessy cheerfully.

"I guess," said Mr. Dooley, "that ye're right about that. Ye'll have a candydate an' he'll have votes. Man an' boy I've seen th' dimmycratic party hangin' to th' ropes a score iv times. I've seen it dead an' burrid an' th' raypublicans kindly buildin' a monymint f'r it an' preparin' to spind their declinin' days in th' custom house. I've gone to sleep nights wondhrin' where I'd throw away me vote afther this an' whin I woke up there was that crazyheaded ol' loon iv a party with its hair sthreamin' in its eyes, an' an axe in its hand, chasin' raypublicans into th' tall grass. 'Tis niver so good as whin 'tis broke, whin rayspictable people speak iv it in whispers, an' whin it has no leaders an' on'y wan principal, to go in an' take it away fr'm th' other fellows. Something will turn up, ye bet, Hinnissy. Th' raypublican party may die iv overfeedin' or all th' leaders pump out so much ile they won't feel like leadin'. An' annyhow they'se always wan ray iv light ahead. We're sure to have hard times. An' when th' la-ads that ar-re baskin' in th' sunshine iv prosperity with

Andhrew Carnaygie an' Pierpont Morgan an' me friend Jawn D. finds that th' sunshine has been turned off an' their fellow-baskers has relieved thim iv what they had in th' dark, we'll take thim boys be th' hand an' say: 'Come over with ye'er own kind. Th' raypublican party broke ye, but now that y're down we'll not turn a cold shoulder to ye. Come in an' we'll keep ye—broke.'

"Yes, sir, ye'll have a candydate. If worst comes to worst I'll offer mesilf again."

"It wud be that," said Mr. Hennessy. "But ye ain't—what —d' ye—call—it?"

"I may not be as illegible as some," said Mr. Dooley, "but I'd get as manny votes as others."

The Vice-President

"It's sthrange about th' vice-prisidincy," said Mr. Dooley. "Th' prisidincy is th' highest office in th' gift iv th' people. Th' vice-prisidincy is th' next highest an' th' lowest. It isn't a crime exactly. Ye can't be sint to jail f'r it, but it's a kind iv a disgrace. It's like writin' anonymous letters. At a convintion nearly all th' dillygates lave as soon as they've nommynated th' prisidint f'r fear wan iv thim will be nommynated f'r vice-prisidint. They offered it to me frind Joe Cannon, and th' language he used brought th' blush iv shame to th' cheeks iv a naygur dillygate fr'm Allybamy. They thried to hand it to Hinnery Cabin Lodge, an' he wept bitterly. They found a man fr'm Wisconsin, who was in dhrink,

Finley Peter Dunne, *Dissertations by Mr. Dooley*, London and New York (1906), pp. 115–120.

an' had almost nommynated him whin his wife came in an' dhragged him away fr'm timptation. Th' way they got Sinitor Fairbanks to accipt was be showin' him a pitcher iv our gr-reat an' noble prisidint thryin' to jump a horse over a six-foot fence. An' they on'y prevailed upon Hinnery Davis to take this almost onequalled honor be tellin' him that th' raison th' Sage iv Esoopus didn't speak earlier was because he has weak lungs.

"Why is it, I wondher, that ivrybody runs away fr'm a nommynation f'r vice-prisidint as if it was an indictment be th' gran' jury? It usen't to be so. I've hollered mesilf black in th' face f'r ol' man Thurman an' Hendricks iv Injyanny. In th' ol' days, whin th' boys had nommynated some unknown man fr'm New York f'r prisidint, they turned in an' nommynated a gr-reat an' well-known man fr'm th' West f'r vice-prisidint. Th' candydate f'r vice-prisidint was all iv th' ticket we iver see durin a campaign. Th' la-ad they put up f'r prisidint stayed down East an' was niver allowed to open his mouth except in writin' befure witnesses, but th' candydate f'r vice-prisidint wint fr'm wan end iv th' counthry to th' other howlin' again' th' tariff an' other immortal issues, now dead. I niver voted f'r Grover Cleveland. I wudden't vote f'r him anny more thin he'd vote f'r me. I voted f'r old man Thurman an' Tom Hendricks an' Adly Stevenson befure he became a profissional vice-prisidint. They thought it was an honor, but if ye'd read their bio-graphies to-day ye'd find at th' end: 'Th' writer will pass over th' closin' years iv Mr. Thurman's career hurriedly. It is enough to say iv this painful peryod that afther a lifetime iv devoted service to his counthry th' statesman's declinin' days was clouded be a gr-reat sorrow. He become vice-prisidint iv th' United States. Oh, how much betther 'twere that we shud be sawed off arly be th' gr-reat reaper Death thin that a life iv honor shud end in ignomy.' It's a turr'ble thing.

"If ye say about a man that he's good prisidintial timber he'll buy ye a dhrink. If ye say he's good vice-prisidintial timber ye man that he isn't good enough to be cut up into shingles, an' ye'd betther be careful.

"It's sthrange, too, because it's a good job. I think a man cud put in four years comfortably in th' place if he was a sound sleeper. What ar-re his jooties, says ye? Well, durin' th' campaign he has to do a good deal iv th' rough outside wurruk. Th' candydate f'r prisidint is at home pickin' out th' big wurruds in th' ditchnry an' firin' thim at us fr'm time to time. Th' candydate f'r th' vice-prisidincy is out in Ioway yellin' fr'm th' back iv a car or a dhray. He goes to all th' church fairs an' wakes an' appears at public meetin's between a cornet solo an' a glee club. He ought to be a man good at repartee. Our now honored (be some) prisidint had to retort with th' very hands that since have signed th' Pannyma Canal bill to a Colorado gintleman who accosted him with a scantling. An' I well raymimber another candydate, an' a gr-reat man, too, who replied to a gintleman in Shelbyville who made a rude remark be threatin' him as though he was an open fireplace. It was what Hogan calls a fine-cut an' incisive reply. Yes sir, th' candydate f'r vice-prisidint has a busy time iv it durin' th' campaign, hoppin' fr'm town to town, speakin', shakin' hands with th' popylace who call him Hal or Charlie, dodgin' bricks, fightin' with his audjeence, an' diggin' up f'r th' fi-nance comity. He has to be an all-round man. He must be a good speaker, a pleasant man with th' ladies, a fair boxer an' rassler, something iv a liar, an' if he's a Raypublican campaignin' in Texas, an active sprinter. If he has all thim qualities, he may or not rayceive a majority at th' polls, an' no wan will know whether they voted f'r him or not.

"Well, he's ilicted. Th' ilictors call on th' candydate f'r prisidint an' hand him th' office. They notify th' candydate f'r vice-prisidint through th' personal columns iv th' pa-apers: 'If th' tall, dark gintleman with hazel eyes, black coat an' white vest, who was nommynated at th' convintion f'r vice-prisidint, will call at headquarters he will hear iv something to his advantage.' So he buys a ticket an' hops to Wash'nton, where he gets a good room suited to his station right above th' kitchen an' overlookin' a wood-yard. Th' prisidint has to live where he is put, but th' vice-prisidint is free to go anny-where he likes, where they are not particklar. Th' Constitu-tion provides that th' prisidint shall have to put up with darky cookin', but th' vice-prisidint is permitted to eat out. Ivry mornin' it is his business to call at th' White House an' inquire afther th' prisidint's health. Whin told that th' prisidint was niver betther he gives three cheers, an' departs with a heavy heart.

"Th' feelin' iv th' vice-prisidint about th' prisidint's well-bein' is very deep. On rainy days he calls at th' White House an' begs th' prisidint not to go out without his rubbers. He has Mrs. Vice-Prisidint knit him a shawl to protect his throat again' th' night air. If th' prisidint has a touch iv fever th' vice-prisidint gets a touch iv fever himsilf. He has th' doctor on th' 'phone durin' th' night. 'Doc, I hear th' prisidint is onwell,' he says. 'Cud I do annything f'r him,— annything like dhrawin' his salary or appintin' th' post-masther at Injynnapolis?' It is princip'lly, Hinnissy, because iv th' vice-prisidint that most iv our prisidints have enjoyed such rugged health. Th' vice-prisidint guards th' prisidint, an' th' prisidint, afther sizin' up th' vice-prisidint, con-cludes that it wud be betther f'r th' counthry if he shud live yet awhile. 'D'ye know,' says th' prisidint to th' vice-prisidint, 'ivry time I see you I feel tin years younger?' 'Ye'er kind wurruds,' says th' vice-prisidint, 'brings tears to me eyes. My wife was sayin' on'y this mornin' how comfortable we ar-re in our little flat.' Some vice-prisidints have been so anxious f'r th' prisidint's safety that they've had to be warned off th' White House grounds.

"Aside fr'm th' arjoos duties iv lookin' afther th' prisidint's health, it is th' business iv th' vice-prisidint to preside over th' deliberations iv th' Sinit. Ivry mornin' between ten an' twelve, he swings his hammock in th' palachial Sinit chamber an' sinks off into dhreamless sleep. He may be awakened by Sinitor Tillman pokin' Sinitor Beveridge in th' eye. This is wan way th' Sinit has iv deliberatin'. If so, th' vice-prisidint rises fr'm his hammock an' says: 'Th' Sinitor will come to ordher.' 'He won't,' says th' Sinitor. 'Oh, very well,' says th' presidin' officer; 'he won't,' an' dhrops off again. It is his jooty to rigorously enforce th' rules iv th' Sinit. There ar-re none. Th' Sinit is ruled be courtesy, like th' longshoreman's union. Th' vice-prisidint is not expected to butt in much. It wud be a breach iv Sinitoryal courtesy f'r him to step down an' part th' Sinitor fr'm Texas an' th' Sinitor fr'm Injyanny in th' middle iv a debate undher a desk on whether Northern gintlemen ar-re more gintlemanly thin Southern gintlemen. I shuddent wondher if he thried to do it if he was taught his place with th' leg iv a chair. He isn't even called upon to give a decision. All that his grateful counthry demands fr'm th' man that she has ilivated to this proud position on th' toe iv her boot is that he shall keep his opinyons to himsilf. An' so he whiles away th' pleasant hours in th' beautiful city iv Wash'nton, an' whin he wakes up he is ayether in th' White House or in th' sthreet. I'll niver say annything again' th' vice-prisidincy. It is a good job, an' is richly deserved be ayether iv th' candydates. An', be Hivens, I'll go further an' say it richly desarves ayether iv thim."

Senatorial Courtesy

"It's a question iv Sinitoryal courtesy. What's that? Well, Hinnissy, ye see, there ain't anny rules in th' Sinit. Ivrybody gets up whin he wants to, an' hollers about annything that comes into his head. Whin Dorgan was in Wash'nton he wint to hear th' debate on th' naval bill, an' a Sinitor was r-readin' the *Life iv Napolyon* to another Sinitor who was asleep.

"Sinitoryal courtesy rules th' body. If ye let me talk I'll let ye sleep. Th' presidin' officer can't come down with his hammer an' bid wan iv thim vin'rable men, grim with thraditions, to chase himsilf fr'm th' flure. In such a case it wud be parlyminthry f'r th' grim Sinitor to heave an ink-well at th' presidin' officer. Undher Sinitoryal courtesy it is proper an' even affable to call a fellow-Sinitor a liar. It is th' hith iv courtesy to rush over an' push his cigar down his throat, to take him be th' hair an' dhrag him around th' room, or to slap him in th' eye on account iv a diff'rence iv opinyon about collectors iv intarnal rivinue. Southern Sinitors have been known to use a small case-knife in a con-throvarsy. It is etiket to take off ye'er boots in th' heat iv debate. It is courteous f'r a Sinitor to go to sleep an' swallow his teeth while another Sinitor is makin' a speech. But wanst a Sinitor is on his feet it is th' hith iv misbehavior to stop him excipt f'r th' purpose iv givin' him a poke in th' nose. Afther a rough-an'-tumble fight, th' Sinitor who previously

Dissertations by Mr. Dooley, pp. 193–195.

had the flure can get up fr'm it if able an' raysume his spectacles, his wig, an' his speech. But while he has wan syllable left in his face he is th' monarch iv all he surveys.

"No rules f'r thim ol' boys. Ye can say annything again' thim, but if ye attack that palajeem iv our liberties, th' sacred right to drool, they rally at wanst. Me frind Sinitor Morgan knew this, an' says he: 'Gintlemen, they'se a bill here I don't want to see passed. It's a mischeevous, foul, criminal bill. I didn't inthrajooce it. I don't wish to obsthruct it. If anny wan says I do, Sinitoryal courtesy will compel me to jam th' libel down his throat with a stove-lifter. I will on'y make a speech about it. In th' year fourteen hundherd an' two——' An' so he goes on. He's been talkin' iver since, an' he's on'y got down to th' sixteenth cinchry, where th' question broadens out. No wan can stop him. Th' air is full iv his wurruds. Sinitors lave Wash'nton an' go home an' spind a week with th' fam'ly an' come back, an' that grim ol' vethran is still there, poorin' out moist an' numerous language. They'se no raison why he shouldn't talk f'river. I hope he will. I don't care whether he does or not. I haven't a frind in th' Sinit. As f'r th' Pannyma Canal, 'tis thirty to wan I'll niver take a ride on it. But that's Sinitoryal courtesy."

"What's to be done about it?" asked Mr. Hennessy.

"What do I do whin ye an' ye'er aged frinds stay here whin ye ought to be home?" asked Mr. Dooley.

"Ye tur-rn out th' gas," said Mr. Hennessy.

"An' that's what I'd do with th' Sinit," said Mr. Dooley.

The Candidate

"I see," said Mr. Hennessy, "that the Dimmycrats have gr-reat confidence."

"They have," said Mr. Dooley. "Th' Dimmycrats have gr-reat confidence, th' Raypublicans ar-re sure, th' Popylists are hopeful, th' Prohybitionists look f'r a landslide or a flood, or whativer you may call a Prohybition victhry, an' th' Socylists think this may be their year. That's what makes pollytics th' gr-reat game an' th' on'y wan to dhrive dull care away. It's a game iv hope, iv jolly-ye'er-neighbor, a confidence game. If ye get a bad hand at poker ye lay it down. But if ye get a bad hand at pollytics ye bet ye'er pair iv deuces as blithe as an Englishman who has jus' larned th' game out iv th' spoortin' columns iv' th' London *Times*. If ye don't win fair ye may win foul. If ye don't win ye may tie an' get th' money in th' confusion. If it wasn't such a game wud there be Dimmycrats in Vermont, Raypublicans in Texas, an' Prohybitionists in the stock-yards ward? Ivry year men crawl out iv th' hospitals, where they've been since last iliction day, to vote th' Raypublican ticket in Mississippi. There's no record iv it, but it's a fact. To-day th' Dimmycrats will on'y concede Vermont, Maine an' Pennsylvania to th' Raypublicans, an' th' Raypublicans concede Texas, Allybammy, an' Mississippi to th' Dimmycrats. But it's arly yet. Wait awhile. Th' wurruk iv th' campaign has not begun. Both sides is inclined to be pessimistic. Th' consarvative business man who thinks that if a little money cud be placed

Dissertations by Mr. Dooley, pp. 199–203.

in Yazoo City th' prejudice again' th' Raypublicans, which is on'y skindeep annyhow, cud be removed, hasn't turned up at headquarters. About th' middle iv October th' Raypublican who concedes Texas to th' Dimmycrats will be dhrummed out iv th' party as a thraitor, an' ye'll hear that th' Dimmycratic party in Maine is so cheered be th' prospects that his frinds can't keep him sober.

"Th' life iv a candydate is th' happiest there is. If I want annythin' pleasant said about me I have to say it mesilf. There's a hundherd thousan' freemen ready to say it to a candydate, an' say it sthrong. They ask nawthin' in rayturn that will require a civil-service examination. He starts in with a pretty good opinyon iv himsilf, based on what his mother said iv him as a baby, but be th' time he's heerd th' first speech iv congratulation he begins to think he had a cold an' indiff'rent parent. Ninety per cint. iv th' people who come to see him tell him he's th' mos' pop'lar thing that iver was, an' will carry th' counthry like a tidal wave. He don't let th' others in. If annybody says annything about him less frindly thin Jacob Riis he knows he's either a sorehead or is in th' pay iv th' other campaign comity. Childher an' dogs ar-re named afther him, pretty women an' some iv th' other kind thry to kiss him, an' th' newspapers publish pitchers iv him as he sets in his libry, with his brow wrinkled in thought iv how fine a man he is. Th' opposition pa-apers don't get up to th' house, an' he niver sees himsilf with a face like Sharkey or reads that th' reason he takes a bath in th' Hudson is because he is too stingy to buy a bathtub f'r th' house an' prefers to sponge on th' gr-reat highway belongin' to th' people.

"If he hasn't done much to speak iv, his frinds rayport his small but handsome varchues. He niver punched his wife, he sinds his boys to school, he loves his counthry, he shaves with a safety razor. A man expicts to be ilicted Prisidint iv th' United States, Hinnissy, f'r th' fine qualities that th' r-rest iv us use on'y to keep out iv th' pinitinchry. All th' time th' rayports fr'm th' counthry become more an' more glowin'. Th' tidal wave is risin', an' soon will amount to a landslide. Victhry is perched upon our banners, and has sint f'r th' family. F'r th' Dimmycrat candydate th' most glowin' rayports iv gains come fr'm New England, where there is always most room f'r Dimmycratic gains. F'r th' Raypublicans, th' news fr'm th' Southwest is so cheerin' as to be almost incredible, or quite so. But iliction day comes at last. Th' people iv this gr-reat counthry gather at th' varyous temples iv liberty in barber-shops an' liv'ry stables an' indicate their choice iv evils. A gr-reat hush falls on th' land as th' public pours out iv th' side dure iv th' saloons an' reverently gathers at th' newspaper offices to await with bated breath th' thrillin' news fr'm th' first precinct iv the foorth ward iv Sheboygan, Wis. An' thin again we hear th' old but niver tiresome story: Texas give a Dimmycrat majority iv five hundred thousan', but will reopen th' polls if more is nicessry; th' Dimmycrats hope, if th' prisint ratio is maintained, th' Raypublican victhry in Pinnsylvanya will not be unanimous. An' wan candydate rayceives six million votes an' is overwhelmingly defeated, an' th' other rayceives five millyon nine hundherd thousan' and is triumphantly ilicted. An' there ye ar-re.

"Why, Hinnissy, wanst whin I was in pollytics, me an' Willum O'Brien put up a German be th' name iv Smeerkase, or some such name, f'r alderman f'r th' fun iv th' thing. It was a gr-reat joke, an' even th' Dutchman knew it. But befure he'd been nommynated two weeks he begun to take it seeryous. 'They'se a good dale iv dissatisfaction in th' ward with th' prisint aldherman,' says he, 'an' ye know I've lived here a long time, an' I'm popylar with th' boys. Sthranger things have happened thin if this joke was to turn out thrue.' 'Well,' says I, 'if ye're ilicted I want ye to make me uncle Mike chief iv polis. He's licked thim all, an' he raaly holds th' job ex-propria vigore, as th' Supreme Coort wud say,' says I. 'Sure I will,' says Smeerkase. Well, he come into me place ivry day to tell me how his campaign was gettin' on. He had assurances fr'm more people thin there were in th' ward that they'd vote f'r him. He had his pitcher took an' hung on th' tillygraft poles. He hired a man to write his obichury fr'm th' time he took his first glass iv beer as a baby to th' moment whin th' indignant citizens iv th' Sixth Ward arose an' demanded that they shud crowd their suffrage on him. That meant me an' O'Brien, d'ye mind? He got up a mass-meeting, with bands an' calceem-lights, an' th' hall was crowded while he talked not on'y broken but, be Hivins, poolverized English on th' issues iv th' day.

"Well, Hinnissy, ye know 'tis not on'y th' candydate himsilf that's confident, it's ivrybody around him. An' befure th' iliction come I begun to think that maybe me frind did have a chance, so I wint around to see him. He was disthributin' th' spendin' money f'r th' polls, an' I had to fight me way in. 'Glad to see ye, Misther Dooley,' says he. 'I wanted to tell ye that I'm sorry I can't appint ye'er uncle chief iv polis. I've inquired into his charackter,' says he, 'an' 'tis not up to th' standard. Besides,' he says, 'I've promised th' job to th' Amalgamated Union iv Can Openers, who ar-re with me to a man.' 'Ar-re ye that sure ye're goin' to be ilicted that ye've already broken ye'er ante-iliction promises?' says I. 'My, but it's you that ar-re th' hurried statesman.' 'It's over,' says he. 'I've ordhered th' flowers f'r me desk in th' council.' 'Make mine a gates-ajar,' says I, an' wint my way.

"How manny votes did he get? Eight. That was th' amount.

'Where did he get thim?' says I to O'Brien. 'They were some we cudden't use,' says he. 'They belonged to a Bohaymian in th' fourth precint, but I give thim to Smeerkase. He's a good fellow,' says he."

Drink and Politics

"Sure, it's a sthrange change has come over our pollyticks since I was captain iv me precinct. We ar-re fallen, as Hogan says, on iffiminate days. Th' hardy an' gloryous peeryod in th' histhry iv th' republic has passed, an' th' times whin Hinnery Clay an' Dan'l Webster wud sit f'r hours pushin' th' scuttle to an' fro acrost th' table has gone to return no more. Booze an' iloquence has both passed out iv our public life. No longer is th' gr-reat statesman carried to th' platform be loving hands an' lashed to th' railin' where him an' King Alcohol sings a duet on th' splindors iv th' blue sky an' th' onfadin' glories iv th' flag, but afther atin' a pepsin tablet an' sippin' a glass iv light gray limonade he reads to th' assimbled multitchood th' financial repoort iv th' Standard Ile comp'ny f'r th' physical year endin' June first.

"Mind ye, all this was befure my time. In my day I niver knew a gr-reat statesman that dhrank, or if he did he niver landed anny job betther thin clerk in th' weather office. But as Hogan says Shakspeare says, they pretinded a vice if they had it not. A pollytician was a baten man if th' story wint around that he was sildom seen dhrunk in public. His aim was to create an imprissyon that he was a gay fellow, a joyval

Finley Peter Dunne, *Mr. Dooley on Making a Will and Other Necessary Evils*, New York (1919), pp. 43–46.

toss pot, that thought nawthin' iv puttin' a gallon iv paint into him durin' an avenin's intertainment. They had to exercise diplomacy, d'ye mind, to keep their repytations goin'. Whin Higgins was runnin' f'r sheriff he always ordhered gin an' I always give him water. Ye undherstand, don't ye? Ye know what gin looks like? Well, wather looks like gin. Wan day Gallagher took up his glass be mistake an' Higgins lost th' precinct be forty votes. Sinitor O'Brien held a bolder coorse. He used to dump th' stuff on th' flure whin no wan was lookin' an' go home with a light foot while I swept out his constitooents. Yes, sir, I've seen him pour into th' saw- dust quarts an' gallons iv me precious old Remorse Rye, aged be me own hands on th' premises.

"Th' most onpopylar prisidint we iver had was Ruther- ford B. Hayes—an' why? Was it because he stole th' prisi- dincy away fr'm Sam'l J. Tilden? It was not. Anny wan wud steal a prisidincy fr'm a Dimmycrat in thim days an' think th' larceny was pathriotism. No, sir, 'twas because whin people wint up to th' White House they got nawthin' to dhrink but sparklin' wather, a bivridge, Hinnissy, that is nayether cheerin' nor ineebratin', but gives ye th' most inconvanient part iv a deebauch, that is th' hiccups. Fr'm 8 o'clock, whin they set down to dinner, to 8:30, whin th' last southren congressman ran shriekin' down th' sthreet, this gr-reat but tactless man pumped his guests full iv imprisoned gas. An' whin his term expired he wint back where he come fr'm an' I niver heerd iv him again. Pollytickally speakin', d'ye mind, he wint down, as ye might say, to a wathry grave.

"But it's all changed now. Pollyticians no longer come into me place. I'm glad iv it. I prefer th' thrade iv prosp'rous steel mannyfacthrers like ye'ersilf. It's more reg'-lar. A states- man wud no more be seen goin' into a saloon thin he wud into a meetin' iv th' Anti-Semitic league. Th' imprissyon he thries to give is that th' sight iv a bock beer sign makes him faint with horror, an' that he's stopped atin' bread because there's a certain amount iv alcohol concealed in it. He wishes to brand as a calumy th' statement that his wife uses an alcohol lamp to heat her curlin' irns. Ivry statesman in this broad land is in danger iv gettin' watherlogged because whiniever he sees a possible vote in sight he yells f'r a pitcher iv ice wather an' dumps into himsilf a basin iv that noble flooid that in th' more rugged days iv th' republic was on'y used to put out fires an' sprinkle th' lawn."

H. L. MENCKEN
(1880-1956)

For nearly half a century, Henry L. Mencken, the sage of Baltimore, bombarded the American public with carefully chosen words from his vast arsenal. He was at his best lampooning politics, especially during the 1920s and 1930s. The real charm of the United States for Mencken lay in the fact that while the country itself was fundamentally comic, its politics were hilarious. Even the platitudinous pomposities of America's elder statesmen, "plainly on furlough from some home for extinct volcanoes," excited his attention and aroused his indignant mirth. Best of all was the quadrennial spectacle provided by each party's national convention, "as fascinating as a revival or a hanging." "Disregarding party affiliation," one of his book jackets trumpeted, "he exuberantly paraded his lineup of dubs, oafs, yahoos, galoots, wowsers, trimmers, stoneheads, and of course the storied boobs, to say nothing of the boob-bumpers and boob-squeezers and other feeders at the public trough."

Mencken thought the trouble with the United States was democracy, whose foundation was the mob. Fact and theory alike disputed the tenet that wisdom was rooted in a popular majority. "If x is the population of the United States and y is the degree of imbecility of the average American," he reasoned, "then democracy is the theory that $x \times y$ is less than y." Democracy led directly to demagoguery. Politics consisted almost entirely of sniffing and snooping, with the witch-hunting mob and its leaders eternally chanting "Fe, Fi, Fo, Fum." Public opinion was nothing else but mob fear sloganized into hysterical outbursts. America's popular heroes were frauds and pretenders. Bryan was the "Fundamentalist Pope," T. R. the "national Barbarossa," and Wilson "the perfect model of the Christian cad." The typical congressman was "a knavish and preposterous nonentity, half way between a Kleagle of the Ku Klux Klan and a grand worthy of the Knights of Zoroaster." Was there hope from better men? Definitely not. Urging gentlemen to go into democratic politics made no more sense to Mencken than trying to end prostitution by filling bawdy houses with virgins. "Either the virgins would leap out of the windows," he predicted, "or they would cease to be virgins."

Mencken was a germanophile and anglophobe, but above all else a states-rights Democrat of the Maryland Free-State persuasion. His writings in the *Smart Set*, the *American Mercury*, and the Baltimore *Evening Sun* revealed his perennial iconoclasm. Inevitably he was an arch-foe of prohibition. "He attained power in a world," noted Gerald W. Johnson, "whose statecraft had flowered in Calvin Coolidge, its economics in Samuel Insull, its morality in Anthony Comstock, its theology in William Jennings Bryan, its philosophy in Orson Swett Marden, and its sociology in prohibition." All these have sunk to their appropriate historical levels. Yet when Mencken assailed them with roars of laughter, these celebrities were not just successful, they were enormously so. In attacking "the bitch-goddess Success," he brought storms of denunciation on himself, but he also provoked gales of laughter and cheers. "There emerged the portrait of a nation," observed Arthur M. Schlesinger, Jr., "in which the business-man and the farmer—in Menckenese, the booboisie and the Bible Belt—had enthroned puritanism and hypocrisy; where the man who likes *potage creole,* Pilsener beer, Rühlander 1903, Brahms, pretty girls, and serious fiction was being suffocated between the Rotarian and the peasant."

Of his "The Declaration of Independence in American," Mencken wrote: "This jocosity was denounced as seditious by various patriotic Americans, and in England it was accepted gravely and deplored sadly as a specimen of current Standard American."

The Last Round

October 4, 1920

After meditation and prayer of excessive virulence for many days and consultation with all the chief political dowsers of the Republic, I conclude with melancholy that God lays upon me the revolting duty of voting for the numskull, Gamaliel, on the first Tuesday in November. It is surely no job to lift the blood pressure and fill the liver with hosannahs. Since I acquired the precious boon of the suffrage, in the year 1901, I have never had to cast my vote for a worse dub. The hon. gentleman is an almost perfect specimen of a 100% American right-thinker. The operations of his medulla oblongata (the organ, apparently, of his ratiocination) resemble the rattlings of a colossal linotype charged with rubber stamps. He invariably utters the expected, which is but another name for the not worth hearing. One half looks for him to abandon connected speech at any moment, and to start a mere chaotic babbling of stereotyped phrases: "Please remit," "Errors and omissions expected," "For review only," "Polizeilich verboten," "Für Damen," "Apartment to let," "Oh, say, can you see," "Less than ½ of 1% of alcohol by volume," "Post no bills," "Tradesmen's entrance," "In God we trust."

Nevertheless, I shall make my crossmark for Gamaliel. And why not? It is not a choice between the succubi and the cherubim; it is a choice between two devils—nay, four. The *Nation,* a gazette I esteem highly, urges me to vote for

H. L. Mencken, *A Carnival of Buncombe.* Edited by Malcolm Moos, Baltimore (1956), pp. 22–27.

Christensen or Debs, but I find it impossible to swallow either. Christensen is a lodge-joiner, and I detest lodge-joiners even more than I detest politicians. Debs is a Socialist, and my last word on the gallows will be a hoot at Socialism. I believe in capitalism, and hope it lasts, at all events, until I am safe in hell. Socialism would cost me even more than it costs me to be robbed by professional patriots. It would be an act of political hari-kari for me to vote for Debs. I simply refuse to do it, despite all the blather of the *Nation*. Or to vote for Christensen, the most worthy supreme archon. If I were a good enough American to believe in laws, I'd propose one making it a felony to be a most worthy supreme archon, punishable by knocking in the head with a footstick. The effect of such a fellow upon me is that of a horse doctor's dose of ipecacuanha, administered *per ora* at a pressure of ten atmospheres.

This leaves Gamaliel—and Jim.*

Well, why not Jim? Here another prejudice rears its obscene and horrendous mask. Next to lodge-joiners, Socialists (and, may I add, forward-lookers, Prohibitionists, evangelical clergymen, stock brokers, anti-vivisectionists, Y.M.C.A. secretaries, boomers, good business men, the judiciary, policemen, women under 30, authors, social pushers, golf players, spiritualists, labor leaders, Christian Scientists, bishops, professors of English, army officers, democrats, war veterans, Single Taxers, collectors for charity, professional Jews, professional patriots, Scotchmen, Armenians, Southerners, suffragettes, uplifters, osteopaths, commuters, children, idealists, motorcyclists, dog-fanciers, horsey women, clarinetists, actors, poets and persons who borrow gin) I detest, beyond all other sentient creatures, the fellow who is fundamentally a fraud. Jim is such a fellow. There is in him an unescapable ob-

* Warren Gamaliel Harding and James M. Cox.

liquity. His opinions are always fluent, but they always strike me as being 95% dishonest. I believe firmly that he would change all of them overnight if he thought that it would make votes for him. In brief, he is essentially a politician, and I regard a politician as a man able to preserve his honor only by dint (a) of an illimitable and pathetic naivete or (b) of a quite extraordinary sapience. Jim is not sharp enough to be a Henry Cabot Lodge and not flat-headed enough to be a Gamaliel. He falls into the middle section. That is to say, he is a professional job-grabber of the standard and familiar type—resilient, sneaking, limber, oleaginous, hollow and disingenuous.

Between such a zig-zag contortionist and an honest oaf of the Gamaliel kidney, I am all in favor of the oaf. The latter at least has the capital merit of representing accurately the mentality of the great masses of the plain people—he may lack cunning, but he is at all events, 100% American. I do not believe in democracy, and am heartily glad that the late war darn nigh ruined it, but so long as the American people admire it they should get it. They will get more of it from Gamaliel, despite his obligation to the Interests, than they will ever get from Jim. Gamaliel is the normal American of the better class—the more honest and reflective class. His thoughts are muddled, but profound. He speaks bad English, but he has a heart. He is the archetype of the *Homo boobus*. Put him into the White House and you will put every president of every Chamber of Commerce into the White House, and every chairman of every Y.M.C.A. boob-squeezing drive, and every sales manager of every shoe-factory, and every reader of the *Saturday Evening Post* and every abhorrer of the Bolsheviki, and every Prominent Baltimorean.

The issues do not interest me. The only one that is of any actual force and weight is the issue of poor Woodrow's astounding unpopularity. Curiously enough, no one has ever thought to inquire into the origins and nature of that unpopularity. I am by profession an explorer of the popular mind, and yet I am as much in the dark about it as the crowd in the nearest cigar store. Some time ago I wrote an article on the subject, perhaps the only full-length effort ever made to penetrate the problem; it was actually all windy theorizing and ended upon an unresolved dissonance. All that seems to be established is that Woodrow came home from Paris ranking with the master-minds of the ages, and that he is now regarded by everyone save a despairing band of last-ditch fanatics as a devious and foolish fellow, of whom the nation will be well rid on March 4. It seems unjust, but there it is. For crimes equally obscure Socrates was hemlocked in a far more civilized land. The public, I suspect, is an ass.

The League issue is pumped-up and of no horse-power. What is chiefly aiding Gamaliel is the fact that the plain people are tired of hearing about it. He promises to scrap it, and so they are in favor of him, save where idealism still flourishes, as in the far West, or where every third white voter has a job that he wants to keep, as in the South. Here in the East the agitation for it is mainly carried on (a) by financial gentlemen who believe that it would safeguard their loot, (b) by politicians who took to good works when the plain people canned them at the polls, *e.g.*, Dr. Taft, Dr. Root and Dr. Marburg, (c) by theorizing professors with their eyes on college presidencies and Oxford LL.D.'s, and (d) by social pushers who are in favor of it because it is English, just as they are in favor of the poetry of Alfred Noyes. The rest is silence. I travel around a good deal and keep my ears open, but it is months since I have met anyone, not belonging to or obviously influenced by one or other of these groups, who was visibly hot for the League. Its chief advocates are all of such character that their advocacy loses ten votes for it to every one gained.

Personally, I am in favor of the League—not that I am under any delusion about its intents and purposes, but precisely because I regard it as thumpingly dishonest. Like democracy, it deserves to be tried. Five years of it will see all the principal members engaged in trying to slaughter one another. In other words, it will make for wars—and I have acquired an evil taste for wars. Don't blame it on any intrinsic depravity. There was a time when I cooed for peace with the best of them, but all the present whoopers for peace insisted upon war, and after viewing war for six years I found that it was better than a revival or a leg-show—nay, even better than a hanging.

Such unspeakable appetites, however, ought to be hidden in the cellar, and not spoken of in public. Moreover, a man is a scoundrel who puts his private yearnings above the honest desires and obvious well-being of the great majority of his fellow citizens. In the present case, that majority is plainly in favor of keeping out of the mess. The bonus agitation has alarmed the taxpayer. In every community there is a one-legged soldier. Another war means another Palmer. Let the heart of the world bust if it will! Let Turk eat Armenian, and Armenian eat Kurd! Let the Poles steal what they can grab, and keep what they can hold! Let the Russians try genuine democracy if they want to! Let the French lift everything that is not nailed down and the English take what is left! Let Europe, Asia and Africa be damned!

Such is *vox populi* as I hear it in the deep silence of these equinoxial nights. The duty of a patriot is clear. I shall vote for Gamaliel. The Binet-Simon test, true enough, may show that he is backward. But even though the indicator runs clear off the gauge on the minus side, he will be born on March 4, 1921.

Gamalielese

March 7, 1921

On the question of the logical content of Dr. Harding's harangue of last Friday I do not presume to have views. The matter has been debated at great length by the editorial writers of the Republic, all of them experts in logic; moreover, I confess to being prejudiced. When a man arises publicly to argue that the United States entered the late war because of a "concern for preserved civilization," I can only snicker in a superior way and wonder why he isn't holding down the chair of history in some American university. When he says that the United States has "never sought territorial aggrandizement through force," the snicker arises to the virulence of a chuckle, and I turn to the first volume of General Grant's memoirs. And when, gaining momentum, he gravely informs the boobery that "ours is a constitutional freedom where the popular will is supreme, and minorities are sacredly protected," then I abandon myself to a mirth that transcends, perhaps, the seemly, and send picture postcards of A. Mitchell Palmer and the Atlanta Penitentiary to all of my enemies who happen to be Socialists.

But when it comes to the style of a great man's discourse, I can speak with a great deal less prejudice, and maybe with somewhat more competence, for I have earned most of my

A Carnival of Buncombe, pp. 38–42.

livelihood for twenty years past by translating the bad English of a multitude of authors into measurably better English. Thus qualified professionally, I rise to pay my small tribute to Dr. Harding. Setting aside a college professor or two and half a dozen dipsomaniacal newspaper reporters, he takes the first place in my Valhalla of literati. That is to say, he writes the worst English that I have ever encountered. It reminds me of a string of wet sponges; it reminds me of tattered washing on the line; it reminds me of stale bean-soup, of college yells, of dogs barking idiotically through endless nights. It is so bad that a sort of grandeur creeps into it. It drags itself out of the dark abysm (I was about to write abscess!) of pish, and crawls insanely up the topmost pinnacle of posh. It is rumble and bumble. It is flap and doodle. It is balder and dash.

But I grow lyrical. More scientifically, what is the matter with it? Why does it seem so flabby, so banal, so confused and childish, so stupidly at war with sense? If you first read the inaugural address and then heard it intoned, as I did (at least in part), then you will perhaps arrive at an answer. That answer is very simple. When Dr. Harding prepares a speech he does not think it out in terms of an educated reader locked up in jail, but in terms of a great horde of stoneheads gathered around a stand. That is to say, the thing is always a stump speech; it is conceived as a stump speech and written as a stump speech. More, it is a stump speech addressed primarily to the sort of audience that the speaker has been used to all his life, to wit, an audience of small town yokels, of low political serfs, or morons scarcely able to understand a word of more than two syllables, and wholly unable to pursue a logical idea for more than two centimeters.

Such imbeciles do not want ideas—that is, new ideas, ideas that are unfamiliar, ideas that challenge their attention.

What they want is simply a gaudy series of platitudes, of threadbare phrases terrifically repeated, of sonorous nonsense driven home with gestures. As I say, they can't understand many words of more than two syllables, but that is not saying that they do not esteem such words. On the contrary, they like them and demand them. The roll of incomprehensible polysyllables enchants them. They like phrases which thunder like salvos of artillery. Let that thunder sound, and they take all the rest on trust. If a sentence begins furiously and then peters out into fatuity, they are still satisfied. If a phrase has a punch in it, they do not ask that it also have a meaning. If a word slides off the tongue· like a ship going down the ways, they are content and applaud it and wait for the next.

Brought up amid such hinds, trained by long practice to engage and delight them, Dr. Harding carries over his stump manner into everything he writes. He is, perhaps, too old to learn a better way. He is, more likely, too discreet to experiment. The stump speech, put into cold type, maketh the judicious to grieve. But roared from an actual stump, with arms flying and eyes flashing and the old flag overhead, it is certainly and brilliantly effective. Read the inaugural address, and it will gag you. But hear it recited through a sound-magnifier, with grand gestures to ram home its periods, and you will begin to understand it.

Let us turn to a specific example. I exhume a sentence from the latter half of the eminent orator's discourse:

> I would like government to do all it can to mitigate, then, in understanding, in mutuality of interest, in concern for the common good, our tasks will be solved.

I assume that you have read it. I also assume that you set it down as idiotic—a series of words without sense. You are quite right; it is But now imagine it intoned as it was designed to be intoned. Imagine the slow tempo of a public speech. Imagine the stately unrolling of the first clause, the delicate pause upon the word "then"—and then the loud discharge of the phrase "in understanding," "in mutuality of interest," "in concern for the common good," each with its attendant glare and roll of the eyes, each with its sublime heave, each with its gesture of a blacksmith bringing down his sledge upon an egg—imagine all this, and then ask yourself where you have got. You have got, in brief, to a point where you don't know what it is all about. You hear and applaud the phrases, but their connection has already escaped you. And so, when in violation of all sequence and logic, the final phrase, "our tasks will be solved," assaults you, you do not notice its disharmony—all you notice is that, if this or that, already forgotten, is done, "our tasks will be solved." Whereupon glad of the assurance and thrilled by the vast gestures that drive it home, you give a cheer.

That is, if you are the sort of man who goes to political meetings, which is to say, if you are the sort of man that Dr. Harding is used to talking to, which is to say, if you are a jackass.

The whole inaugural address reeked with just such nonsense. The thing started off with an error in English in its very first sentence—the confusion of pronouns in the *one-he* combination, so beloved of bad newspaper reporters. It bristled with words misused: *Civic* for *civil*, *luring* for *alluring*, *womanhood* for *women*, *referendum* for *reference*, even *task* for *problem*. "The *task* is to be *solved*"—what could be worse? Yet I find it twice. "The expressed views of world opinion"—what irritating tautology! "The expressed conscience of progress"—what on earth does it mean? "This is not selfishness, it is sanctity"—what intelligible idea do you get out of that? "I know that Congress and the administration will favor every wise government policy to aid the resumption and encourage continued progress"—the resumption of what? "Service is the supreme *commitment* of life"—*ach, du heiliger!*

But is such bosh out of place in a stump speech? Obviously not. It is precisely and thoroughly in place in a stump speech. A tight fabric of ideas would weary and exasperate the audience; what it wants is simply a loud burble of words, a procession of phrases that roar, a series of whoops. This is what it got in the inaugural address of the Hon. Warren Gamaliel Harding. And this is what it will get for four long years—unless God sends a miracle and the corruptible puts on incorruption. . . . Almost I long for the sweeter song, the rubber-stamps of more familiar design, the gentler and more seemly bosh of the late Woodrow.

The Declaration of Independence in American

When things get so balled up that the people of a country got to cut loose from some other country, and go it on their own hook, without asking no permission from nobody, excepting maybe God Almighty, then they ought to let everybody know why they done it, so that everybody can see they are not trying to put nothing over on nobody.

All we got to say on this proposition is this: first, me and you is as good as anybody else, and maybe a damn sight

H. L. Mencken, *The American Language: an Inquiry into the Development of English in the United States,* second edition New York (1921), pp. 388–392. First printed as "Essay in American," in the Baltimore *Evening Sun,* Nov. 7, 1921.

better; second, nobody ain't got no right to take away none
of our rights; third, every man has got a right to live, to
come and go as he pleases, and to have a good time which-
ever way he likes, so long as he don't interfere with nobody
else. That any government that don't give a man them rights
ain't worth a damn; also, people ought to choose the kind of
government they want themselves, and nobody else ought to
have no say in the matter. That whenever any government
don't do this, then the people have got a right to give it the
bum's rush and put in one that will take care of their interests. Of course, that don't mean having a revolution every
day like them South American yellow-bellies, or every time
some jobholder goes to work and does something he ain't got
no business to do. It is better to stand a little graft, etc., than
to have revolutions all the time, like them coons, and any
man that wasn't a anarchist or one of them I.W.W.'s would
say the same. But when things get so bad that a man ain't
hardly got no rights at all no more, but you might almost
call him a slave, then everybody ought to get together and
throw the grafters out, and put in new ones who won't carry
on so high and steal so much, and then watch them. This
is the proposition the people of these Colonies is up against,
and they have got tired of it, and won't stand it no more. The
administration of the present King George III, has been
rotten from the start, and when anybody kicked about it he
always tried to get away with it by strong-arm work. Here is
some of the rough stuff he has pulled:

He vetoed bills in the Legislature that everybody was in
favor of, and hardly nobody was against.

He wouldn't allow no law to be passed without it was first
put up to him, and then he stuck it in his pocket and let on
he forgot about it, and didn't pay no attention to no kicks.

When people went to work and gone to him and asked

him to put through a law about this or that, he give them their choice: either they had to shut down the Legislature and let him pass it all by himself, or they couldn't have it at all.

He made the Legislature meet at one-horse tank-towns, so that hardly nobody could get there and most of the leaders would stay home and let him go to work and do things like he wanted.

He give the Legislature the air, and sent the members home every time they stood up to him and give him a call-down or bawled him out.

When a Legislature was busted up he wouldn't allow no new one to be elected, so that there wasn't nobody left to run things, but anybody could walk in and do whatever they pleased.

He tried to scare people outen moving into these States, and made it so hard for a wop or one of these here kikes to get his papers that he would rather stay home and not try it, and then, when he come in, he wouldn't let him have no land, and so he either went home again or never come.

He monkeyed with the courts, and didn't hire enough judges to do the work, and so a person had to wait so long for his case to come up that he got sick of waiting, and went home, and so never got what was coming to him.

He got the judges under his thumb by turning them out when they done anything he didn't like, or by holding up their salaries, so that they had to knuckle down or not get no money.

He made a lot of new jobs, and give them to loafers that nobody knowed nothing about, and the poor people had to pay the bill, whether they could or not.

Without no war going on, he kept an army loafing around the country, no matter how much people kicked about it.

He let the army run things to suit theirself and never paid no attention whatsoever to nobody which didn't wear no uniform.

He let grafters run loose, from God knows where, and give them the say in everything, and let them put over such things as the following:

Making poor people board and lodge a lot of soldiers they ain't got no use for, and don't want to see loafing around.

When the soldiers kill a man, framing it up so that they would get off.

Interfering with business.

Making us pay taxes without asking us whether we thought the things we had to pay taxes for was something that was worth paying taxes for or not.

When a man was arrested and asked for a jury trial, not letting him have no jury trial.

Chasing men out of the country, without being guilty of nothing, and trying them somewheres else for what they done here.

In countries that border on us, he put in bum governments, and then tried to spread them out, so that by and by they would take in this country too, or make our own government as bum as they was.

He never paid no attention whatever to the Constitution, but he went to work and repealed laws that everybody was satisfied with and hardly nobody was against, and tried to fix the government so that he could do whatever he pleased.

He busted up the Legislatures and let on he could do all the work better by himself.

Now he washes his hands of us and even goes to work and declares war on us, so we don't owe him nothing, and whatever authority he ever had he ain't got no more.

He has burned down towns, shot down people like dogs, and raised hell against us out on the ocean.

He hired whole regiments of Dutch, etc., to fight us, and told them they could have anything they wanted if they could take it away from us, and sicked these Dutch, etc., on us.

He grabbed our own people when he found them in ships on the ocean, and shoved guns into their hands, and made them fight against us, no matter how much they didn't want to.

He stirred up the Indians, and give them arms and ammunition, and told them to go to it, and they have killed men, women and children, and don't care which.

Every time he has went to work and pulled any of these things, we have went to work and put in a kick, but every time we have went to work and put in a kick he has went to work and did it again. When a man keeps on handing out such rough stuff all the time, all you can say is that he ain't got no class and ain't fitten to have no authority over people who have got any rights, and he ought to be kicked out.

When we complained to the English we didn't get no more satisfaction. Almost every day we give them plenty of warning that the politicians over there was doing things to us that they didn't have no right to do. We kept on reminding them who we was, and what we was doing here, and how we come to come here. We asked them to get us a square deal, and told them that if this thing kept on we'd have to do something about it and maybe they wouldn't like it. But the more we talked, the more they didn't pay no attention to us. Therefore, if they ain't for us they must be agin us, and we are ready to give them the fight of their lives, or to shake hands when it is over.

Therefore be it resolved, That we, the representatives of

the people of the United States of America, in Congress assembled, hereby declare as follows: That the United States, which was the United Colonies in former times, is now a free country, and ought to be; that we have throwed out the English King and don't want to have nothing to do with him no more, and are not taking no more English orders no more; and that, being as we are now a free country, we can do anything that free countries can do, especially declare war, make peace, sign treaties, go into business, etc. And we swear on the Bible on this proposition, one and all, and agree to stick to it no matter what happens, whether we win or we lose, and whether we get away with it or get the worst of it, no matter whether we lose all our property by it or even get hung for it.

The Clowns March In

June 2, 1924

At first blush, the Republican National Convention at Cleveland next week promises to be a very dull show, for the Hon. Mr. Coolidge will be nominated without serious opposition and there are no issues of enough vitality to make a fight over the platform. The whole proceedings, in fact, will be largely formal. Some dreadful mountebank in a long-tailed coat will open them with a windy speech; then another mountebank will repeat the same rubbish in other words; then a half dozen windjammers will hymn good Cal as a combination of Pericles, Frederick the Great, Washington, Lincoln, Roose-

A Carnival of Buncombe, pp. 74–78.

velt and John the Baptist; then there will be an hour or two of idiotic whooping, and then the boys will go home. The LaFollette heretics, if they are heard of at all will not be heard of for long; they will be shoved aside even more swiftly than they were shoved aside when Harding was nominated. And the battle for the Vice-Presidency will not be fought out in the hall, but somewhere in one of the hotels, behind locked doors and over a jug or two of bootleg Scotch.

A stupid business, indeed. Nevertheless, not without its charms to connoisseurs of the obscene. What, in truth, could more beautifully display the essential dishonesty and imbecility of the entire democratic process. Here will be assembled all the great heroes and master-minds of the majority party in the greatest free nation ever seen on earth, and the job before them will be the austere and solemn one of choosing the head of the state, the heir of Lincoln and Washington, the peer of Caesar and Charlemagne. And here, after three or four days of bombarding the welkin and calling upon God for help, they will choose unanimously a man whom they regard unanimously as a cheap and puerile fellow!

I don't think I exaggerate. Before the end of the campaign, of course, many of them will probably convince themselves that Cal is actually a man of powerful intellect and lofty character, and even, perhaps, a gentleman. But I doubt seriously that a single Republican leader of any intelligence believes it today. Do you think that Henry Cabot Lodge does? Or Smoot? Or any of the Pennsylvania bosses? Or Borah? Or Hiram Johnson? Or Moses? Or our own Weller? These men are not idiots. They have eyes in their heads. They have seen Cal at close range. . . . But they will all whoop for him in Cleveland.

In such whooping lies the very soul and essence of humor. Nothing imaginable could be more solidly mirthful. Nor will there be any lack of jocosity in the details of the farce: the imbecile paralogy of the speeches; the almost inconceivable nonsense of the platform; the low buffooneries of the Southern delegates, white and black; the swindling of the visitors by the local apostles of Service; the bootlegging and boozing; the gaudy scenes in the hall. National conventions are almost always held in uncomfortable and filthy places; the one at San Francisco, four years ago, is the only decent one I have ever heard of. The decorations are carried out by the sort of morons who arrange street fairs. The hotels are crowded to suffocation. The food is bad and expensive. Everyone present is robbed, and everyone goes home exhausted and sore.

My agents in Cleveland report that elaborate preparations are under way there to slack the thirst of the visitors, which is always powerful at national conventions. The town is very well supplied with bootleggers, and regular lines of rum ships run into it from Canadian ports. Ohio has a State Volstead act and a large force of spies and snoopers, many of them former jail-birds. These agents of the Only True Christianity, no doubt, will all concentrate in Cleveland, and dispute with the national Prohibition blacklegs for the graft. I venture the guess that bad Scotch will sell for $15 a bottle in the hotels and at the convention hall, and that more than one delegate will go home in the baggage car, a victim to methyl alcohol.

Ohio is run by the Anti-Saloon League, and so the city of Cleveland will be unable to imitate the charming hospitality of the city of San Francisco, four years ago. The municipality there ordered 60 barrels of excellent Bourbon for the entertainment of the delegates and alternates, and charged them to the local smallpox hospital. After the convention the Methodist mullahs of the town exposed the transaction, and proved that there had not been a patient in the hospital for four years. But the city officials who were responsible, when they came up for reëlection soon afterward, were re-elected by immense majorities. Despite Prohibition, the people of San Francisco are still civilized, and know the difference between entertaining human beings and entertaining horned cattle.

The managers of the Hon. Mr. Coolidge's campaign are apparently well aware that the nomination of the Hon. Al Smith by the Democrats would plunge them into a very bitter and serious fight, and so they are trying to weaken Al by weakening Tammany Hall. One of the principal arguments used to bring the Democratic convention to New York was that Tammany would see that the delegates and alternates got enough sound drinks at reasonable prices to keep pleasantly jingled—an unbroken tradition at Democratic national conventions since the days of Andrew Jackson. Now the Coolidge managers have hurled hundreds of Prohibition agents into Manhattan, and a desperate effort is under way to make the town bone-dry. The Dogberries of the Federal bench, as usual, lend themselves willingly to the buffoonery: dozens of injunctions issue from their mills every day, and some of the principal saloons of the Broadway region are now padlocked.

But all the New Yorkers that I know are still optimistic. There are, indeed, so many saloons in the town that all the Federal judges east of the Mississippi, working in eight-hour shifts like coal miners, could not close them completely in the month remaining before the convention opens. Every time one saloon is closed two open. Meanwhile, the 12-mile treaty with England seems to have failed absolutely to discourage bootlegging from the Bahamas. On the contrary, the price of Scotch has declined steadily since it was signed, and the stuff now coming in is of very excellent quality. It is my belief that the theory that it is heavily adulterated is spread by Prohibitionists, who are certainly not noted for veracity. I have not only encountered no bad Scotch in New York for a year past; I have never heard of any. All the standard brands are obtainable in unlimited quantities, and at prices, roughly speaking about half those of a year ago.

Moreover, very good beer is everywhere on sale, and nine-tenths of the Italian restaurants, of which there must be at least two thousand in the town, are selling cocktails and wine. Along Broadway the difficulty of concealing so bulky a drink as beer and the high tolls demanded by the Prohibition enforcement officers make the price somewhat high, but in the side streets it is now only 60 per cent above what it was in the days before the Volstead act. The last time I went into a beerhouse in New York, two or three weeks ago, the *Wirt* greeted me with the news that he had just reduced the price 10 cents a *Seidel*. His place was packed to the doors.

I am thus inclined to believe that the efforts of M. Coolidge's partisans to employ the Eighteenth Amendment against M. Smith will fail. When the white, Protestant, Nordic delegates from the Christian Endeavor regions of the South and Middle West arrive in the big town, their tongues hanging out, they will get what they have dreamed of all these months. It will cost them somewhat more than the dreadful corn liquor of their native steppes, but they will quickly get too much aboard to bother about money. In brief, I formally prophesy that the Democratic National Convention will be as wet as Democratic national conventions have always been, and that the Prohibitionist delegates, as always, will do more than their fair share of the guzzling.

The soberest men in the hall, no doubt, will be the Tammany delegates and their brethren from the other big cities of the East. To these cockneys drinking has vastly less fascination than it has for the hinds of the hinterland; decent drinks are always under their noses, and so they are not tortured by the pathological thirst of the rural Ku Kluxers. Moreover, they will have a serious job in hand, and so they will avoid the jug. That job will be to get the bucolic Baptists drunk, and shove Al down their gullets before they recognize the flavor.

The Voter's Dilemma

November 3, 1924

Though he is praised in lush, voluptuous terms by the president of the Johns Hopkins University, the Imperial Wizard of the Ku Klux Klan, the *Wall Street Journal*, the Hon. Frank A. Munsey, the proprietor of the *Saturday Evening Post* and other such agents of a delicate and enlightened patriotism, and though his election, barring some act of God, seems to be as certain as tomorrow's dawn, it is difficult to see how any self-respecting man will be able to vote for the Hon. Mr. Coolidge without swallowing hard and making a face.

For if the campaign has developed anything at all, it has developed the fact that the hon. gentleman, for all the high encomiums lavished upon him, is at bottom simply a cheap and trashy fellow, deficient in sense and almost devoid of any notion of honor—in brief, a dreadful little cad. I doubt that any man of dignity, even among his most ardent supporters,

A Carnival of Buncombe, pp. 114–118.

has any respect for him as a man. His friends are all ninth-raters like himself. Even in the trade of politics, until the martyrdom of the illustrious Harding heaved him into the White House, he was regarded not as a leader, but as a docile camp-follower. He remains essentially a camp-follower today. He will be safe, but he will be ignoble.

Those who support him because of his safeness tend to forget, I fear, the rest of it. They inevitably wriggle themselves into the position of contending that nothing else matters. It is, I believe, a dangerous doctrine. The four years of Coolidge will be four years of puerile and putrid politics. The very worst elements in the Republican party, already corrupt beyond redemption, will be in the saddle, and full of intelligent self-interest. It will be a debauch of grab. And it will be followed by a revolt that will make the cautious radicalism of Dr. LaFollette appear almost like the gospel of Rotary. Let the friends of safety paste that in their hats. They are trying to put out a fire by squirting gasoline upon it.

Compared to Dr. Coolidge, the Hon. Mr. Davis is obviously a man of enormous superiorities—in fact, it is hard to discover a single element in which he is not superior, and clearly so. He knows more, he is of greater dignity, his pronunciamentoes have more apposite and force, his everyday associations are more decent, he has the mien and manner, not of a bookkeeper in a lime-and-cement warehouse in a small town, but of an educated man and a gentleman.

What ails him, as I have more than once argued, is simply his lack of boldness, and particularly of boldness in the purely political sense. I believe that he has been hobbled and his campaign ruined by the professionals who surround him —all of them so stupid that they could not even manage the convention which nominated him. As a result, his arguments have been feeble, and the country has noted the fact. A sturdy believer in the constitutional rights of the citizen, he has been forced to avoid mention of the rights so grossly violated by Prohibition. An honest opponent of corruption in government, and outspoken against the swineries that went on under Harding, he has had to be silent about the far worse swineries that went on under Wilson.

These evasions leave the hon. gentleman with one leg up and one leg down. They have led him, as evasions always do, into downright mendacities, blushful to contemplate in an honorary bencher of the Middle Temple. I allude here to his rumble-bumble to the general effect that no Democratic national administration has ever seen a scandal. If he has forgotten the airship scandal, then surely the country has not forgotten it. Thus an air of equivocation and unreality has got into his discussion of the whole subject, and his campaign has grown progressively feebler. If it were not for the unintelligent support of the South—which is to say, of the Ku Klux that he has denounced—he would be out of it altogether. The East has heard him without attention, and the West has been too busy listening to LaFollette to pay much heed to him.

There remains, then, the Wisconsin Red, with his pockets stuffed with Soviet gold. I shall vote for him unhesitatingly, and for a plain reason: he is the best man in the running, *as a man*. There is no ring in his nose. Nobody owns him. Nobody bosses him. Nobody even advises him. Right or wrong, he has stood on his own bottom, firmly and resolutely, since the day he was first heard of in politics, battling for his ideas in good weather and bad, facing great odds gladly, going against his followers as well as with his followers, taking his own line always and sticking to it with superb courage and resolution.

Suppose all Americans were like LaFollette? What a country it would be! No more depressing goose-stepping. No more gorillas in hysterical herds. No more trimming and trembling. Does it matter what his ideas are? Personally, I am against four-fifths of them, but what are the odds? They are, at worst, better than the ignominious platitudes of Coolidge. They are better than the evasions of Davis. Roosevelt subscribed to most of them, and yet the country survived. Whatever may be said against them, there is at least no concealment about them. LaFollette states them plainly. You may fancy them or you may dislike them, but you can't get away from the fact that they are whooped by a man who, as politicians go among us, is almost miraculously frank, courageous, honest and first-rate.

The older I grow the less I esteem mere ideas. In politics, particularly, they are transient and unimportant. To classify men by examining them is to go back to the stupid days of conscientious Republicans and life-long Democrats. Let us leave such imbecilities to Ku Kluxers, Fundamentalists and readers of the New York *Tribune*. There are only men who have character and men who lack it. LaFollette has it. There is no shaking or alarming him. He is devoid of caution, policy, timidity, baseness—all the immemorial qualities of the politician. He is tremendous when he is right, and he is even more tremendous when he is wrong.

The argument against him seems to follow two lines: that he is a red radical and in secret communion with the Russians, and that he was against the late war and refused to support it. The first allegation is chiefly voiced by the Hon. Mr. Dawes, a man wholly devoid of honor. It is met by the plain fact that all the American communists are opposed to LaFollette and denounce him with great bitterness. The second charge is well-grounded. LaFollette not only voted, as a Senator, against American participation in the war; he also refused flatly to change his views when he failed to prevent it.

What followed is well remembered. While the uproar lasted he was practically barred from the Senate Chamber. His colleagues, eager to escape contamination, avoided him; he was reviled from end to end of the country; all the popularity and influence that he had built up by years of struggle vanished almost completely. Try to imagine any other American politician in that situation. How long would it have taken him to grab a flag and begin howling with the pack? How much would his beliefs and principles have weighed against the complete collapse of his career? I attempt no answer. I simply point to the other Senators who had been, before the declaration of war, in the same boat.

But LaFollette stuck. The stink-bombs burst around him, but still he stuck. The work of his whole life went to pieces, but still he stuck. Weak friends deserted him and old enemies prepared to finish him, but still he stuck. There is no record that he hedged an inch. No accusation, however outrageous, daunted him. No threat of disaster, personal or political, wabbled him for an instant. From beginning to end of those brave and intelligent days he held fast to his convictions, simply, tenaciously, and like a man.

I repeat my question: Suppose all Americans were like him? In particular, suppose all politicians among us were like him? Suppose trimming went out of fashion, and there were an end of skulkers, dodgers and safe men? It is too much, perhaps, to hope for, even to dream of. LaFollette will be defeated tomorrow, as he deserves to be defeated in a land of goose-steppers and rubber-stamps. The robes of Washington and Lincoln will be draped about a man who plays the game according to the American rules.

Twilight

October 17, 1927

Having pussy-footed all his life, it is highly probable that Dr.
Coolidge will go on pussy-footing to the end of the chapter.
There is nothing in the known facts about the man to indicate any change of heart. He was born with that pawky caution which is one of the solid qualities of the peasant, and he
will hang on to it until the angels call him home. It has
made life comfortable for him, as the same quality makes life
comfortable to a bishop or a mud turtle, but what it will cost
him in the long run! The verdict of history upon him is not
hard to forecast. He will be ranked among the vacuums. In
distant ages his career will be cited as proof of the astounding
fact that it is possible to rise to the highest places in this
world, and yet remain as obscure as a bookkeeper in a village
coal-yard. The present age has produced other examples:
King George of England, that King of Italy whose name I
forget, and perhaps six of the nine judges of the Supreme
Court of the United States.

Dr. Coolidge, if he had any enterprise and courage in him,
would be the most enviable man in the world today. For he
faces nearly a year and a half of almost imperial power—and
no responsibility whatever, save to his own conscience. If, as
I believe, he is honest in his withdrawal from the race for
his own shoes, then he is free to do anything he pleases, and
nothing can happen to him. He could, if he would, force
almost any conceivable legislation upon Congress. He could

A Carnival of Buncombe, pp. 123–127.

bring irresistible pressure to bear upon the Supreme Court. He could clear out the frauds and imbeciles who infest the high offices of government, and put in decent men. He could restore the Bill of Rights.

All these things he could do in his seventeen months, and without going outside his constitutional prerogatives. But there is not the slightest chance that he will do any of them, or that doing them will so much as occur to him. He has been plodding along in the goose-step too long for him to attempt any leaping and cavorting now. He will pass from the Presidency as he came into it—a dull and docile drudge, loving the more tedious forms of ease, without imagination, and not too honest.

When I speak of honesty, of course, I mean the higher forms of that virtue—the honesty of the mind and heart, not of the fingers. I suppose that, in the ordinary sense, Dr. Coolidge is one of the most honest men ever heard of in public life in America. True enough, he did his best to hush up the Daugherty scandal, and connoisseurs will recall that a great deal of lying had to be done to hush up his hushing up. But no one ever alleged that he was personally corrupt. The Ohio Gang never took him into its calculations. If he went to its rescue, it was not to protect thieves, but simply to prevent *scandalum magnatum*—a more dangerous thing, in an inflammable democracy, than a little quiet stealing. His motives, one may say, even transcended the partisan; they were, in a certain sense, almost patriotic.

But of intellectual honesty the man apparently knows nothing. He has no taste for cold facts, and no talent for grappling with them. There is no principle in his armamentarium that is worth any sacrifice, even of sleep. Human existence, as he sees it, is something to be got through with the least possible labor and fretting. His ideal day is one on which nothing whatever happens—day sliding into a lazy afternoon upon the *Mayflower,* full of innocent snores. There is no record that he has ever thought anything worth hearing about any of the public problems that have confronted him. His characteristic way of dealing with them is simply to evade them, as a sensible man evades an insurance solicitor or his wife's relatives. In his speeches, though he knows how to write clear English, there is nothing that might not have occurred to a Rotarian, or even to a university president.

All his great feats of derring-do have been bogus. He kept out of the Boston police strike until other men had disposed of it: then he echoed their triumphant whoops in a feeble falsetto. He vetoed the Farm Relief bill because he couldn't help it—because signing it would have made trouble for him. He opened fire upon poor Daugherty only after the man was dead and the smell of his carcass unbearable. He intrigued for a third term until it became obvious that he couldn't get it without a fight, and then he fled ignominiously, leaving his friends upon a burning deck.

There is something deeply mysterious about such a man. It seems incredible that one with such towering opportunities in this world should use them so ill. The rest of us sweat and struggle for our puny chances, and then wreck ourselves trying to turn them into achievements. But here is one who seems content to pass by even great ones: he appears, indeed, to be scarcely conscious of them when they confront him. During his years in the highest office among us the country has seen a huge slaughter of its ancient liberties, a concerted and successful effort to convert every citizen into a mere subject. He has done nothing to stop that, and he has said nothing against it. Instead, he has devoted himself to puerile bookkeeping. The man who had a million in 1923 now has, perhaps, a million and a quarter.

But who, in the long run, will give a damn? Of what use are such achievements to the progress of the human race? Who knows what the tax-rate was in 1847, or who benefited by it, or who was in favor of it or against it? History, it seems to me, deals with larger issues. Its theme, when it is not written by mere pedants, besotted by names and dates, is the upward struggle of man, out of darkness and into light. Its salient men are those who have had a hand in that struggle, on one side or the other. What will such history say of Coolidge? It will say even less, I believe, than it says of John Tyler, who at least had the courage to take himself off the scene in a blaze of treason.

Laws multiply in the land. They grow more and more idiotic and oppressive. Swarms of scoundrels are let loose to harass honest men. The liberties that the Fathers gave us are turned into mockeries. Of all this Dr. Coolidge seems to be almost unaware, as he is apparently unaware of any art or science save party politics. He has to be sure, adverted to the subject in an occasional speech, but only in weasel words. What has he done about it? He has done absolutely nothing.

What he could do if he wanted to, even in the short time remaining to him, is almost past calculation. He could stop the grotesque crimes and oppressions of the Prohibition blacklegs with a stroke of the pen. He could bring a reasonable sanity and order into the whole Prohibition question, and open the way for its candid reconsideration. He could clear out the Department of Justice, and return it to common decency. He could prepare and advocate an intelligent plan for the national defense, and put an end to the disingenuous and dangerous debate which now goes on. He could restore our dealings with foreign nations to frankness and honesty. He could improve the Federal bench by appointing better men. He could shame Congress into some regard for the honor of the nation.

All these things a man of diligent enterprise and laudable ambition could do—and if not all of them, then at least most of them. It might take some fighting, but he would win that fighting, for all men of any decency would be with him. He could turn the flow of national events back to the sound principles upon which the Republic was founded, and get rid of the follies and dishonesties that have displaced those principles. He could confound rogues and hearten honest men. He could leave behind him, win or lose, the memory of an honorable and useful life. He could make it something, once more, to be an American.

But he will do nothing of the sort. The year and a half ahead of him, like the years behind him, will be years of ignoble emptiness. He will keep on playing the politics of the village grocery. The best men of his time will continue to lie beyond his ken, and he will continue to recreate himself with the conversation of cheap-jacks and ignoramuses. There will be the familiar reports of his brave intentions, and the familiar disappointments. He will eat so many more meals, make so many more trips on the *Mayflower* with rogues and bounders, hear so many more reports from herders of votes, and make so many more hollow speeches. The stove will be spit on regularly. The clock will be wound up every night. And so, at last, he will pass from the scene, no doubt well rewarded by those who admire him with intelligent self-interest—an empty and tragic little man, thrown by fate into opportunities beyond his poor talents, and even beyond his imagination.

Imperial Purple

August 17, 1931

Most of the rewards of the Presidency, in these degenerate days, have come to be very trashy. The President continues, of course, to be an eminent man, but only in the sense that Jack Dempsey, Lindbergh, Babe Ruth and Henry Ford are eminent men. He sees little of the really intelligent and amusing people of the country: most of them, in fact, make it a sort of point of honor to scorn him and avoid him. His time is put in mainly with shabby politicians and other such designing fellows—in brief, with rogues and ignoramuses. When he takes a little holiday his customary companions are vermin that no fastidious man would consort with—dry Senators with panting thirsts, the proprietors of bad newspapers in worse towns, grafters preying on the suffering farmers, power and movie magnates, prehensile labor leaders, the more pliable sort of journalists, and so on. They must be pretty dreadful company. Dr. Harding, forced to entertain them, resorted to poteen as an analgesic; Dr. Coolidge loaded them aboard the *Mayflower,* and then fled to his cabin, took off his vest and shirt, and went to sleep; Dr. Hoover hauls them to the Rapidan at 60 miles an hour, and back at 80 or 90.

The honors that are heaped upon a President in this one hundred and fifty-sixth year of the Republic are seldom of a kind to impress and content a civilized man. People send

A Carnival of Buncombe, pp. 241–246.

him turkeys, opossums, pieces of wood from the *Constitution*, goldfish, carved peach-kernels, models of the State capitols of Wyoming and Arkansas, and pressed flowers from the Holy Land. His predecessors before 1917 got demijohns of 12-year-old rye, baskets of champagne, and cases of Moselle and Burgundy, but them times ain't no more. Once a year some hunter in Montana or Idaho sends him 20 pounds of bearsteak, usually collect. It arrives in a high state, and has to be fed to the White House dog. He receives 20 or 30 chain-prayer letters every day, and fair copies of 40 or 50 sets of verse. Colored clergymen send him illustrated Bibles, madstones and boxes of lucky powders, usually accompanied by applications for appointment as collectors of customs at New Orleans, or Register of the Treasury.

His public rewards come in the form of LL.D.'s from colleges eager for the publicity—and on the same day others precisely like it are given to a champion lawn-tennis player, a banker known to be without heirs of his body, and a general in the Army. No one ever thinks to give him any other academic honor; he is never made a Litt.D., a D.D., an S.T.D., a D.D.S., or a J.U.D., but always an LL.D. Dr. Hoover, to date, has 30 or 40 such degrees. After he leaves office they will continue to fall upon him. He apparently knows as little about law as a policeman, but he is already more solidly *legum doctor* than Blackstone or Pufendorf, and the end is not yet.

The health of a President is watched very carefully, not only by the Vice-President but also by medical men detailed for the purpose by the Army or Navy. These medical men have high-sounding titles, and perform the duties of their office in full uniform, with swords on one side and stethoscopes on the other. The diet of their imperial patient is rigidly scrutinized. If he eats a few peanuts they make a pother; if he goes in for a dozen steamed hard crabs at night, washed down by what passes in Washington for malt liquor, they complain to the newspapers. Every morning they look at his tongue, take his pulse and temperature, determine his blood pressure, and examine his eyegrounds and his knee-jerks. The instant he shows the slightest sign of being upset they clap him into bed, post Marines to guard him, put him on a regimen fit for a Trappist, and issue bulletins to the newspapers.

When a President goes traveling he never goes alone, but always with a huge staff of secretaries, Secret Service agents, doctors, nurses, and newspaper reporters. Even so stingy a fellow as Dr. Coolidge had to hire two whole Pullman cars to carry his entourage. The cost, to be sure, is borne by the taxpayers, but the President has to put up with the company. As he rolls along thousands of boys rush out to put pennies on the track, and now and then one of them loses a finger or a toe, and the train has to be backed up to comfort his mother, who, it usually turns out, cannot speak English and voted for Al in 1928. When the train arrives anywhere all the town bores and scoundrels gather to greet the Chief Magistrate, and that night he has to eat a bad dinner, with only gingerale to wash it down, and to listen to three hours of bad speeches.

The President has less privacy than any other American. Thousands of persons have the right of access to him, beginning with the British Ambassador and running down to the secretary of the Republican county committee of Ziebach county, South Dakota. Among them are the 96 members of the United States Senate, perhaps the windiest and most tedious group of men in Christendom. If a Senator were denied admission to the White House, even though he were a Progressive, the whole Senate would rise in indignation, even though it were 80% stand-pat Republican. Such is Senatorial courtesy. And if the minister from Albania were kicked out even the French and German Ambassadors would join in protesting.

Many of these gentlemen drop in, not because they have anything to say, but simply to prove to their employers or customers that they can do it. How long they stay is only partly determined by the President himself. Dr. Coolidge used to get rid of them by falling asleep in their faces, but that device is impossible to Presidents with a more active interest in the visible world. It would not do to have them heaved out by the Secret Service men or by the White House police, or to insult and affront them otherwise, for many of them have wicked tongues. On two occasions within historic times Presidents who were irritable with such bores were reported in Washington to be patronizing the jug, and it took a lot of fine work to put down the scandal.

All day long the right hon. lord of us all sits listening solemnly to quacks who pretend to know what the farmers are thinking about in Nebraska and South Carolina, how the Swedes of Minnesota are taking the German moratorium, and how much it would cost in actual votes to let fall a word for beer and light wines. Anon a secretary rushes in with the news that some eminent movie actor or football coach has died, and the President must seize a pen and write a telegram of condolence to the widow. Once a year he is repaid by receiving a cable on his birthday from King George V. These autographs are cherished by Presidents, and they leave them, *post mortem,* to the Library of Congress.

There comes a day of public ceremonial, and a chance to make a speech. Alas, it must be made at the annual banquet of some organization that is discovered, at the last minute, to be made up mainly of gentlemen under indictment, or at the tomb of some statesman who escaped impeachment by a hair. A million voters with IQ's below 60 have their ears glued to the radio: it takes four days' hard work to concoct a speech with a sensible word in it. Next day a dam must be opened somewhere. Four dry Senators get drunk and make a painful scene. The Presidential automobile runs over a dog. It rains.

The life seems dull and unpleasant. A bootlegger has a better time, in jail or out. Yet it must have its charms, for no man who has experienced it is ever unwilling to endure it again. On the contrary, all ex-Presidents try their level damnedest to get back, even at the expense of their dignity, their sense of humor, and their immortal souls. The struggles of the late Major-General Roosevelt will be recalled by connoisseurs. He was a melancholy spectacle from the moment the White House doors closed upon him, and he passed out of this life a disappointed and even embittered man. You and I can scarcely imagine any such blow as that he suffered in 1912. It shook him profoundly, and left him a wreck.

Long ago I proposed that unsuccessful candidates for the Presidency be quietly hanged, as a matter of public sanitation and decorum. The sight of their grief must have a very evil effect upon the young. We have enough hobgoblins in America without putting up with downright ghosts. Perhaps it might be a good idea to hand over ex-Presidents to the hangman in the same way. As they complete their terms their consciences are clear, and their chances of going to Heaven are excellent. But a few years of longing and repining are enough to imperil the souls of even the most philosophical of them. I point to Dr. Coolidge. He pretends to like the insurance business, but who really believes it? Who can be unaware that his secret thoughts have to do, not with 20-year endowment policies, but with 1600 Pennsylvania Avenue? Who can fail to mark the tragedy that marks his countenance, otherwise so beautifully smooth and vacant, so virginally bare of signs? If you say that he does not suffer, then you say also that a man with cholera morbus does not suffer.

On second thoughts, I withdraw my suggestion. It is probably illegal, and maybe even immoral. But certainly something ought to be done. Maybe it would be a good idea to make every ex-President a Methodist bishop.

RING LARDNER
(1885-1933)

Throughout the 1920s Ringgold Wilmer Lardner was a national celebrity, famous as a sports writer, newspaper columnist, writer of short stories and even one or two plays that briefly caught the public eye. Ring Lardner's fame rested, as it still does, on his satirical, funny short stories written in a racy and authentic Midwestern vernacular about people in ordinary walks of life—bellboys, policemen, housewives, office girls, barbers, athletes, baseball players and their fans.

Lardner steered clear of politics for the most part, both as commentator and participant. Although a registered Republican, his allegiance to the party was perfunctory. He was unable to take politics seriously. Of the fractional nominating vote he received on the forty-second ballot at a national convention he said: "Some folks said it was just a complimentary vote, while others said it was insulting." Reporting the 1924 convention of the Democratic party he invented the characters Abel Woose, neutral delegate from Gangrene, Texas, and Jovial Whee, whose qualifications for the Presidency originated in the fact that his father was "a right-thinking man who believed in God's great out of doors." Messrs. Woose and Whee might in time have developed into full partnership with Jack Keefe of *You Know Me Al* and Alibi Ike among

Lardner's great characters if their creator had been inspired to write further political humor. But he was not, being content to leave that field to Will Rogers and H. L. Mencken. Lardner admired Mencken and shared his contempt for politicians and the democratic process, for the masses and for demagogues and their governments. Individuals alone won Lardner's respect and attention, his comic approach to them deftly concealing a substructure of biting misanthropy.

Late in life, when he was tired and ill, Donald Elder quoted him as writing: "My notion of an ideal President is Al Capone. He would provide his own bodyguard, and see that Congress got good beer instead of whatever it is they have been drinking that makes them act so silly. If he just brought his baggage, the army's artillery would be doubled. As for his social standing he is head of the racket club, and his family can be traced back as far as Sicily." Intriguing, but the result was lame indeed compared to Lardner's best.

The Democrats in 1924

At this writing the name of Al Smith has just been placed in nomination and those on the inside told me that the demonstration would last 2 hours. The demonstration for Mr. McAdoo yesterday only lasted 45 minutes which it looks like that means that Al is either an hour and quarter ahead of him or behind him.

They don't know or care, but if they would hurry up and nominate somebody before Saturday night I would give a demonstration that would last all Summer.

But it looks like the boys is here for the week-end including the month of August. A whole lot of them who did not hire a room with a bath is now talking to the clerk and trying to get themselfs rearranged and a good many of them is beginning to wish they had brought on their brush and comb.

They was a storm here Wednesday night and the papers reported seven people killed. One of them was a bellhop at a hotel I won't mention who died quietly when a delegate from Arkansas gave him a dime.

"Why did you give me that dime?" was his last words and some of the local talent is writing a song about it.

The outlook is beginning to look more terrible every moment, because when they finely do decide on who is going to be president, the next problem is who is to capture the honor of second place on the ticket. This honor has already been offered to me, which means they have got as far as the L's in the telephone directory, but I am proud though poor. Some of the boys has asked me what platform

Ring Lardner, *First and Last*, New York (1934), pp. 200–214.

would I run on if nominated and I said why they are already fixing up their platform ain't they and they said yes but we want your own individual platform.

So I says all right friends I am opposed to the following propositions in every day life:

1. The matter of paper cups on Pullmans.
2. The matter of liquid soap most anywheres.
3. The matter of no hair brushes on Pullmans.
4. The length of a Democratic convention.
5. The matter of paper towels.

If nominated I will fight either for or against any or all of these propositions.

In regards to the programme for the rest of the convention, why it seems that after the demonstration for Mr. Smith gets through they are going to nominate 12 other candidates if it takes all Summer and of course it will take most of the Summer because the keyhole speech makers as Grantland Rice has aptly named them will first half to find out how to spell their names.

It now looks like the convention would be finished by the 1 of September and who won't?

*   *   *

If I was a democrat and if it was me that was running this convention I would see to it that the thing did not drag out over the coming week-end.

Judging from the eagerness with which the visiting firemen has started out to see New York, why if it lasts any more than five or six days the voting strength of the party will be decimated by he whom I sometimes refer to as the grim reaper, and even if the boys is obliged to keep up the pace past Friday it will be hard to get them out of bed in time to vote at the November election.

Abel Woose, the neutral delegate from Gangrene, Texas, who was one of the leading spirits at the Cleveland convention, arrived in New York yesterday in a kiddy kar and at once went to his suite at the Aquarium which he is sharing with a salt mackerel.

"Well, Mr. Woose," I inquired, "how do you like the Big Town?"

"Can a duck swim?" said Mr. Woose. "I had not no more than got off the train when two girls smiled at me."

"Are you sure they was not laughing?" I inquired.

"You seem to feel pretty fresh," said Mr. Woose.

"Well," I says, "anybody that can feel fresh after the Cleveland convention is a hot sketch."

Mr. Woose intends to present his own name to the convention here while the other delegates is out.

Speaking about presenting names, I have been asked by some of the leaders to allow them to present my name as a dark horse.

"You are dark," said one of them, "and you look a good deal like a horse."

I laughed off this flattery but seriously I would not be surprised if they was another landslide towards me like out in San Francisco when I developed unexpected strength along the 42nd ballot and got ½ a vote.

Some folks said it was just a complimentary vote while others said it was insulting.

Be that as it may, if conditions gets to be the same here like they was in San Francisco, they's no telling what will happen, and from all appearances this is going to make San Francisco look like a meeting of the ladies guild.

A good many of the other dark horses that has been men-

tioned won't say whether or not they would accept the so-
called honor if nominated. Personally I don't think it is just
or fair to keep your admirers in the dark in regards to your
intentions and if you ain't got no intentions why come out
and say so and give somebody else a chance.

As far as I am concerned, while I never sought political
honors, why if my friends wants to run me, I will accept on
one condition, namely that Mr. Coolidge withdraw.

*   *   *

The following is a copy of a letter wrote yesterday by
Delegate Abel Woose to his wife in Gangrene, Texas, and I
might state at this junction that this is the first time he has
wrote to her since he left Gangrene as a neutral delegate to
both conventions. It should be explained that when Mr.
Woose come away from home three weeks ago he was 72
years old and is now 103 years old and if this convention
runs another couple weeks he will still be older. It will be
noticed that the letter follows.

DEAR MOTHER. (He calls his wife mother.)

Well mother I suppose you have been wandering what has
became of me. Well mother would of wrote to you sooner
only have been tied up with different committee meetings
and etc.

Well mother we been having a great time here and so far
it don't look like we was no more than started and I was talking to-day to a man named Jefferson from Kansas and he says
Woose so far they have nominated all the democrats in the
United States except Ed Fleming from Chicago and Bill
Lange from San Francisco. He was just joking of course but
they really have nominated most everybody and it looks like

none of them had a chance to get nominated and we are libel to be here till the 1 of August and yesterday they was talking about nominating a girl for vice president and I says why don't they nominate a girl for president too and then her husband would be the first gentleman of the land. Those who overheard this remark laughed hardly.

It was while I was in a barber shop and I asked the barber to give me a shave but he says I could not shave a man like you with a razor, what you need is to be gone over with a thrashing machine. Everybody laughed but he finely shaved me and charged me 25 cents.

The boys is now trying to feign up a platform and they don't know whether to put in a plank vs. the Ku Klux Klan or not say nothing about it. I asked a man today from Michigan named Erskine that if they insist on putting in a plank vs. the klan why they should also ought to express their opinion of the Elks and Kiwanis. He laughed hardly.

Well mother tomorrow is Sunday and we will get a day of rest. I will try and write you another letter and in the meantime don't forget to water the whortle berries.

ABEL WOOSE.

*   *   *

The convention has now took a rest over Sunday and it ain't like they didn't need it. If they was a doctor in the house his advice to the delegates would be to stay quietly in bed a few days and try and sip down a little clam juice.

Newspaper men was yesterday recalling with terror a situation that came up in 1860 when the convention met in Charleston and took plenty of ballots and finally adjourned to Baltimore and took plenty of more ballots and then nominated Mr. Stephen A. Douglas and you know what happened to him. Well any ways please don't leave us adjourn to

Baltimore this time and when I say that I don't mean that I have got anything vs. Baltimore but leave us adjourn to Great Neck, where a man can get a clean shirt and see their family.

The trouble with this convention seems to be that for the first time the women is practically running it and when I say that I don't mean nothing vs. the women, but you know how they are. They never stop to realize that anybody might be in a hurry to get home. And the queer part of that is that when it gets late enough at night, they all want to get home when nobody else does.

Well any ways the most of the gals in this convention so far has all appeared in short hair, but the most of we boys wished they would cut the convention short instead of their hair.

Well a few days ago Mrs. Izetta Brown from West Virginia got up in bobbed hair and seconded the nomination of John W. Davis. Her plea was that he was a handsome man and this country should ought to have a handsome President. I felt like getting up out of what I laughingly call my seat and asking her why did not she second the nomination of Valentino or the younger of the Barrymore boys.

The next woman to get up was a Mrs. Barrett of Virginia, who seconded the nomination of Senator Glass. Everybody applauded her and in response to same she blew kisses instead of continuing to blow glass. Women ain't got no idear of time.

Any ways most of the women delegates and alternates is from out of town and they don't seem to be in no hurry to get home but some of the rest of us is and if the gals don't stop interrupting the proceedings why I for one will try and get the 19th amendment repealed so as women will half to remain in the home and men also.

Yesterday was supposed to be a day of rest and as far as I see it ain't been no different than all the rest of the days we have been having since this convention started and my suggestion is that the next time we have a Democrat convention, make all the delegates be men or women who have got some business to tend to as we can get home some time and go to work.

* * *

Woke up in time to go to what we are laughingly calling the convention and put on my badge which says active press on it and everybody that seen it and looked at bearer laughed outright.

Madison Square Garden was surrounded by what we sometimes call a cordon of police, and they kept questioning my rights to be there and I was tempted one time to say something derogatory to Al Smith but thought of my insurance policies and the anti-suicide clause and decided to let nature take its course.

Well I run into a newspaper man from Washington and he says he thought it would be a good idear to nominate Al and have him run for president of New York and leave the rest of the country if any to Mr. Coolidge.

Went into the convention and run acrost a delegate from my old home state, Mr. Codd of Niles, Michigan. He wanted I should go into the Indiana delegation and get introduced to the boys from down home, but I figured they was having a tough enough time as it was.

As we entered the Garden somebody from Alabama or somewheres was presenting to the convention the name of somebody named Underwood and a good many stenographers cheered as they thought it was the man that makes the typewriters. A lady journalist on my left said she thought it would be grand to have the ticket consist of Underwood and Underwood and maybe we could all get our pictures taken in front of the White House. Girls will be girls.

The boss of the press stand handed me a letter from an admirer in Kansas to the effect that I should ought to be throwed in the ash can because I was trying to make a joke out of a serious convention. Coals to Newcastle is all I can think of to say in reply.

Now a good many of my half witted friends has asked me repeatedly what do I think of the outcome of this convention and who is going to be who and etc. Well friends it looks to me like along about Friday all the visiting firemen is bound to be broke and their wives will be sending them souvenir post cards to come home and milk the cow and etc. and the next name that is mentioned after that, why he will be nominated unanimously and the boys will hustle for their uppers and tickled to death to get back home and tell the rest of the boys what a big time they had in New York. And a few of them will even remember the name of the joint where they held the convention.

At a late hour last night I went down to the Aquarium to visit Neutral Delegate at Large, Mr. Abel Woose from Gangrene, Texas.

"Well, Mr. Woose," I said, "how are you enjoying the convention?"

He was out.

On Prohibition

El Paso, Tex., Aug. 2—Corporal Charley Judson of Company B, Fourth Regiment of the Eighth (Hawkeye) Division, American Prohibitionary Force, was being congratulated by his buddies tonight for shooting the left ear off a two-year-old child who was crossing the bridge from Juarez with a peculiar waddling gait. Corporal Judson said he had witnesses to prove that the fellow had been seen drinking out of a bottle; he fired at his ear instead of his heart because he just wanted to frighten him. The bottle was found to contain a little over an ounce of a liquid identified as milk. "Yeh?" said the Corporal, who has a certain dry humor. "Well, milk don't make people walk funny."

Sault St. Marie, Mich., Aug. 2—Miss Muriel Chapin of this place was scattered all over the Northern Peninsula today by a machine-gun squad in charge of Capt. Felix Lord of Houghton. The captain picked up one of the girl's lips and showed it to his colonel, H. R. King of Calumet. The lip was a pale red. "That's what fooled me," said Captain Lord. "It's just some kind of rouge, but I thought it was grenadine."

Niagara Falls, N. Y., Aug. 2—A depth bomb dropped by Lieut. Ed. Frawley of Herkimer demolished a barrel that was seen shooting the Falls late today. Frawley suspected that

First and Last, pp. 215–220.

the barrel was full of liquor, but it developed that the contents had been John E. Gardner and wife and two children, a Buffalo family out for an outing. "This was self-defense if there ever was one!" declared Lieut. Frawley. "I acted only after assuring myself that the barrel was shooting the Falls."

Plattsburg, N. Y., Aug. 2—A bearded man on a bicycle was stopped here today by Clarence Dutton, an M.P. of the A.P.F. Dutton demanded the man's name and the man said he was Eli Kolp, a farmer residing three miles south of Plattsburg.

"Then why are you wearing a beard?" asked Dutton.

"I look funny without one," replied the bicyclist.

"You look funny with one," retorted Dutton. "You look suspicious to me. How do I know what you've got in those tires?"

"I've got nothing but some air. I'll open them and let it out."

"I'll let some into you," said Dutton, shooting him full of holes.

The bicyclist was later identified as Eli Kolp, a farmer residing three miles south of Plattsburg.

WILL ROGERS

(1879-1935)

William Penn Adair Rogers, cowboy, actor, humorist, and news commentator, first became famous as a trick-rope artist in Broadway musical comedies. Rogers became a star when he learned to joke informally with audiences while spinning a lariat and chewing gum. He reached the peak of his stage success from 1916 to 1925 in Ziegfeld's *Follies,* where he would introduce his fresh and comical comments on news events: "Well, all I know is what I read in the papers." From the beginning the personality of Will Rogers outshone his rope-twirling ability. Dixon Wecter sketched him: "A shock of coarse black hair, later iron-gray, unruly as a schoolboy's, frank blue eyes lifted suddenly in shrewd appraisal, face weatherbeaten and crinkled by his contagious grin, and clothes that looked as if he had taken a long nap in them—this was the image of Will Rogers who 'just played his natchell self.' " This was the beloved figure who, in the decade following 1925, marked the climax of America's long line of cracker-box humorists.

Beginning in 1923, Will Rogers wrote weekly articles of humorous commentary on contemporary affairs for *The New York Times* and syndicated newspapers, which proved enormously popular. He toured Europe in 1926, sending home "Letters of a Self-Made Diplomat to His President."

Included were many cables addressed to Calcool, White-housewash—the first of hundreds of daily telegrams of terse, humorous comment on the news of the day. By this time Will Rogers was concentrating on political subjects. "Politics is the best show in America," he observed once. "I love animals and I love politicians and I love to watch both of 'em play either back home in their native state or after they have been captured and sent to the zoo or to Washington." Behind Rogers' humor there was penetrating wisdom. Unlike Mencken and most of his contemporaries, Rogers blamed Al Smith's defeat in 1928 on the flushness of the times rather than on religion or Prohibition—a judgment supported by recent insights.

Will Rogers was never sharper than when discoursing upon the Depression. Shortly after the Wall Street crash in 1929, Rogers patriotically offered his services for the wide-spread campaign to restore confidence. "But you will have to give me some idea where 'Confidence' is," he added, "and just what you want it restored to." Of President Hoover's speech at Valley Forge, Rogers commented: "He found somebody that was worse off than we are, but he had to go back 150 years in history to do it." And in 1931 he described the whole tragedy: "We got more wheat, more corn, more food, more cotton, more money in the banks, more everything in the world than any nation that ever lived ever had, yet we are starving to death. We are the first nation in the history of the world to go to the poor house in an automobile."

The years of the locust were particularly severe for Republicans, politically speaking, and Rogers was openly a Democrat. Yet he cheerfully and impartially lambasted both major parties. "I don't want to lay the blame on the Republicans for the Depression," he decided in 1932, when it was fashionable to do just that. "They're not smart

enough to think up all those things that have happened."
Free-wheeling political humorist is the best description of
Will Rogers—a humorist outwardly gentle and sparing of
underdogs, but accurate in aim, scoring with every thrust.
If, as he insisted, all he knew about life's wry twists and
turnings could be read in the newspapers, either the papers have slipped, readers have slumped, or the state of
his beloved Cuckooland's humor just ain't what it used
to be.

Selections

June 14, 1920

Only two detrimental things have come out since Nomination in Harding's whole record. One was his middle name, Gamaliel, and the other he used to play a slide trombone in a country band. Musical circles in Washington are now looking towards a big revival.

Ohio claims they are due a President as they haven't had one since Taft. Look at the United States, they haven't had one since Lincoln.

My idea of an honest man is a fellow who will pay income tax on money he sold his vote for. Politicians who buy votes with Wood Alcohol will have to be very careful to not deliver the drink till after the party has voted.

Chicago crooks say it was the poorest convention on record as all the Delegates had were their badges.

July 4, 1920

Harding is sending out his speeches on the Phonograph. Well, us public have one consolation—a record when dropped breaks easily.

Can you imagine anything more cheerful than a party of friends gathered, opening home brew, and listening to a record, "Voters, if I am elected, I will enforce the law to the letter?"

Will Rogers' observations, presented in chronological order, are taken from: *The Autobiography of Will Rogers*, selected and edited by Donald Day, Boston (1949), *passim;* Will Rogers, *How We Elect Our Presidents*, selected and edited by Donald Day, Boston (1952), *passim.*

The Democrats nominated Roosevelt for Vice-President on account of his name, I suppose, figuring that most progressives were so far behind they wouldent know the difference.

Vice Presidents answer about the same purpose as a flank cinch on a saddle. If you break the front one, you are worse off than if you had no other.

The Democrats cant compete with the Republicans in spending money to get in office but after they get in I dont think there is any body can compete with them.

November 11, 1923

If I was running I would be ashamed to let anybody know which one of those Parties I belonged to. Now, take the last three years, it looked like the Democratic Party was the best Party. But the 8 years previous to that it looked like the Republican Party was the best. The only way in the World to make either one look half decent is to keep them out.

Now you take, for instance, a Republican. There is lots of People that wont speak or associate with one. They think they would catch some grafting Disease but I have met several of them and you take one, when he is out of office, and he is as nice a fellow as you would want to meet. You keep a Republican broke and out of office and pretty near anybody can get along with them.

Now, on the other hand, take the Democrats. They are a great deal like France. France wants to so entirely crush Germany that they will never be able to rise up and attack them again. Well, that is the way with the Democrats. Every time they got in office and started to get ahead and accumulated something, why the Republicans would rise and crush them. They didn't even wait for 40 years like the Germans, but would generally pounce on them about every 4 years.

You take a Democrat and a Republican and you keep them both out of office and I bet you they will turn out to be good friends and maybe make useful Citizens and devote their time to some work instead of 'lectioneering all the time.

June 25, 1924

Well, the Democratic scandals got started yesterday. The thing was almost an hour late in starting. You could tell the delegates who had been entertained by Tammy men the night before. They looked awful, and must have felt terrible.

The building is literally lined with flags. I could never understand the exact connection between the flag and a bunch of politicians. Why a political speaker's platform should be draped in flags any more than a factory where men work, or an office building, is beyond me.

A man handed around in the press stands some thick paperback books. I asked, "Is this the life of Old Hickory?" He said, "No, that is Pat Harrison's keynote speech." He told things on the Republicans that would have made anybody but Republicans ashamed of themselves.

When he mentioned old Andy Jackson, he just knocked those Democrats off their seats. Then, as he saw they were recovering, he hit 'em with the name of Thomas Jefferson, and that rocked them back. Then he mentioned Woodrow Wilson, and that sent them daffy.

I am not up on political etiquette, but it struck me as rather strange, after paying a tribute to a wonderful man, that the delegates should raise up and start shouting and singing "Hail, Hail, the Gang's All Here, What the Hell Do We Care." They hollered and shouted and sang "John

Brown's Body" and "Tipperary." Even my old Side-Kick Bryan, was prancing around the hall shouting.

Now, he has been brought up different. He has read the Bible, even if it was just to get quotations from, but he knows, even if those other delegates didn't, that that was no way to pay tribute to a martyred President.

As poor as the Republican Convention was I will give them credit, they didn't sing "Hail, Hail, the Gang's All Here" when the speaker mentioned Lincoln.

The whole thing looked like a sure stampede for Wilson. So there will be a terrible disappointment when the delegates find that he has passed beyond and won't be able to accept.

Chairman Cordell Hull read what the convention was gathered here for: "That it was to nominate a man to run for President and take any other drastic means necessary."

Mayor Hylan made a welcoming speech to the convention. It was on "Honesty in Private and Government Affairs." I don't see why he should lecture the delegates. They are not going to get away with anything in this town.

But he did have a sure fire finish to his act. He said, "I have told them to issue you little cards that will be good for every so-called private place in New York."

July 9, 1924

Well, it was 6:30 and they had just read the platform. I had it before me, forty-five pages. If it had come out in the open on every question and told just where they stood, they could have saved themselves, not only forty-two pages of paper, but perhaps their election in November.

When you straddle a thing it takes a long time to explain it.

It favors fixing everything the Republicans have ruined, keeping everything that they haven't, right up to its present standard. In the Republican platform at Cleveland they promised to do better.

I don't think they have done so bad this time. Everybody's broke but them.

July 10, 1924

Who said miracles don't happen? Didn't the Democratic National Convention nominate a man at last?

That should bring more people back to religion than any other one thing. It has been a demonstration of faith, because, after all, God is good.

This convention wound up in a personal triumph for William Jennings Bryan. My old friend W. J. is the greatest character we have in this country today. He is a very unique man. Most of us only attract attention twice on earth. One is when we are born and the other is when we die.

But Mr. Bryan even improves on a bear; a bear hibernates all Winter, but Bryan hibernates for four years, and then emerges, and has a celebration every four years at every Democratic Convention.

In the meantime, he lectures in tents, shooting galleries, grain elevators, snow sheds or any place that he can find a bunch of people that haven't got a radio.

No one has ever been able to understand the unique and uncanny power that he seems to hold over the Democratic Party, especially near nominating time. Since 1896 he has either run himself or named the man that would run.

And then all during the convention here you would hear

the expression, "Well, poor old man Bryan! He has lost his grip on the delegates. Here is one where he won't be able to name the man." But not me; I never wavered.

When he came out *against* Davis, Davis was a nominated man. Those eleven hundred delegates said, "If Bryan is so set against him he must be the right man."

Next to Bryan the New York papers have killed off more deserving candidates by supporting them.

October 19, 1924

I have been trying to read the papers and see just what it is in this election that one Party wants that the other one don't. To save my soul I can't find any difference. The only thing that I can see where they differ is that the Democrats want the Republicans to get out and let them in, and the Republicans don't want to get out.

They are so hard up for an issue that Mr. Coolidge has finally announced his policy will be Common Sense. Well, don't you know the Democrats will claim that too? Do you think they will call their campaign "Darn Foolishness"? Besides, Common Sense is not an Issue in Politics; it's an affliction.

Davis announced that his Policy will be Honesty. Neither is that an issue in Politics; it's a Miracle, and can he get enough people that believes in Miracles to elect him?

The only thing I see now that the two old line Parties are divided on is the question, "Who will have the Post Offices?" No matter how many Parties you have they are all fighting for the same thing—SALARY. You abolish salaries and you will abolish Politics and TAXES.

February 15, 1925

Well, I see where Judge Gary, the head of the Steel Trust and Mr. John D. Rockefeller, Jr., head of the Oil Trust went down to Washington and had breakfast with President Coolidge. They are going to fix up the Prohibition enforcement. They haven't had time to get around to it before. They took down a Pamphlet thanking Mr. Coolidge for his good example in not breaking the law. The Automobile men are going to draw up one now and take it down and give it to him for not stealing a car during his term of office.

They don't have to have men like Mr. Gary and Mr. Rockefeller compliment Mr. Coolidge for keeping the law. He has always kept the law. His worst political enemy could never say he ever broke a law. You remember a few years ago this country had to pass a special law called the Anti Trust Law, aimed primarily at these two Trusts, the Oil and the Steel. Now if you have to pass a law to curb men like that they are not exactly the men to give confidence to the rest of our Nation in regard to keeping the law. Getting them to arrange our Morals would be like appointing me as Teacher of English at Harvard.

February 22, 1925

The last few days I have read various addresses made on Lincoln's Birthday. Every Politician always talks about him, but none of them ever imitate him. They always make that a day of delivering a Lecture on "Americanism." When an Office Holder, or one that has been found out, can't think of anything to deliver a speech on, he always falls back on the good old subject, AMERICANISM. Now that is the one thing that I have never delivered an essay on, either written or spoken. They have all had a crack at it every Fourth of July and Lincoln's Birthday. So now I am going to take up the subject and see what I can wrestle out of it. Let's get our rope ready and turn it out, and we will catch it and see really what brands it has on it. Here it comes out of the Corral. We got it caught; now it's throwed and Hog Tied; and we will pick the brands and see what they are.

The first thing I find out is that there ain't any such animal. This American Animal that I thought I had here is nothing but the big Honest Majority, that you might find in any Country. He is not a Politician. He is not a 100 percent American. He is not any organization, either uplift or downfall. In fact I find he don't belong to anything. He is no decided Political faith or religion. I can't even find out what religious brand is on him. From his earmarks he has never made a speech, and announced that he was An American. He hasn't denounced anything. It looks to me like he is just an Animal that has been going along, believing in right, doing right, tending to his own business, letting the other fellows alone.

He don't seem to be simple enough minded to believe that EVERYTHING is right and he don't appear to be Cuckoo enough to think that EVERYTHING is wrong. He don't seem to be a Prodigy, and he don't seem to be a Simp. In fact, all I can find out about him is that he is just NORMAL. After I let him up and get on my Horse and ride away I look around and I see hundreds and hundreds of exactly the same marks and Brands. In fact they so far outnumber the freakly branded ones that the only conclusion I can come to is that this Normal breed is so far in majority that there is no use to worry about the others. They are a lot of Mavericks, and Strays.

A bunch of Bobbed Haired men gathered in Madison Square Garden last Sunday at a meeting of these Reds, or Bolsheviki, or whatever they call themselves. It was one of their denouncement meetings. They denounced the heavy snow, Declaration of Independence, 5 cent Street Car Fare, Floods in Georgia, Mayor Hylan's Bathing Suit, Twin Beds, and the Eclipse. A Kid 14 years old delivered such a tribute to Lenine that he made it look like George Washington or Abe Lincoln couldn't have caddied for Lenine. Oh, this Boy had got disgusted with America young in life. Incidentally, while he was making this tirade, NORMALISM of his age, at least a million of them were out skating.

Now some say that a thing like that should not be allowed. Why sure it should be allowed! England can teach any Country in the World how to handle discontent. (Maybe it's because they have more of it.) They give 'em a Park, Hyde Park, they even furnish the Soap Boxes (as the former contents of the Box is generally as foreign to the Speakers as his Nationality is to the Country he is speaking in). Give 'em a Hall or a Box to stand on and say "Sic 'em; knock everything in sight" and when they have denounced everything from Bunions to Capitalistic Bath Tubs, then they will go home, write all week on another speech for the following Sunday and you will never have any trouble with them.

It's just like an exhaust on an Automobile. No matter how high priced the Car, you have to have an exit for its bad Air, and Gasses. They have got to come out. It don't do any particular harm, unless you just stand around behind smelling of it all the time, but who would want to follow a Car to smell of its exhaust when you could just as well be in the Car riding?

Now sometimes there is a loud explosion and everybody on the Streets will turn round and see what it is. The minute they see, they will go right on their business. They know there has been no damage done. So that's how it is with the so called Radical element. Let them have a Park or a Hall as an exhaust Pipe. Then when they have some particular Noted Denouncer, why, you will hear a loud report. You will listen, or read what he said and go on about your business the same as the listeners to a back fire. You know its necessary.

Now I am not much on History but I don't think any of these people were drafted over here, nor that there are any Immigration Laws in Europe against this Country. I have often thought what would happen if the Government sent somebody to one of those meetings and he got up and announced that he was instructed to send every one of them back to the Country where they come from, and had been raving about. Say there would be such a stampede they would tear down the building to keep from going. You couldn't Shanghai them out of here.

No sir! This country is too big now. To stop this Country now would be like spitting on a Railroad track to stop a Train. These Reds are on their backs snoring and they ain't keeping anybody awake but each other. No Element, no Party, not even Congress or the Senate can hurt this Country now; it's too big. There are too many men just like those Dog Team drivers and too many Women like that Nurse up in Nome for anything to ever stampede this old Continent of ours. That's why I never can take a Politician seriously. They are always shouting that "such and such a thing will ruin us, and that this is the eventful year in our Country's life."

Say, all the years are the same. Each one has its little temporary setbacks, but they don't mean a thing in the general result. Nobody is making History. Everybody is just drifting along with the tide. If any office holder feels he is carrying a burden of responsibility, some Fly will light on his back and scratch it off for him some day. Congress can pass a bad law and as soon as the old Normal Majority find it out they have scratched it off the books.

We lost Roosevelt TR, a tough blow. But here we are still kicking. So, if we can spare men like Roosevelt and Wilson there is no use in any other Politician ever taking himself serious.

Henry Ford has been a big factor in the Industrial Development of the Country. Yet if he was gone there would still be enough of those things left to clutter up the Highways for Years. John D. Rockefeller who has done a lot for humanity with his Gifts; yet when he is gone and Gasoline raises 2 Cents, and all expenses and the Estate is settled we will kick along. *Even when our next War comes we will through our shortsightedness not be prepared, but that won't be anything fatal. The real energy and minds of the Normal Majority will step in and handle it and fight it through to a successful conclusion.* A war didn't change it before. It's just the same as it was, and always will be, because its founded on right and even if everybody in Public Life tried to ruin it they couldn't. This Country is not where it is today on account of any man. It is here on account of the real common sense of the big Normal Majority. A Politician is just like a Necktie Salesman in a big Department Store. If he decides to give all the Ties away, or decided to pocket all the receipts, it don't affect the Store. It don't close. He closes, as soon as he is found out.

So I can find nothing for alarm in our immediate future. The next time a Politician gets spouting off about what this Country needs, either hit him with a tubercular tomato or lay right back in your seat and go to sleep. Because THIS COUNTRY HAS GOT TOO BIG TO NEED A DAMN THING.

March 1, 1925

It may interest you to know that five of the Will Rogers articles have been read on the floor of Congress and printed in the Congressional Record as representing a typical American view of important public subjects.

When a Gentleman quoted me on the floor of Congress the other day, another member took exception and said he objected to the remarks of a Professional Joke Maker going into the Congressional Record.

Now can you beat that for jealousy among people in the same line? Calling me a Professional Joke Maker! He is right about everything but the Professional. THEY are the Professional Joke Makers. Read some of the Bills that they have passed, if you think they ain't Joke makers. I could study all my life and not think up half the amount of funny things they can think up in one Session of Congress. Besides my jokes don't do anybody any harm. You don't have to pay any attention to them. But everyone of the jokes those Birds make is a LAW and hurts somebody (generally everybody).

"Joke Maker!" He couldn't have coined a better term for Congress if he had been inspired. But I object to being called a Professional. I am an Amateur beside them. If I had that Guy's unconscious Humor, Ziegfeld couldn't afford to pay me I would be so funny.

Of course I can understand what he was objecting to was any common Sense creeping into the *Record*. It was such a Novelty, I guess it did sound funny.

And, by the way, I have engaged counsel and if they ever put any more of my material in that "Record of Inefficiency" I will start suit for deformation of Character. I don't want my stuff buried away where Nobody ever reads it. I am not going to lower myself enough to associate with them in a Literary way.

June 28, 1925

America has a great habit of always talking about protecting American interests in some foreign Country. PROTECT 'EM HERE AT HOME! There is more American Interests right here than anywhere. If an American goes to Mexico and his Horse dies, we send them a Note wanting American Interests preserved and the horse paid for.

We don't guarantee investments here at home. Why should we make Mexico guarantee them? Our Papers are always harping on US developing Mexico. Suppose Mexico don't want developing. Maybe they want it kept as it was years ago. How much do Americans spend in the Summer to get to some places where there is no development—No Street Cars, Elevators, Fords, Telephones, Radios, and a million and one other things that you just like to get away from once in awhile? Well, suppose they don't want 'em at all down there. Why don't you let every Nation do and act as they please? What business is it of yours how Mexico acts or lives?

If America is not good enough for you to live in, why, then you are privileged to go to some other Country. But don't ask protection from a Country that was not good enough for you. If you want to make money out of a Country, why, take out their Citizenship Papers and join them. **Don't use one Country for Money and another for convenience.** The difference in our exchange of people with Mexico is; they send workmen here to work, while we send Americans there to "work" Mexico.

America and England, especially, are regular old Busy-bodies when it comes to telling somebody else what to do. But you notice they (England and America) never tell each other what to do. You bet your life they don't!

Big Nations are always talking about Honor. Yet England promised to protect France against Germany, IF FRANCE WOULD PAY THEM WHAT THEY OWED THEM. They act as a Police Force for Pay.

What is the consequence? As soon as Germany gets strong enough so she thinks she can lick both of them there will be another War.

*   *   *   *   *

The Lord put all these millions of people all over the earth. They don't all agree on how they got there, and ninety percent don't care. But he was pretty wise when he did see to it that they all do agree on one thing, (whether Christian, Heathen, or Mohammedan) and that is the better lives you live the better you will finish.

Paris, France, September 17, 1926

France said at the League the other day that she and Germany were old pals again. I guess they are. I floated down the Rhine in Germany all day yesterday and there were so many French soldiers in the way I couldn't see the castles.

Ottawa, Ontario, October 13, 1926

More sentiment here to be annexed by Mexico than America. They know us too well. If we get any nation to join us it will have to be some stranger. We only have one reason for wanting Canada. And modification of the Volstead act will eliminate that.

Montgomery, Alabama, October 21, 1926

It took two weeks to coach New York politicians how to dress and act to meet Queen Marie of Roumania so they all looked like twins and spoke the same little piece. Americans are getting like a Ford car—they all have the same parts, the same upholstering and make exactly the same noises.

Oklahoma City, Oklahoma, October 29, 1926

The South is dry and will vote dry. That is everybody that is sober enough to stagger to the polls will.

January 16, 1927

We better start doing something about our defense. We are not going to be lucky enough to fight Nicaragua forever. Build all we can, and we will never have to use it. If you think preparedness don't give you prestige, look at Japan. We are afraid to look at them cross eyed now for fear we will hurt their "Honor." Before they got a Navy neither them, nor us, knew they had any honor. Japan or England either would have just as much honor without any Navy at all, but the Navy helps to remind you of it.

All we got to go by is the History, and History **don't** record that "Economy" ever won a war. So I believe I **would** save my money somewhere else even if I had to work a little shorter handed, around the Capitol there.

San Francisco, March 12, 1927

See by the newspapers this morning Secretary Wilbur says there is no danger from Europe from airplanes. WHEN WE NEARLY LOSE THE NEXT WAR, AS WE PROBABLY WILL, WE CAN LAY IT ONTO ONE THING AND THAT WILL BE THE JEALOUSY OF THE ARMY AND NAVY TOWARD AVIATION.

They have belittled it since it started and will keep on doing it till they have something dropped on them from one.

Sacramento, March 16, 1927

Just addressed the California State Legislature and helped them pass a bill to form a lawyers' association to regulate their conduct.

Personally I don't think you can make a lawyer honest by an act of Legislature. You've got to work on his conscience. And his lack of conscience is what makes him a lawyer.

Cleveland, Ohio, April 18, 1927

Al Smith explains that if elected President all Protestants would not be exterminated; that even a few of the present Senators would be retained, including Tom Heflin; that the Knights of Columbus would not replace the Boy Scouts and Kiwanis; that mass would not replace golf on Sunday morning; and, that those that were fortunate enough to have meat could eat it on Friday.

It's no compliment to a nation's intelligence when these things have to be explained.

Morgantown, W. Va., April 21, 1927

This is the home State of John W. Davis, the last Democratic sacrifice on the altar of "no policy to run on." Notice to Democrats— Get a policy and stick to it, even if it's wrong.

April 25, 1927

Can you imagine? This town of Cleveland wants the Republican and Democratic conventions both in 1928.

A town that don't know any more than that is liable to ask for a sesquicentennial. The Republican convention will be held further West, for that's the way they are going to relieve the farmers—to let 'em see a convention. And as for the Democratic one, a sanity test will follow any town purposely asking for it.

Beverly Hills, August 18, 1927

Herb Hoover is out here among us. He is just waiting around between calamities. When we, as individuals, get sick we send for Hoover. He is America's family physician. He is a great guy, is Doc Hoover, and I hope they don't spoil him by putting him into politics.

October, 1927

Will in an article in the Saturday Evening Post *advised Al Smith to write all Democratic organizations as follows:*

"I, Al Smith, of my own free will and accord, do this day relinquish any claim or promise that I might have of any support or Deligates at the next Democratic Convention. I don't want to hinder what little harmony there is left in the party.

"I not only do not choose to run, but I refuse to run. But will give all my time and talents to work faithfully for whoever is nominated by the party."

Now, Al, if you will send 'em this letter you will look like you are sacrificing yourself, and in '32 they will nominate you by radio; they can't help it, and you will have a united party. A half-wit knew you all couldent win in '24. Well, it's the same this year; you couldent put on a revival of Thomas Jefferson and get away with it.

Al, don't let those New Yorkers kid you. You got no Platform, you got no Issue, you can't ask people to throw somebody out just because somebody else wants in. You meet too many Democratic Leaders—that's what's the matter with the Party—these same leaders not knowing any more about Public Opinion than they do. That's why they are Democratic Leaders.

Then, you New Yorkers get a wrong prospectus of things. The outsiders don't care nothing about New York, and if you think Tammany Hall is an asset, you just run and try to carry them with you and you will find you have been overhandicapped. Now it ain't that you ain't strong, Al; you are strong—you are strong—you are the strongest thing the Democrats have had in years. No Democrat could come near you— But it's not a Democrat that you meet in the finals; it's a Republican. Everybody is always asking, "What's the matter with the Democratic Party?" There ain't nothing wrong with it; it's a Dandy Old Party. The only thing wrong with it is the law killed it. It won't let a man vote but once, and there just ain't enough voters at one vote each to get it anywhere. You can't lick this Prosperity thing; even the fellow that hasent got any is all excited over the idea. You Politicians have got to look further ahead; you always got a putter in your hands, when you ought to have a Driver. Now, Al, I am trying to tell you how to be President, not how to be a Candidate.

Orlando, Florida, March 12, 1928

See by today's paper where Senator Borah made an appeal to the country to donate a dollar or more each to save the respect of the Republican Party. I just mailed $5 to make five Republicans respectable. Wish I could afford more, but this continued prosperity has just about got me broke.

New York, April 16, 1928

I received my $5 back from Senator Borah that I sent him to clean up five Republicans. I even named the five that he was to clean up. He wasn't able to raise the fund because people realized that it was a lost cause. You can't make the Republican Party pure by more contributions, because contributions are what got it where it is today.

This was a noble idea of Borah's, but noble ideas don't belong in politics.

April 22, 1928

Corruption has supplanted the Tariff, as a National issue. But its awful hard to get people interested in corruption unless they can get some of it. You take a fellow that hasent received any corruption, and its kinder like the fellow that has never drank Sour Kraut Juice, he aint much interested in whether its good or bad. People just figure "Well there couldent be so much corruption, or some of it would have come my way." And the fellow that has received any of it naturally he is in favor of a continuation of the policy.

The Democrats were supposed to have started it in what was called Tammany Hall. But a good thing cant be restricted and is bound to spread. So the Republicans had their eyes open for all new wrinkles that would help them stay on the U. S. Pension list. So like everything else they took it and improved on it and brought corruption up to the high standard that it is today.

The Democrats always were a kind of a cheap lot. They never had much money to operate on. They were always kinder doing business on a shoe string basis. The type of Man they had with them went in more for Oratory than he did for Stocks and Bonds. They would rather make a Speech than a Dollar. They cultivated their voices instead of their finances.

You give a Democrat a high hat and a frock coat and put him on the speakers list, and he would turn down the chairmanship of the board of a big corporation. Give him a horse in the parade every year and that was just about all the glory he wanted.

The Democratic graft was mostly confined to sorter rounding the Saloon keepers into line with a Campaign collection every year. They thought that was just about the height of

"Big Business." I guess it was because they dident know there was any other business. They dident know that a man that was owner of some mines, or lumber or coal, might also dig up something for the pot. (If promised a little break in the Tarriff, or Railroad rates, or suppressed opposition.) But their mind was on a Saloon and thats as high as they could elevate it. So the Republicans just was wise enough to see that the same principal applied to one business as to the other. If it was good for the Saloons to stand in with the Government, why it was good for all other business. So they commenced working out the idea in a big way. The men who were thinking of running for office got to looking 'round their various States and seeing what some other men wanted, and they went to them and said, "If you will sorter help me out at the poles, I think I can help you out getting these big things."

While the Democrat was still fooling his time away with the "Jitney" fellow the Republicans said, "There is only one way to be in Politics and thats to be in a big way. Whats the use of being a Piker?" So instead of getting a hundred dollars from some poor little Guy, they grabbed off a couple of thousand from the big fellow that was looking for something worth while, and they just kept working and building their business right up, till, look what it is today.

There is two types of Larceny, Petty and Grand, and the courts will really give you a longer sentence for Petty than they do for Grand. They are supposed to be the same in the eyes of the law, but the Judges always put a little extra on you for Petty, which is a kind of a fine for stupidness. "If thats all you got you ought to go to jail longer."

But the parties will never be changed as long as we live, for you cant change human nature. You cant broaden a mans vision if he wasent born with one. And another thing, its hard to get people to believe a thing as Corruption, when its something that has always been going on. These deals gradually come under the heading of legitimate Campaign business.

You promise something in return for something whether it is a Post Office, or an Oil well. Its what the Lawyers call "Sharp practice."

Its going to be awful hard to make an issue of corruption. Its like the poor, its always been with us.

If you promise a man that if you are made Senator, that he will be made a Judge, why you have sold him something. His votes have helped you to get your salary. You might promise him a river to get a damn built on, but you have always promised something, either directly or indirectly, and you cant get voters to distinguish the difference, IF *there is any.*

June 10, 1928

Today being Sunday (even in a political convention) I just got an idea I would see just how religious all these politicians really are, as I had heard that religion might play some part in the Fall festivities. So I grab a cab and rush from one church to the other all over town, and not a single candidate, or delegate, or even alternate, was among the worshipers.

Still, this Fall, in the campaign, you will hear them get up and shout "Our religion is the bulwark of our great and glorious country; we must continue to be God-fearing people; our Church is our salvation." Well, our churches are our salvation, but some of those babies won't be among those rescued.

June 11, 1928

Well, I just got tired milling around the Hotel Lobbies all this time and I just made up my mind to go right where the Convention was being held. So when Andy Mellon come I just headed for his quarters. He had always been mighty nice to me and laughed at my little Jokes at the Dinners. So he had a Senator who was acting as a Doorman let me right in. To make sure that I would get in I took my tax receipt with me to show him that I did all I could to make his Department make a good showing, for I knew how hard he is trying to make us forget Alexander Hamilton.

"How are you, Mr. Mellon, the whole town has been waiting for you?"

"Hello, Will, I am glad to see you. How is your personal Campaign getting on?"

"I am doing about as well as all the other Candidates here with the exception of the one that will be nominated. Who are your Pennsylvania Delegation for?"

"Well, I haven't told them yet."

"If Hoover will keep you in your present job will you be for him?"

"Certainly, but he hasn't said that he would."

"Would you like to be President yourself?"

"No, I care not who is a Country's President, just so I can handle its money."

June 15, 1928

Wow! She is all over, Hoover and Curtis. The Republican Party owed Curtis something, but I didn't think they would be so low down as to pay him that way. He used to be floor walker of the Republican Party on the Senate floor. Now he will be Timekeeper.

Another Preacher prayed this morning and had to read his Prayer. There hasn't been a one that could make an impromptu prayer. This one was Methodist, and he wanted us "to look to the Hills for wisdom" and here we were nominating Charley Curtis from the plains of Kansas, where a five foot ash head would constitute a precipice. This Preacher prayed for Plymouth Rock. But it's Boulder Dam we are after now. There is no appropriation goes with Plymouth Rock.

I hate to say it, but the Women that spoke were all terrible. Well, they were pretty near as bad as the men, that will give you an idea how bad they were.

June 24, 1928

Everything is as quiet, restful, and beautiful, you wouldn't think there was a Democrat in a thousand miles. Been here three days, haven't heard a cheer, a Band, an Argument, or even an echo.

I wouldn't stay for the thing, but I know that a Democrat is just like a Baby. If it's hollering and making a lot of noise, there is nothing serious the matter with it. But if it's quiet and still and don't pay much attention to anything, why that's when it's really dangerous.

The Kansas City Convention took the life out of this one in more ways than one. You know you wouldn't feel so good either, if someone had just announced to you ten days ago, that it was Tunney that you were to meet in the finals.

But there is bound to be some comedy coming and here is the reason.

Since Prohibition was unearthed nine years ago, there has only been one argument invented that a Politician when he is cornered can duck behind, and that is the old Applesauce, "I am for Law Enforcement."

Now the Republicans held their Convention first, and naturally they grabbed this lone tree to hide behind. Now that leaves the Democrats out in the open. If they say anything about Prohibition, they either got to say, "It ought to be modified," or "It shouldn't be modified." They can't duck behind the old "Alibi" tree, "I am for Law Enforcement," for there is only room for one back there, and a Republican is already hiding there.

If I had been the Democrats I would have held my Convention first so I could have grabbed that "Alibi" first, if I had had to hold it three years ago.

Now naturally, the logical thing to do if it was a "Legitimate" business would be to nominate with Smith another wet as Vice President, and also put into the Platform a plank on modification, and have the whole prohibition thing out, on a straight out issue, and let the Voters settle it once and for all. But Politics is not a "Legitimate" business, and they won't do it that way.

Why? Because they don't know if there is more Wet Votes, or Dry Votes. So they are afraid to take a chance. So they will try to "straddle" the same way the Republicans did.

So, if these Boys are not shouting and singing down here, it's because they not only have a Convention on their hands, but a PROBLEM.

So there is bound to be some laughs, and they will be serious and Unintentional, which are the best laughs in the World.

June 28, 1928

Senator George rallied the drys about him last night. But when they left the Hall and the Smith delegates got their corkscrews working, George was left stranded on a pile of emptys higher than the Convention Hall.

Franklin Roosevelt, a fine and wonderful man who has devoted his life to nominating Al Smith, did his act from memory.

Franklin Roosevelt could have gotten far in the Democratic party himself, but he has this act all perfected, and don't like to go to the trouble of learning something else.

It was a fine speech. It always has been, but it's always been ahead of its time. Now he has 'em believing it. The only part I didn't agree with is where he said that Al was "Good to Women, and Children, and Dumb animals," and he insinuated that the Republican President and nominee were not.

Now Franklin, you are wrong about the Republicans and the Dumb Animals. They just thrive on Dumb Animals. They are like Lincoln with the poor. They must love 'em for they have so many of them in the party. And I even believe that the Republicans like children. Not perhaps as children, but they are the material of which voters are made in a few years. So I believe the Republicans would be kind to 'em just so they would grow into manhood quicker.

I have heard so much at this Convention about "Getting back to the old Jeffersonian principles" that being an amateur, I am in doubt as to why they LEFT THEM in the first place.

All you hear about here is the amount of graft and corruption. But each man wants to put his Nominee where it is going on. Why if these offices are as bad as they say they are, I wouldn't want a decent friend of mine to even want to go in them.

They are stalling with the Platform, and when it is ready there is not a wire walker in America that can stand on it.

It's got to a point here now where State Delegations will "caucus" on a half quart.

August 17, 1928

From now till November neither of the boys can be themselves. They are on parade. They are eating and sleeping in a show window. They are acting every minute.

Coolidge is the only one nobody ever knew when he was acting and when he wasn't. He was like a ukelele. You can't tell when somebody is playing one or just monkeying with it.

October 2, 1928

Al Smith unanimously nominated Franklin D. Roosevelt today for Governor of New York.

Roosevelt will always be remembered as the man that any time as many as three persons met, either in conference or convention, would arise and nominate Al Smith for President. You could just wake him in the middle of the night and he would start to nominate Al.

His nominating days over, he is now going to take up politics seriously. He is a Roosevelt by blood, but a namesake politically. If he had retained his splendid qualities and stayed with the Republican end of the family, he would have been President, but I doubt if he could have retained those qualities and been Republican.

October 31, 1928

Well, the promising season ends next Tuesday, and at about 8 o'clock that same night the "Alibi" season opens and lasts for the next four years.

To show you what campaign promises amount to, can you remember back a few weeks ago when the promise was made on both sides that "the campaign was to be run on a high plane"?

This campaign ends Tuesday, but it will take two generations to sweep up the dirt.

November 4, 1928

I have been studying the two parties and here is the difference: Hoover wants all the drys and as many wets as possible. Smith wants all the wets and as many drys as he can get. Hoover says he will relieve the farmer even if he has to appoint a commission.

Hoover says the tariff will be kept up. Smith says the tariff will not be lowered.

Hoover is strongly in favor of prosperity. Smith highly indorses prosperity.

Hoover wants no votes merely on account of religion. Smith wants no votes solely on religious grounds. Both would accept Mohammedan votes if offered.

Hoover would like to live in the White House. Smith is not adverse to living in the White House. In order to get in there either one will promise the voters anything from perpetual motion to eternal salvation.

February 28, 1929

No wonder Hoover can't get a Cabinet.

Big men won't take it for they won't take a chance on a Senate insult. If he has ever earned more than a Senator, he is in League with big business. If he ever drove a Standard Oil truck, or was a bookkeeper in a Morgan bank, he is in league with monopolies. If he is independently rich, he is in league with the devil.

But if he has never done anything, and been a financial failure at that, he will pass the Senate as a brother, and every time Hoover finds a man of that type he is a Democrat.

And that's another stanch rule. You can't use even an able man from the other party. That would revert to democracy, and not politics.

Beverly Hills, June 9, 1929

There is an epidemic of towns trying to claim the birth of the Republican Party.

All they have to do to find where the Republican Party was formed is find where the first corporation was formed. It was incorporated for the sole purpose of taking over the management and finances of the United States.

Its slogan is: "Stay with us, we can afford to pay more than our competitors."

November 1, 1929

Mr. Hoover is becoming a typical American President by becoming disgusted with the Senate early in his Administration.

Distrust of the Senate by Presidents started with Washington who wanted to have 'em courtmartialed. Jefferson proposed life imprisonment for 'em, old Andy Jackson said "To hell with 'em," and got his wish. Lincoln said the Lord must have hated 'em for he made so few of 'em. Roosevelt whittled a big stick and beat on 'em for six years. Taft just laughed at 'em and grew fat. They drove Wilson to an early grave. Coolidge never let 'em know what he wanted, so they never knew how to vote against him, and Mr. Hoover took 'em serious, thereby making his only political mistake.

November 19, 1929

America already holds the record for freak movements. Now we have a new one. It's called, "Restoring Confidence." Rich men who never had a mission in life outside of watching a stock ticker, are working day and night "Restoring Confidence."

Now I am not unpatriotic, and I want to do my bit, so I hereby offer my services to my President, my Country, and my friends around Old Trinity Church, New York, to do anything (outside of serving on a Commission) that I can, in this great movement.

But you will have to give me some idea where "Confidence" is, and just what you want it restored to.

Beverly Hills, February 21, 1930

On account of us being a democracy and run by the people, we are the only nation in the world that has to keep a government for four years, no matter what it does.

September 7, 1930

There is going to be a lot of changes in Washington when the boys gather after the next election.

Democrats are going to make some big gains for the people are sore at Hoover because they had to go back to work and couldent just make a living by buying a stock and selling it to the other fellow at a raise.

Beverly Hills, October 7, 1930

Nick Longworth on the air last night hit on a humorous angle that I had never thought of, and I bet none of you had either. He blamed the Democratic Party for the financial depression that is enveloping the world. Its really the biggest advertisement that the Democratic Party have ever had. Why if they was that important, they wouldn't be Democrats. Did you ever notice, there has never been a year when alibis were as scarce?

Los Angeles, November 2, 1930

Come pretty near having two holidays of equal importance in the same week, Halloween and Election, and of the two election provides us the most fun. On Halloween they put pumpkins on their heads, and on Election they don't have to.

Los Angeles, November 4, 1930

Did you ever figure what constitutes our modern "representative"? The one that can bring home the new Federal postoffice, even if they wasn't using the old one; Federal aid for roads, that nobody may ever drive on, and a government Dam. That's the height of Statesmanship is to come home with a dam. Even if you got nowhere to put it. Just raid the national treasury enough and you will soon be referred to as a "Statesman."

November 16, 1930

Well all I know is just what I read in the papers, and all I have read in the past week is about the Democratic uprising of November 4th. It was my birthday and the Boys of the party really did themselves proud in my honor. The Republicans were looking for a punch in the jaw, but not for a kick in the pants at the same time. Why there was men beat at this wake that thought they had a deed on their seat.

Joe Robinson is mighty liable to be the Democratic Nominee in '32. It will be between him and Franklyn D. Roosevelt, and they are both mighty fine men. Joe if they want a dry, and Roosevelt if they want a wet. But the wets seemed to kinder swamp everything at this meelee and are gaining strength every day, so in '32 it looks like the wet Candidate will have the edge at the Nomination. Looks like the Democrats nominated their president yesterday, Franklin D. Roosevelt.

January 6, 1931

I dont want to discourage Mr. Mellon and his carefully balanced budget, but you let this country get hungry and they are going to eat, no matter what happens to budgets, income taxes or Wall Street values.

Washington mustent forget who rules when it comes to a showdown.

May 31, 1931

President Hoover made a speech Saturday at Valley Forge. He found somebody that was worse off than we are but he had to go back 150 years in history to do it.

Beverly Hills, June 22, 1931

When some nation wants us to help 'em out they use the same old "gag" that we should exert our "moral leadership" and we, like a yap, believe it, when as a matter of truth no nation wants any other nation exerting a "Moral leadership" over 'em even if they had one. If we ever pass out as a great nation we ought to put on our tombstone "America died from a delusion that she had moral leadership."

June 28, 1931

Will you do me one favor. If you see or hear of anybody proposing my name either humorously or semiseriously for any political office will you maim said party and send me the bill.

A comedian can only last till he either takes himself serious or his audience takes him serious and I dont want either one of those to happen to me.

I wont run no matter how bad the country will need a comedian by that time. I couldent run anyhow because I cant make up my mind which side to run on, "wet" or "dry."

I dont know which side the most votes is on and I cant straddle it for that's where all the rest of the candidates are.

What is there to worry anybody over the next nominations anyhow? It's one year away but the candidates will be Hoover and Curtis versus Franklyn D. Roosevelt and some Western or Southern Democratic Governor.

I have looked politics and the movies both over and while they have much in common I believe politics is the most common, so I will stay with the movies. It's hard to give up the old White House but it would be much harder to take politics seriously.

So long, Boys, the first ex-candidate.

Beverly Hills, August 19, 1931

The Russians got a five year plan. Maybe it's terrible, but they got one. We been two years just trying to get a plan.

We will just have to save ourselves accidentally. That's the way we stumbled upon prosperity.

Asking a Democrat [Owen D. Young] to feed the country is almost a "believe it or not." Young is in a tough spot. If he feeds 'em through the winter he will only be keeping 'em alive to vote the Republican ticket next fall. Voters can't remember back over two months.

October 25, 1931 [radio broadcast]

We used to be told that depression was just a state of mind but starvation has changed that impression. Depression is a state of health. It's moved from the mind to the stomach. And it aint really depression either; it's just a return to normalcy. We are just getting back to earth. We are back to two-bit meals and cotton underwear and off $1.50 steaks and silk under rompers. The trouble is America is just muscle bound from holding a steering wheel. The only place we are calloused from work is the bottom of our driving toe.

This country has just got one problem: it's not the balancing of Mr. Mellon's budget (that's his problem); it's not the League of Nations; it's not the silver question; not a one of those problems mean a thing in the world to us *as long as we have seven million of our own out of work*. Our only problem is to arrange the affairs of this prosperous country (yes, prosperous right now) so that a man that wants to work can get work and give him a more equal division of the wealth the country produces.

Now if our big men in the next year cant fix that, well they just aint big men, that's all.

What does prohibition amount to if your neighbor's children are not eating? It's food, not drink is our problem now. We were so afraid the poor people might drink, now we fixed it so they cant eat.

We got more wheat, more corn, more food, more cotton, more money in the banks, more everything in the world than any nation that ever lived ever had, yet we are starving to death.

We are the first nation in the history of the world to go to the poor house in an automobile.

Our potter's fields are surrounded by granaries full of grain. Now if there ain't something "cockeyed" in an arrangement like that, then this microphone in front of me is a mousetrap.

Now a miracle can't happen and all these people get a job over night. It's going to take time. So they must be fed and cared for perhaps all winter.

Every one of us that have anything got it by the aid of

these very people. There is not an unemployed man in the country that hasent contributed to the wealth of every millionaire in America.

The working classes dident bring this one. It was the big boys that thought the financial drunk was going to last forever and over bought, over merged and over capitalized.

Now the people are not asking for money. They are asking for a job. But there is no job, towns and cities cant say they havent got the money. For the same amount of money is in the country as when these folks had their share. Somebody's got it.

Last winter we dident realize the need. But this winter we got no excuse. Its been shown to us all summer.

Now dont wait for the government to feed these people. I have seen lots of audiences and heard lots of appeals, but I have yet to see one where the people knew the need, and the cause was there, that they dident come through. Even Europe who hates us and thinks we are arrogant, bad-mannered and everything else, will tell you that we are liberal.

Dog-gone it, our folks are liberal. I don't know anything about America's being "fundamentally sound" and all that after-dinner "hooey," but I do know that America is "fundamentally generous."

October 27, 1931

Well, this was Navy Day. We celebrated it this year by lopping off its appropriations. Wake up some morning with a war on our hands then the mad rush will be on to build battleships, give the companies big bonuses to get 'em done quick. Then we will have to go through that silk-shirt buying period again.

England is a pretty wise old bird. She relinquished her world's financial supremacy but didn't relinquish any ships. Shows which she thinks the most valuable to a country.

January 22, 1932

See where Congress passed a two billion dollar bill to relieve Banker's mistakes and loan to new industries. You can always count on us helping those who have lost part of their fortunes but our whole history records nary a case where the loan was for the man who had absolutely nothing. Our theory is to help those who can get along even if they don't get it.

February 12, 1932

This is an election year. Every statesman wants to vote appropriations but is afraid to vote taxes. The oratory of Washington is on "reconstruction" but the heart of Washington is on November fourth 1932.

February 24, 1932

You cant get a room in Washington. Every hotel is jammed to the doors with bankers from all over America to get their "hand out."

I have asked the following prominent men in America this question: "What group have been more responsible for this financial mess, the farmers? labor? Manufacturers? Tradesmen or who?" And every man—Henry Ford, Garner, Newt. Baker, Borah, Curtis, and a real financier, Barney Baruch—without a moment's hesitation said, "Why, the bankers."

Yet they have the honor of being the first group to go on the "dole" in America.

Beverly Hills, May 3, 1932

See where the two English scientists were able, headline said, "to split the atom." The world is not bad enough as it was, now they go and split up the atom. That's the last straw. We expect the Democrats to split, the country to split over prohibition, but we always felt that the old "atom" would remain intact. It was certainly a big disappointment to me. Come on boys, lets up and atom.

June 28, 1932

Ah! They was Democrats today. They fought, they fit, they split and adjourned in a dandy wave of dissension. Thats the old Democratic spirit.

A whole day fighting over what? A President? No. A Platform? No. "Well then what did they take up eleven hundred deligates and 12 thousand spectators time for?" Why to see whether Huey Long (the Louisiana porcupine) was to sit on the floor or in the gallery. Well the "porcupine sticks right on the floor." And the other four hours was fighting over who would be chairman of a convention thats already a week old.

You cant beat the old Democrats for comedy. Time means no more to them than to a Mexican "Burro."

The Democrats are the only known race of people that give a dinner and then wont decide who will be toastmaster till they all get to the dinner and fight over it. No job is ever too small for them to split over. But you would a loved 'em today. They was real **Democrats**.

July 13, 1932

Here is a funny situation. The women Anti-prohibitionists said, "We will support the party that comes out for direct repeal." And they would if it had been the Republican Party. But as luck would have it, it was those "mangy" Democrats instead. Now most of these women are wealthy Republicans. And they are having a time now trying to get out of it.

They want prohibition repealed all right but not bad enough to repeal the Republican Party with it. They want it wet but not wet enough to be Democratic.

In other words politics is thicker than beer.

August 1, 1932

This is not an election of partys or policies this fall. Its an election where both sides really need the work.

August 5, 1932

Every year it gets harder and harder to tell the difference between a Republican and a Democrat (course outside of the looks). But I believe I have found out the sure way to tell one from another this year. Its just the way they talk.

The Republican says, "Well things could have been worse" and the Democrat says "How?"

September 16, 1932

Roosevelt is headed West. Says he is just out to meet the folks. But he will give preference to anyone of legal age and a registered voter.

Mr. Hoover who originally wasnt going further west during the campaign than the Potomac, has started looking at time tables. Politicians in order to hold the real dyed-in-the-wool radio nut are crooning their speeches.

San Antonio, October 6, 1932

Been flying, train-riding, automobiling, horseback and buggy riding over Texas for thirty-three years and I've never seen a tenth of it. If it had been Europe, eighty wars would have been fought over it. There is single ranches here bigger than France. Counties bigger than England. Saddle horse pastures big as Alsace-Lorraine. The lakes of Switzerland would be buffalo wallows in Texas. It's located between Mexico and the United States to keep Mexico from annexing the United States. It's so far to town that the cowboys started in to vote for "Teddy" and arrived in time to register for "Franklin." Its "Vatican" is the town of Uvalde, its pope is John Nance Garner. Its sole industry is internal politics. It's so big that no one Governor can handle it; they have to have a man and his wife. It's the only State where a Republican has to have a passport to enter.

P.S. They would use California for a telephone booth down here.

New York, November 1, 1932

There should be a moratorium called on candidates speeches. They have both called each other everything in the world they can think of. From now on they are just talking themselves out of votes. The high office of President of the United States has degenerated into two ordinarily fine men being goaded on by their political leeches into saying things that if they were in their right minds, they wouldn't think of saying. Imagine Mr. Hoover last night "any change of policies will bring disaster to every fireside in America." Of all the conceit. This country is a thousand times bigger than any two men in it, or any two parties in it. These big politicians are so serious about themselves and their parties. This country has gotten where it is in spite of politics, not by the aid of it. That we have carried as much political bunk as we have and still survived shows we are a super nation. If by some divine act of Providence we could get rid of both these parties and hired some good man, like any other big business does, why that would be sitting pretty. This calamity was brought on by the actions of the people of the whole world and its weight will be lifted off by the actions of the people of the whole world, and not by a Republican or a Democrat. So you two boys just get the weight of the world off your shoulders and go fishing. Both of you claim you like to fish, now instead of calling each other names till next Tuesday, why you can do everybody a big favor by going fishing, and you will be surprised but the old U.S. will keep right on running while you boys are sitting on the bank. Then come back next Wednesday and we will let you know which one is the lesser of the two evils of you.

November 10, 1932

Well the returns are pretty much all in. All but Kentucky. They got a law they can't count their votes till everybody sobers up, so it will be quite a little bit before we get them.

I was surprised at the vote the Republicans poled in Mississippi and Louisiana. I thought there was more postoffices there than there is.

By the way what ever become of the Roosevelts that claimed they was only eighth couzins to this one?

November 14, 1932

Herbert has invited Franklyn down to see him. Now on the face of it that looks like the last word in hospitality. But lets look that gift horse in the face. Is Herbert just crazy about Franklyn? No, "Children," prominent men are never crazy about each other. Herbert's in a hole. But if Franklyn confers with him and then something is done why they split the blame 50-50.

November 26, 1932

The last few years under Mr. Coolidge and Mr. Hoover there had grown the old original idea of the Republican Party that it was the Party of the rich. And I think that was the biggest contributing part in their defeat.

This last election was a revulsion of feeling that went back a long way ahead of the hard times. Mr. Hoover reaped the benefits of the arrogance of the party when it was going strong.

Well after that twenty-eight election there was no holding

'em. They really did think they had "Hard Times" cornered once and for all. Merger on top of merger. Get two non-paying things merged and then issue more stock to the Public. Consolidations and "Holding Companies." Those were the "Inventions" that every voter that had bought during the "Cuckoo" days were gunning for at this last election.

Saying that all the big vote was just against hard times is not all so. They was voting against not being advised that all those foreign loans was not too solid. They was voting because they had never been told or warned to the contrary that every big consolidation might not be just the best investment. You know the people kinder look on our Government to tell 'em and kinder advise 'em. A many an old bird really got sore at Coolidge but could only take it out on Hoover.

Big business sure got big, but it got big by selling its stocks and not by selling its products. No scheme was halted by the Government as long as somebody would buy the stock. It could have been a plan to deepen the Atlantic Ocean and it would have had the indorsement of the proper department in Washington, and stocks would have gone on the market.

This election was lost four and five and six years ago, not just this year. They dident start thinking of the old common fellow till just as they started out on the election tour. The money was all appropriated for the top in the hopes that it would trickle down to the needy. Mr. Hoover was an engineer. He knew that water trickled down. Put it uphill and let it go and it will reach the dryest little spot.

But he dident know that money trickled up. Give it to the people at the bottom and the people at the top will have it before night anyhow. But it will at least have passed through the poor fellow's hands. They saved the big banks but the little ones went up the flue.

No, sir, the little fellow felt that he never had a chance and he dident till November the Eighth. And did he grab it?

The whole idea of Government relief for the last few years has been to loan somebody more money, so they could go further in debt. It aint much relief to just transfer your debts from one party to another adding a little more in the bargain.

No, I believe the "Boys" from all they had and hadent done had this coming to 'em.

December 22, 1932

I dont want to lay the blame on the Republicans for the depression. They're not smart enough to think up all those things that have happened.

February 21, 1933

Every man, every industry in the United States was hit by depression. Before you start dealing out public funds to help, you should first find out if we have enough money to give part of them a sandwich and leave the rest to go hungry.

But, no, they didn't do that. They just started right in by helping the bankers, so every man, woman and child in the U.S. thinks, and rightfully that they have got as much right to get some sort of government aid as the bankers, the railroads, and big business. They got the first U.S. dole, and it will never be finished till the last one hundred and twenty million reach in and get theirs.

The Rogue's gallery photograph show us that three of Roosevelt's cabinet escaped from the Senate. That's like going to the Old Men's Home to get athletes.

July 13, 1933

This fellow Roosevelt can close the banks, he can tell industry how much to pay, and how many hours to work, he
can hold back the sun, he can evaporate the water. But when
he demands that a postmaster has to be able to read, that's
carrying dictatorship too far. He is monkeying with the very
fundamentals of American political parties. I tell you this
suggestion of his is bordering on treason.

The idea of a postmaster being able to read! It looks like
an undemocratic move to favor the college man. I tell you
he will ruin the Democratic Party. We mustn't let him get
away with it.

Beverly Hills, September 20, 1933

To inflate, or not to inflate, that is the Democratic question. Whether its nobler in the minds to suffer the slings and
arrows of southern politicians, or to take up inflation against
a sea of economists, and by opposing, end them. To expand,
to inflate, to inflate perchance to dream. Aye, there's the rub.
For in that sleep of inflation, what dreams may come, puzzle
the will, and makes us doubtful whether to bear those ills
we have, than fly to others we know not of.

January 4, 1934

Mr. Roosevelt proposed in his speech that the NRA and a
lot of these other government regulated business ethics
would be made permanent. Well that was a terrible blow to
some business men. They had figured they would only be

required to be honest by the government till the emergency was over.

Beverly Hills, February 12, 1934

Papers today say, "what would Lincoln do today?" Well, in the first place he wouldn't chop any wood, he would trade his ax in on a Ford. Being a Republican he would vote the Democratic ticket. Being in sympathy for the under dog he would be classed as a Radical Progressive. Having a sense of humor he would be called eccentric.

Santa Monica, April 22, 1934

Saturday President Roosevelt had at the White House, his graduating class of Harvard, 1904. There was over 300 of em, and all Republicans. I think he was just quietly rubbing it in on em. For the press couldent name a one of em that anybody had ever heard of. I think F.D. with his usual sense of humor, was just in a subtle way impressing on the boys "if there hadent been a Democrat in the class youse guys would never got to even see the inside of the White House." It only illustrates that every Harvard class should have one Democrat to rescue it from oblivion.

Beverly Hills, May 29, 1934

Walking Monday afternoon through one of the most famous of the historical California missions, San Juan Capistrano, (half way to San Diego) and who should I find in meditation before a wonderful old picture (depicting the joy of harvest, and the merrymaking at the sale of the crops), it was Secretary of Agriculture Wallace, tears were in his eyes, and he kept murmuring lowly, as he turned to the altar, "Oh What have I done Father that I couldent have been Secretary of Agriculture in days like those."

June 10, 1934

I am going to tell you something that hasent been brought up in public for years. I am going to say a few words for the Republican Party.

Spelled, R-E-P-U-B-L-I-C-A-N.

Your fathers and grandfathers will remember the name. The reason I know it's not been spoken of is that you cant speak of something unless you think of it and you cant think of it unless something happens to bring the name up. I got to thinking of the Johnston flood, the Galveston tidal wave, the Chicago fire, and my thoughts naturally drifted to the Republicans. Not that they were responsible for the above events, but there has been lots of people always been awful suspicious.

Now where has that Republican party gone? Such extermination of an entire race has never before been recorded. History records that they were rather a kindly people and were good to their young. Never warlike—in fact, they would step aside and egg the Democrats on till they declared war, then afterwards say, It was you that did it.

They were a thrifty race. Controlled most of the money. They had a certain foresight and would take over the reigns of government about the time things were going good. And when they saw pestilence and famine was about to be visited on the land, they would slip it back to the Democrats.

The Democrats were a kind of a semi-heathen tribe. They were a nomad race. They could live on little because they had never had much.

But they don't live on little when they get in office.

Their greatest traits were optimism and humor. You had to have optimism to join the Democratic Party and you had to have humor to stick with 'em. But they had a certain native shrewdness. They figured out that the one way to get the money away from the Republicans was to put a—bounty —or (as the Latin calls it) taxes on 'em.

Bounty or taxes is a thing you pay if you have anything, and if you havent you dont. Well, the Democrats knowing the Republicans had it, and knowing they dident, put it on 'em.

The theory was that while the Republicans are smart enough to make money the Democrats are smart enough to get in office every 2 or three times a century and take it away from 'em. And do these Republicans howl when this bounty —or taxes—hits 'em! They yowl like a she bear being deprived of its young.

And the Democrats are heartless. If they can get their hands in a Republican's pocket to get it out is just like trying to pull a badger out.

So the whole thing is just a revolving wheel. One party gets in and through a full stomach and a swell head oversteps themselves and out they go. And the other gets in. And that's as it should be. For there would be no living with one of 'em if they knew the other one dident exist.

Now the Republicans admit they are the rich ones, that they are smarter and can make money faster, so it's a good thing the old Democrats come along and level 'em off every once in a while. If they are so smart let 'em go out and make some more.

So they tell me that in quite a few places around over the country there is scattering Republican campfires. They are coming out of their caves and hidden valleys, director's meetings, and coupon clipping rooms and are sharpening up their campaign speeches to try and get back into the old teepees and post offices.

So that about concludes the bedside story of the two great Political parties which we work night and day to support.

November 25, 1934

This Election changed a lot of folks' idea of things. They have kinder become reconciled to the fact that the folks are not so excited about this great debt that is piling up as they thought they were. This thing of worrying about what our grand children are going to have to pay, well most folks say, "Well our children seem to think they are smarter than we are, so if they are the chances are that their children will be smarter than they are, so if they are that smart why maybe they can think of some substitute for money that they can pay off their national debt with, and they will wonder why we dident have a bigger one. Maybe we wont print the money, but they will, so what difference does it make to us?

Beverly Hills, March 13, 1935

Say did you read about what Mr. Roosevelt said about those "Holding Companies." A Holding Company is a thing where you hand an accomplice the goods while the policeman searches you.

July 4, 1935

That liberty we got 159 years ago was a great thing. Never was as much politics indulged in under the guise of "Freedom and liberty."

They was 5 percent what George Washington did, and 95 percent what the speaker intended to do. What this country needs on July the Fourth is not more "Liberty or more freedom." Its a Roman candle that only shoots out of one end.

A Century Ago

Voices from the Cracker Barrel

Voices from the Cracker Barrel
(1815–1885)

Between the American Revolution and the triumph of popular sovereignty, the literary development of the humorous possibilities inherent in native traits and characters proceeded apace. The struggles to safeguard the newly created nation against great odds widened Americans' awareness of their own regional and national peculiarities. Poor Richard, Yankee Doodle, and Brother Jonathan in various ways captured qualities of personality identifiable among rural New Englanders—thrift, industry, and godliness, to be admired, penury, cautiousness, and simplicity, to be ridiculed. In almanacs and travel books, read from one end of the country to the other, comic figures emerged such as the Yankee, the dull-witted Dutchman, the Southern fire-eater, the militiaman bumpkin, the heavy-drinking, hard-fighting frontiersman, the roistering keelboatman of the half-horse and half-alligator species. Newspaper portrayals of comic types appeared only sporadically, however. "At almost any time," Walter Blair observed, "had these characterizations gone a few steps farther, handled by competent authors, widespread and extensive depiction might have resulted."

By 1830, Down East and frontier styles of humor were abundantly represented in almanacs, newspapers, and popular dramas, and they would flourish thereafter. British models of humorous fiction and satiric essays afforded workable hints to American writers. The better humorists were native to the sections of the United States they described. Their function was to distill the comic essence of regional life. Everywhere they portrayed local scenes in lively vernacular. They uncovered the humorous depths of village society Down East, explored the outcroppings of backwoods wit and slapstick along the rivers, turnpikes, and canals stretching into the interior, and recorded mirthfully the roistering flavor of the Old Southwest. By the middle of the nineteenth century, Americans were familiar with the fundamental elements of their countrymen's humor. And for several decades afterward literary humorists in great numbers practiced, as Blair put it, "variations on themes already announced." A great deal of the best of their writings was political in content.

SEBA SMITH
[Major Jack Downing]
(1792-1868)

Seba Smith's first Jack Downing letter appeared in the
Daily Courier of Portland, Maine, in January 1830. The
Daily Courier, the first daily newspaper north or east of
Boston, had just been launched by Smith. It professed
political independence, an attitude at that time more likely
to win distrust than popular support. Yet Smith shrewdly
foresaw that witty observations on the political state of
Maine could add both spice and circulation to his newspaper.

A deadlock in the legislature and strong partisan feelings among Maine's citizenry afforded the right atmosphere. There was little outright novelty in Downing's letters and "other dockyments." The ingredients of Downing's
letters were the regional humor of the Down East variety,
frontier gusto, almanac witticism, wry folk wisdom, and
an epistolary style, though none was the invention of Seba
Smith. Whatever was new and unusual was the regularity
of Downing's adventures and his continuous popular acclaim. Politics was Downing's central interest from the
very beginning. With his appearance a vibrant strand of
American literary humor began to be regularly heard.

It was at a critical juncture in Maine's public affairs that
Seba Smith, as he later recalled, "wishing to show the ridiculous position of the legislature in its true light, and

also by something out of the common track of newspaper writing, to give increased interest and popularity to his little daily paper, bethought himself of the plan to bring a green, unsophisticated lad from the country into town with a load of ax-handles, hoop poles, and other notions for sale, and while waiting the movements of a dull market let him blunder into the halls of the legislature, and after witnessing for some days their strange doings sit down and write an account of them to his friends at home in his own plain language."

Smith's plan was enormously successful. Within about a year Downing's letters became national in character, their purely regional quality diminishing. Major Jack Downing assumed the guise of confidential adviser to Presidents, from Andrew Jackson to Franklin Pierce. Downing's grotesque accounts of political goings on were soon being copied and imitated by newspapers throughout the entire country. Even the character Jack Downing was appropriated by other writers. The *Major Jack Downing Letters* written by Charles Augustus Davis for the New York *Advertiser* enjoyed a wider acclaim for a time than the original creation, owing perhaps to the sharper bite of Davis' satire.

Three decades after it all began, Seba Smith's accumulated wit and wisdom was published as Major Jack Downing's *My Thirty Years Out of the Senate.* This was a telling thrust at Thomas Hart Benton's *Thirty Years' View* of his long career in the United States Senate. It was also a measure of Smith's superiority. Seba Smith and his popular mouthpiece, Major Jack Downing, knew that there was "an *outside* as well as an inside to everything," including politics. The immortal Sam Patch had postulated, it was widely known, that "some things can be done as well as others."

Readers should be aware of certain facts. Both Whigs and Democrats claimed victory at Maine's polls in 1830. Hence it took six weeks merely to organize the legislature. The social status of the second wife of President Jackson's Secretary of War, John H. Eaton, became a political issue in 1831 dividing the supporters of Vice-President John C. Calhoun and Martin Van Buren. The Democrats' nomination of Franklin Pierce for President in 1852 filled many a loyal heart with dark forebodings at the party's apparently slim prospects for victory.

Letter I

Portland, Monday, Jan. 18, 1830.

To Cousin Ephraim Downing, up in Downingville:

DEAR COUSIN EPHRAIM:—I now take my pen in hand to let you know that I am well, hoping these few lines will find you enjoying the same blessing. When I come down to Portland I didn't think o' staying more than three or four days, if I could sell my load of ax handles, and mother's cheese, and cousin Nabby's bundle of footings; but when I got here I found Uncle Nat was gone a freighting down to Quoddy, and Aunt Sally said as how I shouldn't stir a step home till he come back agin, which won't be this month. So here I am, loitering about this great town, as lazy as an ox. Ax handles don't fetch nothing; I couldn't hardly give 'em away. Tell Cousin Nabby I sold her footings for nine-pence a pair, and took it all in cotton cloth. Mother's cheese come to seven-and-sixpence; I got her half a pound of shushon, and two ounces of snuff, and the rest in sugar. When Uncle Nat comes home I shall put my ax handles aboard of him, and let him take 'em to Boston next time he goes; I saw a feller tother day, that told me they'd fetch a good price there. I've been here now a whole fortnight, and if I could tell ye one half I've seen, I guess you'd stare worse than if you'd seen a catamount. I've been to meeting, and to the museum, and to both Legislaters, the one they call the House, and the one they call the Sinnet. I spose Uncle Joshua is in a great hurry to hear something about these Legislaters; for you know he's always reading

Seba Smith [Major Jack Downing], *My Thirty Years Out of the Senate,* New York (1859), pp. 36–40.

newspapers, and talking politics, when he can get anybody to talk with him. I've seen him when he had five tons of hay in the field well made, and a heavy shower coming up, stand two hours disputing with Squire W. about Adams and Jackson—one calling Adams a tory and a fed, and the other saying Jackson was a murderer and a fool; so they kept it up, till the rain began to pour down, and about spoilt all his hay.

Uncle Joshua may set his heart at rest about the bushel of corn that he bet 'long with the postmaster, that Mr. Ruggles would be Speaker of that Legislater they call the House; for he's lost it, slick as a whistle. As I hadn't much to do, I've been there every day since they've been a setting. A Mr. White, of Monmouth, was the Speaker the first two days; and I can't see why they didn't keep him in all the time; for he seemed to be a very clever, good-natured sort of man, and he had such a smooth, pleasant way with him, that I couldn't help feeling sorry when they turned him out and put in another. But some said he wasn't put in hardly fair; and I don't know as he was, for the first day, when they were all coming in and crowding round, there was a large, fat man, with a round, full, jolly sort of a face, I suppose he was the captain, for he got up and commanded them to come to order, and then he told this Mr. White to whip into the chair quicker than you could say Jack Robinson. Some of 'em scolded about it, and I heard some, in a little room they called the lobby, say 'twas a mean trick; but I couldn't see why, for I thought Mr. White made a capital Speaker, and when *our* company turns out, the cap'n always has a right to do as he's a mind to.

They kept disputing most all the time the first two days about a poor Mr. Roberts, from Waterborough. Some said he shouldn't have a seat because he adjourned the town meeting and wasn't fairly elected. Others said it was no such thing, and that he was elected as fairly as any of 'em. And Mr. Roberts himself said he was, and said he could bring men that would swear to it, and good men too. But, notwithstanding all this, when they came to vote, they got three or four majority that he shouldn't have a seat. And I thought it a needless piece of cruelty, for they wan't crowded, and there was a number of seats empty. But they would have it so, and the poor man had to go and stand up in the lobby.

Then they disputed awhile about a Mr. Fowler's having a seat. Some said he shouldn't have a seat, because when he was elected some of his votes were given for his father. But they were more kind to him than they were to Mr. Roberts, for they voted that he *should* have a seat; and I suppose it was because they thought he had a lawful right to inherit whatever was his father's. They all declared there was no party politics about it, and I don't think there was; for I noticed that all who voted that Mr. Roberts *should* have a seat, voted that Mr. Fowler should *not;* and all who voted that Mr. Roberts should *not* have a seat, voted that Mr. Fowler *should.* So, as they all voted *both* ways, they must have been conscientious, and I don't see how there could be any party about it.

It's a pity they couldn't be allowed to have two Speakers, for they seemed to be very anxious to choose Mr. Ruggles and Mr. Goodenow. They two had every vote except one, and if they had had *that,* I believe they would both have been chosen; as it was, however, they both came within a humbird's eye of it. Whether it was Mr. Ruggles voted for Mr. Goodenow, or Mr. Goodenow for Mr. Ruggles, I can't exactly tell; but I rather guess it was Mr. Ruggles voted for Mr. Goodenow, for he appeared to be very glad to see Mr. Goodenow in the chair, and shook hands with him as good-natured as could be. I would have given half my load of ax handles, if they could both have been elected and set up there together, they would have been so happy. But as they can't have but one Speaker at a time, and as Mr. Goodenow appears to understand the business very well, it is not likely Mr. Ruggles will be Speaker any this winter. So Uncle Joshua will have to shell out his bushel of corn, and I hope it will learn him better than to bet about politics again. Before I came from home, some of the papers said how there was a majority of ten or fifteen *National Republicans* [Whigs] in the Legislater, and the other party said there was a pretty clever little majority of *Democratic Republicans* [Democrats]. Well, now everybody says it has turned out jest as that queer little paper, called the Daily Courier, said 'twould. That paper said it was such a close rub it couldn't hardly tell which side would beat. And it's jest so, for they've been here now most a fortnight acting jest like two boys playin see-saw on a rail. First one goes up, and then 'tother; but I reckon one of the boys is rather heaviest, for once in a while he comes down chuck, and throws the other up into the air as though he would pitch him head over heels. Your loving cousin till death.

JACK DOWNING.

Letter XXII

MR. DOWNING TELLS HOW HE STRIPT UP HIS SLEEVES AND DEFENDED MR. INGHAM ON HIS FRONT DOOR-STEPS, DURING THE AFTER-CLAP THAT FOLLOWED THE BLOW-UP OF GINERAL JACKSON'S FIRST CABINET.

[*Seba Smith's editorial note of 1859:*] It will be remembered, by those whose political reminiscences extend back

My Thirty Years . . . , pp. 119–126.

so far, that General Jackson's first Cabinet blew up. In other words, the whole Cabinet resigned in a body. This came upon the country something like a thunder-clap. Very soon upon the heels of the thunder-clap came an *after-clap,* which produced a sensation throughout the country scarcely inferior to that of the thunder-clap. The thunder-clap and the after-

The Battle of the After-Clap

clap were believed to be intimately connected, and some even went so far as to say that the after-clap was the real cause of the thunder-clap. Major Downing's letter gives some of the exciting scenes of the after-clap, and perhaps a few words should be added here explanatory of the whole affair.

There was an inside view and an outside view to this Cabinet difficulty, as well as most other things in the world.

The inside view, the Senatorial view, such as Colonel Benton would take in his "Thirty Years," was something like this: Mr. Calhoun, the Vice-President, and Mr. Van Buren, the Secretary of State, were rival competitors for the successor-ship to the office of President. It came to the knowledge of the President that a proposition had been made in Mr. Monroe's Cabinet to punish General Jackson for his conduct and doings in Florida, in the Seminole War. For some time General Jackson believed that this proposition in the Cabinet came from Mr. Crawford, and that he was triumphantly de-fended by Mr. Calhoun and Mr. Adams, a statement having been published in a Western newspaper to this effect. After-ward the General learned, on the authority of Mr. Crawford and from other sources, that it was Mr. Calhoun who made the proposition to punish him, and that he was protected in the Cabinet by Mr. Crawford and Mr. Adams. And he be-lieved, as did also Mr. Crawford, that the reverse and false statement in the papers had been published at the instiga-tion of Mr. Calhoun. This, of course, produced a decided coolness, or rather a warm difficulty, between the President and the Vice-President. Mr. Calhoun thereupon published a pamphlet, addressed to the people of the United States, to explain the cause of the difficulty, and charging Mr. Van Buren with being at the bottom of all the mischief. The President and Vice-President were at sword-points, the mem-bers of the Cabinet were divided on the points of the quarrel —some of them were for Mr. Van Buren for the succession and some for Calhoun. An explosion was inevitable. The President had become attached to Mr. Van Buren, and was ready to do anything in the world for him.

It was finally determined that there must be a re-organiza-tion of the Cabinet. Mr. Ingham, Secretary of the Treasury, Mr. Branch, Secretary of the Navy, and Mr. Berrien, Attorney-General, were in favor of Mr. Calhoun; and Major Eaton, Secretary of War, and Mr. Barry, Postmaster-General, were in favor of Mr. Van Buren. In order to relieve the President from the necessity of dismissing any members of the Cabinet, Mr. Van Buren proposed that the whole Cabinet should resign, which was promptly done. Their places were filled as follows: Edward Livingston, of Louisiana, Secretary of State; Louis McLane, of Delaware, Secretary of the Treasury; Lewis Cass, of Ohio, Secretary of War; Levi Woodbury, of New Hampshire, Secretary of the Navy; Amos Kendall, of Kentucky, Postmaster-General; Roger B. Taney, of Maryland, Attorney-General. Mr. Downing, who "footed it" from Portland to Washington for the express purpose of filling one of these offices, was a little too late, it seems, as other people are sometimes who go to Washington on a similar errand. So much for the inside view.

The outside view of this matter, such as Mr. Downing would take in his "Thirty Years," and such as a good many outside folks took at the time, showed "a lady in the case." Mr. Eaton had married Mrs. Timberlake, widow of an officer of the navy, and Mr. Eaton and his wife were pets and protégés of President Jackson. But, in consequence of certain gossip or slanders about this lady, the wives of the other members of the Cabinet refused to visit or associate with her. Then, of course, "the fat was all in the fire." No Cabinet could stand an ordeal like that without an explosion. General Jackson was furious as a roaring lion, and Major Eaton a little more so. He challenged Mr. Ingham to a duel, but Ingham would not fight. Then followed the scenes of attempted redress with canes and bowie-knives, and an assault upon Mr. Ingham's house at night, which was so bravely defended by Mr. Downing, and so graphically described in his letter.

Washington City, June 21, 1831.

To Uncle Joshua Downing, up in Downingville, or else to Cousin Nabby, it isn't much matter which, being that some of it is about the ladies:

DEAR UNCLE JOSHUA:—It's pretty trying times here. They carry on so like the old smoker, I don't hardly know what to make of it. If I hadn't said I wouldn't leave Washington till I got an office, I don't know but I should come back to Downingville and go to planting potatoes. Them are Huntonites and Jacksonites down there in Maine last winter were pretty clever sort of folks to what these chaps are here. Cause down there if they got ever so mad, they didn't do nothing but talk and jaw one another; but here, if anybody doesn't do to suit 'em, fact they'll up and shoot him in a minute. I didn't think getting an office was such dangerous kind of business, or I don't know as I should have tried it. Howsomever, it's neck or nothing with me now, and I must do something to try to get some money here, for I about as lieves die as to undertake to foot it away back agin clear to the State of Maine. And as the folks have to go armed here, I want you to put my old fowling piece into the stage and send it on here as quick as possible. I hope you'll be as quick as you can about it, for if I get an office I shan't dare to take it till I get my gun. They come pretty near having a shooting scrape here yesterday. The Telegraph paper said something about Mr. Eaton's wife. It was nothing that I should think they need to make such a fuss about; it only said that some of the ladies here refused to visit her. But some how or other it made Mr. Eaton as mad as a March hair. He declared he'd fight somebody, he didn't care who.

The first man he happened to come at was Mr. Ingham. So he dared Mr. Ingham out to fight. Not to box, as they do sometimes up in Downingville, but to stand and shoot at each other. But Mr. Ingham wouldn't touch to, and told him he was crazy. That made Mr. Eaton ten times more mad than he was before; and he declared he'd flog him anyhow, whether he was willing or not. So he got a gang of gentlemen yesterday to go with him to the Treasury Office, where Mr. Ingham does his writing, and waited there and in a grog shop close by as much as two hours for a chance to catch him and give it to him. Mr. Ingham was out a visiting in the city, and when he got home his folks told him what was going on, and begged him not to go to the office, for he would certainly be killed. "Poh," says he, "do you think I'm afraid of them are blustering chaps? There's more smoke than fire there, I can tell ye; give me my pistols, it is time for me to go to the office." Some of the ladies cried, and some almost fainted away. But he pacified 'em as well as he could, and then set out for the office, and three or four men went with him, and I guess they carried something under their arms that would make daylight shine through a feller pretty quick. And I guess the gang of gentlemen waiting for him begun to smell a rat, for they cleared out pretty soon and never touched him. But their courage came again in the evening, and this same gang of gentlemen turned out and marched up to Mr. Ingham's house, and threatened to burst the doors open and drag him out by the hair of the head and skin him alive. I thought this was carrying the joke rather too far, so I tho't I'd put in my oar; for when I see any body run upon too hard I can't help taking their part.

So I stepped up to Mr. Ingham's front door steps, and threw my hat down, and rolled up my sleeves, and spit on my hands; and by that time the chaps began to stare at me a little. And now says I, "Major Eaton, this is quite too bad. A man's house is his castle. Here's Mr. Ingham in his house as peaceable as a lamb; he isn't a meddling with nobody, and you needn't think to drag him out here to-night, I can tell ye. If you really want to take a bit of a box, just throw away your powder and ball and here's the boy for you. I'll take a fist or two with you and glad of the chance."

"You impudent scoundrel," says he, "who are you? what business is it to you what I *done?* Clear out, or I'll send you where you ought to have been long ago."

"Well, then, you'll send me into some good office," says I, "for there's where I ought to have been more than two years ago."

"Well," says he, "clear out;" and up he come blustering along toward the steps. But I jest put my foot down, and doubled up my fist, and now, says I, "Major Eaton, it won't be healthy for you to come on to these steps to-night."

Says he, "I'm going through that door whether or no." Says I, "you don't go through this door to-night, without you pass over the dead body of *Jack Downing,* of the State of Maine." My stars, when they heard that, they dropt their heads as quick as though they had been cut off, for they didn't know who I was before. Major Eaton and the whole gang of gentlemen with him turned right about and marched away as whist as mice. They were afraid I should have 'em all before the President to-day, and have 'em turned out of office; for it's got whispered round the city that the President sets a great deal by me, and that I have a good deal of influence with him.

This morning Mr. Ingham started for Philadelphy. Before he left, he thanked me a thousand times for defending his house so well last night, and he wrote a letter to the President, telling him all about the scrape. I went a piece with him to see him safe out of the city on the great road toward Baltimore.

About my prospects for an office, I can't tell you yet how I shall come out. I've been in to see the President a number of times, and he talks very favorable. I have some chance to get in to be Secretary of War, if old Judge White don't take it; and if I don't get that the president says he'll do the best he can for me.

I never had to be so strict a Republikan before in my life as I've had to be since I've been here, in order to get the right side of the President. I'll tell you something about it in my next, and about my visits to the President, and a good many other famous things here.

P.S.—Be sure and send the old gun as quick as possible.

> Your loving neffu,
> JACK DOWNING.

Letter LXXI

SHOWING HOW THE MAJOR PERSUADED UNCLE JOSHUA TO TAKE
HOLD AND HELP ELECT GENERAL PIERCE TO THE PRESIDENCY,
AND HOW DOWNINGVILLE RATIFIED THE NOMINATION

> DOWNINGVILLE, *Away Down East*
> *In the State of Maine, July 20, 1852.*

MR. GALES AND SEATON—

MY DEAR OLD FRIENDS:—We've made out to ratify at last; but it was about as hard a job as it was for the Baltimore Convention to nominate. And I'm afraid the worst on't

My Thirty Years . . . , pp. 383–391.

ain't over yet; for Uncle Joshua shakes his head and says to
me, in a low tone, so the rest shan't hear, "Between you and
me, Major, the 'lection will be a harder job still." I put great
faith in Uncle Joshua's feelins. He's a regular political weath-
erglass, and can always tell whether we are going to have it
fair or foul a good ways ahead. So when he shakes his head,
I naterally look out for a tough spell of weather. When I got
home from Baltimore, says I, "Well, Uncle Joshua, you got
my letter in the *Intelligencer,* didn't you?" And says he,
"Yes."

"Well, didn't we do that business up well?" says I.

"I don't know about that," said Uncle Joshua; "I have my
doubts about it."

"Why, don't you think," says I, "the nomination of Gineral
Pierce will put the Democratic party on its legs again, and
give it a fine start?"

Uncle Joshua looked up to me kind of quizical, and says
he, "It *has* gin the party a pretty considerable of a start
already, it come so unexpected." And then he sot as much
as two minutes drumming his finger on the table, and didn't
say nothin'.

And then he looked up again, and says he, "Major, *who is
Gineral Pierce?* It ain't a *fictious* name, is it?"

"Why, Uncle Joshua," says I, "how you talk! It is Gineral
Franklin Pierce of New Hampshire."

"Gineral Franklin Pierce of New Hampshire, is it?" says
he. "Well, now, Major, are you sure there *is* such a person,
or did somebody play a hoax on the Baltimore Convention?"

"Yes," says I. "Uncle, I'm as sure of it as I am that there is
such a person as Uncle Joshua Downing. To make all sure
of it and no mistake, I come through New Hampshire, and
went to Concord, where they said he lived, and inquired all
about it. The neighbors there all knew him perfectly well,

and showed me the house he lives in. He wasn't at home, or I should a seen him myself, and should got his promise to keep the Downingville Post-Office for you. But you needn't be afraid but what you'll have it, for I sent a telegraph to him from Baltimore, as soon as he was nominated, to keep it for you."

Here I see by the looks of Uncle Joshua's eyes that he begun to get hold of some new ideas. Says he, "Well, Major, it is a fact then, is it, that he was nominated in real earnest, and 'twasn't no joke?"

"Upon my word and honor," says I, "there isn't a particle of joke about it—it was all done in real arnest."

"Well, then, if you've really got a candidate," says Uncle Joshua, "I should like to know something about him. Does he belong to the Old Fogy class or Young America class?"

"I guess about half and half," says I, "and he'll be all the stronger for that, because he can draw votes on both sides."

"After all," says he, "I'm afraid it's a bad nomination. Them old pillars of the Democratic party, Gineral Cass, and Mr. Buchanan, and Governor Marcy, and Gineral Houston, and the rest, will feel so insulted and mortified at being pushed aside for strangers to take the lead, that they'll all be agin the nomination, and their friends, too, and that'll upset the whole kettle of fish."

"Don't you never fear that, Uncle Joshua," says I; "them old pillars that you speak of are all very much tickled with the nomination. Ye see, it broke the nose of Young America, and they was delighted with it. As soon as the nomination was out of the mould, before it had time to cool, they all telegraphed right to Baltimore that nothin' in the world could have happened to suit 'em better; it was a most excellent nomination, and they felt under everlasting obligations to the Baltimore Convention. You needn't have no fears that they'll feel any coldness towards the nomination. They'll turn to and work for it like beavers."

"Well, how is it," said Uncle Joshua, "about that boy candidate for the Presidency that they call Young America? If his nose is knocked out of joint he'll of course oppose the nomination, tooth and nail."

"There's where you are mistaken again, Uncle Joshua," says I. "On the contrary, he goes for it hotter than any of 'em; and he telegraphed back to Baltimore, as quick as lightning could carry it, that the nomination was jest the thing; it couldn't be no better. Ye see, he looks upon it in the light that it chokes off all the Old Fogies, and leaves the field clear for him next time. He thinks so highly of the nomination, and feels so patriotic about it, they say he is going to stump it through all the States, and make speeches in favor of Gineral Pierce's election. You may depend upon it, Uncle Joshua, we've got a very strong nomination—one that'll carry all afore it—and everybody is delighted with it, and everybody's going to go for it. I didn't expect you to hold back a moment. I thought you would have things all cut and dried for a rousin' ratification meeting by the time I got home."

"Well, you know, Major," said Uncle Joshua, "I always follow Colonel Crockett's rule, and never go ahead till I know I'm right. How foolish we should look to call a ratification meeting here in Downingville, and be voted right plump down. You know the Free-Soilers are very strong among us; they are strong in all the Northern States. And you know the Baltimore Convention fixed up a platform to stand on, that's all in favor of the Compromise and the Fugitive law, and is dead set agin the Free-Soilers. Now, Major, you must have more understanding than to think the Free-Soilers will ever swallow that platform; and if they don't, we are dished."

"You are wrong again, Uncle Joshua," says I, "for the biggest Free-Soiler in all America swallowed it right down, and didn't make a wry face about it."

"Who do you mean?" says he.

"I mean Mr. John Van Buren," says I.

"But you don't mean," says Uncle Joshua, "that Mr. John Van Buren accepts this platform, and is willing to stand on it."

"Yes I do, exactly so," says I, "for he got right up in Tammany Hall and made a speech about it; and he said he would go the nomination, and he'd stand the platform; at all events, he'd stand the platform for *this election,* anyhow. You needn't be at all afraid of the Free-Soilers, Uncle; they ain't so stiff as you think for, and they are as anxious to get the offices as anybody, and will work as hard for 'em. Now let us go to work and get up our ratification, and blow it out straight. The Democracy of the country expects Downingville to do its duty."

"Well, Major," says Uncle Joshua, "you've made out a better case than I thought you could. I'm willing to take hold and see what we can do. But I declare I can't help laughing when I think it's Gineral Franklin Pierce, of New Hampshire, that we've got to ratify. I wish we knew something about him; something that we could make a little flusteration about, and wake up the Democracy."

"Good gracious, Uncle Joshua," says I, "have you been Postmaster of Downingville this twenty years, and always reading the papers, and don't know that Gineral Pierce was one of the heroes of the Mexican war?"

At that, Uncle Joshua hopped out of his chair like a boy, and says he, "Major, is that a fact?"

"Yes," says I, " 'tis a fact. You know Mr. Polk sent me out

there as a private ambassador to look after Gineral Scott and Mr. Trist. And Gineral Pierce *was* out there; I knew all about it, and about his getting wounded."

"Good!" says Uncle Joshua, snapping his fingers; "that's lucky, then we've got something to go upon; something that the boys can hoorah about. And if we don't have too strong a team agin us we may carry the day yet. Who do you think the other party will put up?"

"Well," says I, "it's pretty likely to be Mr. Webster or Mr. Fillmore, and they can't either of 'em hold a candle to Gineral Pierce."

"Of course not," says Uncle Joshua, "if he was the hero of the Mexican war. I s'pose it was Gineral Scott's part of the war that he was in, because that's where you was. Which of the battles did he fight the bravest in, and mow down most of the Mexicans? Did he help storm that Gibralta castle at Vera Cruz?"

"No," says I, "that little matter was all over before Gineral Pierce got to Mexico."

"Well, the great battle of Cerro Gordo come next," said Uncle Joshua; "I dare say Gineral Pierce was foremost in marching up that bloody Bunker Hill and driving off Santa Anna and his fifteen thousand troops."

"I'm sure he would a been foremost, if he'd been there," says I, "but he hadn't got into the country yet, and Gineral Scott wouldn't wait for him. It seems as if Gineral Scott is always in a hurry when there is any fightin' to do, and won't wait for nobody."

"Well, the next great battle, if I remember the newspapers right," said Uncle Joshua, "was Contreras; and after that came the bloody and hot times of Cherubusco, and the King's Mill, and Chepultepec, and marching into the City of

Mexico. These was the battles, I s'pose, where Gineral Pierce fit like a lion, and became the hero of the Mexican war. But which battle did he shine the brightest in, and cut down most of the enemy?"

"The truth is," says I, "he got wounded at Contreras, and so wasn't able to take a part in them bloody affairs of Cherubusco, King's Mill, and Chepultepec."

"Then he *was* in the battle of Contreras," said Uncle Joshua, "and that can't be disputed?"

"O yes," says I, "he certainly was in the first part of it, when they was getting the battle ready, for there's where he got wounded."

"Good," said Uncle Joshua, "he was in one battle, and got wounded; that's enough to make a handle of, anyhow. Whereabouts was his wound?"

"Well, he had several hurts," said I; "I believe in his foot and ancle, and other parts."

"Rifle balls?" said Uncle Joshua, very earnest.

"O no, nothing of that kind," says I.

"What then; sword cuts? Or did the Mexicans stick their bayonets into him?"

"No, no; nothin' of that kind, nother," says I.

"Then it must be grape or bombshells," said Uncle Joshua, "how was it?"

"No, no, 'twasn't none of them things," says I. "The fact was, when they was skirmishing round, getting ready for the battle, his horse fell down with him and lamed him very bad."

Uncle Joshua colored a little, and sot and thought. At last he put on one of his knowing looks, and says he, "Well, Major, a wound is a wound, and we can make a handle of it without being such fools as to go into the particulars of how he came by it. I say let's go ahead and ratify Gineral Pierce, and who knows but what we can make something out of this Mexican business?"

Well, Mr. Gales and Seaton, the thing was done. We ratified on the 21st of June, in the evening, and it was a tall piece of business. When I begun, I meant to give you a full account of it, with some of the speeches and resolutions; but I've made my preamble so long that I can't do it in this letter. *We had a torchlight procession.* Cousin Ephraim took his cart and oxen, and went into the woods and got a whole load of birch bark and pitch-pine knots, and all the boys in Downingville turned out and carried torches. The schoolhouse was illuminated with fifty candles. Uncle Joshua presided, as usual. Banners were hung round the room, with large letters, giving the names of all the great battles in Mexico; and the enthusiasm was immense. When we'd got about through, and was just winding up with three tremendous cheers for the "Hero of Mexico," a message came up to Uncle Joshua from the Post-Office, stating that the telegraph had just brought news that the Whig Convention at Baltimore had nominated Gineral Scott for President. It gin the whole Convention the cold shuggers in a minute. Uncle Joshua looked very serious, and says he, "Feller-Democrats, to prevent any mistakes, I think you had better give them three last cheers over again, and put in the name of Gineral Pierce." So we did, and gin three rousin cheers for *Gineral Franklin Pierce, of New Hampshire, the Hero of Mexico.*

Downingville is wide awake, and will do her duty in November.

So I remain your old friend,
MAJOR JACK DOWNING.

JAMES RUSSELL LOWELL
[Hosea Biglow]
(1819-1891)

James Russell Lowell wrote his first series of *The Biglow Papers* to oppose war against Mexico and any extension of slave territory. It was a time of intense agitation over the slavery question. *The Biglow Papers* were published first in newspapers, where they excited widespread attention and invited comparison with the letters of Seba Smith and his imitators. Lowell evoked the mental quirks, the popular sense of humor aimed at politics, and the dialects characteristic of New England's Yankees. Yet Lowell's efforts were patently superior. He was a first-rate craftsman, destined to become America's literary tastemaker for the Gilded Age.

The polish and cleverness of Lowell's pen grow more apparent with closer reading of *The Biglow Papers*. These sophisticated satires required more than a single Yankee character. Lowell's principals were Hosea Biglow and his father, both ordinary but sensible farmers, Birdofredum Sawin, a volunteer soldier fighting in Mexico, at once a clown and the twisted incarnation of Manifest Destiny, and Homer Wilbur, an elderly clergyman representing New England's more cautious facets of personality and its pedantry "with an infinite capacity of sermonizing muscularized by long practice."

Sometimes Lowell overdid what he set out to do. His acerbic verses and satirical commentaries suffer from didactic zeal. Lowell purposely used his humor to battle for the right. His message against slavery and its proponents come across clearly, though too emphatically for any lingering humorous effect. His humor betrays a lack of sympathy, an all-important element of democracy's laughter at its best. With Seba Smith's Jack Downing and others, the blows were softened as soon as they were struck.

The two selections from *The Biglow Papers* require a brief explanation. "What Mr. Robinson Thinks" satirized the reckless spirit for expansion and conquest, and what Parson Wilbur regarded as "the pernicious sentiment of 'Our Country, right or wrong.' " The somewhat cryptic cast of characters included Governor Briggs of Massachusetts, notorious for never wearing a shirt collar as well as for his distrust of spread-eagle imperialism, John P. Robinson, a local spokesman for Manifest Destiny, and Caleb Cushing, a distinguished officer of the United States Army in Mexico and later Minister to China. It was claimed that this poem tipped the gubernatorial election in favor of Briggs. "The Debate in the Sennit" lampooned a speech by Senator John C. Calhoun favoring an extension of slave territory. Heard in the background was a chorus of well-known senators echoing Calhoun's stand.

What Mr. Robinson Thinks

Guvener B. is a sensible man;
  He stays to his home an' looks arter his folks;
He draws his furrer ez straight ez he can,
  An' into nobody's tater-patch pokes;—
    But John P.
    Robinson he
  Sez he wunt vote fer Guvener B.

My! aint it terrible? Wut shall we du?
  We can't never choose him, o' course,—thet's flat;
Guess we shall hev to come round, (don't you?)
  An' go in fer thunder an' guns, an' all that;
    Fer John P.
    Robinson he
  Sez he wunt vote fer Guvener B.

Gineral C. is a dreffle smart man:
  He's been on all sides thet give places or pelf;
But consistency still wuz a part of his plan,—
  He's ben true to *one* party,—an' thet is himself;
    So John P.
    Robinson he
  Sez he shall vote fer Gineral C.

Gineral C. he goes in fer the war;
  He don't vally principle more'n an old cud;
Whut did God make us raytional creeturs fer,
  But glory an' gunpowder, plunder an' blood?

James Russell Lowell, *The Biglow Papers*, 2d English edition, London (1861), pp. 52–57.

438

So John P.
Robinson he
Sez he shall vote for Gineral C.

We were gittin' on nicely up here to our village,
   With good old idees o' wut's right an' wut aint,
We kind o' thought Christ went agin war an' pillage,
   An' thet eppyletts worn't the best mark of a saint;
      But John P.
      Robinson he
Sez this kind o' thing's an exploded idee.

The side of our country must ollers be took,
   An' President Polk, you know, *he* is our country;
An' the angel that writes all our sins in a book
   Puts the *debit* to him, an' to us the *per contry;*
      An' John P.
      Robinson he
Sez this is his view o' the thing to a T.

Parson Wilbur he calls all these argimunts lies;
   Sez they're nothin' on airth but jest *fee, faw, fum;*
An' thet all this big talk of our destinies
   Is half on it ignorance, an' t'other half rum;
      But John P.
      Robinson he
Sez it aint no sech thing; an', of course, so must we.

Parson Wilbur sez *he* never heard in his life
   Thet the' Apostles rigged out in their swaller-tail coats
An' marched round in front of a drum an' a fife,
   To git some on 'em office, an' some on 'em votes,
      But John P.
      Robinson he
Sez they didn't know everythin' down in Judee.

Wal, it's a marcy we've gut folks to tell us
　　The rights an' the wrongs o' these matters, I vow,—
God sends country lawyers, an' other wise fellers,
　　To drive the world's team wen it gits in a slough;
　　　　Fer John P.
　　　　Robinson he
Sez the world'll go right, ef he hollers out Gee!

The Debate in the Sennit, Sot to a Nusry Rhyme

TO MR. BUCKENAM.

MR. EDITER, As i wuz kinder prunin round, in a little nussry sot out a year or 2 a go, the Dbait in the sennit cum inter my mine. An so i took & Sot it to wut I call a nussry rime. I hev made sum onnable Gentlemun speak that dident speak in a Kind uv Poetikul lie sense the seeson is dreffle backerd up This way

　　　　　　　　　ewers as ushul
　　　　　　　　　HOSEA BIGLOW

"Here we stan' on the Constitution, by thunder!
　　It's a fact o' wich ther's bushils o' proofs;
Fer how could we trample on 't so, I wonder,
　　Ef't worn't thet it's ollers under our hoofs?"
　　　　Sez John C. Calhoun, sez he;—
　　　　　　"Human rights haint no more
　　　　　　Right to come on this floor,
　　　　No more'n the man in the moon," sez he.

"The North haint no kind o' bisness with nothin',
　　An' you've no idee how much bother it saves;

The Biglow Papers, pp. 84–92.

We aint none riled by their frettin' and frothin'
  We're *used* to layin' the string on our slaves,"
    Sez John C. Calhoun, sez he;—
      Sez Mister Foote,
      "I should like to shoot
      The holl gang, by the gret horn spoon!" sez he.

"Freedom's Keystone is Slavery, that ther's no doubt on,
  It's sutthin' thet's—wha'd'ye call it?—divine,—
An' the slaves that we ollers *make* the most out on
  Air them north o' Mason an' Dixon's line,"
    Sez John C. Calhoun, sez he;—
      "Fer all thet," sez Mangum,
      " 'Twould be better to hang 'em,
      An' so git red on 'em soon," sez he.

"The mass ough' to labour an' we lay on soffies,
  Thet's the reason I want to spread Freedom's aree;
It puts all the cunninest on us in office,
  An' reelises our Maker's orig'nal idee,"
    Sez John C. Calhoun, sez he;—
      "Thet's ez plain," sez Cass,
      "Ez thet some one's an ass,
      It's ez clear ez the sun is at noon," sez he.

"Now don't go to say I'm the friend of oppression,
  But keep all your spare breath fer coolin' your broth,
Fer I ollers hev strove (at least thet's my impression)
  To make cussed free with the rights o' the North,"
    Sez John C. Calhoun, sez he;—
      "Yes," sez Davis o' Miss.,
      "The perfection o' bliss
      Is in skinnin' thet same old coon," sez he.

"Slavery's a thing thet depends on complexion,
    It's God's law that fetters on black skins don't chafe;
Ef brains wuz to settle it (horrid reflection!)
    Wich of our onnable body'd be safe?"
        Sez John C. Calhoun, sez he;—
            Sez Mister Hannegan,
            Afore he began agin,
        "Thet exception is quite oppertoon," sez he.

"Gen'nle Cass, Sir, you needn't be twitchin' your collar,
    Your merit's quite clear by the dut on your knees,
At the North we don't make no distinctions o' color;
    You can all take a lick at our shoes wen you please,"
        Sez John C. Calhoun, sez he;—
            Sez Mister Jarnagin,
            "They wunt hev to larn agin,
        They all on 'em know the old toon," sez he.

"The slavery question ain't no ways bewilderin'.
    North an' South hev one int'rest, it's plain to a glance;
No'thern men, like us patriarchs, don't sell their childrin,
    But they *du* sell themselves, ef they git a good chance,"
        Sez John C. Calhoun, sez he;—
            Sez Atherton here,
            "This is gittin' severe,
        I wish I could dive like a loon," sez he.

"It'll break up the Union, this talk about freedom,
    An' your fact'ry gals (soon ez we split) 'll make head,
An' gittin' some Miss chief or other to lead 'em,
    'll go to work raisin' promiscoous Ned,"
        Sez John C. Calhoun, sez he;—
            "Yes, the North," sez Colquitt,

"Ef we Southerners all quit,
    Would go down like a busted balloon," sez he.

"Jest look wut is doin', what annyky's brewin'
    In the beautiful clime o' the olive an' vine,
All the wise aristoxy is tumblin' to ruin,
    An' the sankylots drorin' an' drinkin' their wine,"
        Sez John C. Calhoun, sez he;—
            "Yes," sez Johnson, "in France
            They're beginnin' to dance
        Beelzebub's own rigadoon," sez he.

"The South's safe enough, it don't feel a mite skeery,
    Our slaves in their darkness an' dut air tu blest
Not to welcome with proud hallylugers the ery
    Wen our eagle kicks yourn from the naytional nest,"
        Sez John C. Calhoun, sez he;—
            "O," sez Westcott o' Florida,
            "Wut treason is horrider
        Then our priv'leges tryin' to proon?" sez he.

"It's 'coz they're so happy, thet, wen crazy sarpints
    Stick their nose in our bizness, we git so darned riled,
We think it's our dooty to give pooty sharp hints,
    That the last crumb of Edin on airth shan't be spiled,"
        Sez John C. Calhoun, sez he;—
            "Ah," sez Dixon H. Lewis,
            "It perfectly true is
        Thet slavery's airth's grettest boon," sez he.

DAVY CROCKETT
(1786-1836)

The life and writings of Davy Crockett are shrouded in legend and mystery. His real personality has been almost lost to view. He served under Andrew Jackson in the war against the Creek Indians, and was elected to represent Tennessee in the 20th, 21st, and 23rd congresses. Defeated for re-election by a Jackson supporter (having turned Whig against his old commander), Crockett vowed: "You may all go to Hell, and I will go to Texas." He died at the Alamo.

It is likely that several pens contributed to the sum total of Davy Crockett's published works. For many years and in various anthologies James Strange French was credited with their authorship, and A. S. Clayton presumably added his bit. Scholars point to Matthew St. Clair Clarke, clerk of the United States House of Representatives from 1822 through 1833, as the ghost-writer of the biographies of Crockett published in 1833. Conclusive proof is lacking, however. It is certain, as the *Dictionary of American Biography* states, that works attributed to Davy Crockett "bear little resemblance, either in substance or manner, to such of his letters that have come down to us."

At any rate, Davy Crockett's "Coon Story," extracted from his biography, contains a fresh, humorous flavor of political campaigning on the frontier. The message of its last line is timely.

444

Death of Col. Crockett

Coon Story

That Colonel Crockett could avail himself, in electioneering, of the advantages which well-applied satire ensures, the following anecdote will sufficiently prove.

In the canvass of the congressional election of 18—, Mr. ****** was the Colonel's opponent—a gentleman of the most pleasing and conciliating manners—who seldom addressed a person or a company without wearing upon his countenance a peculiarly good humoured smile. The Colonel, to counter-act the influence of this winning attribute, thus alluded to it, in a stump speech:

"Yes, gentlemen, he may get some votes by grinning, for he can *out-grin* me, and you know I ain't slow—and to prove to you that I am not, I will tell you an anecdote. I was con-cerned myself—and I was fooled a little of the wickedest. You all know I love hunting. Well, I discovered a long time ago that a 'coon couldn't stand my grin. I could bring one tumbling down from the highest tree. I never wasted powder and lead, when I wanted one of the creatures. Well, as I was walking out one night, a few hundred yards from my house, looking carelessly about me, I saw a 'coon planted upon one of the highest limbs of an old tree. The night was very *moony* and clear, and old Ratler was with me; but Ratler won't bark at a 'coon—he's a queer dog in that way. So, I thought I'd bring the lark down, in the usual way, *by a grin.* I set myself—and, after grinning at the 'coon a reasonable time, found that he didn't come down. I wondered what was the reason—and I took another steady grin at him. Still, he

Sketches and Eccentricities of Colonel David Crockett of West Tennessee, New York (1833), pp. 125–127.

was *there*. It made me a little mad; so I felt round and got an old limb about five feet long—and, planting one end upon the ground, I placed my chin upon the other, and took *a rest*. I then grinned my best for about five minutes—but the cursed 'coon hung on. So, finding I could not bring him down by grinning, I determined to have him—for I thought he must be a droll chap. I went over to the house, got my axe, returned to the tree, saw the 'coon still there, and began to cut away. Down it come, and I run forward; but d——n the 'coon was there to be seen. I found that what I had taken for one, was a large knot upon a branch of the tree—and, upon looking at it closely, I saw that *I had grinned all the bark off, and left the knot perfectly smooth*.

"Now fellow-citizens," continued the Colonel, "you must be convinced that, in the *grinning line*, I myself am not slow—yet, when I look upon my opponent's countenance, I must admit that he is my superior. You must all admit it. Therefore, be wide awake—look sharp—and do not let him grin you out of your votes." . . .

JOHN S. ROBB
[Solitaire]
(Fl. 1847-1858)

John S. Robb of St. Louis, Missouri, relished the vitality and natural humor of western life before the Civil War. As "Solitaire," the proud though pseudonymous author of *Swallowing Oysters Alive,* Robb wrote tongue-in-cheek sketches about the settlement of the West as though it constituted a continuous enterprise in hilarity. He even devised a frontier thesis long before Frederick Jackson Turner. The farther west and the later the hour, the funnier it all became. Wrote Robb: "It would indeed seem that the nearer sundown, the more original the character and odd the expression, as if the sun with his departing beams had shed a new feature upon the back-woods inhabitants."

Robb's pen portrait of "the standing candidate," Old Sugar, is a compact masterpiece. Old Sugar's comic aspects fall well short of ludicrousness. His outlines are soft, as if it was precisely at such bridging points of human nature where frontier crudity blended into urbane civilization. Engagingly he lured "sniggers" from his whiskey-drinking clientele. Patriotically, in vulgarized imagery reminiscent of Andrew Jackson's rebuff to Calhoun. he toasted national unity: "Here is to the string that binds

the states; may it never be bit apart by political *rats!*"
Old Sugar reminds us of the pupil about to receive a thrashing from his tutor: "If you can't be easy,
be as easy as you can!" It would be helpful if Old Sugar
were still around to keep a watchful, if bloodshot, eye on
the state of the nation. Perhaps he is. "Whar politicians
congregate," quoth he, "I'm always thar at any rate!"

The Standing Candidate—His Excuse
for Being a Bachelor

At Buffalo Head, Nianga county, state of Missouri, during the canvass of 1844, there was held an extensive political *Barbecue,* and the several candidates for congress, legislature, county offices, &c., were all congregated at this southern point for the purpose of making an *immense* demonstration. Hards, softs, whigs and Tylerites were represented, and to hear their several expositions of state and general policy, a vast gathering of the Missouri sovereigns had also assembled. While the impatient candidates were awaiting the signal to mount the "stump," an odd-looking old man made his appearance at the brow of a small hill bounding the place of meeting.

"Hurrah for old *Sugar!*" shouted an hundred voices, while on, steadily, progressed the object of the cheer.

Sugar, as he was familiarly styled, was an old man, apparently about fifty years of age, and was clad in a coarse suit of brown linsey-woolsey. His pants were patched at each knee, and around the ankles they had worn off into picturesque points—his coat was not of the modern close-fitting cut, but hung in loose and easy folds upon his broad shoulders, while the total absence of buttons upon this garment, exhibited the owner's contempt for the storm and the tempest. A coarse shirt, tied at the neck with a piece of twine, completed his body covering. His head was ornamented with an old woollen cap, of divers colors, below which beamed a broad, humorous countenance, flanked by a pair of short,

Henry Clay Lewis [John S. Robb; "Solitaire"], *Streaks of Squatter Life, and Far-West Scenes* . . . , Philadelphia (1847), pp. 91–100.

funny little grey whiskers. A few wrinkles marked his brow, but time could not count them as sure chronicles of his progress, for Sugar's hearty, sonorous laugh oft drove them from their hiding place. Across his shoulder was thrown a sack, in each end of which he was bearing to the scene of political action, a keg of *bran new whiskey,* of his own manufacture, and he strode forward on his moccasin covered feet, encumbered as he was, with all the agility of youth. *Sugar* had long been the *standing candidate* of Nianga county, for the legislature, and founded his claim to the office upon the fact of his being the first "squatter" in that county—his having killed the first *bar* there, ever killed by a white man, and, to place his right beyond cavil, he had *'stilled* the first keg of whiskey! These were strong claims, which urged in his comic rhyming manner would have swept the "diggins," but *Sugar,* when the canvass opened, always yielded his claim to some liberal purchaser of his fluid, and duly announced himself a candidate for the *next* term.

"Here you air, old fellar!" shouted an acquaintance, "allays on hand 'bout 'lection."

"Well, Nat," said *Sugar,* "You've jest told the truth as easy as ef you'd taken sum of my mixtur—

> "Whar politicians congregate,
> I'm always thar, at any rate!"

"Set him up!—set the old fellar up somewhar, and let us take a universal liquor!" was the general shout.

"Hold on, boys,—keep cool and shady," said old *Sugar,* "whar's the candidates?—none of your splurgin round till I git an appropriation fur the sperits. Send em along and we'll negotiate fur the *fluid,* arter which I shall gin 'em my instructions, and they may then *percede* to

'Talk away like all cre-a-tion,
What they knows about the nation.' "

The candidates were accordingly summoned up to pay
for *Sugar's* portable grocery, and to please the crowd and
gain the good opinion of the owner, they made up a purse
and gathered round him. *Sugar* had placed his two kegs
upon a broad stump and seated himself astride of them,
with a small tin cup in his hand and a paper containing
brown sugar lying before him—each of his kegs was furnished
with a *spiggot*, and as soon as the money for the whole contents was paid in, *Sugar* commenced addressing the crowd as
follows:

"Boys, fellars, and candidates," said he, "I, *Sugar*, am the
furst white man ever seed in these yeur diggins—I killed
the furst *bar* ever a white skinned in this county, and I
kalkilate I hev hurt the feelings of his relations sum sence,
as the *bar-skin* linin' of my cabin will testify;—'sides that,
I'm the furst manufacturer of whiskey in the range of this
district, and powerful mixtur' it is, too, as the hull bilin' of
fellars in this crowd will declar';—more'n that, I'm a candidate for the legislatur', and intend to gin up my claim, *this*
term, to the fellar who kin talk the *pootyest;*—now, finally at
the eend, boys, this mixtur' of mine will make a fellar talk
as iley as goose-grease,—as sharp as lightnin' and as *per*suadin'
as a young gal at a quiltin', so don't spar it while it lasts, and
the candidates kin drink furst, 'cause they've got to do the
talkin'!"

Having finished his charge he filled the tin cup full of
whiskey, put in a handful of brown sugar, and with his forefinger stirred up the sweetening, then surveying the candidates he pulled off his cap, remarking, as he did so:

"Old age, allays, afore beauty!—your daddy furst, in

course," then holding up the cup he offered a toast, as follows:

"Here is to the string that binds the states; may it never be bit apart by political *rats!*" Then holding up the cup to his head he took a hearty swig, and passed it to the next oldest looking candidate. While they were tasting it, *Sugar* kept up a fire of lingo at them:

"Pass it along lively, gentle*men,* but don't spar the *fluid.* You can't help tellin' truth arter you've swaller'd enough of my mixtur', jest fur this reason, its ben 'stilled in honesty, rectified in truth, and poured out with wisdom! Take a *leetle* drop more," said he to a fastidious candidate, whose stomach turned at thought of the way the "mixtur'" was mixed. "Why, Mister," said *Sugar,* coaxingly.

> "Ef you wur a babby, jest new born,
> 'Twould do you good, this juicy *corn!*"

"No more, I thank you," said the candidate, drawing back from the proffer.

"*Sugar* winked his eye at some of his cronies, and muttered—"He's got an *a*-ristocracy stomach, and can't go the *native licker.*" Then dismissing the candidates he shouted,—"crowd up, constitoo*ents,* into a circle, and let's being fair—your daddy furst, allays; and mind, no changin' places in the circle to git the sugar in the bottom of the cup. I know you're arter it, Tom Williams, but none of your yankeein' round to git the sweetnin'—it's all syrup, fellars, cause *Sugar* made and mixed it. The gals at the frolicks allays git me to prepar' the cordials, 'cause they say I make it mity drinkable. Who next? What *you,* old Ben Dent!—Well, hold your hoss for a minit, and I'll strengthen the tin with a speck more, jest because you can kalkilate the valee of the licker, and do it jestiss!"

Thus chatted *Sugar* as he measured out and sweetened up

the contents of his kegs, until all who would drink had taken their share, and then the crowd assembled around the speakers. We need not say that the virtues of each political party were duly set forth to the hearers—that follows as a matter of course, candidates dwell upon the strong points of their argument, always. One among them, however, more than his compeers, attracted the attention of our friend *Sugar*, not because he had highly commended the contents of his kegs, but because he painted with truth and feeling the claims of the western *pioneers!* Among these he ranked the veteran Col. Johnson and his compatriots, and as he rehearsed their struggles in defence of their firesides, how they had been trained to war by conflict with the ruthless savage, their homes oft desolated, and their children murdered,—yet still, ever foremost in the fight, and last to retreat, winning the heritage of these broad valleys for their children, against the opposing arm of the red man, though aided by the civilized power of mighty Britain, and her serried cohorts of trained soldiery! We say as he dwelt upon these themes *Sugar's* eye would fire up, and then, at some touching passage of distress dwelt upon by the speaker, tears would course down his rude cheek. When the speaker concluded he wiped his eyes with his hard hand, and said to those around him:—

"That arr true as the yearth!—thar's suthin' like talk in that fellar!—he's the right breed, and his old daddy has told him about them times. So did mine relate 'em to me, how the ony sister I ever had, when a babby had her brains dashed out by one of the red skinned devils! But didn't we pepper them fur it? Didn't I help the old man, afore he grew too weak to hold his shootin' iron, to send a few on 'em off to rub out the account? Well, *I did!—Hey!*" and shutting his teeth together he yelled through them the exultation of full vengeance.

The speaking being done, candidates and hearers gathered around old *Sugar*, to hear his comments upon the speeches, and to many inquiries of how he liked them, the old man answered:—

"They were all pooty good, but that tall fellar they call Tom, from St. Louis; *you*, I mean, *stranger*," pointing at the same time to the candidate, "you jest scart up my feelin's to the right pint—you jest made me feel wolfish as when I and old dad war arter the red varmints; and now what'll *you* take? I'm goin' to publicly *de*cline in your favor."

Pouring out a tin full of the liquor, and stirring it as before, he stood upright upon the stump, with a foot on each side of his kegs, and drawing off his cap, toasted:—

"The memory of the western *pioneers!*"

A shout responded to his toast, which echoed far away in the depths of the adjoining forest, and seemed to awaken a response from the spirits of those departed heroes.

"That's the way to sing it out, boys," responded old *Sugar*, "sich a yell as that would *scar* an inimy into ager fits, and make the United States Eagle scream 'Hail Columby.'"

"While you're up, *Sugar*," said one of the crowd, "give us a stump speech, yourself."

"Bravo!" shouted an hundred voices, "a speech from *Sugar*."

"Agreed, boys," said the old man, "I'll jest gin you a few words to wind up with, so keep quiet while your daddy's talkin'

> 'Sum tell it out jest like a song,
> I'll gin it to you sweet and strong.'

"The only objection ever made to me in this arr county, as a legislatur', was made by the *wimin*, 'cause I war a *bachelor*, and I never told you afore why I *re*-mained in the state of number *one*—no fellar stays single *pre*-meditated, and, in course, a hansum fellar like me, who all the gals declar' to be as enticin' as a jay bird, warn't goin' to stay alone, ef he could help it. I did see a creatur' one, named *Sofy Mason,* up the Cumberland, nigh onto Nashville, Tenn*esee,* that I tuk an orful hankerin' arter, and I sot in to lookin' anxious fur matrimony, and gin to go reglar to meetin', and tuk to dressin' tremengeous finified, jest to see ef I could win her good opinion. She did git to lookin' at me, and one day, cumin' from meetin', she was takin' a look at me a kind of shy, jest as a hoss does at suthin' he's scart at, when arter champin' at a distance fur awhile, I sidled up to her and blarted out a few words about the sarmin'—she said yes, but cuss me ef I know whether that wur the right answer or not, and I'm a thinkin' she didn't know then, nuther! Well, we larfed and talked a leetle all the way along to her daddy's, and thar I gin her the best bend I had in me, and raised my bran new hat as peert and *per*lite as a minister, lookin' all the time so enticin' that I sot the gal tremblin'. Her old daddy had a powerful numerous lot of healthy niggers, and lived right adjinin' my place, while on tother side lived Jake Simons—a sneakin', cute varmint, who war wusser than a miser fur stinginess, and no sooner did this cussed sarpint see me sidlin' up to Sofy, than he went to slickin' up, too, and sot himself to work to cut me out. That arr wur a struggle ekill to the battle of Orleans. Furst sume new fixup of Jake's would take her eye, and then I'd sport suthin' that would outshine him, until Jake at last gin in tryin' to outdress me, and sot to thinkin' of suthin' else. Our farms wur jest the same number of acres, and we both owned three niggers apiece. Jake knew that Sofy and her dad kept a sharp eye out fur the main chance, so he thort he'd clar me out by buyin' another nigger; but I jest follor'd suit, and bought one the day arter he got his, so he had no advantage thar; he then got a *cow,* and so did I, and jest about then both on our *pusses* gin out. This put Jake to his wits' eend, and I war a wunderin' what in the yearth he would try next. We stood so, hip and thigh, fur about two weeks, both on us talkin' sweet to Sofy, whenever we could git her alone. I thort I seed that Jake, the sneakin' cuss, wur gittin' a mite ahead of me, 'cause his tongue wur so iley; howsever, I didn't let on, but kep a top eye on him. One Sunday mornin' I wur a leetle mite late to meetin', and when I got thar the furst thing I seed war Jake Simons, sittin' close bang up agin Sofy, in the same pew with her daddy! I biled a spell with wrath, and then tarned sour; I could taste myself! Thar they wur, singin' *himes* out of the same book. Je-e-eminy, fellars, I war so *enormous* mad that the new silk handkercher round my neck lost its color! Arter meetin' out they walked, linked arms, a smilin' and lookin' as pleased as a young couple at thar furst christenin', and Sofy tarned her 'cold shoulder' at me so orful pinted, that I wilted down, and gin up right straight—Jake had her, thar wur no disputin' it! I headed toward home, with my hands as fur in my trowsers pockets as I could push 'em, swarin' all the way that she wur the last one would ever git a chance to rile up my feelin's. Passin' by Jake's plantation I looked over the fence, and thar stood an explanation of the marter, right facin' the road, whar every one passin' could see it—his consarned *cow* was tied to a stake in the gardin', *with a most promisin' calf alongside of her!* That *calf* jest soured my milk, and made Sofy think, that a fellar who war allays gittin' ahead like Jake, wur a right smart chance for a lively husband!"

A shout of laughter here drowned *Sugar's* voice, and as soon as silence was restored he added, in a solemn tone, with one eye shut, and his forefinger pointing at his auditory:—

"What is a cussed sight wusser than his gittin' Sofy war the fact, that he *borrowed that calf the night before from Dick Harkley!* Arter the varmint got Sofy hitched, he told the joke all over the settle*ment,* and the boys never seed me arterwards that they didn't *b-a-h* at me fur lettin' a *calf* cut me out of a gal's affections. I'd a shot Jake, but I thort it war a free country, and the gal had a right to her choice without bein' made a widder, so I jest sold out and travelled! I've allays thort sence then, boys, that *wimin* wur a good deal like *licker,* ef you love 'em too hard thar sure to throw you some way:

'Then here's to *wimin,* then to *licker,*
Thar's nuthin' swimmin' can be slicker!' "

CHARLES FARRAR BROWNE
[Artemus Ward]
(1834-1867)

While reporting for the Cleveland (Ohio) *Plain Dealer,*
Charles Farrar Browne created the delightful character of
Artemus Ward, a traveling showman of volatile personality. A. Ward, as he signed his name, resembled P. T. Bar-
num drawn to smaller scale. Before crowds of gaping vil-
lagers and rustics, Ward paraded his "moral wax figgers"
and certain "sagashus beasts," which included "three moral bares" and a "kangaroo (a amoozing little raskal)."

By 1862 Artemus Ward was spectacularly successful as
a lecturer and writer, while Browne's original identity was lost to view behind the popular personality he had
created. The cream of Ward's "goaks," sketches, and tall
tales were appearing in *Vanity Fair,* "the grate komick
paper" launched to compete with London's *Punch.* Lincoln
even took the time of his War Cabinet to read aloud
Ward's "A High-handed Outrage at Utica" before turning
solemnly to consideration of his Emancipation Proclamation.

On the lecture platform, Ward's humor, like that of
his intimate friend Mark Twain, depended on his mastery of timing and especially of anticlimax. His appearance of personal distress and ignorance, his electrify-

ing flashes of interest followed by a resurgence of despair, deadpan seriousness, and meandering vagueness,
could not be duplicated in print. The comic visage of
Ward's writings originated in his outrageous spelling, rus-
ticisms, and puns. "Had this been all," as Stephen Lea-
cock observed, "Artemus Ward would long since have
been forgotten. But beneath the comic superficiality
of his written work, as behind the 'mask of melancholy,'
there was always the fuller, deeper meaning of the true
humorist, based on reality, on the contrasts, the incongruities, and the shortcomings of life itself."

Artemus Ward devoted only part of his literary talents
to the subject of politics, albeit a good part indeed. In
this respect he presents a contrast to Seba Smith's Jack
Downing, who admittedly influenced him, as well as to
Petroleum V. Nasby and Mr. Dooley. Ward could be cun-
ningly neutral in political disputes. His classic shilly-shally
compels admiration: "My perlitical sentiments agree with
yourn exactly. I know they do, becaws I never saw a man
whose didn't." George Washington was Ward's own hero
among his country's statesmen for a reason that still carries conviction: "He never slopt over!" Ward's distaste
for the Afro-American slave and his laissez-faire attitude
toward secession obscured his true colors. "I'm a Union
man," he proclaimed.

Like the Union he loved, Ward's own "kareer"
was "tremenjis." He was "the first comic man," as Walter Blair pointed out, "to make a really good living from
humor alone." His efforts were being warmly received in
England, where Artemus Ward died of consumption
at the age of thirty-three, as laughter from both sides of
the Atlantic saluted his last and greatest tour as a "moral lecturer."

The context of Ward's writings was the mid-century

turbulence of reform, secession, and fractricidal strife. Their content is self-explanatory, and, as in the essay on "Woman's Rights," measures our progress, or lack of it, ever since.

Woman's Rights

I pitcht my tent in a small town in Injianny one day last seeson & while I was standin at the dore takin money, a deppytashun of ladies came up & sed they wos members of the Bunkumville Female Reformin & Wimin's Rite's Associashun, and thay axed me if thay cood go in without payin.

"Not exactly," sez I, "but you can pay without goin in."

"Dew you know who we air?" said one of the wimin—a tall and feroshus lookin critter, with a blew Kotton umbreller under her arm—"do you know who we air, Sur?"

"My impreshun is," sed I, "from a kersery view, that you air females."

"We air, Sur," said the feroshus woman—"we belong to a Society whitch beleeves wimin has rites—whitch beleeves in razin her to her proper speer—whitch beleeves she is indowed with as much intelleck as man is—whitch beleeves she is trampled on and aboozed—& who will resist hense4th & forever the incroachments of proud & domineering men."

Durin her discourse, the exsentric female grabed me by the coat-kollor & was swinging her umbreller wildly over my hed.

"I hope, marm," sez I, starting back, "that your intensions is honorable! I'm a lone man hear in a strange place. Besides, Ive a wife to hum."

"Yes," cried the female, "& she's a slave! Doth she never dream of freedom—doth she never think of throwin of the yoke of tyrrinny & votin for herself?—Doth she never think of these here things?"

Charles Farrar Browne, *The Complete Works of Artemus Ward*, London (1889), pp. 84–85.

"Not bein a natral born fool," sed I, by this time a little riled, "I kin safely say that she dothunt."

"Oh, whot—whot!" screamed the female, swingin her umbreller in the air. "O, what is the price that woman pays for her expeeriunce!"

"I don't know," sez I; "the price of my show is 15 cents pur individooal."

"& can't our Sosiety go in free?" asked the female.

"Not if I know it," sed I.

"Crooil, crooil man!" she cried, & bust into teers.

"Won't you let my darter in?" sed anuther of the exsentric wimin, taken me afeckshunitely by the hand. "O, please let my darter in—shee's a sweet gushin child of natur."

"Let her gush!" roared I, as mad as I cood stick at their tarnal nonsense—"let her gush!" Where upon they all sprung back with the simultanious observashun that I was a Beest.

"My female friends," sed I, "be4 you leve, Ive a few remarks to remark; wa them well. The female woman is one of the greatest institooshuns of which this land can boste. It's onpossible to get along without her. Had there bin no female wimin in the world, I should scarcely be here with my unparalleld show on this very occashun. She is good in sickness—good in wellness—good all the time. O woman, woman!" I cried, my feelins worked up to a hi poetick pitch, "You air a angle when you behave yourself; but when you take off your proper appairel & (mettyforically speaken)—get into pantyloons—when you desert your firesides, & with your heds full of wimin's rites noshuns go round like roarin lyons, seekin whom you may devour someboddy—in short, when you undertake to play the man, you play the devil and air an emfatic noosance. My female friends," I continued, as they were indignantly departin, "wa well what A. Ward has sed!"

Artemus Ward

Fourth of July Oration

Delivered July 4th, at Weathersfield, Connecticut, 1859

[*I delivered the follerin, about two years ago, to a large and discriminating awjince. I was 96 minits passin a given pint. I have revised the orashun, and added sum things which makes it approposser to the times than it otherwise would be. I have also corrected the grammers and punktooated it. I do my own punktooatin nowdays. The Printers in* VANITY FAIR *offiss can't punktooate worth a cent.*]

FELLER CITIZENS,—I've been honored with a invite to norate before you to-day; and when I say that I skurcely feel ekal to the task, I'm sure you will believe me.

Weathersfield is justly celebrated for her onyins and patritism the world over, and to be axed to paws and address you on this, my fust perfeshernal tower threw New England, causes me to feel—to feel—I may say it causes me to *feel*. (Grate applaws. They thought this was one of my eccentricities, while the fact is I was stuck. This between you and I.)

I'm a plane man. I don't know nothin about no ded languages and am a little shaky on livin ones. There4, expect no flowry talk from me. What I shall say will be to the pint, right strate out.

I'm not a politician, and my other habits air good. I've no enemys to reward, nor friends to sponge. But I'm a Union man. I luv the Union—it is a Big thing—and it makes my hart bleed to see a lot of ornery peple a-movin' heaven—no, not heaven, but the other place—and earth, to bust it up.

Artemus Ward, *Complete Works* . . . , pp. 122–126.

Too much good blud was spilt in courtin and marryin that hily respectable female the Goddess of Liberty to git a divorce from her now. My own State of Injianny is celebrated for unhitchin marrid peple with neatness and dispatch, but you can't git a divorce from the Goddess up there. Not by no means. The old gal has behaved herself too well to cast her off now. I'm sorry the picters don't give her no shoes or stockins, but the band of stars upon her hed must continner to shine undimd, forever. Ime for the Union as she air, and whithered be the arm of every ornery cuss who attempts to bust her up. That's me. I hav sed! [It was a very sweaty day, and at this pint of the orashun a man fell down with sun-stroke. I told the awjince that considerin the large number of putty gals present I was more fraid of a DAWTER STROKE. This was impromptoo, and seemed to amoose them very much.]

Feller Citizens,—I hain't got time to notis the growth of Ameriky frum the time when the Mayflowers cum over in the Pilgrim and brawt Plymmuth Rock with him, but every skool boy nose our kareer has bin tremenjis. You will excuse me if I don't prase the erly settlers of the Kolonies. Peple which hung idiotic old wimin for witches, burnt holes in Quakers' tongues and consined their feller critters to the tredmill and pillery on the slitest provocashun may have bin very nice folks in their way, but I must confess I don't admire their stile, and will pass them by. I spose they ment well, and so, in the novel and techin langwidge of the nuse-papers, "peas to their ashis." Thare was no diskount, how-ever, on them brave men who fit, bled and died in the American Revolushun. We needn't be afraid of setting 'em up two steep. Like my show, they will stand any amount of prase. G. Washington was abowt the best man this world ever sot eyes on. He was a clear-heded, warm-harted, and stiddy

goin man. He never slopt over! The prevailin weakness of
most public men is to SLOP OVER! [Put them words in large
letters—A.W.] They git filled up and slop. They Rush Things.
They travel too much on the high presher principle. They git
on to the fust poplar hobby-hoss whitch trots along, not carin
a sent whether the beest is even-goin, clear sited and sound,
or spavined, blind and bawky. Of course they git throwed
eventooually, if not sooner. When they see the multitood
goin it blind they go Pel Mel with it, instid of exertin theirselves to set it right. They can't see that the crowd which is
now bearin them triumfuntly on its shoulders will soon
diskiver its error and cast them into the hoss pond of Obliv-
yun, without the slitest hesitashun. Washington never slopt
over. That wasn't George's stile. He luved his country dearly.
He wasn't after the spiles. He was a human angil in a 3
kornerd hat and knee britches, and we shan't see his like
right away. My frends, we can't all be Washington's, but we
kin all be patrits & behave ourselves in a human and a
Christian manner. When we see a brother goin down hill to
Ruin let us not give him a push, but let us seeze rite hold of
his coat-tails and draw him back to Morality.

Imagine G. Washington and P. Henry in the character of
seseshers! As well fancy John Bunyan and Dr. Watts in
spangled tites, doin the trapeze in a one-horse circus!

I tell you, feller-citizens, it would have bin ten dollars in
Jeff Davis's pocket if he'd never bin born!

*   *   *

Be shure and vote at leest once at all elecshuns. Buckle on
yer Armer and go to the Poles. See two it that your naber
is there. See that the kripples air provided with carriages.
Go to the poles and stay all day. Bewair of the infamous
lise whitch the Opposishun will be sartin to git up fur

perlitical effek on the eve of eleckshun. To the poles! and when you git there vote jest as you darn please. This is a privilege we all persess, and it is 1 of the booties of this grate and free land.

I see mutch to admire in New Englan. Your gals in particklar air abowt as snug bilt peaces of Calliker as I ever saw. They air fully equal to the corn fed gals of Ohio and Injianny, and will make the bestest kind of wives. It sets my Buzzum on fire to look at 'em.

> Be still, my sole, be still,
> & you, Hart, stop cuttin up!

I like your skool houses, your meetin houses, your enterprise, gumpshun, &c., but your favorite Bevridge I disgust. I allude to New England Rum. It is wuss nor the korn whisky of Injianny, which eats threw stone jugs & will turn the stummuck of the most shiftliss Hog. I seldom seek consolashun in the flowin Bole, but tother day I wurrid down some of your Rum. The fust glass indused me to swear like a infooriated trooper. On takin the secund glass I was seezed with a desire to break winders, & arter imbibin the third glass I knockt a small boy down, pickt his pocket of a New York Ledger, and wildly commenced readin Sylvanus Kobb's last Tail. Its drefful stuff—a sort of lickwid litenin, gut up under the personal supervishun of the devil—tears men's inards all to peaces and makes their noses blossum as the Lobster. Shun it as you would a wild hyeny with a fire brand tied to his tale, and while you air abowt it you will do a first rate thing for yourself and everybody abowt you by shunnin all kinds of intoxicatin lickers. You don't need 'em no more'n a cat needs 2 tales, sayin nothin abowt the trubble and sufferin they cawse. But unless your inards air cast iron, avoid New Englan's favorite Bevridge.

My friends, I'm dun. I tear myself away from you with tears in my eyes & a pleasant oder of Onyins abowt my close. In the langwidge of Mister Catterline to the Rummuns, I go, but perhaps I shall cum back agin. Adoo, peple of Wethersfield. Be virtoous & you'll be happy.

Interview with President Lincoln

I hav no politics. Nary a one. I'm not in the bizniss. If I was I spose I should holler versiffrusly in the streets at nite, and go home to Betsy Jane smellen of coal ile and gin in the mornin. I should go to the Poles arly. I should stay there all day. I should see to it that my nabers was thar. I should git carriges to take the kripples, the infirm, and the indignant thar. I should be on guard agin frauds and sich. I should be on the look out for the infamus lise of the enemy, got up jest be4 elecshun for perlitical effeck. When all was over, and my candydate was elected, I should move heving & arth—so to speak—until I got orfice, which if I didn't git a orfice I should turn around and abooze the Administration with all my mite and maine. But I'm not in the bizniss. I'm in a far more respectful bizniss nor what pollertics is. I wouldn't giv two cents to be a Congresser. The wus insult I ever received was when sertin citizens of Baldinsville axed me to run fur the Legislater. Sez I, "My frends, dostest think I'd stoop to that there?" They turned as white as a sheet. I spoke in my most orfullest tones, & they knowd I wasn't to be trifled with. They slunked out of site to onct.

Artemus Ward, *Complete Works* . . . , pp. 109–113.

There4, havin no politics, I made bold to visit Old Abe at his humstid in Springfield. I found the old feller in his parler, surrounded by a perfeck swarm of orfice seekers. Knowin he had been capting of a flat boat on the roarin Mississippy I thought I'd address him in sailor lingo, so sez I, "Old Abe, ahoy! Let out yer main-suls, reef hum the fore-castle & throw yer jib-poop over-board! Shiver my timbers, my harty!" [N.B.—This is ginuine mariner langwidge. I know, becawz I've seen sailor plays acted out by them New York theater fellers.] Old Abe lookt up quite cross & sez, "Send in yer petition by & by. I can't possibly look at it now. Indeed I can't. It's onpossible, sir!"

"Mr Linkin, who do you spect I air?" sed I.

"A orfice-seeker, to be sure!" sed he.

"Wall, sir," sed I, "you's never more mistaken in your life. You hain't gut a orfiss I'd take under no circumstances. I'm A. Ward. Wax figgers is my perfeshun. I'm the father of Twins, and they look like me—both of them. I cum to pay a frendly visit to the President eleck of the United States. If so be you wants to see me, say so—if not, say so, & I'm orf like a jug handle."

"Mr Ward, sit down. I am glad to see you, sir."

"Repose in Abraham's Buzzum!" sed one of the orfice seekers, his idee bein to git orf a goak at my expense.

"Wall," sez I, "ef all you fellers repose in that there Buzzum thare'll be mity poor nussin for sum of you!" where-upon Old Abe buttoned his weskit clear up and blusht like a maidin of sweet 16. Jest at this pint of the conversation another swarm of orfice-seekers arrove & cum pilin into the parler. Sum wanted post-orfices, sum wanted collectorships, sum wantid furrin missions, and all wanted sumthin. I thought Old Abe would go crazy. He hadn't more than had time to shake hands with 'em, before another tremenjis crowd cum porein onto his premises. His house and door-yard was now perfeckly overflowed with orfice-seekers, all clameruss for a immejit interview with Old Abe. One man from Ohio, who had about seven inches of corn whisky into him, mistook me for Old Abe, and addrest me as "The Pra-hayrie Flower of the West!" Thinks I, *you* want a offiss putty bad. Another man with a gold heded cane and a red nose, told Old Abe he was "a seckind Washington & the Pride of the Boundless West."

Sez I, "Squire, you wouldn't take a small post-offis if you could git it, would you?"

Sez he, "A patrit is abuv them things, sir!"

"There's a putty big crop of patrits this season, aint there, Squire?" sez I, when *another* crowd of offiss-seekers pored in. The house, dooryard, barn, & woodshed was now all full, and when *another* crowd cum I told 'em not to go away for want of room, as the hog-pen was still empty. One patrit from a small town in Michygan went up on top the house, got into the chimney and slid down into the parler where Old Abe was endeverin to keep the hungry pack of orfice-seekers from chawin him up alive without benefit of clergy. The minit he reached the fire-place, he jumpt up, brusht the soot out of his eyes, and yelled: "Don't make eny pint-ment at the Spunkville post-offiss till you've read my papers. All the respectful men in our town is signers to that there dockyment!"

"Good God!" cride Old Abe, "they cum upon me from the skize—down the chimneys, and from the bowels of the yearth!" He hadn't more'n got them words out of his delikit mouth before two fat offiss-seekers from Wisconsin, in en-deverin to crawl atween his legs for the purpuss of applyin for the tollgateship at Milwawky, upsot the President eleck, & he would hev gone sprawlin into the fire-place if I hadn't caught him in these arms. But I hadn't morn'n stood him up strate, before another man cum crashin down the chimney, his head strikin me vilently agin the inards and prostrating my voluptoous form onto the floor. "Mr Linkin," shoutid the infatooated being, "my papers is signed by every clergyman in our town, and likewise the skoolmaster!"

Sez I, "You egrejis ass," gitting up & brushin the dust from my eyes, "I'll.sign your papers with this bunch of bones, if you don't be a little more keerful how you make my breadbasket a depot in the futer. How do you like that air perfumery?" sez I, shuving my fist under his nose. "Them's the kind of papers I'll giv you! Them's the papers *you* want!"

"But I workt hard for the ticket; I toiled night and day! The patrit should be rewarded!"

"Virtoo," sed I, holdin the infatooated man by the coat-collar, "virtoo, sir, is its own reward. Look at me!" He did look at me, and qualed be4 my gase. "The fact is," I continued, lookin round on the hungry crowd, "there is scacely a offiss for every ile lamp carrid round durin this campane. I wish thare was furrin missions to be filled on varis lonely Islands where eppydemics rage incessantly, and if I was in Old Abe's place I'd send every mother's son of you to them. What air you here for?" I continnered, warmin up considerable, "can't you giv Abe a minit's peace? Don't you see he's worrid most to death? Go home, you miserable men, go home & till the sile! Go to peddlin tinware—go to choppin wood—go to bilin sope—stuff sassengers—black boots—git a clerkship on sum respectable manure cart—go round as original Swiss Bell Ringers—becum 'origenal and only' Campbell Minstrels—go to lecturin at 50 dollars a nite—imbark in the peanut bizniss—*write for the Ledger**—saw off your legs and go round givin concerts, with techin appeals to

* A New York newspaper famous for its numerous contributors.—*A. Ward.*

a charitable public, printed on your handbills—anything for a honest livin, but don't come round here drivin Old Abe crazy by your outrajis cuttings up! Go home. 'Stand not upon the order of your goin,' but go to onct! Ef in five minits from this time," sez I, pullin out my new sixteen dollar huntin cased watch, and brandishin it before their eyes,—"Ef in five minits from this time a single sole of you remains on these here premises, I'll go out to my cage near by, and let my Boy Constructor loose! & ef he gits amung you, you'll think old Solferino has cum again and no mistake!" You ought to hev seen them scamper, Mr Fair. They run orf as though Satun hisself was after them with a red hot ten pronged pitchfork. In five minits the premises was clear.

"How kin I ever repay you, Mr Ward, for your kindness?" sed Old Abe, advancin and shakin me warmly by the hand. "How kin I repay you, sir?"

"By givin the whole country a good, sound administration. By poerin ile upon the troubled waturs, North and South. By pursooin a patriotic, firm, and just course, and then, if any State wants to secede, let 'em Sesesh!"

"How 'bout my Cabinit, Mister Ward?" sed Abe.

"Fill it up with Showmen, sir! Showmen is devoid of politics. They hain't got any principles! They know how to cater for the public. They know what the public wants, North & South. Showmen, sir, is honest men. Ef you doubt their literary ability, look at their posters, and see small bills! Ef you want a Cabinit as is a Cabinit, fill it up with showmen, but don't call on me. The moral wax figger perfeshun musn't be permitted to go down while there's a drop of blood in these vains! A. Linkin, I wish you well! Ef Powers or Walcutt wus to pick out a model for a beautiful man, I scacely think they'd sculp you; but ef you do the fair thing by your country, you'll make as putty a angel as any of us!

A. Linkin, use the talents which Nature has put into you judishusly and firmly, and all will be well! A. Linkin, adoo!"

He shook me cordyully by the hand—we exchanged picters, so we could gaze upon each others' liniments when far away from one another—he at the hellum of the ship of State, and I at the hellum of the show bizness—admittance only 15 cents.

The Show Is Confiscated

You hav perhaps wondered wharebouts I was for these many dase gone and past. Perchans you sposed I'd gone to the Tomb of the Cappyletts, tho I don't know what those is. It's a poplar noospaper frase.

Listen to my tail, and be silent that ye may here. I've been among the Seseshers, a earnin my daily peck by my legitimit perfeshun, and havn't had no time to weeld my facile quill for "the Grate Komick paper," if you'll allow me to kote from your troothful advertisement.

My success was skaly, and I likewise had a narrer scape of my life. If what I've been threw is "Suthern hosspitality," 'bout which we've hearn so much, then I feel bound to obsarve that they made too much of me. They was altogether too lavish with their attenshuns.

I went among the Seseshers with no feelins of annermosity. I went in my perfeshernal capacity. I was actooated by one of the most Loftiest desires which can swell the human Buzzum, viz.:—to giv the people their money's worth, by showin them Sagashus Beests, and Wax Statoots, which I

Artemus Ward, *Complete Works* . . . , pp. 113–118.

venter to say air onsurpast by any other statoots anywheres.
I will not call that man who sez my statoots is humbugs a
lier and a hoss thief, but bring him be4 me and I'll wither
him with one of my scornful frowns.

But to proceed with my tail. In my travels threw the Sonny
South I heared a heap of talk about Seceshon and bustin up
the Union, but I didn't think it mounted to nothin. The
politicians in all the villages was swearin that Old Abe
(sometimes called the Prahayrie flower) shouldn't never be
noggerated. They also made fools of theirselves in varis ways,
but as they was used to that I didn't let it worry me much,
and the Stars and Stripes continued for to wave over my
little tent. Moor over, I was a Son of Malty and a member
of several other Temperance Societies, and my wife she was
a Dawter of Malty, an I sposed these fax would secoor me
the infloonz and pertectiun of all the fust families. Alas! I
was dispinted. State arter State seseshed, and it growed hotter and hotter for the undersined. Things came to a climb-
macks in a small town in Alabamy, where I was premp-
torally ordered to haul down the Stars & Stripes. A deppytashun of red-faced men cum up to the door of my tent
ware I was standin takin money (the arternoon exhibishun
had commenst, an' my Italyun organist was jerkin his sole-
stirrin chimes). "We air cum, Sir," said a millingtary man
in a cockt hat, "upon a hi and holy mishun. The Southern
Eagle is screamin threwout this sunny land—proudly and
defiantly screamin, Sir!"

"What's the matter with him?" sez I; "don't his vittles sit
well on his stummick?"

"That Eagle, Sir, will continner to scream all over this
Brite and tremenjus land!"

"Wall, let him *scream*. If your Eagle can amuse hisself by

screamin, let him went!" The men annoyed me, for I was Bizzy makin change.

"We are cum, Sir, upon a matter of dooty——"

"You're right, Capting. It's every man's dooty to visit my show," sed I.

"We air cum——"

"And that's the reason you are here!" sez I, larfin one of my silvery larfs. I thawt if he wanted to goak I'd give him sum of my sparklin eppygrams.

"Sir, you're inserlent. The plain question is, will you hand down the Star-Spangled Banner, and hist the Southern flag!"

"Nary hist!" Those was my reply.

"Your wax works and beests is then confisticated, & you air arrested as a Spy!"

Sez I, "My fragrant roses of the Southern clime and Bloomin daffodils, what's the price of whisky in this town, and how many cubic feet of that seductive flooid can you individooally hold?"

They made no reply to that, but said my wax figgers was confisticated. I axed them if that was ginerally the stile among thieves in that country, to which they also made no reply, but sed I was arrested as a Spy, and must go to Montgomry in iuns. They was by this time jined by a large crowd of other Southern patrits, who commenst hollerin "Hang the bald-headed aberlitionist, and bust up his immoral exhibition!" I was ceased and tied to a stump, and the crowd went for my tent—that water-proof pavilion, wherein instruction and amoosment had been so muchly combined, at 15 cents per head—and tore it all to pieces. Meanwhile dirty faced boys was throwin stuns and empty beer bottles at my massive brow, and takin other improper liberties with my person. Resistance was useless, for a variety of reasons, as I readily observed.

The Seseshers confisticated my statoots by smashin them to attums. They then went to my money box and confisticated all the loose change therein contaned. They then went and bust in my cages, lettin all the animils loose, a small but helthy tiger among the rest. This tiger has a excentric way of tearin dogs to peaces, and I allers sposed from his gineral conduck that he'd have no hesitashun in servin human beins in the same way if he could git at them. Excuse me if I was crooil, but I larfed boysterrusly when I see that tiger spring in among the people. "Go to it, my sweet cuss!" I inardly exclaimed; "I forgive you for bitin off my left thum with all my heart! Rip 'em up like a bully tiger whose Lare has bin inwaded by Seseshers!"

I can't say for certain that the tiger serisly injured any of them, but as he was seen a few days after, sum miles distant, with a large and well selected assortment of seats of trowsis in his mouth, and as he lookt as tho he'd bin havin sum vilent exercise, I rayther guess he did. You sill therefore perceive that they didn't confisticate him much.

I was carried to Montgomry in iuns and placed in durans vial. The jail was a ornery edifiss, but the table was librally surplied with Bakin and Cabbidge. This was a good variety, for when I didn't hanker after Bakin I could help myself to the cabbige.

I had nobody to talk to nor nothin to talk about, however, and I was very lonely, specially on the first day; so when the jailer parst my lonely sell I put the few stray hairs on the back part of my hed (I'm bald now, but thare was a time when I wore sweet auburn ringlets) into as dish-hevild a state as possible, & rollin my eyes like a manyyuck, I cride: "Stay, jaler, stay! I am not mad but soon shall be if you don't bring me suthing to Talk!" He brung me sum noospapers, for which I thanked him kindly.

At larst I got a interview with Jefferson Davis, the President of the Southern Conthieveracy. He was quite perlite, and axed me to sit down and state my case. I did it, when he larfed and said his gallunt men had been a little 2 enthoosiastic in confisticatin my show.

"Yes," sez I, "they confisticated me too muchly. I had sum hosses confisticated in the same way onct, but the confisticaters air now poundin stun in the States Prison in Injinnapylus."

"Wall, wall, Mister Ward, you air at liberty to depart; you air frendly to the South, I know. Even now we hav many frens in the North, who sympathise with us, and won't mingle with this fight."

"J. Davis, there's your grate mistaik. Many of us was your sincere frends, and thought certin parties amung us was fussin about you and meddlin with your consarns intirely too much. But J. Davis, the minit you fire a gun at the piece of dry-goods called the Star-Spangled Banner, the North gits up and rises en massy, in defence of that banner. Not agin you as individooals,—not agin the South even—but to save the flag. We should indeed be weak in the knees, unsound in the heart, milk-white in the liver, and soft in the hed, if we stood quietly by and saw this glorus Govyment smashed to pieces, either by a furrin or a intestine foe. The gentleharted mother hates to take her naughty child across her knee, but she knows it is her dooty to do it. So we shall hate to whip the naughty South, but we must do it if you don't make back tracks at onct, and we shall wallup you out of your boots! J. Davis, it is my decided opinion that the Sonny South is makin a egrejus mutton-hed of herself!"

"Go on, sir, you're safe enuff. You're too small powder for me!" sed the President of the Southern Conthieveracy.

"Wait till I go home and start out the Baldinsvill Mounted

Hoss Cavalry! I'm Capting of that Corpse, I am, and J. Davis, beware! Jefferson D., I now leave you! Farewell, my gay Saler Boy! Good bye my bold buccaneer! Pirut of the deep blue sea, adoo! adoo!"

My tower threw the Southern Conthieveracy on my way home was thrillin enuff for yeller covers. It will form the subjeck of my next. Betsy Jane and the progeny air well.—

Yours respectively,

A. WARD.

Thrilling Scenes in Dixie

I had a narrer scape from the sonny South. "The swings and arrers of outrajus fortin," alluded to by Hamlick, warn't nothin in comparison to my troubles. I come pesky near swearin sum profane oaths more'n onct, but I hope I didn't do it, for I've promist she whose name shall be nameless (except that her initials is Betsy J.) that I'll jine the Meetin House at Baldinsville, jest as soon as I can scrape money enuff together so I can 'ford to be piuss in good stile, like my welthy nabers. But if I'm confisticated agin I'm fraid I shall continner on in my present benited state for sum time.

I figgered conspicyusly in many thrillin scenes in my tower from Montgomry to my humstead, and on sevril occasions I thought "the grate komick paper" wouldn't be inriched no more with my lubrications. Arter biddin adoo to Jefferson D. I started for the depot. I saw a nigger sittin on a fence a-playin on a banjo. "My Afrikan Brother," sed I,

Artemus Ward, *Complete Works* . . . , pp. 118–122.

coting from a Track I onct red, "you belong to a very interesting race. Your masters is going to war excloosively on
your account."

"Yes, boss," he replied, "an' I wish 'em honorable graves!"
and he went on playin the banjo, larfin all over and openin
his mouth wide enuff to drive in an old-fashioned 2 wheeled
chaise.

The train of cars in which I was to trust my wallerable
life was on the scaliest, rickytiest lookin lot of consarns that
I ever saw on wheels afore. "What time does this string of
second-hand coffins leave?" I inquired of the depot master.
He sed direckly, and I went & sot down. I hadn't more'n
fairly squatted afore a dark lookin man with a swinister expression onto his countenance entered the cars, and lookin
very sharp at me, he axed what was my principles?

"Secesh!" I answered. "I'm a Dissoluter. I'm in favor of
Jeff Davis, Bowregard, Pickens, Capt. Kidd, Bloobeard,
Munro Edards, the devil, Mrs Cunningham, and all the
rest of 'em."

"You're in favor of the war!"

"Certingly. By all means. I'm in favor of this war and
also of the next war. I've been in favor of the next war for
over sixteen years!"

"War to the knive!" sed the man.

"Blud, Eargo, blud!" sed I, tho them words isn't origgernal
with me. Them words was rit by Shakspeare, who is ded.
His mantle fell onto the author of "The Seven Sisters," who's
goin to hav a Spring overcoat made out of it.

We got under way at larst, an' proceeded on our jerney at
about the rate of speed which is ginrally obsarved by prop-
erly-conducted funeral processions. A hansum yung gal, with
a red musketer bar on the back side of her hed, and a sassy
little black hat tipt over her forrerd, sot in the seat with me.

She wore a little Sesesh flag pin'd onto her hat, and she was a goin for to see her troo love, who had jined the Southern army, all so bold and gay. So she told me. She was chilly, and I offered her my blanket.

"Father livin?" I axed.

"Yes, sir."

"Got any Uncles?"

"A heap. Uncle Thomas is ded, tho."

"Peace to Uncle Thomas's ashes, and success to him! I will be your Uncle Thomas! Lean on me, my pretty Secesher, and linger in Blissful repose!" She slept as secoorly as in her own housen, and didn't disturb the sollum stillness of the night with 'ary snore!

At the first station a troop of Sojers entered the cars and inquired if "Old Wax Works" was on bored. That was the disrespectiv stile in which they referred to me. "Becawz if Old Wax Works is on bored," sez a man with a face like a double-brested lobster, "we're going to hang Old Wax Works!"

"My illustrious and patriotic Bummers!" sez I, a gittin up and takin orf my Shappo, "if you allude to A. Ward, it's my pleasin dooty to inform you that he's ded. He saw the error of his ways at 15 minits parst 2 yesterday, and stabbed his-self with a stuffed sled-stake, dying in five beautiful tabloos to slow moosic! His larst words was: "My perfeshernal career is over! I jerk no more!"

"And who be you?"

"I'm a stoodent in Senator Benjamin's law offiss. I'm going up North to steal some spoons and things for the Southern Army."

This was satisfactry, and the intossicated troopers went orf. At the next station the pretty little Secesher awoke and sed she must git out there. I bid her a kind adoo and giv her sum pervisions. "Accept my blessin and this hunk of ginger-bread!" I sed. She thankt me muchly and tript galy away. There's considerable human nater in a man, and I'm fraid I shall allers giv aid and comfort to the enemy if he cums to me in the shape of a nice young gal.

At the next station I didn't get orf so easy. I was dragged out of the cars and rolled in the mud for several minits, for the purpose of "takin the conseet out of me," as a Secesher kindly stated.

I was let up finally, when a powerful large Secesher came up and embraced me, and to show that he had no hard feelins agin me, put his nose into my mouth. I returned the compliment by placin my stummick suddenly agin his right foot, when he kindly made a spittoon of his able-bodied face. Actooated by a desire to see whether the Secesher had bin vaxinated I then fastened my teeth onto his left coat-sleeve and tore it to the shoulder. We then vilently bunted our heads together for a few minits, danced around a little, and sot down in a mud puddle. We riz to our feet agin & by a sudden and adroit movement I placed my left eye agin the Secesher's fist. We then rushed into each other's arms and fell under a two-hoss wagon. I was very much exhaustid and didn't care about gittin up agin, but the man said he reckoned I'd better, and I conclooded I would. He pulled me up, but I hadn't bin on my feet more'n two seconds afore the ground flew up and hit me in the hed. The crowd sed it was high old sport, but I couldn't zackly see where the lafture come in. I riz and we embraced agin. We careered madly to a steep bank, when I got the upper hands of my antaggernist and threw him into the raveen. He fell about forty feet, striking a grindstone pretty hard. I understood he was injured. I haven't heard from the grindstone.

A man in a cockt hat cum up and sed he felt as though a

apology was doo me. There was a mistake. The crowd had taken me for another man! I told him not to mention it, and axed him if his wife and little ones was so as to be about, and got on bored the train, which had stopped at that station "20 minits for refreshments." I got all I wantid. It was the hartiest meal I ever et.

I was rid on a rale the next day, a bunch of blazin fire crackers bein tied to my coat tales. It was a fine spectycal in a dramatic pint of view, but I didn't enjoy it. I had other adventers of a startlin kind, but why continner? Why lasserate the Public Boozum with these here things? Suffysit to say I got across Mason & Dixie's line safe at last. I made tracks for my humsted, but she to whom I'm harnist for life failed to recognize, in the emashiated bein who stood before her, the gushin youth of forty-six summers who had left her only a few months afore. But I went into the pantry, and brought out a certain black bottle. Raisin it to my lips, I sed "Here's to you, old gal!" I did it so natral that she knowed me at once. "Those form! Them voice! That natral stile of doin things! 'Tis he!" she cried, and rushed into my arms. It was too much for her & she fell into a swoon. I cum very near swoundin myself.

No more today from yours for the Pepetration of the Union, and the bringin of the Goddess of Liberty out of her present bad fix.

CHARLES HENRY SMITH
[Bill Arp]
(1826-1903)

Charles Henry Smith, or Bill Arp, "so called," was Georgia-born and Georgia-bred. After brief study, he was admitted to the bar, entering into a partnership in Rome, Georgia. He served in the Confederate army throughout the War Between the States, after which he resumed practicing law. He held office briefly as state senator and as mayor of Rome, but around 1877 abandoned law for farming. Eleven years later he moved into Cartersville to devote himself to study and writing.

Four letters signed Bill Arp and addressed to "Mr. Abe Linkhorn" appeared in the Rome *Southern Confederacy* in 1861–1862. The first three comprise the selections to follow. Their quaint spelling and dialect were typical of the times, while their sentiments afford insights into Southern attitudes. Bill Arp (the name was borrowed from a local wit) blended genial humor, forceful satire, and common sense. "I'm a good Union man—'so-called'—but I'll bet on Dixie as long as I've got a dollar," he declared. Arp put his money where his convictions lay: "I joined the army and succeeded in killing about as many of them as they of me." Small wonder that as a comic writer and lecturer during the ordeal of Reconstruction he was hailed as "the best loved man in all the Southland." The Savannah *Press* eulogized him: "In the dark days he kept southern hearts from breaking."

To Abe Lincoln

Rome, Geo., April, 1861.

Mr. Lincoln—

Sir: These are to inform you that we are all well, and hope these lines may find you in *statu quo*. We received your proclamation, and as you have put us on very short notice, a few of us boys have concluded to write you, and ask for a little more time. The fact is, we are most obliged to have a few more days, for the way things are happening, it is utterly impossible for us to disperse in twenty days. Old Virginia, and Tennessee, and North Carolina are continually aggravating us into tumults and carousments, and a body can't disperse until you put a stop to such unruly conduct on their part. I tried my darn'dst yesterday to disperse and retire, but it was no go; and besides, your marshal here ain't doing a darn'd thing—he don't read the riot-act, nor remonstrate, nor nothing, and ought to be turned out. If you conclude to do so, I am authorized to recommend to you Colonel Gibbons or Mr. McClung, who would attend to the business as well as most anybody.

The fact is, the boys around here want watching, or they'll take something. A few days ago I heard they surrounded two of our best citizens because they were named Fort and Sumter. Most of them are so hot that they fairly siz when you pour water on them, and that's the way they make up their military companies here now—when a man applies to

Charles Henry Smith, *Bill Arp, So Called: A Side Show of The Southern Side of The War*, New York (1866), pp. 18–20.

join the volunteers, they sprinkle him, and if he sizzes they take him, and if he don't they don't.

Mr. Lincoln, sir, privately speaking, I'm afraid I'll get in a tight place here among these bloods, and have to slope out of it, and I would like much to have your Scotch cap and cloak that you travelled in to Washington. I suppose you wouldn't be likely to use the same disguise again when you left, and therefore I would propose to swap. I am five feet five, and could get my plough breeches and coat to you in eight or ten days if you can wait that long. I want you to write to me immediately about things generally, and let us know where you intend to do your fighting. Your proclamation says something about taking possession of all the private property at "All Hazards." We can't find no such a place on the map. I thought it must be about Charleston, or Savannah, or Harper's Ferry, but they say it ain't anywhere down South. One man said it was a little factory on an island in Lake Champlain, where they make sand-bags. My opinion is, that sand-bag business won't pay, and it is a great waste of money. Our boys here carry their sand in their gizzards, where it keeps better, and is always handy. I'm afraid your Government is giving you and your Kangaroo a great deal of unnecessary trouble, and my humble advice is, if things don't work better soon, you'd better grease it, or trade the darn'd old thing off. I'd take rails or any thing for it. If I could see you, I'd show you a sleight-of-hand trick that would change the whole concern into buttons quick. If you don't trade or do something else with it soon, it will spoil or die on your hands certain.

Give my respects to Bill Seward and the other members of the Kangaroo. What's Hannibal doing? I don't hear any thing from him now-a-days.

Yours, with care,

BILL ARP.

P.S.—If you can possibly extend that order to thirty days, do so. We have sent you a CHECK at Harper's Ferry (who keeps that darn'd old Ferry now? it's giving us a heap of trouble), but if you positively won't extend, we'll send you a check, drawn by Jeff. Davis, Beauregard endorser, payable on sight anywhere.

Yours,

B. A.

To Mr. Abe Lincoln

Centreville, January 12, 1862.

Mr. Lincoln—

Sir: In the spring of the year I wrote to you a letter from my native soil, asking for a little more time to disperse. I told you then that twenty days were not enough—that the thing could not be done in that brief interval. You can look back and see I was right. We tried our durndest to comply with your schedule, but as you kept calling for volunteers, our Cherokee Georgia Democrats kept coming out from under their clay roots. They shook themselves and spit fire, and wouldn't go back so long as the Whigs would read them the news about this fuss.

Mr. Abe Lincoln, sir, the spring has shed its fragrance, the summer is over and gone, the yellow leaves of autumn have covered the ground, old Winter is slobbering his froth on the earth, but we have not been able to disperse as yet. Me and the boys started last May to see you personally, and ask for an extension of your brief furlough, but we got on a bust in old Virginia, about the 21st of July, and like to have got run over by a parcel of fellows running from Bull Run to your city. After that we tried to get to you by the Potomac River, but Mr. Whiting said you were not running that machine *at these presents.* We next went to Mr. Harper's Ferry, to take the Baltimore Railroad, but we couldn't find the conductor, and cars seemed scarce, and the folks said

Bill Arp, So Called, pp. 21–23.

you were not running that machine *much*. We thought, however, to take a deck passage on the canal, but a dam had broke and General Jackson said you were not running that machine, *scarcely any*. After all that we came back, and thought we'd get Captain Wilkes to ship us over, but Mr. Bennett sent us word that the captain had quit a seafaring life. Mr. Seward made him quit, to pacify an old English Bull that was bellowing about and pawing dirt in the air. Mr. Lincoln, sir, if that Bull is of the same stock as the one your folks saw here in July, he is dangerous, and will have a bad effect on your population. You had better circumscribe him before he hurts somebody.

Mr. Lincoln, sir, what are your factories doing now-a-days? I heard you had quit running their machines, owing to a thin crop of cotton. If you would put sweet oil on your factories, they wouldn't rust while standing idle. I was glad to hear that you had got enough cotton to do yours and Seward's families. The boys say you got enough to make as many shirts as Falstaff had in his company.

Mr. Lincoln, sir, how do you come on with your stone fleet—does it pay expenses—is it a safe investment—could I get any stock in it at a fair price? Don't you think it is most too far to haul rocks, and won't it impoverish New England soil to take the rocks off of it?

Mr. Abe Lincoln, sir, the 18th is the anniversary of the day when Georgia tore herself frantically loose from the abolition dynasty—when she ripped her star from off the striped rag, and spread a new shirting to the breeze. We calculate to celebrate that day, and I am authorized to invite you and Bill Seward over to partake of our hospitalities. Where is Hamlin? I allow that he is dead, or I would ask him too. Let me know if you and Seward are coming, so we can fix up and swap a lie or two with you. Couldn't you all come along with Mack when he makes that advance he has been talking about so long? Bring your knitting with you when you come, and a clean shirt or two. Do you chaw tobacco? We have got some that is good. Ely chawed, and Mr. Davis gave him a whole warehouse at Richmond.

Mr. Lincoln, sir, I wish you would ask Banks to send me a codfish. Polecats are bad around here, and we want something to drive 'em away. If you bring Banks and Picayune Butler with you, you needn't bring the cod.

Yours, till death,

BILL ARP.

P.S.—Where is Fremont? I hear he has gone up a spout.

Another Letter to Mr. Lincoln

December 2, 1862.

Mr. Lincoln—

Sir: A poet has said that "Time untied waiteth for no man." To my opinion it is untied now and hastens on to that eventful period which you have fixed when Africa is to be unshackled, when Niggerdom is to feel the power of your proclamation, when Uncle Tom is to change his base and evacuate his cabin, when all the emblems of darkness are to rush frantically forth into the arms of their deliverers, and with perfumed and scented gratitude embrace your Excellency and Madam Harriet Beecher Stowe! What a glorious day that is to be! What a sublime era in history! What a

Bill Arp, So Called, pp. 24–26.

proud culmination and consummation and corruscation of your political hopes! After a few thousand have clasped you in their ebony arms it will be a fitting time, Mr. Lincoln, for you to lay yourself down and die. Human ambition can have no higher monument to climb. After such a work you might complete the immortal heroism of your character, by leaping from the topmost pinnacle of your glory upon the earth below.

But alas for human folly—alas for all sublunary things—our people will not believe, these crazy rebels will not consider; Christmas is already here, only one more brief week to slide away before we must part, forever part, with all our negro heritage, and yet our stubborn people continue to buy and sell them, and the shorter the lease, the higher the price they are paying. What infatuation! I do verily believe they will keep up their old ways until next Wednesday night, just as though they did not have to give them all up the next morning before breakfast. Some say the stay law affects the niggers and will operate to make them stay at home—some say you have not got transportation nor rations for four millions of darkeys—some say your call is premature; but the majority are of the opinion that a little difficulty you met at Fredericksburg has interfered with your arrangements, and extended the time like a sine die.

Mr. Lincoln, sir, I forewarned you about crossing those sickly rivers. The Lee side of any shore is unhealthy to your population; keep away from those Virginia watercourses, go around them or under them, but for the sake of economy don't try to cross them. It is too hard upon your burial squads and ambulance horses.

Mr. Lincoln, sir, when is this war to close? How much longer can you renew your note of ninety days which you said was time enough to settle this difficulty—do you pay the interest? How much territory have you subjugated—what makes cotton sell at 67 cents a pound in your diggins—is it not awful scarce—what do your bony women do for stuffing and padding? I heard they had to use hay and saw-dust and such like, and I thought it must be very painful to their tender bosoms to have to resort to such scarce commodity; I would like to send you a bale, but Governor Brown would seize it. It is said by many that the war is about to close because of the Governor's late raid on leather—they say the war begun with a John Brown raid in Virginia, and will end with a Joe Brown raid in Georgia—I allow not, for I think the Governor only took that way of getting the State rid of its surplus, for he wanted to drive it into the adjoining States where things were scarcer. I would like to see you personally, Mr. Lincoln, and hear you talk and tell some of your funny anecdotes, like you told Governor Morehead. I laughed when I read them till the tears fairly rained from my eyelids—I know I could make my fortune, Mr. Lincoln, compiling your wit. May I be your Boswell, and follow you about?

But fare thee well, my friend, and, before you cross another Rubicon, I advise you, in the eloquent language of Mr. Burke, "consider, old cow, consider."

Yours, till death,

BILL ARP.

P.S.—Give my respects to Johnny Van Buren; I heard you and him were mighty thick and affectionate.

B. A.

ROBERT HENRY NEWELL
[Orpheus C. Kerr]
(1836-1901)

Robert Henry Newell, newspaper and magazine editor, wrote novels and poems as well as the Civil War "papers" of Orpheus C. Kerr, on which his fame endures. He is frequently ranked with Downing, Ward, Arp, Nasby, and Nye among the great builders of newspaper humor and the tellers of tall tales. His pseudonym was a pun on "office seeker." It was by all odds the funniest product of his wit.

Letter XIV

SHOWING HOW OUR CORRESPONDENT MADE A SPEECH OF
VAGUE CONTINUITY, AFTER THE MODEL OF THE LATEST
APPROVED STUMP ORATORY.

WASHINGTON, D.C., September 30th, 1861.

Another week has fled swiftly by, my boy, on those
wings which poets and other long-haired creatures suppose to be eternally flapping through the imaginary atmosphere of time; yet the high old battle so long expected
has not got any further than "heavy firing near the Chain
Bridge," which takes place every afternoon punctually at
three o'clock—just in time for the evening papers. I have
been thinking, my boy, that if this heavy firing in the vicinity of Chain Bridge lasts a few years longer, it will finally become a nuisance to the First Families living in that
vicinity. But sometimes what is thought to be heavy firing
is not that exactly; the other day, a series of loud explosions were heard on Arlington Heights, and twenty-four
reporters immediately telegraphed to twenty-four papers
that five hundred thousand rebels had attacked our lines
with two thousand rifled cannon, and had been repulsed
with a loss of fourteen thousand killed. Federal loss—one
killed, and two committed suicide. But when General Mc-
Clellan came to inquire into the cause of the explosions,
this report was somewhat modified:

"What was that firing for?" he asked an orderly, who
had just come over the river.

"If you please, sir," responded the sagacious animal, "there was no firing at all. It was Villiam Brown, of Regiment 5, Mackerel Brigade, which has a horrible cold, and sneezes in that way."

Villiam has since been ordered to telegraph to the War Department whenever he sneezes, so that no more of these harrowing mistakes may be made.

Last night, my boy, an old rooster from Cattaraugus, who wants a one-horse post-office, and thinks I've got some influence with Abe the Venerable, brought six big Dutchmen to serenade me; and, as soon I opened the window to damn them, he called unanimously for a speech. At this time, my boy, an immense crowd, consisting of two policemen and a hackman, were drawn to the spot, and greeted me with great applause. Feeling that their intentions were honorable, I could not bear to disappoint my fellow-citizens, and so I was constrained to make the following

SPEECH.

Men of America:—It is with feelings akin to emotion that I regard this vast assemblage of Nature's noblemen, and reflect that it comes to do honor to me, who have only performed my duty. Gentlemen, my heart is full; as the poet says:

> "The night shall be filled with burglars,
>   And the chaps that infest the day
> Shall pack up their duds like peddlers,
>   And carry the spoons away."

It seems scarcely five minutes ago that this vast and otherwise large country sprung from chaos at the call of

Columbus, and immediately commenced to produce wood-
en nutmegs for a foreign shore. It seems but three seconds
ago that all this beautiful scene was a savage wild, and
echoed the axe-falls of the sanguinary pioneer, and the
footfalls of the Last of the Mohicans. Now what do I see
before me? A numerous assembly of respectable Dutchmen, and other Americans, all ready to prove to the world
that

> "Truth crushed to earth shall rise again,
>   The immortal ears of jack are hers;
> But Sarah languishes in pain
>   And dyes, amid her worshipers."

I am convinced, fellow-citizens, that the present outrageous war is no ordinary row, and that it cannot be
brought to a successful termination without some action
on the part of the Government. If to believe that a war
cannot rage without being prosecuted, is abolitionism,
then I am an abolitionist; if to believe that a good article
of black ink can be made out of black men, is republicanism, then I am a republican; but we are all brothers now,
except that fat Dutchman, who has gone to sleep on his
drum, and I pronounce him an accursed secessionist:

> "How doth the little busy bee
>   Improve each shining hour,
> And gathers beeswax all the day,
>   From every opening flower."

Men of America, shall these things longer be?—I address myself particularly to that artist with the accordeon,
who don't understand a word of English—shall these
things longer be? That's what I want to know. The majestic shade of Washington listens for an answer, and I

intend to send it by mail as soon as I receive it. Fellow citizens, it can no longer be denied that there is treason at our very hearthstones. Treason—merciful Heavens!

> "Come rest in this bosom, my own little dear,
>   The Honourable R. M. T. Hunter is here;
> I know not, I care not, if jilt's in that heart,
>   I but know that I love thee, whatever thou art."

And now the question arises, is Morrill's tariff really a benefit to the country? Gentlemen, it would be unbecoming in me to answer this question, and you would be incapable of understanding what I might say on the subject. The present is no time to think about tariffs: our glorious country is in danger and there is a tax of three per cent on all incomes over eight hundred dollars. Let each man ask himself in Dutch: "Am I prepared to shoulder my musket if I am drafted, or to procure a reprobate to take my place?" In other words:

> "The minstrel returned from the war,
>   With insects at large in his hair,
> And having a tuneful catarrh,
>   He sung through his nose to his fair."

Therefore, it is simply useless to talk reason to those traitors, who forget the words of Jackson—words, let me add, which I myself do not remember. Animated by an unholy lust for arsenals, rifled cannon, and mints, and driven to desperation by the thought that Everett is preparing a new Oration on Washington, and Morris a new song on a young woman living up the Hudson River, they are overturning the altars of their country and issuing treasury bonds, which cannot be justly called objects of interest.

What words can express the horrors of such unnatural crime?

> "Oft in the chilly night,
>   When slumber's chains have bound me,
> Soft Mary brings a light,
>   And puts a shawl around me."

Such, fellow-citizens, is the condition of our unhappy country at present, and as soon as it gets any better I will let you know. An Indian once asked a white man for a drink of whisky. "No!" said the man, "you red skins are just ignorant enough to ruin yourselves with liquor." The sachem looked calmly into the eyes of the insulter, as he retorted: "You say I am ignorant. How can that be when I am a well-red man?"

And so it is, fellow-citizens, with this Union at present, though I am not able to show exactly where the parallel is. Therefore,

> "Let us then be up and wooing,
>   With a heart for any mate,
> Still proposing, still pursuing,
>   Learn to court her, and to wait."

At the conclusion of this unassuming speech, my boy, I was waited upon by a young man, who asked me if I did not want to purchase some poetry; he had several yards to sell, and warranted it to wash.

Yours, particularly,

ORPHEUS C. KERR.

Robert Henry Newell [Orpheus C. Kerr], *The Orpheus C. Kerr Papers*, First Series, New York (1862–1865), pp. 99–104.

DAVID ROSS LOCKE

[Petroleum Vesuvius Nasby]

(1833-1888)

Petroleum Vesuvius Nasby's first letter to the public appeared in April 1863. Its title was "Negro Emancipation," its author, the publisher of the Findlay (Ohio) *Jeffersonian,* David Ross Locke. Thereafter Locke's serialized letters appeared until 1882 as the "Divers Views and Opinions and Prophecies" of Petroleum V. Nasby, who claimed to serve in turn as the Late Pastor of the Church of the New Dispensation, the Chaplain to His Excellency the President, and Postmaster "at Confederit X Roads which is in the State uv Kentucky." Their influence was great. Lincoln reportedly exclaimed over Nasby's letters: "For the genius to write these things I would gladly give up my office." General Grant asserted that he "couldn't get through a Sunday without one." Secretary of the Treasury Boutwell attributed the defeat of the Confederacy to "three great forces—the Army and Navy, the Republican Party, and the letters of Petroleum V. Nasby."

Here again was the tradition of Jack Downing, but acidified by Locke into the most withering satire of his day. During the Civil War the figure of Petroleum V. Nasby emerged as an overdrawn Copperhead, a caricature of what Locke considered to be the stupidity and corrup-

tion of the Democrats. Nasby's first success lay in his recognition of a fear widespread among Northern workingmen
that emancipation of the South's slaves would release a
flood of colored immigrants into the North. As Petroleum
V. Nasby resolved in protest: "Wareas—In the event uv
this emigrashun our feller-townsman, Abslum Kitt, and uthers whose familis depend upon their labor fur support,
wood be throde out uv employment."

"Abslum Kitt," according to the Toledo correspondent
of the Detroit *Post,* was actually a town charge named
Flenner living in Findlay, "a lazy, drunken, good-for-noth-
ing sort of a fellow" who was more bother than he was
worth. "In fact his father was already in the poor-house,"
the correspondent added, "and if Flenner, Jr. had been
there too he would have cost the town less trouble and
money." A prominent Findlay Democrat, ashamed to do
so himself, employed Flenner to circulate a petition asking the legislature to prohibit Negro immigration and to
remove those Negroes already living in the state. Locke
saw the petition in Flenner's hands. He was "at once
struck with its absurdity, especially when presented by a
man like Flenner."

Locke borrowed Flenner's petition, intending to publish
it with adverse editorial comment. But so ridiculous did
the affair seem to him that he contrived instead to "support" the petition through the heavy and deadly irony
of Petroleum V. Nasby's first letter to an editor. Within
a short time, leading journals throughout the country reprinted Nasby's views. Encouraged by his initial success,
Locke continued to write letter after letter on the public
affairs of the Civil War era and the turbulent Reconstruction period that followed.

The following selections belong to a sorely troubled period of American history. They demonstrate the truth
that wars do not end when the firing ceases, but only when

the bitter issues for which men fight are laid to rest by history. Nasby's own "Prefis, or Interductry Chapter," is offered for its original purposes, as well as to remind us that the popular attitudes of earlier periods in history are not to be equated with our own. Once in his guise of Lait Pastor uv the Church uv the Noo Dispensashun, Petroleum V. Nasby drew a refrain from an old revival hymn that suggests something of the secret of his appeal:

> There's a lite about to gleam,
> There's a fount about to stream,
> Wait a little longer!

Prefis,
or
Interductry Chapter

There is a vacany in the mind uv the public for jist sich a book ez this, else it had never bin published. There is a vacancy in my pockit for the money I am to reseeve ez copy-rite, else I hed never slung together, in consecootive shape, the ijees wich I hev from time to time flung out thro the public press, for the enlitenment uv an ongrateful public and the guidance uv an obtoose Dimocracy.

I didn't put these thots uv mine upon paper for amooze-ment. There hezn't bin anythin amoozin in Dimocrisy for the past five years, and the standardbearers, the captins uv fifties and hundreds, the leaders uv the hosts, hev hed a ruther rough time uv it. Our prominence made us uncom-fortable, for we hev bin the mark uv every writer, every orator, ez well ez uv every egg-thrower, in the country. When that gileless patriot, Jeems Bookannon, retired to private life, regretted by all who held office under him, Dimocracy felt that she wuz entrin upon a period uv darknis and gloom. The effort our Suthern brethrin made for their rites, ren-dered the position uv us Northern Dimocrats eggstremely precarious. We coodent go back on our friends South, for, knowin that peace must come, and that when it did come we wood hev to, ez in the olden time, look to them for support and maintenance, it behooved us to keep on their good side. This wood hev bin easy enuff, but alars! there are laws agin

David Ross Locke [Petroleum V. Nasby], *Swingin' Round the Cirkle*, Boston (1867), pp. 7–12.

treason, and two-thirds uv the misguided people north hed got into a way uv thinkin that the Dimocrasy South had committed that crime, and they intimated that ef we overstepped the line that divides loyalty from treason by so much ez the millionth part uv a hair, they'd make us suffer the penalty they hoped to mete out to them, but which, owin to Johnson, they dident, and wat's more, can't. Halleloogy!

But I anticipate. Twict I wuz drafted into a service I detested—twict I wuz torn from the buzzum uv my family, wich I wuz gittin along well enough, even ef the wife uv my buzzum wood occasionally git obstinit, and refooze to give me sich washin money ez wuz nessary to my existence, preferrin to squander it upon bread and clothes for the children,— twict, I say, I wuz pulled into the servis, and twict I wuz forced to desert to the Dimocrisy uv the south, rather than fite agin em. When finally the thumb uv my left hand wuz acksidentally shot off, owin to my foot becomin entangled into the lock uv my gun, wich thumb wuz also accidentally across the muzzle thereof, and I wuz no longer liable to military dooty and cood bid Provost Marshels defiance, I only steered clear uv Scylla to go bumpin onto Charybdis. I coodent let Dimocrisy alone, and the eggins—the ridin upon rails—the takin uv the oath—but why shood I harrow up the public buzzum? I stood it all till one nite I wuz pulled out uv bed, compelled to kneel onto my bare knees in the cold snow, the extremity uv my under garment, wich modesty forbids me to menshun the name uv it, fluttrin in a Janooary wind, and by a crowd uv laffin soljers compelled to take the oath and drink a pint uv raw, undilooted water! That feather broke the back uv the camel. The oath give me inflamashen uv the brane and the water inflamashen uv the stumick, and for six long weeks I lay, a wreck uv my former self. Ez I arose from that bed and saw in a glass the remains uv my pensive beauty, I vowed to wage a unceasin war on the party wich caused sich havoc, and I hev kept my oath.

I hev bin in the Apossel biznis more extensively than any man sence the time uv Paul. First I established a church uv Democrats in a little oasis I diskivered in the ablishn state uv Ohio, to wit, at Wingert's Corners, where ther wuz four groceries, but nary church or skool-house within four miles, and whose populashen wuz unanimously Dimocratic, the grocery keepers hevin mortgages on all the land around em—but alars! I wuz forced to leeve it after the election of Linkin in 1864. Noo Gersey bein the only state North wich wuz onsquelched, to her I fled, and at Saint's Rest (wich is in Noo Gersey) I erected another tabernacle. There I stayed, and et and drank and wuz merry, but Ablishnism pursood me thither, and in the fall uv '65 that state got ornery and cussid, and went Ablishn, and agin, like the wandrin Jew, I wuz forced to pull up, and wend my weary way to Kentucky, where, at Confedrit X Roads, I feel that I am safe. Massychoosets ideas can't penetrate us here. The aristocracy bleeve in freedom uv speech, but they desire to exercise a supervision over it, that they may not be led astray. They bleeve they'r rite, and for fear they'd be forced to change their minds, whenever they git into argument with anybody, ef the individooal gits the better uv them, they to-wunst shoot him ez a disturber. Hence Massychoosits can't disturb us here; the populashen is unanimously Democratic, and bids fair to continyoo so.

Here I hope to spend the few remainin years uv a eventful life. Here in the enjoyment uv that end uv the hopes uv all Democrats, a Post Offis, with four well-regulated groceries within a stun's throw, and a distillery ornamentin the landscape only a quarter uv a mile from where I rite these lines, with the ruins uv a burnt nigger school house within site uv my winder, from wich rises the odor, grateful to a Democratic nostril, and wich he kin snuff afar off, and say ha! ha! to, uv a half dozen niggers wich wuz consumed when it wuz burned, wat more kin I want? I feel that I am more than repaid for all my suffrins, and that I shel sale smoothly down the stream uv time, unvexed and happy.

It is proper to state that the papers uv which this volume is composed wuz written at various times and under various circumstances. They reflect the mind uv the author doorin a most eventful year in his history, and mark the condition uv the Dimocrisy from week to week. Consekently they shift from grave to gay, from lively to severe, with much alacrity, the grate party seemin at times to be lifted onto the top wave uv success, and at other times being down in the trough uv despondency and despair.

I mite say more, but wherefore? Ez the record uv a year uv hopes and fears, uv exaltation and depression, it may possess interest or may not—'cordin to the style uv the reader. Whatever may be its fate, one thing I am certin uv, to wit: I am a reglerly commissioned P. M.; and while the approval of the public mite lighten the toils uv offishl life and sweeten the whisky wich the salary purchases, the frowns uv the said public can't redoose me to the walks uv private life. They can't frown me out uv offis, nor frown P. M. General Randall's name off my commishn.

P. V. N.

POST OFFIS, CONFEDRIT X ROADS
(wich is in the State uv
Kentucky) , Oct. 1, 1866

The Assassination

[*Locke's editorial note:*]

The northern secessionists had, from the beginning, represented President Lincoln as worse than a brute. The leading men of the party were in a peculiar situation at his death. The loyal people compelled them to conceal the satisfaction they felt at his tragical taking off. Like the Parson, they "wept profusely the moment they saw a squad of returned soldiers coming round the corner."

SAINT'S REST
(wich is in the Stait of Noo Jersey),
April the 20th, 1865.

The nashen mourns! The hand uv the vile assassin hez bin raised agin the Goril—the head uv the nashen, and the people's Father hez fallen beneath the hand uv a patr—vile assassin.

While Aberham Linkin wuz a livin, I need not say that I did not love him. Blessed with a mind uv no ordinary dimensions, endowed with all the goodness uv Washington, I alluz bleeved him to hev bin guilty uv all the crimes uv a Nero.

No man in Noo Jersey laments his untimely death more than the undersined. I commenst weepin perfoosely the minit I diskivered a squad uv returned soljers comin round the corner, who wuz a forcin constooshnel Dimekrats to hang out mournin.

Troo, he didn't agree with me, but I kin overlook that—it

David Ross Locke, *The Struggles Social, Financial and Political of Petroleum V. Nasby*, Boston (1888), pp. 171–172.

wuz his misforchoon. Troo, he hung unoffendin men, in Kentucky, whose only crime wuz in bein loyal to wat *they* deemed *their* guverment, ez tho a man in this free country coodent choose which guverment he'd live under. Troo, he made cold-blooded war, in the most fiendish manner, on the brave men uv the South, who wuz only assertin the heaven-born rite uv roolin theirselves. Troo, he levied armies, made up uv pimps, whose chiefest delite wuz in ravishin the wives and daughters uv the South, and a miscellaneous burnin their houses. Troo, he kept into offis jist sich men ez wood sekund him in his hell-begotten skeems, and dismist every man who refused to becum ez depraved ez he wuz. Troo, he wood read uv these scenes uv blood and carnage, and in high glee tell filthy anecdotes; likewise wood he ride over the field uv battle, and ez the wheels uv his gorjus carriage crushed into the shuddrin earth the bodies uv the fallen braves, sing Afrikin melodies. Yet I, in common with all troo Dimekrats, weep! We weep! We wish it to be distinkly understood, we weep! Ther wuz that in him that instinktivly forces us to weep over his death, and to loathe the foul assassin who so suddenly removed so much loveliness uv character. He had ended the war uv oppression—he hed subjoogatid a free and brave people, who were strugglin for their rites, and hed em under his feet; but I, in common with all Dimekrats, mourn his death!

Hed it happened in 1862, when it wood hev been uv sum use to us, we wood not be so bowed down with woe and anguish. It wood hev throwd the guverment into confusion, and probably hev sekoored the independence uv the South.

But alas! the tragedy cum at the wrong time!

Now, we are saddled with the damnin crime, when it will prodoose no results. The war wuz over. The game wuz up when Richmond wuz evacuated. Why kill Linkin then? For

revenge? Revenge is a costly luxury—a party so near bankrupt ez the Dimokrasy cannot afford to indulge in it. The
wise man hez no sich word ez revenge in his dictionary—the
fool barters his hope for it.

Didst think that Linkin's death wood help the South?
Linkin's hand wuz velvet—Johnson's may be, to the eye, but
to the feel it will be found iron. Where Linkin switched,
Johnson will flay. Where Linkin banished, Johnson will
hang.

Davis wuz shocked when he heard it—so wuz I, and, in
common with all troo Dimekrats, I weep.

PETROLEUM V. NASBY.

Lait Paster uv the Church uv the Noo Dispensashun.

After the New Jersey Election, 1865

SAINT'S REST
(wich is in the State uv Noo Gersey),
November 9, 1865.

Never wuz I in so pleasant a frame uv mind as last night. All
wuz peace with me, for after bein buffeted about the world
for three skore years, at last it seemed to me ez tho forchune,
tired uv persekootin a unforchnit bein, hed taken me into
favor. I hed a solemn promise from the Dimekratic State
Central Committy in the great State uv Noo Gersey, that ez
soon ez our candidate for Governor wuz dooly elected, I
shood hev the position uv Dorekeeper to the House uv the
Lord (wich in this State means the Capital, & wich is cer-

Swingin' Round the Cirkle, pp. 13–18.

tainly better than dwellin in the tents uv wicked grosery keepers, on tick, ez I do), and a joodishus exhibition uv this promise hed prokoored for me unlimited facilities for bor-rerin, wich I improved, muchly.

On Wednesday nite I wuz a sittin in my room, a enjoyin the pleasin reflection that in a few days I should be placed above want & beyond the contingencies uv fortune. Wood! oh wood! that I hed died then and there, before that dream ov bliss wuz roodly broken. A wicked boy cum runnin past with a paper wich he hed brot from the next town where there lives a man who takes one. He flung it thro the window to me and past on. I opened it eagerly, and glanced at the hed lines!

"NOO GERSEY—5,000 REPUBLIKIN!"

One long and piercin shreek wuz heard thro that house, and wen the inmates rushed into the room they found me in-anymate on the floor. The fatal paper lay near me, explainin the cause uv the catastrophe. The kind-hearted landlord, after feelin uv my pockets and diskiverin that the contents thereof wood not pay the arrearages uv board, held a hurried consultation with his wife as to the propriety uv bringin me to; he insisting that it wuz the only chance uv gittin what wuz back—she insistin that ef I was brung to I'd go on runnin up the bill, bigger and bigger, and never pay at last. While they was argooin the matter, pro and con, I happened to git a good smell uv his breath, wich restored me to con-sciousniss to-wunst, without further assistance.

When in trouble my poetic sole alluz finds vent in song. Did ever poet who delited in tombs, and dark rollin streams, and consumption, and blighted hopes, and decay, and sich themes, ever hev such a pick of subjects ez I hev at this time? The follerin may be a consolation to the few Dimokrats uv the North who have gone so far into copperheadism that they can't change their base:—

A WALE!

In the mornin we go forth rejoicin in our strength—in the evenin we are bustid and wilt!

Man born uv woman (and most men are) is uv few days, & them is so full uv trouble that it's skarsely worth while bein born at all.

In October I waded in woe knee-deep, and now the waters uv afflickshun are about my chin.

I look to the east, and Massychusets rolls in Ablishun.

To the west I turn my eyes, and Wisconsin, and Minnesota, and Illinoy ansers Ablishun.

Southward I turn my implorin gaze, and Maryland sends greetin—Ablishun.

In New York we had em, for lo! we run a soljer, who fought valiantly, and we put him on a platform, wich stunk with nigger—yea, the savor thereof wuz louder than the Ablishun platform itself.

But behold! the people jeer and flout, and say "the platform stinketh loud enough, but the smell thereof is *not* the smell uv the Afrikin—it is of the rotten material uv wich it is composed, and the corrupshun they hev placed upon it"—and New York goes Ablishun.

Slocum held hisself up, and sed, "Come and buy." And our folds bought him and his tribe, but he getteth not his price.

NOO GERSEY—ABLISHUN!!

Job's cattle wuz slain by murrain and holler horn and sich, and, not livin near Noo York, the flesh thereof he cood not sell.

But Job hed suthin left—still cood he sell the hides and tallow!

Lazarus hed sores, but he hed dorgs to lick them.

Noo Gersey wuz the hide & tallow uv the Dimocrisy, and lo! that is gone.

What little is left uv the Dimocrisy is all sore, but where is the dorg so low as to lick it!

Noo Gersey wuz our ewe lamb—lo! the strong hand uv Ablishnism hez taken it.

Noo Gersey wuz the Aryrat on wich our ark rested—behold! the dark waves uv Ablishnism sweep over it!

Darkness falls over me like a pall—the shadder uv woe encompasseth me.

Down my furrowed cheeks rolleth the tears uv anguish, varyin in size from a large Pea to a small tater.

Noo Gersey will vote for the Constooshnel Amendment, and lo! the Nigger will possess the land.

I see horrid visions!

On the Camden and Amboy, nigger brakesmen; and at the polls, niggers!

Where shall we find refuge?

In the North? Lo! it is barred agin us by Ablishnism.

In the South? In their eyes the Northern copperhead findeth no favor.

In Mexico? There is war there, and we might be drafted.

Who will deliver us? Who will pluck us from the pit into wich we hev fallen?

Where I shel go the Lord only knows, but my impression is, South Karliny will be my future home. Wade Hampton is electid Governor, certin, and in that noble State, one may perhaps preserve enough uv the old Dimokratic States Rites to leaven the whole lump.

"I'm aflote—I'm aflote
On the dark rollin sea."

And into what harbor fate will drive my weatherbeaten bark, the undersigned can not trooly say.

Noo Gersey—farewell! The world may stand it a year or two, but I doubt it.

> Mournfly and sadly,
> PETROLEUM V. NASBY,

Lait Paster uv the Church uv the Noo Dispensashun.

A Change of Base—Kentucky

A Change of Base—Kentucky.—A Sermon which was interrupted by a Subjugated and Subdued Confederate.

> CONFEDRIT X ROADS
> (*wich is in the Stait uv Kentucky*),
> *December 9, 1865.*

Here is the grate Stait uv Kentucky, the last hope uv Democrisy, I hev pitched my tent, and here I propose to lay these old bones when Deth, who has a mortgage onto all uv us, shall see fit to 4close. I didn't like to leave Washinton. I luv it for its memories. Here stands the Capitol where the President makes his appintments; there is the Post Offis Department, where all the Postmasters is appinted. Here it was that Jaxon rooled. I had a respex for Jaxon. I can't say I luved him, for he never yoosed us rite. He hated the Whigs ez bad ez we did, but after we beat em and elevated him to

Swingin' Round the Cirkle, pp. 33–40.

the Presidency, the stealins didn't come in ez fast ez we expected. Never shel I forgit the compliment he paid me. Jest after his election I presented myself afore him with my papers, and applicant for a place. He read em, and scanned me with a critic's eye.

"Can't yoo make yoose uv sich a man ez me?" sez I, inquirinly.

"Certinly," sez he; "I kin and alluz hev. Its sich ez yoo I use to beet the whigs with, and I am continyooally astonished to see how much work I accomplish with sich dirty tools. My dear sir," sed he, pintin to the door, "when I realize how many sich cusses ez yoo there is, and how cheap they kin be bought up, I really tremble for the Republic."

I didn't get the office I wantid.

Yet ez much ez I love Washinton, I wuz forced to leave it. I mite hev stayed there, but the trooth is, the planks uv that city and the pavements are harder, and worse to sleep on, than those uv any other city in the Yoonited Staits. I hed lived two months by passin myself off ez Dimekratic Congressmen, but that cood only last a short time, there not bein many uv that persuasion here to personate. I had gone the rounds uv the House ez often ez it wuz safe, and one nite commenced on the Senit. Goin into Willard's, I called for a go uv gin, wich the gentlemanly and urbane bar keeper sot afore me, and I drank. "Put it down with the rest uv mine," sez I, with a impressive wave uv the hand.

"Yoor name?" sez he.

Assoomin a intellectual look, I retorted, "Do you know Charles Sumner?"

Here I over did it; here vaultin ambition o'erleaped herself. Hed I sed "Saulsbury," it mite have ansered, but to give Sumner's name for a drink uv gin wuz a peece uv lunacy for wich I kan't account. I wuz ignominiously kicked into

Do You Know Charles Sumner?

the street. Drinks obtained at the expense uv bein kicked is cheep, but I don't want em on them terms; my pride revolted, and so I emigrated. The gentlemanly and urbane conductors uv the Pennsylvania Central passed me over their road. They did it with the assistance uv two gentlemanly and urbane brakesmen, wich dropped me tenderly across the track, out uv the hind eend uv the last car.

I found here a church buildin, uv wich the congregation had bin mostly killed in bushwhackin expeditions, and announsin myself ez a constooshnel preacher from Noo Gersey, succeeded in drawin together a highly respectable awjience last Sunday.

Takin for a text the passage, "The wagis uv sin is death," I opened out ez follows:—

"Wat is sin? Sin, my beloved hearers, is any deviashen from yer normal condishen. Yoor beloved pastor hez a stumick and a head, wich is in close sympathy with each other, so much so, indeed, that the principal biznis uv the head is to fill the stumick, and mighty close work its been for many years, yoo bet. Let your beloved pastor drink, uv a nite, a quart or two more than his yoosual allowance, more than his stumick absolootely demands, and his head swells with indignashen. The excess is sin, and the ache is the penalty.

"The wagis uv sin is death! Punishment and sin is ez unseperable ez the shadder is from the man—one is ez shoor to foller the other ez the assessor is to kum around—ez nite is to foller day. The Dimekratic party, uv wich I am a ornament, hez experienced the trooth uv this text. When Douglas switched off, he sinned, and ez a consekence, Linkin wuz elected, and the Sceptre departed from Israel. When——"

At this pint in the discourse, a old man in the back part uv the house ariz and interrupted me. He sed he hed a word to say on that subjick which must be sed, and ef I interrupted him till he got through he'd punch my hed; whereupon I let him go on.

"Trooly," sez he, "the wages of sin is deth. I hev alluz bin a Dimecrat. The old Dimocracy hez bin in the service uv sin for thirty years, and the assortment uv death it hez received for wages is trooly surprisin. Never did a party commence better. Jaxon wus a honist man, who knew that righteousnis wuz the nashun's best holt. But he died, and a host uv tuppenny politicians, with his great name for capital, jumped into his old clothes, an undertook to run the party. Ef the Dimocracy coold hev elected a honist man every fourth or fifth term, they mite hev ground along for a longer period, but alars! Jaxon wuz the last of that style we hed, and so many dishonist cusses wuz then in the Capital that his ghost coodent watch the half uv them.

"The fust installment uv deth we reseeved wuz when Harrison beet us. The old pollytishens in our party didn't mind it, for, sez they, 'The Treasurey woodent hev bin wuth mutch to us ennyhow after the suckin it has experienced for 12 years; it needs 4 years uv rest.' We elected Poke, and here it wuz that Sin got a complete hold uv us. Anshent compacts made with the devil wuz alluz ritten in blud. We made a contract with Calhoonism, and that wuz ritten in blud wich wuz shed in Mexico. Here we sold ourselves out, boots and britches, to the cotton Democricy, and don't our history ever sence prove the trooth uv the text, 'The wages uv sin is deth?' O, my frends! in wat hevy installments, and how regularly, hez these wages bin pade us.

"Our men uv character commenst leavin us. Silas Write kicked out, and wood hev gone over agin us hed he not fortunately died too soon, and skores uv uthers followed soot. Things went on until Peerse wuz elected. The Devil (wich is cotton), whom we wuz servin, brot Kansas into the ring, and wat a skatterin ensood.

"Agin, the men uv character got out, and gradually but shoorly the work uv deth went on. Bookannon wuz elected, but wuz uv no yoose to us. After Peerse hed run the machine four yeers, wat wuz there left? Eko ansers. Anuther siftin follered, and the old party wich wunst boasted a Jaxon hed got down to a Vallandigum. The Devil, to wich we hed sold ourselves, wood not let us off with this, however. 'The wages uv sin is deth,' and we hed not reseeved full pay ez yet. He instigated South Karliny to rebel; he indoosed the other Democratic States to foller; he forced the Northern Democrisy to support em, and so on. That wuz the final stroke. Dickinson, and Cass, and Dix, and Todd, and Logan, all left us, and wun by wun the galaxy uv Northern stars disappeared from the Democratic firmament, leaving Noo Gersey alone, and last fall, my brethrin, she sot in gloom.

"Oh, how true it is! We served sin faithfully, and where are we? We went to war for slavery, and slavery is dead. We fit for a confederacy, and the confederacy is dead. We fit for States Rites, and States Rites is dead. And Democracy tied herself to all these corpses, and they hev stunk her to death.

"Kentucky went heavy into the sin biznis, and whar is Kentucky? We sent our men to the confedrit army and none uv em cum back, ceptin the skulkers, who comprised all uv that class wich we wood hev bin glad to hev killed. Linkin wantid to hev us free our niggers, and be compensatid for em. We held on to the sin uv niggers, and now they are taken from us with nary a compensate. In short, whatever uv good the Devil promised us in pollytix hez resulted in evil. My niggers is gone, my plantashen here hez fed alternately both armies, ez they cavorted backerds and forrerds through the Stait, my house and barns wuz burnt, and all I hev to show

for my property is Confedrit munny, which is a very dead
article uv death. I know not what the venerable old sucker
in the pulpit wuz a goin to say, but ef he kin look over this
section uv the heritage, and cant preach a elokent sermon on
that text, he aint much on the preach. I'm dun."

Uv coarse, after a ebulition of this kind, I cooldn't go on.
I dismist the awdience with a benedickshun, hopin to get em
together when sich prejudiced men aint present.

PETROLEUM V. NASBY,
Lait Paster uv the Church uv the Noo Dispensashun.

The Reward of Virtue

The Reward of Virtue.—After Months of waiting, the
Virtuous Patriot secures his Loaf.—The Jollification.

CONFEDRIT X ROADS
(*wich is in the Stait uv Kentucky*),
August 12, 1866.

At last I hev it! Finally it come! After five weary trips to
Washington, after much weary waitin and much travail, I hev
got it. I am now Post Master at Confedrit X Roads, and am
dooly installed in my new position. If I ever hed any doubts
ez to A. Johnson bein a better man than Paul the Apossle,
a look at my commission removes it. Ef I ketch myself a
feelin that he deserted us onnecessarily five years ago, another
look, and my resentment softens into pity. Ef I doubt his
Democrisy, I look at that blessed commission, and am reas-
sured, for a President who cood turn out a wounded Federal

Swingin' Round the Cirkle, pp. 187–195.

soldier, and appoint sich a man ez ME, must be above suspicion.

I felt it wuz coming two weeks ago. I received a cirkler from Randall, now my sooperior in offis, propoundin these questions:—

1. Do yoo hev the most implicit faith in Androo Johnson, in all that he hez done, all that he is doin, and all he may hereafter do?

2. Do yoo bleeve that the Philadelphia Convenshun will be a convocashen uv saints, all actuated by pure motives, and devoted to the salvation uv our wunst happy, but now distractid country?

3. Do yoo bleeve that, next to A. Johnson, Seward, Doolittle, Cowan, and Randall are the four greatest, and purest, and bestest, and self-sacrificinest, and honestest, and righteousist men that this country hez ever prodost?

4. Do yoo bleeve that there is a partikelerly hot place reserved in the next world for Trumbull, a hotter for Wade, and the hottest for Sumner and Thad Stevens?

5. Do yoo approve uv the canin uv Grinnell by Rosso?

6. Do yoo consider the keepin out uv Congris eleven sovrin states a unconstooshnel and unwarrantid assumption uv power by a secshnal Congris?

7. Do yoo bleeve the present Congris a rump, and that (eleven states bein unrepresented) all their acts are unconstooshnel and illegal, ceptin them wich provides for payin salaries?

8. Do yoo bleeve that the Memphis and Noo Orleans unpleasantnesses wuz brot about by the unholy machinashens uv them Radical agitators, actin in conjunction with ignorant and besotted niggers, to wreak their spite on the now loyal citizens uv those properly reconstructed cities?

9. Are yoo not satisfied that the Afrikin citizens uv Ameri-

kin descent kin be safely trusted to the operations uv the universal law wich governs labor and capital?

10. Are yoo willin to contribute a reasonable per cent. uv yoor salary to a fund to be used for the defeat uv objectionable Congrismen in the disloyal states North?

To all uv these inquiries I not only answered yes, but went afore a Justis uv the Peace and took an affidavit to em, forwarded it back, and my commission wuz forthwith sent to me.

There wuz a jubilee the nite it arriv. The news spread rapidly through the four groceries uv the town, and sich anuther spontaneous outburst uv joy I never witnessed.

The bells rung, and for an hour or two the Corners wuz in the wildest stait uv eggsitement. The citizens congratoolated each other on the certainty uv the acceshun uv the President to the Dimocrisy, and in their enthoosiasm five nigger families were cleaned out, two uv em, one a male and the tother a female, wuz killed. Then a perceshun wuz organized as follers:—

Two grocery keepers with bottles.

Deekin Pogram.

ME, with my commishun pinned onto a banner, and under it written, "In this Sign we Conker."

Wagon with tabloo onto it: A nigger on the bottom boards, Bascom, the grocery keeper, with one foot onto him, holdin a banner inscribed, "The Nigger where he oughter be."

Citizen with bottle.

Deekin Pogram's daughter Mirandy in a attitood uv wallopin a wench. Banner: "We've Regained our Rites."

Two citizens with bottles tryin to keep in perceshun.

Two more citizens, wich hed emptyd their bottles, fallin out by the way side.

Citizens, two and two, with bottles.

Wagon, loaded with the books and furnitur uv a nigger skool, in a stait uv wreck, with a ded nigger layin on top uv it, wich hed bin captoored within the hour. Banner: "My Policy."

The perceshun mooved to the meetin hous, and Deekin Pogram takin the Chair, a meetin wuz to wunst organized.

The Deekin remarked that this wuz the proudest moment uv his life. He wuz gratified at the appintment uv his esteemed friend, becoz he appreciated the noble qualities wich wuz so conspikuous into him, and becoz his arduous services in the coz uv Dimokrisy entitled him to the posishun. All these wuz aside uv and entirely disconnected from the fact that thare wood now be a probability uv his gittin back a little matter uv nine dollars and sixty-two cents ("Hear! hear!") wich he hed loaned him about eighteen months ago, afore he had knowed him well, or larned to luv him. But thare wuz anuther reason why he met to rejoyce to-nite. It showed that A. Johnson meant biznis; that A. Johnson wuz troo to the Dimokrasy, and that he hed fully made up his mind to hurl the bolts uv offishl thunder wich he held in his Presidenshal hands at his enemies, and to make fight in earnest; that he wuz goin to reward his friends—them ez he cood trust. Our venerable friend's bein put in condishun to pay the confidin residents uv the Corners the little sums he owes them is a good thing ("Hear!" "Hear!" "Troo!" "Troo!" with singular unanimity from every man in the bildin), but wat wuz sich considerashuns when compared to the grate moral effect uv the decisive movement? ("A d——d site!" shouted one grocery keeper, and "We don't want no moral effect!" cried another.) My friends, when the news uv this bold step uv the President goes forth to the South, the price uv Confedrit skript will go up, and the shootin uv niggers will cease; for the redempshun uv the first I consider ashoored, and the redoosin uv the latter to their normal condishun I count ez good ez done.

Squire Gavitt remarked that he wuz too much overpowered with emoshun to speak. For four years, nearly five, the only newspaper wich come to that offis hed passed thro' the polluted hands uv a Ablishnist. He hed no partikler objecshun to the misguided man, but he wuz a symbol uv tyranny, and so long ez he sot there, he reminded em that they were wearin chains. Thank the Lord, that day is over! The Corners is redeemed, the second Jaxson hez risin, and struck off the shackles. He wood not allood to the trifle uv twelve dollars and a half that he loaned the appintee some months ago, knowin that it wood be paid out uv the first money——

Bascom, the principal grocery keeper, rose, and called the Squire to order. He wanted to know ef it wuz fair play to talk sich talk. No man cood feel a more hartfelt satisfaction at the appintment uv our honored friend than him, showin, ez it did, that the President hed cut loose from Ablishnism, wich he dispised, but he protestid agin the Squire undertakin to git in his bill afore the rest hed a chance. Who furnisht him his licker for eight months, and who hez the best rite for the first dig at the proceeds uv the position? He wood never——

The other three grocery keepers rose, when Deekin Pogram rooled em all out uv order, and offered the followin resolutions:—

Whereas, the President hez, in a strikly constooshnel manner, relieved this commoonity uv an offensive Ablishunist, appinted by that abhorred tyrant Linkin, and appinted in his place a sound constooshnel Demokrat—one whom to know is to lend; therefore, be it

Resolved, That we greet the President, and ashoor him uv our continyood support and confidence.

Resolved, That we now consider the work uv Reconstruction, so far ez this community is concerned, completed, and that we feel that we are wunst more restored to our proper relations with the federal government.

Resolved, That the glorious defence made by the loyal Democracy uv Noo Orleans agin the combined conventioners and niggers, shows that freemen kin not be conkered, and that white men shel rule America.

Resolved, That, on this happy occasion, we forgive the Government for what we did, and cherish nary resentment agin anybody.

The resolutions wuz adopted, and the meetin adjourned with three cheers for Johnson and his policy.

Then came a scene. Every last one uv em hed come there with a note made out for the amount I owed him at three months. Kindness of heart is a weakness of mine, and I signed em all, feelin that ef the mere fact of writin my name wood do em any good, it wood be crooel in me to object to the little laber required. Bless their innocent soles! they went away happy.

The next mornin I took possesshun uv the offis.

"Am I awake, or am I dreamin?" thought I. No, no! It is no dream. Here is the stamps, here is the blanks, and here is the commisshun! It is troo! it is troo!

I heerd a child, across the way, singin,—

> "I'd like to be a angel,
> And with the angels stand."

I woodn't, thought I. I woodn't trade places with an angel, even up. A Offis with but little to do, with four grocerys within a stone's throw, is ez much happiness ez my bilers will stand without bustin. A angel 4sooth!

PETROLEUM V. NASBY, P.M.
(wich is Postmaster).

Nasby's Dream of Perfect Bliss

The Presidential Tour Continued

The Presidential Tour Continued—From Detroit to Indianapolis.

POST OFFIS, CONFEDRIT X ROADS
(wich is in the Stait uv Kentucky),
September 11, 1866.

I am at home, and glad am I that I am at home. Here is
Kentucky, surrounded by Dimicrats, immersed a part of the
time in my offishel dooties, and the balance uv the time in
whiskey, with the privilege uv wallopin niggers, and the
more inestimable and soothing privilege uv assistin in mob-
bin uv Northern Ablishnists, who are not yet all out uv the
State, time passes pleasantly, and leaves no vain regrets. I

Swingin' Round the Cirkle, pp. 214–221.

alluz go to bed nites, feeling that the day hez not bin wasted.

From Detroit the Presidential cavalcade, or ez the in-famous Jacobin Radical party irrevelently term it, the me-najery, proceeded to Chicago. The recepshuns his Imperial Highniss received through Michigan were flatterin in the extreme. I continue my diary:

IPSLANTY.—At this pint the President [Andrew Johnson] displayed that originality and fertility uv imaginashun kar-acteristic uv him. The recepshun wuz grand. The masses called for Grant, and His Highness promptly responded. He asked em, ef he was Judis Iskariot who wuz the Saviour? Thad Stevens? If so, then after swingin around the cirkle, and findin traitors at both ends of the line, I leeve the 36 States with 36 stars onto em in yoor hands, and——

The train wuz off amid loud shouts uv "Grant! Grant!" to wich the President responded by wavin his hat.

ANN ARBOR.—At this pint the train moved in to the in-spiring sounds uv a band playin "Hale to the Cheef," and vocifrous cries uv "Grant! Grant!" His Majesty smilinly appeared and thanked em for the demonstration. It was soothin, he remarked. The air their band wuz playin, "Hail to the Chief," wuz appropit, ez he wuz Chief Magistrate uv the nashen, to wich posishen he hed reached, hevin bin Alderman uv his native village, U.S. Senator, etsettry. The crowd hollered "Grant! Grant!" and the President thanked em for the demonstration. It showed him that the people wuz with him in his efforts to close his eyes on a Union uv 36 States and a flag uv 36 stars onto it. Ef I am a traitor, sed he, warmin up, who is the Judis Iskariot? Ez I'm swingin around the cirkle, I find Thad Stevens on the one side and Jeff Davis on the——

The conductor cruelly startid the train, without givin him time to finish.

The crowd proposed three cheers for Grant, and the President waved his hat to em, sayin that he thanked em, showing as it did that the people wuz with him.

BATTLE CREEK.—A large number was assembled here, who, ez the train stopped, yelled "Grant! Grant!" Affected to tears by the warmth uv the reception, the President thanked em for this mark of confidence. Ef he ever hed any doubts ez to the people's being with him, these doubts wuz removed. He wood leave in their hands the flag and the Union uv 36 States, and the stars thereto appertaining. Ef he wuz a Joodis Iskariot who wuz——

The crowd gave three hearty cheers for Grant ez the train moved off, to wich the President responded by wavin his hat.

KALAMAZOO.—The offishels were on hand at this pint, and so wuz the people—4 offishels and several thousand people, which the latter greeted us with cheers for Grant! Grant! The President responded, sayin, that in swingin around the cirkle, he had bin called Joodis Iskariot for sacrificin uv hisself for the people! Who wuz the Saviour? Wuz Thad Stevens? No! Then cleerly into yoor hands I leave the Constitution uv 36 stars with 36 States onto em, intact and undissevered.

The offishels received the stars and States, and amid cheers for Grant, for wich the President thanked em, the train glode off magestically.

And so on to Chicago, where we didn't get off our speech, though from the manner in wich the people hollered Grant! Grant! we felt cheered at realizin how much they wuz with us. His eminence wanted to sling the 36 States and the flag with the stars at em, but ez General Logan wuz there, ready to fling em back, it wuz deemed highly prudent not to do it.

Here my trials commenst. At the Biddle House, in Detroit, the nigger waiters showed how much a African kin be spiled by bein free. *They hed the impudence to refoose to wait on us,* and for a half hour the imperial stumick wuz forced to fast. This alarmin manifestation uv negro malignancy alarmed His Eggsalency. "Thank God!" sed he, "that I vetoed the Freedmen's Buroo Bill. I hev bin Alderman uv my native town—I hev swung around the entire cirkle, but this I never dreemed uv. What would they do if they hed their rites?" The insident made an impression onto him, and at Chicago he resolved to trust em no longer. He ordered his meals to his room, and sent for me. "My friend," sed he, "taste evrything onto this table."

"Why? my liege," sed I.

"Niggers is cooks," sed he, "and this food may be pizoned. They hate me, for I ain't in the Moses bizness. Taste, my friend."

"But spozn," sed I, "that it *shood* be pizoned? Wat uv *my* bowels? My stomick is uv ez much valyoo to me ez yourn is to yoo."

"Nasby," sez he, "taste! Ef yoo die, who mourns? Ef I die, who'd swing around the cirkle? Who'd sling the flag and the 36 stars at the people, and who'd leave the Constooshn in their hands? The country demands the sacrifice; and besides, ef yoo don't off goes yoor offishl head."

That last appele fetched me. Ruther than risk that offis I'd chaw striknine, for uv what akkount is a Dimokrat, who hez wunst tasted the sweets uv place, and is ousted? And from Chicago on I wuz forced to taste his food and likker— to act ez a sort uv a litenin-rod to shed off the vengeance uv the nigger waiters. I wood taste uv every dish and drink from each bottle, and ef I didn't swell up and bust in 15 minits His serene Highness wood take hold. I suffered several deaths. I resoom my diary:

JOLIET.—The crowd wuz immense. The peasantry, ez the

train approached, rent the air with shouts uv "Grant!" "Grant!" His Potency, the President, promptly acknowledged the compliment. He was sacrificin hisself for them— who hed made greater sacrifices? He hed bin Alderman uv his native town, and Vice-President; he wuz Joodas Iskariot, who wuz the Saviour? He hed swung around the cirkle, and hedn't found none so far. He left in their hands the—

And so on, until near St. Louis, when we penetrated a Democratic country, uv wich I informed his Majesty. "How knowest thou?" sez he. "Easy," sez I. "I observe in the crowds a large proportion uv red noses, and hats with the tops off. I notice the houses unpainted, with pig pens in front ov em; and what is more, I observe that crowds compliment yoo direct, instead of doin it, ez heretofore, over Grant's shoulders. The Knights uv the Golden Cirkle, wich I spect is the identical cirkle yoo've bin swingin around lately, love yoo and approach yoo confidently."

The President brisked up, and from this to Indianapolis he spoke with a flooidity I never observed in him before. I may say, to yoose a medikle term, that he had a hemorrhage uv words. At the latter city our reception was the most flatrin uv eny we have experienced. The people, when the President appeared on the balcony uv the Bates House, yelled so vociferously for Grant, that the President, when he stepped forward to acknowledge the compliment, coodent be heard at all. He waved his hat; and the more he waved it the more complimentary the crowd became. "Grant!" "Grant!" they yelled; and the more they yelled Grant, until, overpowered by the warmth uv the recepshun, and unwillin to expose his health, the President retired without slingin a speech at em, but entirely satisfied that the people wuz with him.

The next mornin the office-holders uv the State, without

the people, assembled, and he made his regler speech to em, wich appeared to be gratifyin to both him and them. The President does not like to sleep with a undelivered speech on his mental stumick. It gives him the nitemare.

Here I left the party, for a short time, that I mite go home and attend to my official dooties. There is five Northern families near the Corners wich must hev notice to leave, and eight niggers to hang. I hed orders to report to the party somewhere between Looisville and Harrisburgh, wich I shall do, ez, travelin by order, I get mileage and sich.

PETROLEUM V. NASBY, P.M.
(wich is Postmaster),
and likewise Chaplin to the expedishn.

SAMUEL LANGHORNE CLEMENS
[Mark Twain]
(1835-1910)

The greatness of Mark Twain's writings defies facile cat-
egorization. Mark Twain dealt with mankind's foibles and
follies on a spectrum far broader than politics alone. Indeed, politics and politicians increasingly summoned his
sense of personal outrage. His political reporting was serious and disciplined for the Virginia City (Nevada)
Territorial Enterprise (1862-1864), yet the editorial comments which he inserted in his dispatches reporting the
third Territorial Legislature were personal and comic.

He vented spleen as a wrathful witness to betrayal,
evidencing little of his customary delight at mortal foolishness betrayed. If the quality of his humor suffered somewhat from the withering fire he leveled at governments and their leaders, it was unavoidable. For Mark
Twain was ever the man to recognize colossal humbug
whenever it was present (which it patently was in the
politics of the Gilded Age) and to recoil from it instinc-
tively. "I have been reading the morning paper," he
wrote to William Dean Howells in 1899. "I do it every
morning—well knowing that I shall find in it the usual
depravities and basenesses and hypocrisies and cruelties

that make up civilization, and cause me to put in the rest of the day pleading for the damnation of the human race."

Sam Clemens' life story is an integral part of America's history: a boy in Hannibal, Missouri, tramp printer throughout the East, river pilot on the Mississippi, Confederate soldier for less than a month, miner and speculator, feature writer and reporter for Viginia City and San Francisco newspapers, early friend and admirer of Artemus Ward. The celebrated story of the jumping frog was his first notable success. *Innocents Abroad* established his reputation so firmly that almost anything else he wrote was guaranteed an extraordinary financial success. Comic lecturing swelled his income and made him a familiar sight to his countrymen and admirers all over the world. *Tom Sawyer* and *Huckleberry Finn* elevated him to immortality.

The selections to follow represent a motley assortment culled from Twain's less well-known writings. They express his indignation at the confusion and corruption characteristic of America's political system in all its branches and offices. His major satirical effort along these lines was *The Gilded Age,* the novel he co-authored with Charles Dudley Warner following Grant's re-election to the Presidency in 1872.

"Political Economy" seems to be a curious exception, with politics at first glance less to the point than lightning rods. But this is a wonderfully comic achievement on two levels. The lower level of "Political Economy" captures the popular image of the ubiquitous lightning-rod salesman, the high-pressure huckster of Twain's day. The higher level, the disquisition on "political economy," appears to be nothing at all, and remains incomplete as if to prove its unimportance. Yet it is funny for at least two reasons—its straight-faced, apparently high-minded contrast with the madcap affair of the lightning rods, and its own delicious idiocies—for example, Twain's extending the "great lights" of all time, including the biological deviates, from Zoroaster at the beginning down to Horace Greeley at the end.

The total impact confirms one of Mark Twain's most captivating observations about the United States: "It is by the goodness of God that in our country we have these three unspeakably precious things: freedom of speech, freedom of conscience, and the prudence never to practice either of them."

Cannibalism in the Cars

I visited St. Louis lately, and on my way West, after changing cars at Terre Haute, Indiana, a mild, benevolent-looking gentleman of about forty-five, or maybe fifty, came in at one of the way-stations and sat down beside me. We talked together pleasantly on various subjects for an hour, perhaps, and I found him exceedingly intelligent and entertaining. When he learned that I was from Washington, he immediately began to ask questions about various public men, and about Congressional affairs; and I saw very shortly that I was conversing with a man who was perfectly familiar with the ins and outs of political life at the Capital, even to the ways and manners, and customs of procedure of Senators and Representatives in the Chambers of the national Legislature. Presently two men halted near us for a single moment, and one said to the other:

"Harris, if you'll do that for me, I'll never forget you, my boy."

My new comrade's eye lighted pleasantly. The words had touched upon a happy memory, I thought. Then his face settled into thoughtfulness—almost into gloom. He turned to me and said, "Let me tell you a story; let me give you a secret chapter of my life—a chapter that has never been referred to by me since its events transpired. Listen patiently, and promise that you will not interrupt me."

I said I would not, and he related the following strange adventure, speaking sometimes with animation, sometimes with melancholy, but always with feeling and earnestness.

Samuel L. Clemens [Mark Twain], *Sketches New and Old,* New York (1875), pp. 370–384.

The Stranger's Narrative

"On the 19th of December, 1853, I started from St. Louis on the evening train bound for Chicago. There were only twenty-four passengers, all told. There were no ladies and no children. We were in excellent spirits, and pleasant acquaint-anceships were soon formed. The journey bade fair to be a happy one; and no individual in the party, I think, had even the vaguest presentiment of the horrors we were soon to undergo.

"At 11 P.M. it began to snow hard. Shortly after leaving the small village of Welden, we entered upon that tremendous prairie solitude that stretches its leagues on leagues of house-less dreariness far away toward the Jubilee Settlements. The winds, unobstructed by trees or hills, or even vagrant rocks, whistled fiercely across the level desert driving the falling snow before it like spray from the crested waves of a stormy sea. The snow was deepening fast; and we knew, by the diminished speed of the train, that the engine was plowing through it with steadily increasing difficulty. Indeed, it almost came to a dead halt sometimes, in the midst of great drifts that piled themselves like colossal graves across the track. Conversation began to flag. Cheerfulness gave place to grave concern. The possibility of being imprisoned in the snow, on the bleak prairie, fifty miles from any house, pre-sented itself to every mind, and extended its depressing influence over every spirit.

"At two o'clock in the morning I was aroused out of an uneasy slumber by the ceasing of all motion about me. The appalling truth flashed upon me instantly—we were captives in a snow-drift! 'All hands to the rescue!' Every man sprang to obey. Out into the wild night, the pitchy darkness, the billowy snow, the driving storm, every soul leaped, with the consciousness that a moment lost now might bring destruction to us all. Shovels, hands, boards—anything, everything that could displace snow, was brought into instant requisition. It was a weird picture, that small company of frantic men fighting the banking snows, half in the blackest shadow and half in the angry light of the locomotive's reflector.

"One short hour sufficed to prove the utter uselessness of our efforts. The storm barricaded the track with a dozen drifts while we dug one away. And worse than this, it was discovered that the last grand charge the engine had made upon the enemy had broken the fore-and-aft shaft of the driving wheel! With a free track before us we should still have been helpless. We entered the car wearied with labor, and very sorrowful. We gathered about the stoves, and gravely canvassed our situation. We had no provisions whatever—in this lay our chief distress. We could not freeze, for there was a good supply of wood in the tender. This was our only comfort. The discussion ended at last in accepting the disheartening decision of the conductor, viz., that it would be death for any man to attempt to travel fifty miles on foot through snow like that. We could not send for help, and even if we could it would not come. We must submit, and await, as patiently as we might, succor or starvation! I think the stoutest heart there felt a momentary chill when those words were uttered.

"Within the hour conversation subsided to a low murmur here and there about the car, caught fitfully between the rising and falling of the blast; the lamps grew dim; and the majority of the castaways settled themselves among the flickering shadows to think—to forget the present, if they could—to sleep, if they might.

"The eternal night—it surely seemed eternal to us—wore its lagging hours away at last, and the cold gray dawn broke in the east. As the light grew stronger the passengers began to stir and give signs of life, one after another, and each in turn pushed his slouched hat up from his forehead, stretched his stiffened limbs, and glanced out of the windows upon the cheerless prospect. It was cheerless, indeed!—not a living thing visible anywhere, not a human habitation; nothing but a vast white desert; uplifted sheets of snow drifting hither and thither before the wind—a world of eddying flakes shutting out the firmament above.

"All day we moped about the cars, saying little, thinking much. Another lingering dreary night—and hunger.

"Another dawning—another day of silence, sadness, wasting hunger, hopeless watching for succor that could not come. A night of restless slumber, filled with dreams of feasting—wakings distressed with the gnawings of hunger.

"The fourth day came and went—and the fifth! Five days of dreadful imprisonment! A savage hunger looked out at every eye. There was in it a sign of awful import—the foreshadowing of a something that was vaguely shaping itself in every heart—a something which no tongue dared yet to frame into words.

"The sixth day passed—the seventh dawned upon as gaunt and haggard and hopeless a company of men as ever stood in the shadow of death. It must out now! That thing which had been growing up in every heart was ready to leap from every lip at last! Nature had been taxed to the utmost—she must yield. RICHARD H. GASTON of Minnesota, tall, cadaverous, and pale, rose up. All knew what was coming. All prepared—every motion, every semblance of excitement was smothered—only a calm, thoughtful seriousness appeared in the eyes that were lately so wild.

"Gentlemen: It cannot be delayed longer! The time is at hand! We must determine which of us shall die to furnish food for the rest!"

"MR. JOHN J. WILLIAMS of Illinois rose and said: 'Gentlemen—I nominate the Rev. James Sawyer of Tennessee.'

"MR. WM. R. ADAMS of Indiana said: 'I nominate Mr. Daniel Slote of New York.'

"MR. CHARLES J. LANGDON: 'I nominate Mr. Samuel A. Bowen of St. Louis.'

"MR. SLOTE: 'Gentlemen—I desire to decline in favor of Mr. John A. Van Nostrand, Jun., of New Jersey.'

"MR. GASTON: 'If there be no objection, the gentleman's desire will be acceded to.'

"MR. VAN NOSTRAND objecting, the resignation of Mr. Slote was rejected. The resignations of Messrs. Sawyer and Bowen were also offered, and refused upon the same grounds.

"MR. A. L. BASCOM of Ohio: 'I move that the nominations now close, and that the House proceed to an election by ballot.'

"MR. SAWYER: 'Gentlemen—I protest earnestly against these proceedings. They are, in every way, irregular and unbecoming. I must beg to move that they be dropped at once, and that we elect a chairman of the meeting and proper officers to assist him, and then we can go on with the business before us understandingly.'

"MR. BELL of Iowa: 'Gentlemen—I object. This is no time to stand upon forms and ceremonious observances. For more than seven days we have been without food. Every moment we loose in idle discussion increases our distress. I am satisfied with the nominations that have been made—every gentleman present is, I believe—and I, for one, do not see why we should not proceed at once to elect one or more of them. I wish to offer a resolution——'

"MR. GASTON: 'It would be objected to, and have to lie

over one day under the rules, thus bringing about the very delay you wish to avoid. The gentleman from New Jersey——'

"MR. VAN NOSTRAND: 'Gentlemen—I am a stranger among you; I have not sought the distinction that has been conferred upon me, and I feel a delicacy——'

"MR. MORGAN of Alabama (interrupting): 'I move the previous question.'

"The motion was carried, and further debate shut off, of course. The motion to elect officers was passed, and under it Mr. Gaston was chosen chairman, Mr. Blake, Secretary, Messrs. Holcomb, Dyer, and Baldwin, a committee on nominations, and Mr. R. M. Howland, purveyor, to assist the committee in making selections.

"A recess of half an hour was then taken, and some little caucusing followed. At the sound of the gavel the meeting reassembled, and the committee reported in favor of Messrs. George Ferguson of Kentucky, Lucien Herrman of Louisiana, and W. Messick of Colorado as candidates. The report was accepted.

"MR. ROGERS of Missouri: 'Mr. President—The report being properly before the House now, I move to amend it by substituting for the name of Mr. Herrman that of Mr. Lucius Harris of St. Louis, who is well and honorably known to us all. I do not wish to be understood as casting the least reflection upon the high character and standing of the gentleman from Louisiana—far from it. I respect and esteem him as much as any gentleman here present possibly can; but none of us can be blind to the fact that he has lost more flesh during the week that we have lain here than any among us —none of us can be blind to the fact that the committee has been derelict in its duty, either through negligence or a graver fault, in thus offering for our suffrages a gentleman who, however pure his own motives may be, has really less nutriment in him——'

"THE CHAIR: 'The gentleman from Missouri will take his seat. The Chair cannot allow the integrity of the committee to be questioned save by the regular course, under the rules. What action will the House take upon the gentleman's motion?'

"MR. HALLIDAY of Virginia: 'I move to further amend the report by substituting Mr. Harvey Davis of Oregon for Mr. Messick. It may be urged by gentlemen that the hardships and privations of a frontier life have rendered Mr. Davis tough; but, gentlemen, is this a time to cavil at toughness? Is this a time to be fastidious concerning trifles? Is this a time to dispute about matters of paltry significance? No, gentlemen, bulk is what we desire—substance, weight, bulk—these are the supreme requisites now—not talent, not genius, not education. I insist upon my motion.'

"MR. MORGAN (excitedly): 'Mr. Chairman—I do most strenuously object to this amendment. The gentleman from Oregon is old, and furthermore is bulky only in bone—not in flesh. I ask the gentleman from Virginia if it is soup we want instead of solid sustenance? if he would delude us with shadows? if he would mock our suffering with an Oregonian specter? I ask him if he can look upon the anxious faces around him, if he can gaze into our sad eyes, if he can listen to the beating of our expectant hearts, and still thrust his famine-stricken fraud upon us? I ask him if he can think of our desolate state, of our past sorrows, of our dark future, and still unpityingly foist upon us this wreck, this ruin, this tottering swindle, this gnarled and blighted and sapless vagabond from Oregon's inhospitable shores? Never!' [Applause.]

"The amendment was put to vote, after a fiery debate, and lost. Mr. Harris was substituted on the first amendment. The balloting then began. Five ballots were held without a choice. On the sixth, Mr. Harris was elected, all voting for him but himself. It was then moved that his election should be ratified by acclamation, which was lost, in consequence of his again voting against himself.

"MR. RADWAY moved that the House now take up the remaining candidates, and go into an election for breakfast. This was carried.

"On the first ballot there was a tie, half the members favoring one candidate on account of his youth, and half favoring the other on account of his superior size. The President gave the casting vote for the latter, Mr. Messick. This decision created considerable dissatisfaction among the friends of Mr. Ferguson, the defeated candidate, and there was some talk of demanding a new ballot; but in the midst of it a motion to adjourn was carried, and the meeting broke up at once.

"The preparations for supper diverted the attention of the Ferguson faction from the discussion of their grievance for a long time, and then, when they would have taken it up again, the happy announcement that Mr. Harris was ready drove all thought of it to the winds.

"We improvised tables by propping up the backs of car-seats, and sat down with hearts full of gratitude to the finest supper that had blessed our vision for seven torturing days. How changed we were from what we had been a few short hours before! Hopeless, sad-eyed misery, hunger, feverish anxiety, desperation, then—thankfulness, serenity, joy too deep for utterance now. That I know was the cheeriest hour of my eventful life. The wind howled, and blew the snow wildly about our prison-house, but they were powerless to distress us any more. I liked Harris. He might have been better done, perhaps, but I am free to say that no man ever agreed with me better than Harris, or afforded me so large a degree of satisfaction. Messick was very well, though rather high-flavored, but for genuine nutritiousness and delicacy of fiber, give me Harris. Messick had his good points—I will not attempt to deny it, nor do I wish to do it—but he was no more fitted for breakfast than a mummy would be, sir—not a bit. Lean?—why, bless me!—and tough? Ah, he was very tough! You could not imagine it—you could never imagine anything like it."

"Do you mean to tell me that——"

"Do not interrupt me, please. After breakfast we elected a man by the name of Walker, from Detroit, for supper. He was very good. I wrote his wife so afterwards. He was worthy of all praise. I shall always remember Walker. He was a little rare, but very good. And then the next morning we had Morgan of Alabama for breakfast. He was one of the finest men I ever sat down to—handsome, educated, refined, spoke several languages fluently—a perfect gentlemen—he was a perfect gentleman, and singularly juicy. For supper we had that Oregon patriarch, and he *was* a fraud, there is no question about it—old, scraggy, tough, nobody can picture the reality. I finally said, gentlemen, you can do as you like, but *I* will wait for another election. And Grimes of Illinois said, 'Gentlemen, *I* will wait also. When you elect a man that has *something* to recommend him, I shall be glad to join you again.' It soon became evident that there was general dissatisfaction with Davis of Oregon, and so, to preserve the good will that had prevailed so pleasantly since we had had Harris, an election was called, and the result of it was that Baker of Georgia was chosen. He was splendid! Well, well—after that we had Doolittle, and Hawkins, and McElroy (there was some complaint about McElroy, because he was uncommonly short and thin), and Penrod, and two Smiths, and Bailey (Bailey had a wooden leg, which was clear loss, but he was otherwise good), and an Indian boy, and an organ-grinder, and a gentleman by the name of Buckminster—a poor stick of a vagabond that wasn't any good for company and no account for breakfast. We were glad we got him elected before relief came."

"And so the blessed relief *did* come at last?"

"Yes, it came one bright, sunny morning, just after election. John Murphy was the choice, and there never was a better, I am willing to testify; but John Murphy came home with us, in the train that came to succor us, and lived to marry the widow Harris——"

"Relict of——"

"Relict of our first choice. He married her, and is happy and respected and prosperous yet. Ah, it was like a novel, sir—it was like a romance. This is my stopping-place, sir; I must bid you good-by. Any time that you can make it convenient to tarry a day or two with me, I shall be glad to have you. I like you, sir; I have conceived an affection for you. I could like you as well as I liked Harris himself, sir. Good day, sir, and a pleasant journey."

He was gone. I never felt so stunned, so distressed, so bewildered in my life. But in my soul I was glad he was gone. With all his gentleness of manner and his soft voice, I shuddered whenever he turned his hungry eye upon me; and when I heard that I had achieved his perilous affection, and that I stood almost with the late Harris in his esteem, my heart fairly stood still!

I was bewildered beyond description. I did not doubt his word; I could not question a single item in a statement so stamped with the earnestness of truth as his; but its dreadful details overpowered me, and threw my thoughts into helpless confusion. I saw the conductor looking at me. I said, "Who is that man?"

"He was a member of Congress once, and a good one. But he got caught in a snow-drift in the cars, and like to have been starved to death. He got so frost-bitten and frozen up generally, and used up for want of something to eat, that he was sick and out of his head two or three months afterward. He is all right now, only he is a monomaniac, and when he gets on that old subject he never stops till he has eat up that whole car-load of people he talks about. He would have finished the crowd by this time, only he had to get out here. He had got their names as pat as A B C. When he gets all eat up but himself, he always says: 'Then the hour for the usual election for breakfast having arrived, and there being no opposition, I was duly elected, after which, there being no objections offered, I resigned. Thus I am here.' "

I felt inexpressibly relieved to know that I had only been listening to the harmless vagaries of a madman instead of the genuine experiences of a bloodthirsty cannibal.

1868

The Facts in the Great Beef Contract

In as few words as possible, I wish to lay before the nation what share, howsoever small, I have had in this matter—this matter which has so exercised the public mind, engendered so much ill-feeling, and so filled the newspapers of both

Sketches New and Old, pp. 121–131.

continents with distorted statements and extravagant comments.

The origin of this distressful thing was this—and I assert here that every fact in the following résumé can be amply proved by the official records of the General Government:

John Wilson Mackenzie, of Rotterdam, Chemung County, New Jersey, deceased, contracted with the General Government, on or about the 10th day of October, 1861, to furnish to General Sherman the sum total of thirty barrels of beef.

Very well.

He started after Sherman with the beef, but when he got to Washington Sherman had gone to Manassas; so he took the beef and followed him there, but arrived too late; he followed him to Nashville, and from Nashville to Chattanooga, and from Chattanooga to Atlanta—but he never could overtake him. At Atlanta he took a fresh start and followed him clear through his march to the sea. He arrived too late again by a few days; but hearing that Sherman was going out in the *Quaker City* excursion to the Holy Land, he took shipping for Beirut, calculating to head off the other vessel. When he arrived in Jerusalem with his beef, he learned that Sherman had not sailed in the *Quaker City,* but had gone to the Plains to fight the Indians. He returned to America and started for the Rocky Mountains. After sixty-eight days of arduous travel on the Plains, and when he had got within four miles of Sherman's headquarters, he was tomahawked and scalped, and the Indians got the beef. They got all of it but one barrel. Sherman's army captured that, and so, even in death, the bold navigator partly fulfilled his contract. In his will, which he had kept like a journal, he bequeathed the contract to his son Bartholomew W. Bartholomew W. made out the following bill, and then died:

THE UNITED STATES

> *In account with* JOHN WILSON MACKENZIE, of New
> Jersey, deceased, ... Dr.
> To thirty barrels of beef for General Sherman, at
> $100, ... $ 3,000
> To traveling expenses and transportation, ... 14,000
>
> Total, ... $17,000
>
> Rec'd Pay't.

He died then; but he left the contract to Wm. J. Martin, who
tried to collect it, but died before he got through. *He* left it
to Barker J. Allen, and he tried to collect it also. He did not
survive. Barker J. Allen left it to Anson G. Rogers, who attempted to collect it, and got along as far as the Ninth
Auditor's Office, when Death, the great Leveler, came all
unsummoned, and foreclosed on *him* also. He left the bill to
a relative of his in Connecticut, Vengeance Hopkins by
name, who lasted four weeks and two days, and made the
best time on record, coming within one of reaching the
Twelfth Auditor. In his will he gave the contract bill to his
uncle, by the name of O-be-joyful Johnson. It was too under-
mining for Joyful. His last words were: "Weep not for me—*I
am willing to go.*" And so he was, poor soul. Seven people
inherited the contract after that; but they all died. So it came
into my hands at last. It fell to me through a relative by the
name of Hubbard—Bethlehem Hubbard, of Indiana. He
had had a grudge against me for a long time; but in his last
moments he sent for me, and forgave me everything, and
weeping, gave me the beef contract.

This ends the history of it up to the time that I succeeded
to the property. I will now endeavor to set myself straight
before the nation in everything that concerns my share in
the matter. I took this beef contract, and the bill for mileage

and transportation, to the President of the United States.

He said, "Well, sir, what can I do for you?"

I said, "Sire, on or about the 10th day of October, 1861, John Wilson Mackenzie, of Rotterdam, Chemung County, New Jersey, deceased, contracted with the General Government to furnish to General Sherman the sum total of thirty barrels of beef——"

He stopped me there, and dismissed me from his presence—kindly, but firmly. The next day I called on the Secretary of State.

He said, "Well, sir?"

I said, "Your Royal Highness: on or about the 10th day of October, 1861, John Wilson Mackenzie, of Rotterdam, Chemung County, New Jersey, deceased, contracted with the General Government to furnish to General Sherman the sum total of thirty barrels of beef——"

"That will do, sir—that will do; this office has nothing to do with contracts for beef."

I was bowed out. I thought the matter all over, and finally, the following day, I visited the Secretary of the Navy, who said, "Speak quickly, sir; do not keep me waiting."

I said, "Your Royal Highness, on or about the 10th day of October, 1861, John Wilson Mackenzie, of Rotterdam, Chemung County, New Jersey, deceased, contracted with the General Government to furnish to General Sherman the sum total of thirty barrels of beef——"

Well, it was as far as I could get. *He* had nothing to do with beef contracts for General Sherman either. I began to think it was a curious kind of a government. It looked somewhat as if they wanted to get out of paying for that beef. The following day I went to the Secretary of the Interior.

I said, "Your Imperial Highness, on or about the 10th day of October——"

"That is sufficient, sir. I have heard of you before. Go, take your infamous beef contract out of this establishment. The Interior Department has nothing whatever to do with subsistence for the army."

I went away. But I was exasperated now. I said I would haunt them; I would infest every department of this iniquitous government till that contract business was settled. I would collect that bill, or fall, as fell my predecessors, trying. I assailed the Postmaster-General; I besieged the Agricultural Department; I waylaid the Speaker of the House of Representatives. *They* had nothing to do with army contracts for beef. I moved upon the Commissioner of the Patent Office.

I said, "Your August Excellency, on or about——"

"Perdition! have you got *here* with your incendiary beef contract, at last? We have *nothing* to do with beef contracts for the army, my dear sir."

"Oh, that is all very well—but *somebody* has got to pay for that beef. It has got to be paid *now,* too, or I'll confiscate this old Patent Office and everything in it."

"But, my dear sir——"

"It don't make any difference, sir. The Patent Office is liable for that beef, I reckon; and, liable or not liable, the Patent Office has got to pay for it."

Never mind the details. It ended in a fight. The Patent Office won. But I found out something to my advantage. I was told that the Treasury Department was the proper place for me to go to. I went there. I waited two hours and a half, and then I was admitted to the First Lord of the Treasury.

I said, "Most noble, grave, and reverend Signor, on or about the 10th day of October, 1861, John Wilson Macken——"

"That is sufficient, sir. I have heard of you. Go to the First Auditor of the Treasury."

I did so. He sent me to the Second Auditor. The Second Auditor sent me to the Third, and the Third sent me to the First Comptroller of the Corn-Beef Division. This began to look like business. He examined his books and all his loose papers, but found no minute of the beef contract. I went to the Second Comptroller of the Corn-Beef Division. He examined his books and his loose papers, but with no success. I was encouraged. During that week I got as far as the Sixth Comptroller in that division; the next week I got through the Claims Department; the third week I began and completed the Mislaid Contracts Department, and got a foothold in the Dead Reckoning Department. I finished that in three days. There was only one place left for it now. I laid siege to the Commissioner of Odds and Ends. To his clerk, rather— he was not there himself. There were sixteen beautiful young ladies in the room, writing in books, and there were seven well-favored young clerks showing them how. The young women smiled up over their shoulders, and the clerks smiled back at them, and all went merry as a marriage bell. Two or three clerks that were reading the newspapers looked at me rather hard, but went on reading, and nobody said anything. However, I had been used to this kind of alacrity from Fourth Assistant Junior Clerks all through my eventful career, from the very day I entered the first office of the Corn-Beef Bureau clear till I passed out of the last one in the Dead Reckoning Division. I had got so accomplished by this time that I could stand on one foot from the moment I entered an office till a clerk spoke to me, without changing more than two, or maybe three, times.

So I stood there till I had changed four different times. Then I said to one of the clerks who was reading:

"Illustrious Vagrant, where is the Grand Turk?"

"What do you mean, sir? whom do you mean? If you mean the Chief of the Bureau, he is out."

"Will he visit the harem to-day?"

The young man glared upon me awhile, and then went on reading his paper. But I knew the ways of those clerks. I knew I was safe if he got through before another New York mail arrived. He only had two more papers left. After a while he finished them, and then he yawned and asked me what I wanted.

"Renowned and honored Imbecile: on or about——"

"You are the beef-contract man. Give me your papers."

He took them, and for a long time he ransacked his odds and ends. Finally he found the Northwest Passage, as *I* regarded it—he found the long-lost record of that beef contract—he found the rock upon which so many of my ancestors had split before they ever got to it. I was deeply moved. And yet I rejoiced—for I had survived. I said with emotion, "Give it me. The government will settle now." He waved me back, and said there was something yet to be done first.

"Where is this John Wilson Mackenzie?" said he.

"Dead."

"When did he die?"

"He didn't die at all—he was killed."

"How?"

"Tomahawked."

"Who tomahawked him?"

"Why, an Indian, of course. You didn't suppose it was the superintendent of a Sunday-school, did you?"

"No. An Indian, was it?"

"The same."

"Name of the Indian?"

"His name? *I* don't know his name."

"*Must* have his name. Who saw the tomahawking done?"

"I don't know."

"You were not present yourself, then?"

"Which you can see by my hair. I was absent."

"Then how do you know that Mackenzie is dead?"

"Because he certainly died at that time, and I have every reason to believe that he has been dead ever since. I *know* he has, in fact."

"We must have proofs. Have you got the Indian?"

"Of course not."

"Well, you must get him. Have you got the tomahawk?"

"I never thought of such a thing."

"You must get the tomahawk. You must produce the Indian and the tomahawk. If Mackenzie's death can be proven by these, you can then go before the commission appointed to audit claims with some show of getting your bill under such headway that your children may possibly live to receive the money and enjoy it. But that man's death *must* be proven. However, I may as well tell you that the government will never pay that transportation and those traveling expenses of the lamented Mackenzie. It *may* possibly pay for the barrel of beef that Sherman's soldiers captured, if you can get a relief bill through Congress making an appropriation for that purpose; but it will not pay for the twenty-nine barrels the Indians ate."

"Then there is only a hundred dollars due me, and *that* isn't certain! After all Mackenzie's travels in Europe, Asia, and America with that beef; after all his trials and tribulations and transportation; after the slaughter of all those innocents that tried to collect that bill! Young man, why didn't the First Comptroller of the Corn-Beef Division tell me this?"

"He didn't know anything about the genuineness of your claim."

"Why didn't the Second tell me? why didn't the Third? why didn't all those divisions and departments tell me?"

"None of them knew. We do things by routine here. You have followed the routine and found out what you wanted to know. It is the best way. It is the only way. It is very regular, and very slow, but it is very certain."

"Yes, certain death. It has been, to the most of our tribe. I begin to feel that I, too, am called. Young man, you love the bright creature yonder with the gentle blue eyes and the steel pens behind her ears—I see it in your soft glances; you

wish to marry her—but you are poor. Here, hold out your hand—here is the beef contract; go, take her and be happy! Heaven bless you, my children!"

This is all I know about the great beef contract that has created so much talk in the community. The clerk to whom I bequeathed it died. I know nothing further about the contract, or any one connected with it. I only know that if a man lives long enough he can trace a thing through the Circumlocution Office of Washington and find out, after much labor and trouble and delay, that which he could have found out on the first day if the business of the Circumlocution Office were as ingeniously systematized as it would be if it were a great private mercantile institution.

1870.

Political Economy

Political Economy is the basis of all good government. The wisest men of all ages have brought to bear upon this subject the——

[Here I was interrupted and informed that a stranger wished to see me down at the door. I went and confronted him, and asked to know his business, struggling all the time to keep a tight rein on my seething political economy ideas, and not let them break away from me or get tangled in their harness. And privately I wished the stranger was in the bottom of the canal with a cargo of wheat on top of him. I was all in a fever, but he was cool. He said he was sorry to disturb me, but as he was passing he noticed that I needed

Sketches New and Old, pp. 16–24.

some lightning-rods. I said, "Yes, yes—go on—what about it?" He said there was nothing about it, in particular—nothing except that he would like to put them up for me. I am new to housekeeping; have been used to hotels and boarding-houses all my life. Like anybody else of similar experience, I try to appear (to strangers) to be an old housekeeper; consequently I said in an offhand way that I had been intending for some time to have six or eight lightning-rods put up, but —— The stranger started, and looked inquiringly at me, but I was serene. I thought that if I chanced to make any mistakes, he would not catch me by my countenance. He said he would rather have my custom than any man's in town. I said, "All right," and started off to wrestle with my great subject again, when he called me back and said it would be necessary to know exactly how many "points" I wanted put up, what parts of the house I wanted them on, and what quality of rod I preferred. It was close quarters for a man not used to the exigencies of housekeeping; but I went through creditably, and he probably never suspected that I was a novice. I told him to put up eight "points," and put them all on the roof, and use the best quality of rod. He said he could furnish the "plain" article at 20 cents a foot; "coppered," 25 cents; "zinc-plated spiral-twist," at 30 cents, that would stop a streak of lightning any time, no matter where it was bound, and "render its errand harmless and its further progress apocryphal." I said apocryphal was no slouch of a word, emanating from the source it did, but philology aside, I liked the spiral-twist and would take that brand. Then he said he *could* make two hundred and fifty feet answer; but to do it right, and make the best job in town of it, and attract the admiration of the just and the unjust alike, and compel all parties to say they never saw a more symmetrical and hypothetical display of lightning-rods since they were born, he supposed he really

couldn't get along without four hundred, though he was not
vindictive, and trusted he was willing to try. I said, go ahead
and use four hundred, and make any kind of a job he pleased
out of it, but let me get back to my work. So I got rid of him
at last; and now, after half an hour spent in getting my
train of political economy thoughts coupled together again,
I am ready to go on once more.]

*richest treasures of their genius, their experience of life, and
their learning. The great lights of commercial jurisprudence,
international confraternity, and biological deviation, of all
ages, all civilizations, and all nationalities, from Zoroaster
down to Horace Greeley, have*——

[Here I was interrupted again, and required to go down
and confer further with that lightning-rod man. I hurried off,
boiling and surging with prodigious thoughts wombed in
words of such majesty that each one of them was in itself a
straggling procession of syllables that might be fifteen minutes passing a given point, and once more I confronted him
—he so calm and sweet, I so hot and frenzied. He was standing in the contemplative attitude of the Colossus of Rhodes,
with one foot on my infant tuberose, and the other among
my pansies, his hands on his hips, his hat-brim tilted forward,
one eye shut and the other gazing critically and admiringly
in the direction of my principal chimney. He said now *there*
was a state of things to make a man glad to be alive; and
added, "I leave it to *you* if you ever saw anything more de-
liriously picturesque than eight lightning-rods on one chimney?" I said I had no present recollection of anything that
transcended it. He said that in his opinion nothing on earth
but Niagara Falls was superior to it in the way of natural
scenery. All that was needed now, he verily believed, to make

my house a perfect balm to the eye, was to kind of touch up the other chimneys a little, and thus "add to the generous *coup d'œil* a soothing uniformity of achievement which would allay the excitement naturally consequent upon the *coup d'état.*" I asked him if he learned to talk out of a book, and if I could borrow it anywhere? He smiled pleasantly, and said that his manner of speaking was not taught in books, and that nothing but familiarity with lightning could enable a man to handle his conversational style with impunity. He then figured up an estimate, and said that about eight more rods scattered about my roof would about fix me right, and he guessed five hundred feet of stuff would do it; and added that the first eight had got a little the start of him, so to speak, and used up a mere trifle of material more than he had calculated on—a hundred feet or along there. I said I was in a dreadful hurry, and I wished we could get his business permanently mapped out, so that I could go on with my work. He said, "I *could* have put up those eight rods, and marched off about my business—some men *would* have done it. But no; I said to myself, this man is a stranger to me, and I will die before I'll wrong him; there ain't lightning-rods enough on that house, and for one I'll never stir out of my tracks till I've done as I would be done by, and told him so. Stranger, my duty is accomplished; if the recalcitrant and dephlogistic messenger of heaven strikes your——" "There, now, there," I said, "put on the other eight—add five hundred feet of spiral-twist—do anything and everything you want to do; but calm your sufferings, and try to keep your feelings where you can reach them with the dictionary. Meanwhile, if we understand each other now, I will go to work again."

I think I have been sitting here a full hour this time, trying to get back to where I was when my train of thought was

broken up by the last interruption; but I believe I have accomplished it at last, and may venture to proceed again.]
wrestled with this great subject, and the greatest among them have found it a worthy adversary, and one that always comes up fresh and smiling after every throw. The great Confucius said that he would rather be a profound political economist than chief of police. Cicero frequently said that political economy was the grandest consummation that the human mind was capable of consuming; and even our own Greeley has said vaguely but forcibly that "Political——

[Here the lightning-rod man sent up another call for me. I went down in a state of mind bordering on impatience. He said he would rather have died than interrupt me, but when he was employed to do a job, and that job was expected to be done in a clean, workmanlike manner, and when it was finished and fatigue urged him to seek the rest and recreation he stood so much in need of, and he was about to do it, but looked up and saw at a glance that all the calculations had been a little out, and if a thunder-storm were to come up, and that house, which he felt a personal interest in, stood there with nothing on earth to protect it but sixteen lightning-rods——"Let us have peace!" I shrieked. "Put up a hundred and fifty! Put some on the kitchen! Put a dozen on the barn! Put a couple on the cow—Put one on the cook!—scatter them all over the persecuted place till it looks like a zinc-plated, spiral-twisted, silver-mounted cane-brake! Move! use up all the material you can get your hands on, and when you run out of lightning-rods put up ram-rods, cam-rods, stair-rods, piston-rods—*anything* that will pander to your dismal appetite for artificial scenery, and bring respite to my raging brain and healing to my lacerated soul!" Wholly unmoved—further than to smile sweetly—this iron being simply turned back his wrist-bands daintily, and said that he would now proceed to hump himself. Well, all that was nearly three hours ago. It is questionable whether I am calm enough yet to write on the noble theme of political economy, but I cannot resist the desire to try, for it is the one subject that is nearest to my heart and dearest to my brain of all this world's philosophy.]

"economy is heaven's best boon to man." *When the loose but gifted Byron lay in his Venetian exile he observed that, if it could be granted him to go back and live his misspent life over again, he would give his lucid and unintoxicated intervals to the composition, not of frivolous rhymes, but of essays upon political economy. Washington loved this exquisite science; such names as Baker, Beckwith, Judson, Smith, are imperishably linked with it; and even imperial Homer, in the ninth book of the* Iliad, *has said:*

> *Fiat justitia, ruat cælum,*
> *Post mortem unum, ante bellum,*
> *Hic jacet hoc, ex-parte res,*
> *Politicum e-conomico est.*

The grandeur of these conceptions of the old poet, together with the felicity of the wording which clothes them, and the sublimity of the imagery whereby they are illustrated, have singled out that stanza, and made it more celebrated than any that ever——

["Now, not a word out of you—not a single word. Just state your bill and relapse into impenetrable silence for ever and ever on these premises. Nine hundred dollars? Is that all? This check for the amount will be honored at any respectable bank in America. What is that multitude of people gathered in the street for? How?—'looking at the lightning-rods!' Bless my life, did they never see any lightning-rods before? Never saw 'such a stack of them on one establish-ment,' did I understand you to say? I will step down and critically observe this popular ebullition of ignorance."]

THREE DAYS LATER.—We are all about worn out. For four-and-twenty hours our bristling premises were the talk and wonder of the town. The theaters languished, for their hap-piest scenic inventions were tame and commonplace com-pared with my lightning-rods. Our street was blocked night and day with spectators, and among them were many who came from the country to see. It was a blessed relief on the second day when a thunder-storm came up and the lightning began to "go for" my house, as the historian Josephus quaintly phrases it. It cleared the galleries, so to speak. In five minutes there was not a spectator within half a mile of my place; but all the high houses about that distance away were full, windows, roof, and all. And well they might be, for all the falling stars and Fourth-of-July fireworks of a generation, put together and rained down simultaneously out of heaven in one brilliant shower upon one helpless roof, would not have any advantage of the pyrotechnic display that was making my house so magnificently conspicuous in the general gloom of the storm. By actual count, the lightning struck at my establishment seven hundred and sixty-four times in forty minutes, but tripped on one of those faithful rods every time, and slid down the spiral-twist and shot into the earth before it probably had time to be surprised at the way the thing was done. And through all that bombardment only one patch of slates was ripped up, and that was because, for a single instant, the rods in the vicinity were transporting all the lightning they could possibly accommodate. Well, nothing was ever seen like it since the world began. For one

Political Economy

whole day and night not a member of my family stuck his head out of the window but he got the hair snatched off it as smooth as a billiard-ball; and, if the reader will believe me, not one of us ever dreamt of stirring abroad. But at last the awful siege came to an end—because there was absolutely no more electricity left in the clouds above us within grappling distance of my insatiable rods. Then I sallied forth, and gathered daring workmen together, and not a bite or a nap did we take till the premises were utterly stripped of all their terrific armament except just three rods on the house, one on the kitchen, and one on the barn—and, behold, these remain there even unto this day. And then, and not till then, the people ventured to use our street again. I will remark here, in passing, that during that fearful time I did not continue my essay upon political economy. I am not even yet settled enough in nerve and brain to resume it.

TO WHOM IT MAY CONCERN.—Parties having need of three thousand two hundred and eleven feet of best quality zinc-plated spiral-twist lightning-rod stuff, and sixteen hundred and thirty-one silver-tipped points, all in tolerable repair (and, although much worn by use, still equal to any ordinary emergency), can hear of a bargain by addressing the publisher.

1870

The Facts Concerning the Recent Resignation

Washington, Dec. 2, 1867.

I have resigned. The Government appears to go on much the same, but there is a spoke out of its wheel, nevertheless.

Sketches New and Old, pp. 348–358.

I was clerk of the Senate Committee on Conchology, and I have thrown up the position. I could see the plainest disposition on the part of the other members of the Government to debar me from having any voice in the counsels of the nation, and so I could no longer hold office and retain my self-respect. If I were to detail all the outrages that were heaped upon me during the six days that I was connected with the Government in an official capacity, the narrative would fill a volume. They appointed me clerk of that Committee on Conchology, and then allowed me no amanuensis to play billiards with. I would have borne that, lonesome as it was, if I had met with that courtesy from the other members of the Cabinet which was my due. But I did not. Whenever I observed that the head of a department was pursuing a wrong course, I laid down everything and went and tried to set him right, as it was my duty to do; and I never was thanked for it in a single instance. I went, with the best intentions in the world, to the Secretary of the Navy, and said:

"Sir, I cannot see that Admiral Farragut is doing anything but skirmishing around there in Europe, having a sort of picnic. Now, that may be all very well, but it does not exhibit itself to me in that light. If there is no fighting for him to do, let him come home. There is no use in a man having a whole fleet for a pleasure excursion. It is too expensive. Mind, I do not object to pleasure excursions for the naval officers— pleasure excursions that are in reason—pleasure excursions that are economical. Now, they might go down the Mississippi on a raft——"

You ought to have heard him storm! One would have supposed I had committed a crime of some kind. But I didn't mind. I said it was cheap, and full of republican simplicity, and perfectly safe. I said that, for a tranquil pleasure excursion, there was nothing equal to a raft.

Then the Secretary of the Navy asked me who I was; and when I told him I was connected with the Government, he wanted to know in what capacity. I said that, without remarking upon the singularity of such a question, coming, as it did, from a member of that same Government, I would inform him that I was clerk of the Senate Committee on Conchology. Then there was a fine storm! He finished by ordering me to leave the premises, and give my attention strictly to my own business in future. My first impulse was to get him removed. However, that would harm others beside himself, and do me no real good, and so I let him stay.

I went next to the Secretary of War, who was not inclined to see me at all until he learned that I was connected with the Government. If I had not been on important business, I suppose I could not have got in. I asked him for a light (he was smoking at the time), and then I told him I had no fault to find with his defending the parole stipulations of General Lee and his comrades in arms, but that I could not approve of his method of fighting the Indians on the Plains. I said he fought too scattering. He ought to get the Indians more together—get them together in some convenient place, where he could have provisions enough for both parties, and then have a general massacre. I said there was nothing so convincing to an Indian as a general massacre. If he could not approve of the massacre, I said the next surest thing for an Indian was soap and education. Soap and education are not as sudden as a massacre, but they are more deadly in the long run; because a half-massacred Indian may recover, but if you educate him and wash him, it is bound to finish him sometime or other. It undermines his constitution; it strikes at the foundation of his being. "Sir," I said, "the time has come when blood-curdling cruelty has become necessary. Inflict soap and a spelling-book on every Indian that ravages the Plains, and let them die!"

The Secretary of War asked me if I was a member of the Cabinet, and I said I was. He inquired what position I held, and I said I was clerk of the Senate Committee on Conchology. I was then ordered under arrest for contempt of court, and restrained of my liberty for the best part of the day.

I almost resolved to be silent thenceforward, and let the Government get along the best way it could. But duty called, and I obeyed. I called on the Secretary of the Treasury. He said:

"What will *you* have?"

The question threw me off my guard. I said, "Rum punch."

He said, "If you have got any business here, sir, state it— and in as few words as possible."

I then said that I was sorry he had seen fit to change the subject so abruptly, because such conduct was very offensive to me; but under the circumstances I would overlook the matter and come to the point. I now went into an earnest expostulation with him upon the extravagant length of his report. I said it was expensive, unnecessary, and awkwardly constructed; there were no descriptive passages in it, no poetry, no sentiment—no heroes, no plot, no pictures—not even woodcuts. Nobody would read it, that was a clear case. I urged him not to ruin his reputation by getting out a thing like that. If he ever hoped to succeed in literature, he must throw more variety into his writings. He must beware of dry detail. I said that the main popularity of the almanac was derived from its poetry and conundrums, and that a few conundrums distributed around through the Treasury report would help the sale of it more than all the internal revenue he could put into it. I said these things in the kindest spirit, and yet the Secretary of the Treasury fell into a violent passion. He even said that I was an ass. He abused me in the most vindictive manner, and said that if I came there again meddling with his business, he would throw me out of the window. I said I would take my hat and go, if I could not be treated with the respect due to my office, and I did go. It was just like a new author. They always think they know more than anybody else when they are getting out their first book. Nobody can tell *them* anything.

During the whole time that I was connected with the Government it seemed as if I could not do anything in an official capacity without getting myself into trouble. And yet I did nothing, attempted nothing, but what I conceived to be for the good of my country. The sting of my wrongs may have driven me to unjust and harmful conclusions, but it surely seemed to me that the Secretary of State, the Secretary of War, the Secretary of the Treasury, and others of my *confrères,* had conspired from the very beginning to drive me from the Administration. I never attended but one Cabinet meeting while I was connected with the Government. That was sufficient for me. The servant at the White House door did not seem disposed to make way for me until I asked if the other members of the Cabinet had arrived. He said they had, and I entered. They were all there; but nobody offered me a seat. They stared at me as if I had been an intruder. The President said:

"Well, sir, who are *you?*"

I handed him my card, and he read—"The HON. MARK TWAIN, Clerk of the Senate Committee on Conchology." Then he looked at me from head to foot, as if he had never heard of me before. The Secretary of the Treasury said:

"This is the meddlesome ass that came to recommend me to put poetry and conundrums in my report, as if it were an almanac."

The Secretary of War said: "It is the same visionary that came to me yesterday with a scheme to educate a portion of the Indians to death, and massacre the balance."

The Secretary of the Navy said: "I recognize this youth as the person who has been interfering with my business time and again during the week. He is distressed about Admiral Farragut's using a whole fleet for a pleasure excursion, as he terms it. His proposition about some insane pleasure excursion on a raft is too absurd to repeat."

I said: "Gentlemen, I perceive here a disposition to throw discredit upon every act of my official career; I perceive, also, a disposition to debar me from all voice in the counsels of the nation. No notice whatever was sent to me to-day. It was only by the merest chance that I learned that there was going to be a Cabinet meeting. But let these things pass. All I wish to know is, is this a Cabinet meeting, or is it not?"

The President said it was.

"Then," I said, "let us proceed to business at once, and not fritter away valuable time in unbecoming fault-findings with each other's official conduct."

The Secretary of State now spoke up, in his benignant way, and said, "Young man, you are laboring under a mistake. The clerks of the Congressional committees are not members of the Cabinet. Neither are the doorkeepers of the Capitol, strange as it may seem. Therefore, much as we could desire your more than human wisdom in our deliberations, we cannot lawfully avail ourselves of it. The counsels of the nation must proceed without you; if disaster follows, as follow full well it may, be it balm to your sorrowing spirit, that by deed and voice you did what in you lay to avert it. You have my blessing. Farewell."

These gentle words soothed my troubled breast, and I went away. But the servants of a nation can know no peace. I had hardly reached my den in the Capitol, and disposed my feet on the table like a representative, when one of the Senators on the Conchological Committee came in in a passion and said:

"Where have you been all day?"

I observed that, if that was anybody's affair but my own, I had been to a Cabinet meeting.

"To a Cabinet meeting? I would like to know what business you had at a Cabinet meeting?"

I said I went there to consult—allowing for the sake of argument, that he was in anywise concerned in the matter. He grew insolent then, and ended by saying he had wanted me for three days past to copy a report on bomb-shells, egg-shells, clam-shells, and I don't know what all, connected with conchology, and nobody had been able to find me.

This was too much. This was the feather that broke the clerical camel's back. I said, "Sir, do you suppose that I am going to *work* for six dollars a day? If that is the idea, let me recommend the Senate Committee on Conchology to hire somebody else. I am the slave of *no* faction! Take back your degrading commission. Give me liberty or give me death!"

From that hour I was no longer connected with the Government. Snubbed by the department, snubbed by the Cabinet, snubbed at last by the chairman of the committee I was endeavoring to adorn, I yielded to persecution, cast far from me the perils and seductions of my great office, and forsook my bleeding country in the hour of her peril.

But I had done the State some service, and I sent in my bill:

The United States of America in account with the Hon. Clerk of the Senate Committee on Conchology, Dr.

To consultation with Secretary of War, ... $ 50
To consultation with Secretary of Navy, ...   50
To consultation with Secretary of Treasury, ...   50
Cabinet consultation, ... No charge ..
To mileage to and from Jerusalem,* *via* Egypt, Al-
 giers, Gibraltar, and Cadiz, 14,000 miles at 20c. a
 mile, ...   2800
To salary as Clerk of Senate Committee on Conchol-
 ogy, six days, at $6 per day, ...   36
                                 Total $2986

Not an item of this bill has been paid, except that trifle of thirty-six dollars for clerkship salary. The Secretary of the Treasury, pursuing me to the last, drew his pen through all the other items, and simply marked in the margin "Not allowed." So, the dread alternative is embraced at last. Repudiation has begun! The nation is lost.

I am done with official life for the present. Let those clerks who are willing to be imposed on remain. I know numbers of them, in the Departments, who are never informed when there is to be a Cabinet meeting, whose advice is never asked about war, or finance, or commerce, by the heads of the nation, any more than if they were not connected with Government, and who actually stay in their offices day after day and work! They know their importance to the nation, and they unconsciously show it in their bearing, and the way they order their sustenance at the restaurant—but they work. I know one who has to paste all sorts of little scraps from the newspaper into a scrap-book—some-

---

* Territorial delegates charge mileage both ways, although they never go back when they get here once. Why my mileage is denied me is more than I can understand.—*Mark Twain.*

times as many as eight or ten scraps a day. He doesn't do it well, but he does it as well as he can. It is very fatiguing. It is exhausting to the intellect. Yet he only gets eighteen hundred dollars a year. With a brain like his, that young man could amass thousands and thousands of dollars in some other pursuit, if he chose to do it. But no—his heart is with his country, and he will serve her as long as she has got a scrap-book left. And I know clerks that don't know how to write very well, but such knowledge as they possess they nobly lay at the feet of their country, and toil on and suffer for twenty-five hundred dollars a year. What they write has to be written over again by other clerks sometimes; but when a man has done his best for his country, should his country complain? Then there are clerks that have no clerkships, and are waiting, and waiting, and waiting, for a vacancy—waiting patiently for a chance to help their country out—and while they are waiting, they only get barely two thousand dollars a year for it. It is sad—it is very, very sad. When a member of Congress has a friend who is gifted, but has no employment wherein his great powers may be brought to bear, he confers him upon his country, and gives him a clerkship in a department. And there that man has to slave his life out, fighting documents for the benefit of a nation that never thinks of him, never sympathizes with him—and all for two thousand or three thousand dollars a year. When I shall have completed my list of all the clerks in the several departments, with my statement of what they have to do, and what they get for it, you will see that there are not half enough clerks, and that what there are do not get half enough pay.

Letter Read at a Dinner of the Knights
of St. Patrick

Hartford, Ct., March 16, 1876.

To the Chairman:

Dear Sir,—I am very sorry that I cannot be with the Knights of St. Patrick to-morrow evening. In this centennial year we ought to find a peculiar pleasure in doing honor to the memory of a man whose good name has endured through fourteen centuries. We ought to find pleasure in it for the reason that at this time we naturally have a fellow-feeling for such a man. He wrought a great work in his day. He found Ireland a prosperous republic, and looked about him to see if he might find some useful thing to turn his hand to. He observed that the president of that republic was in the habit of sheltering his great officials from deserved punishment, so he lifted up his staff and smote him, and he died. He found that the secretary of war had been so unbecomingly economical as to have laid up $12,000 a year out of a salary of $8000, and he killed him. He found that the secretary of the interior always prayed over every separate and distinct barrel of salt beef that was intended for the unconverted savage, and then kept that beef himself, so he killed him also. He found that the secretary of the navy knew more about handling suspicious claims than he did about handling a ship, and he at once made an end of him. He found that a very foul private secretary had been engineered through

Samuel L. Clemens [Mark Twain], *Tom Sawyer Abroad, Tom Sawyer, Detective and Other Stories*, New York (1894), pp. 409–410.

a sham trial, so he destroyed him. He discovered that the congress which pretended to prodigious virtue was very anxious to investigate an ambassador who had dishonored the country abroad, but was equally anxious to prevent the appointment of any spotless man to a similar post; that this congress had no God but party; no system of morals but party policy; no vision but a bat's vision, and no reason or excuse for existing anyhow. Therefore he massacred that congress to the last man.

When he had finished his great work, he said, in his figurative way, "Lo, I have destroyed all the reptiles in Ireland."

St. Patrick had no politics; his sympathies lay with the right—that was politics enough. When he came across a reptile, he forgot to inquire whether he was a democrat or a republican, but simply exalted his staff and "let him have it." Honored be his name—I wish we had him here to trim us up for the centennial. But that cannot be. His staff, which was the symbol of real, not sham reform, is idle. However, we still have with us the symbol of Truth—George Washington's little hatchet—for I know where they've buried it.

Yours truly,

MARK TWAIN.

CHARLES HEBER CLARK
[Max Adeler]
(1841-1915)

Charles Heber Clark was a Philadelphia journalist who published several volumes of light humor, poetry, and fiction under the nom de plume Max Adeler. He served on the editorial staff of the *Evening Bulletin,* which back then nearly everybody in Philadelphia read, and he edited the *Textile Record.* A minor humorist, Clark merits remembrance nevertheless as a contributor toward popular amusement, as someone who, according to a reviewer in the *Nation,* got "most of his fun out of the peculiar life of a small place." In the following selection Clark pokes his fun at the peculiar political life of a small place.

My First Political Speech

. . . The chairman began with a short speech in which he
went over almost precisely the ground covered by my introduction; and as that portion of my oration was . . . reduced to a fragment . . . , I quietly resolved to begin, when
my turn came, with point number two.

The chairman introduced to the crowd Mr. Keyser, who
was received with cheers. He was a ready speaker, and he began, to my deep regret, by telling in capital style my story
number three, after which he used up some of my number
six arguments, and concluded with the remark that it was
not his purpose to occupy the attention of the meeting for
any length of time, because the executive committee in Wil-
mington [Delaware] had sent an eloquent orator who was
now upon the platform and would present the cause of the
party in a manner which he could not hope to approach.

Mr. Keyser then sat down, and Mr. Schwartz was introduced. Mr. Schwartz observed that it was hardly worth while
for him to attempt to make anything like a speech, because
the gentleman from New Castle had come down on purpose
to discuss the issues of the campaign, and the audience, of
course, was anxious to hear him. Mr. Schwartz would only
tell a little story which seemed to illustrate a point he wished
to make, and he thereupon related my anecdote number
seven . . . The point illustrated I was shocked to find was
almost precisely that which I had attached to my story number seven. The situation began to have a serious appearance.
Here, at one fell swoop, two of my best stories and three of

Charles Heber Clark [Max Adeler], *Out of the Hurly-Burly, or Life in an
Odd Corner*, Philadelphia (1874), pp. 381–386.

my sets of arguments were swept off into utter uselessness.

When Schwartz withdrew, a man named Krumbauer was brought forward. Krumbauer was a German, and the chairman announced that he would speak in that language for the benefit of those persons in the audience to whom the tongue was pleasantly familiar. Krumbauer went ahead, and the crowd received his remarks with roars of laughter. After one particularly exuberant outburst of merriment, I asked the man who sat next to me, and who seemed deeply interested in the story,

"What was that little joke of Krumbauer's? It must have been first rate."

"So it was," he said. "It was about a Dutchman up in Berks county, Penna., who got mixed up in his dates."

"What dates?" I gasped, in awful apprehension.

"Why, his Fourths of July, you know. Got seven or eight years in arrears and tried to make them all up at once. Good, wasn't it?"

"Good? I should think so; ha! ha! My very best story, as I'm a sinner!"

It was awfully bad. I could have strangled Krumbauer and then chopped him into bits. The ground seemed slipping away beneath me; there was the merest skeleton of a speech left. But I determined to take that and do my best, trusting to luck for a happy result.

But my turn had not yet come. Mr. Wilson was dragged out next, and I thought I perceived a demoniac smile steal over the countenance of the cymbal player as Wilson said he was too hoarse to say much; he would leave the heavy work for the brilliant young orator who was here from New Castle. He would skim rapidly over the ground and then retire. He did. Wilson rapidly skimmed all the cream off of my arguments numbers two, five and six, and wound up by offering the whole of my number four argument. My hair fairly stood on end when Wilson bowed and left the stand. What on earth was I to do now? Not an argument left to stand upon; all my anecdotes gone but two, and my mind in such a condition of frenzied bewilderment that it seemed as if there was not another available argument or suggestion or hint or anecdote remaining in the entire universe. In an agony of despair, I turned to the man next to me and asked him if I would have to follow Wilson.

He said it was his turn now.

"And what are you going to say?" I demanded, suspiciously.

"Oh, nothing," he replied—"nothing at all. I want to leave room for you. I'll just tell a little story or so, to amuse them, and then sit down."

"What story, for instance?" I asked.

"Oh, nothing, nothing; only a little yarn I happen to remember about a farmer who married a woman who said she could cut four cords of wood, when she couldn't."

My worst fears were realized. I turned to the man next to me, and said, with suppressed emotion.

"May I ask your name, my friend?"

He said his name was Gumbs.

"May I inquire what your Christian name is?"

He said it was William Henry.

"Well, William Henry Gumbs," I exclaimed, "gaze at me! Do I look like a man who would slay a human being in cold blood?"

"HM-m-m, n-no; you don't," he replied, with an air of critical consideration.

"But I AM!" said I, fiercely—"I AM; and I tell you now that if you undertake to relate that anecdote about the farmer's wife I will blow you into eternity without a moment's warning; I will, by George!"

Mr. Gumbs instantly jumped up, placed his hand on the railing of the porch, and got over suddenly into the crowd. He stood there pointing me out to the bystanders, and doubtless advancing the theory that I was an original kind of a lunatic, who might be expected to have at any moment a fit which would be interesting when studied from a distance.

The chairman looked around, intending to call upon my friend Mr. Gumbs; but not perceiving him, he came to me and said:

"Now is your chance, sir; splendid opportunity; crowd worked up to just the proper pitch. We paved the way for you; go in and do your best."

"Oh yes; but hold on for a few moments, will you? I can't speak now; the fact is I am not quite ready. Run out some other man."

"Haven't got another man. Kept you for the last purposely, and the crowd is waiting. Come ahead and pitch in, and give it to 'em hot and heavy."

It was very easy for him to say "give it to them," but I had nothing to give. Beautifully they paved the way for me! Nicely they had worked up the crowd to the proper pitch! Here I was in a condition of frantic despair, with a crowd of one thousand people expecting a brilliant oration from me who had not a thing in my mind but a beggarly story about a fire-extinguisher and a worse one about a farmer's wife. I groaned in spirit and wished I had been born far away in some distant clime among savages who knew not of mass meetings, and whose language contained such a small number of words that speech-making was impossible.

But the chairman was determined. He seized me by the

arm and fairly dragged me to the front. He introduced me
to the crowd in flattering, and I may say outrageously ridiculous, terms, and then whispering in my ear, "Hit 'em hard,
old fellow, hit 'em hard," he sat down.

The crowd received me with three hearty cheers. As I
heard them I began to feel dizzy. The audience seemed to
swim around and to increase tenfold in size. By a resolute
effort I recovered my self-possession partially, and determined to begin. I could not think of anything but the two
stories, and I resolved to tell them as well as I could. I said,

"Fellow-citizens: It is so late now that I will not attempt
to make a speech to you." (Cries of "Yes!" "Go ahead!"
"Never mind the time!" etc., etc.) Elevating my voice, I
repeated: "I say it is so late now that I can't make a speech as
I intended on account of its being so late that the speech
which I intended to make would keep you here too late if I
made it as I intended to. So I will tell you a story about a
man who bought a patent fire-extinguisher which was warranted to split four cords of wood a day; so he set fire to his
house to try her, and—No, it was his wife who was warranted
to split four cords of wood—I got it wrong; and when the
flames obtained full headway, he found she could only split
two cords and a half, and it made him—What I mean is that
the farmer, when he bought the exting—courted her, that is,
she said she could set fire to the house, and when he tried
her, she collapsed the first time—the extinguisher did, and
he wanted a divorce because his house—Oh, hang it, fellow-
citizens, you understand that this man, or farmer, rather,
bought a—I should say courted a—that is, a fire-ex——"
(Desperately.) "Fellow-citizens! IF ANY MAN SHOOTS THE
AMERICAN FLAG, PULL HIM DOWN UPON THE SPOT; BUT AS FOR
ME, GIVE ME LIBERTY OR GIVE ME DEATH!"

As I shouted this out at the top of my voice, in an ecstasy

of confusion, a wild, tumultuous yell of laughter came up from the crowd. I paused for a second . . . , and then, dashing through the throng at the back of the porch, I rushed down the street to the dépôt, with the shouts of the crowd and the uproarious music of the band ringing in my ears. I got upon a freight train, gave the engineer five dollars to take me along on the locomotive, and spent the night riding to New Castle.

EDGAR WILSON NYE
[Bill Nye]
(1850-1896)

"Bill" Nye's letter accepting the office of postmaster at Laramie, Wyoming Territory, brought him widespread acclaim as a comic writer. It appeared in the Laramie *Boomerang,* which he and Judge Jacob Blair had founded in 1881. By 1885 Nye's reputation as a humorist was nationwide. He was performing regularly before lyceum audiences, frequently on the same bill with his close friend, the Hoosier poet James Whitcomb Riley, against whose calculated bathos Nye's humor and satire stood out effectively. Syndication of Nye's articles by the New York *World* assured his reputation and income.

Nye was born in Maine, and grew up in the St. Croix Valley of Wisconsin. After brief schooling, he was apprenticed in a lawyer's office, which meant only that the shelves of law books were at his disposal whenever his menial tasks were done. Later he taught school. In 1876 he removed to the Wyoming Territory. There, by his own account, he was admitted to the bar by a generous committee of examiners. He became justice of the peace in Laramie, earning his living from letters and sketches published in the Cheyenne *Sun,* the Laramie *Daily Sentinel,* and the Denver *Tribune.* In 1882, Nye was appointed postmaster of Laramie. Simultaneously he was superintendent of schools, a member of the territorial legislature, and United States Commissioner. His experiences in these political offices supplied all the humorous material he could possibly use.

Bill Nye's political humor belongs to the pattern of Downing, Ward, Nasby and Will Rogers, with whom he came to be compared. There was familiar correspondence with persons in high places and folksy reliance on homespun situations. Nye's wit, unlike Nasby's, was suffused with a cheerful, mellow sense of the ludicrous. He mixed understatement with sly exaggeration, while his style was distorted by grotesque sentence structure and softened into mirthfulness by pervasive good cheer.

Admirers said that Nye's writings exercised a restraining influence upon the public affairs of his time, a gentle rein against the tendency of politics to grow remote, corrupt, and threatening. His own appointment as postmaster of Laramie, "a great triumph of eternal truth over error and wrong," filled him with satisfaction. His resignation, he professed to fear, might mean financial panic for Europe. But no matter. Whatever happened, Bill Nye would emerge on top. "I can write up things that never occurred with a masterly and graphic hand," he once observed. "Then if they occur I am grateful," he added, "if not I bow to the inevitable and smother my chagrin."

Accepting the Laramie Postoffice

Office of Daily Boomerang,
Laramie City, Wy.
August 9, 1882.

My dear General:

I have received by telegraph the news of my nomination by the President and my confirmation by the Senate, as postmaster at Laramie, and wish to extend my thanks for the same.

I have ordered an entirely new set of boxes and post-office outfit, including new corrugated cuspidors for the lady clerks.

I look upon the appointment as a great triumph of eternal truth over error and wrong. It is one of the epochs, I may say, in the Nation's onward march toward political purity and perfection. I do not know when I have noticed any stride in the affairs of state, which so thoroughly impressed me with its wisdom.

Now that we are co-workers in the same department, I trust that you will not feel shy or backward in consulting me at any time relative to matters concerning postoffice affairs. Be perfectly frank with me, and feel free to bring anything of that kind right to me. Do not feel reluctant because I may at times appear haughty and indifferent, cold or reserved. Perhaps you do not think I know the difference between a general delivery window and a three-em quad, but that is a mistake.

My general information is far beyond my years.

Edgar Wilson Nye, *Remarks by Bill Nye,* Chicago (1887), p. 161.

With profoundest regard, and a hearty endorsement of the policy of the President and the Senate, whatever it may be,

I remain, sincerely yours,

BILL NYE, P.M.

Strict Attention to Business

A Resign

Postoffice, Divan,
Laramie City, W.T.,
Oct. 1, 1883.

To the President of the United States:

Sir: I beg leave at this time officially to tender my resignation as postmaster at this place, and in due form to deliver the great seal and the key to the front door of the office. The safe combination is set on the numbers 33, 66 and 99, though I do not remember at this moment which comes first, or how many times you revolve the knob, or in which direction you should turn it first to make it operate.

There is some mining stock in my private drawer in the safe, which I have not yet removed. It is a luxury, but you may have it. I have decided to keep a horse instead of this mining stock. The horse may not be so pretty, but it will cost less to keep him.

You will find the postal cards that have not been used under the distributing table, and the coal down in the cellar. If the stove draws too hard, close the damper in the pipe and shut the general delivery window.

Looking over my stormy and eventful administration as postmaster here, I find abundant cause for thanksgiving. At the time I entered upon the duties of my office the department was not yet on a paying basis. It was not even self-sustaining. Since that time, with the active coöperation of

Remarks by Bill Nye, pp. 180–182.

the chief executive and the heads of the department, I have been able to make our postal system a paying one, and on top of that I am now able to reduce the tariff on average-sized letters from three cents to two. I might add that this is rather too too, but I will not say anything that might seem undignified in an official resignation which is to become a matter of history.

Acting under the advice of Gen. Hatton, a year ago, I removed the feather bed with which my predecessor, Deacon Hayford, had bolstered up his administration by stuffing the window, and substituted glass. Finding nothing in the book of instructions to postmasters which made the feather bed a part of my official duties, I filed it away in an obscure place and burned it in effigy, also in the gloaming.

It was not long after I had taken my official oath before an era of unexampled prosperity opened for the American people. The price of beef rose to a remarkable altitude, and other vegetables commanded a good figure and a ready market. We then began to make active preparations for the introduction of the strawberry-roan two-cent stamps and the black-and-tan postal note. One reform has crowded upon the heels of another, until the country is to-day upon the foam-crested wave of permanent prosperity.

Mr. President, I cannot close this letter without thanking yourself and the heads of the departments at Washington for your active, cheery and prompt coöperation in these matters. You may do as you see fit, of course, about incorporating this idea into your Thanksgiving proclamation, but rest assured it would not be ill-timed or inopportune. It is not alone a credit to myself. It reflects credit upon the administration also.

I need not say that I herewith transmit my resignation with great sorrow and genuine regret. We have toiled on together month after month, asking for no reward except the innate consciousness of rectitude and the salary as fixed by law. Now we are to separate. Here the roads seem to fork, as it were, and you and I, and the cabinet, must leave each other at this point.

You will find the key under the door-mat, and you had better turn the cat out at night when you close the office. If she does not go readily, you can make it clearer to her mind by throwing the cancelling stamp at her.

If Deacon Hayford does not pay up his box-rent, you might as well put his mail in the general delivery, and when Bob Head gets drunk and insists on a letter from one of his wives every day in the week, you can salute him through the box delivery with an old Queen Anne tomahawk, which you will find near the Etruscan water-pail. This will not in any manner surprise either of these parties.

Tears are unavailing! I once more become a private citizen, clothed only with the right to read such postal cards as may be addressed to me, and to curse the inefficiency of the postoffice department. I believe the voting class to be divided into two parties; viz., those who are in the postal service, and those who are mad because they cannot receive a registered letter every fifteen minutes of each day, including Sunday.

Mr. President, as an official of this Government I now retire. My term of office would not expire until 1886. I must, therefore, beg pardon for my eccentricity in resigning. It will be best, perhaps, to keep the heart-breaking news from the ears of European powers until the dangers of a financial panic are fully past. Then hurl it broadcast with a sickening thud.

Revolutionary Times

Libels and Satires

Libels and Satires
(1775–1815)

These satires and innuendoes of the young Republic exemplify the eighteenth century's practice of attacking or mocking public personages circumspectly enough to avoid criminal charges of libel, challenges to duel, or mob violence against authors, printers, and booksellers alike. Such anonymous or pseudonymous libels and discreet satires persisted well into the nineteenth century, until Seba Smith and others led the way into the gentler age of the crackerbarrel humorists.

The selections begin with a spoofing account of George Washington's first appearance before his troops of the Continental Army after becoming their commander-in-chief. Severely dealt with are General Anthony Wayne by Major John André of the treasonous connection with Benedict Arnold, the revolutionary Sons of Liberty, the agitator Tom Paine, Loyalists equivocating between ties to Crown and menacing mobs, the neutralists and pacifists of the Society of Friends or Quakers, traitor Benedict Arnold, doubtful patriots, King George III, aristocrats disdaining the principles of 1776, and windy congressmen.

The lives of Philip Freneau and Henry Hugh Brackenridge, whose pieces bring this section to a close, were interlocked from their student years together at the College of New Jersey, now Princeton University, during the last years of colonial America, through the struggle for independence, and into the early years of the United States. Freneau, "the poet of the American Revolution," and Brackenridge dedicated their talents to the national cause. Even in the War of 1812, Freneau's ballads and satires traveled far and wide, while Brackenridge's last effort to reduce democracy's absurdities, a sample of which is included herein, was published in 1815.

ANONYMOUS

George Washington
(Tune: "Yankee Doodle")

Away from camp, 'bout three miles off,
　From Lily he dismounted,
His sergeant brush'd his sun-burnt wig
　While he the specie counted.

All prinked up in *full* bag-wig;
　The shaking notwithstanding,
In leathers tight, oh! glorious sight!
　He reach'd the Yankee landing.

Old mother Hancock with a pan
   All crowded full of butter,
Unto the lovely Georgius ran,
   And added to the splutter.

Says she, "Our brindle has just calved,
   And John is wondrous happy.
He sent this present to you, dear,
   As you're the 'country's papa.'"

Full many a child went into camp,
   All dressed in homespun kersey,
To see the greatest rebel scamp
   That ever cross'd o'er Jersey.

Upon a stump, he placed (himself,)
   Great Washington did he,
And through the nose of lawyer Close
   Proclaimed great Liberty.

1775?

Entitled "Adam's Fall," in Frank Moore, ed., *Songs and Ballads of the American Revolution*, New York (1856), pp. 99–102. John Hancock is, of course, the "signer." Lawyer "Close" could be Major General Charles Lee, who journeyed northward with Washington from Philadelphia. For a comprehensive treatment and numerous specimens, including the above, see Bruce Ingham Granger, *Political Satire in the American Revolution, 1763–1783*, Ithaca, N. Y. (1960), pp. 203–204, *et passim*.

JOHN TRUMBULL
[M'Fingal]

Sons of Liberty

For Liberty, in your own by-sense,
Is but for crimes a patent license;
To break of law th' Egyptian yoke,
And throw the world in common stock,
Reduce all grievances and ills
To Magna Charta of your wills;

From dungtills deep of blackest hue,
Your dirt-bred patriots spring to view,
To wealth and power and honor rise,
Like new-wing'd maggots changed to flies.

You've push'd and turn'd the whole world up-
Side down and got yourselves at top,
While all the great ones of your state,
Are crush'd beneath the pop'lar weight.

Your Commonwealth's a common harlot,
The property of every varlet,

Which now in taste, and full employ,
All sorts admire, as all enjoy;
But soon a batter'd strumpet grown,
You'll curse and drum her out of town.

John Trumbull [M'Fingal], *The Poetical Works.* . . , Hartford (1820),
Volume I, pp. 88–94; reprinted in Bruce Ingham Granger, *Political Satire* . . . ,
p. 239.

ANONYMOUS

Tom Paine

Tom mounted on his sordid load,
And bawling, d--n ye, clear the road;
His shovel grasp'd firm in his hands,
Which far and near the street commands,
No hardy mortal dares approach,
Whether on horseback, foot, or coach;
None in his wits the risque would choose,
Who either wears a coat or nose.
  So----in pomp, on Billingsgate,
His arms display'd in burlesque state;
Scurrility and impudence,
Bombast and Bedlam eloquence,
Defiance bids—to COMMON SENSE

This rejoinder to Paine's *Common Sense,* his inflammatory appeal for revolution, appeared in the *Pennsylvania Evening Post,* February 6, 1776; reprinted in Bruce Ingham Granger, *Political Satire* . . . , pp. 244–245.

ANONYMOUS

The Pausing Loyalist

To sign, or not to sign!—That is the question:
Whether 'twere better for an honest man
To sign—and so be safe; or to resolve,
Betide what will, against "associations,"
And by retreating, shun them. To fly—I reck
Not where—and, by that flight, t'escape
Feathers and tar, and thousand other ills
That Loyalty is heir to: 'tis a consummation
Devoutly to be wished. To fly—to want—
To want?—perchance to starve! Ay, there's the rub!
For in that chance of want, what ills may come
To patriot rage when I have left my all,
Must give us pause! . . .

Reprinted in Leonard C. Lewin, ed., *A Treasury of American Political Humor*, New York, Delacorte, 1964, p. 337.

[COMUS]

The Quakers

Our quiet principles compel us
To put no finger to the bellows,
But mind what our forefathers tell us,
Which is, To have no hand therein
Till truth decrees which side shall win.
Yet as the wisest men may fail
To judge which shall at last prevail,
It may most probably occur
That *Friends* like worldly men may err,
And humbly thinking to obey,
The light within, mistake their way.
But error, when it's well design'd,
Is an obedience of the mind,
And shews, in colours clear and strong,
Friends may be right in doing wrong.

It doth suce that we are true
To any side we join unto,
So long, and not a moment longer,
Than truth shall make that side the stronger;
For as the truth can never fail,
Or that which is not truth prevail,

So by the same unerring guide
The strongest is the rightest side,
Which we shall serve with all our might,
Not as the *strongest*—but the *right*—
And all we wish or want to know
Is simply this—*which side is so.*

[Comus], "The Quakers," or "A *MODERN TESTIMONY* for the Year 1778," *Pennsylvania Packet*, September 29, 1778; reprinted in Bruce Ingham Granger, *Political Satire* . . . , p. 255.

ANONYMOUS

The American Vicar of Bray

When Royal George rul'd o'er this land,
And loyalty no harm meant,
For Church and King I made a stand
And so I got preferment. . . .

After repeal of the Stamp Act, however—

I quickly joined the common cry,
That we should all be slaves, Sir;
The House of Commons was a sty;
The King and Lords were knaves, Sir. . . .

*Independence was declared; the outlook was unpromis-
ing, so he—*

Declar'd it was Rebellion base
To take up arms—I curs'd it.
For faith it seem'd a settled case
That we should soon be worsted. . . .

*As the fortunes of war swung back and forth, the Vicar
swung with them, until finally—*

Since Fate has made us great and free,
And Providence can't falter;
So Cong. till death my King shall be,
Unless the times shall alter.

"The American Vicar of Bray," *Royal Gazette,* June 30, 1779, included in Winthrop Sargent, ed., *The Loyalist Poetry of the Revolution,* Philadelphia (1857), pp. 94–98; reprinted with continuity in Leonard C. Lewin, ed., *A Treasury* . . . p. 336.

JOHN ANDRE

Anthony Wayne

"Their fort and block-houses we'll level,
　And deal a horrid slaughter;
We'll drive the scoundrels to the devil,
　And ravish wife and daughter.

"I, under cover of attack,
　Whilst you are all at blows,
From English neighb'rhood and Nyack
　Will drive away the cows;

"For well you know the latter is
　The serious operation,
And fighting with the refugees
　Is only demonstration."

At noon the men, now "drunk as pison," prepare for the
assault.

The sounds confus'd of boasting oaths,
　Re-echo'd through the wood;
Some vow'd to sleep in dead men's clothes,
　And some to swim in blood.

At Irving's nod 'twas fine to see,
  The left prepare to fight;
The while, the drovers, Wayne and Lee,
  Drew off upon the right.

At the blockhouse the "loyal heroes" stand firm against Irving.

Now, as the fight was further fought,
  And balls began to thicken,
The fray assum'd, the generals thought,
  The color of a lickin'.

Yet undismay'd the chiefs command,
  And to redeem the day;
Cry, Soldiers, charge! they hear, they stand,
  They turn and run away.

While Lee is busy driving off the cattle, Wayne is quite willing to be distracted.

For now a prey to female charms,
  His soul took more delight in
A lovely hamadryad's arms,
  Than cow-driving or fighting.

She takes him by the "bridle of his jade" and convinces him that he should give over the expedition.

The hamadryad had but half
  Receiv'd address from Wayne,
When drums and colors, cow and calf,
  Came down the road amain.

And in a cloud of dust was seen
  The sheep, the horse, the goat,
The gentle heifer, ass obscene,
  The yearling and the shoat.

And pack-horses with fowls came by,
  Befeather'd on each side;
Like Pegasus, the horse that I
  And other poets ride.

Sublime upon his stirrups rose
  The mighty Lee behind,
And drove the terror-smitten cows
  Like chaff before the wind.

Suddenly this drove encounters another. It is the fleeing
cavalry, "Irving and terror in the van."

As when two kennels in the street,
  Swell'd with a recent rain,
In gushing streams together meet,
  And seek the neighboring drain;

So met these dung-born tribes in one,
  As swift in their career,
And so to Newbridge they ran on—
  But all the cows got clear.

At this juncture a frantic parson prophesies brighter days
ahead. His words console all save Wayne, who has lost his
horse—

His horse that carried all his prog,
  His military speeches;

His corn-stock whiskey for his grog,
  Blue stockings and brown breeches.

And now I've clos'd my epic strain,
  I tremble as I show it,
Lest this same warrior-drover, Wayne,
  Should ever catch the poet.

"The Cow-Chace," *Royal Gazette*, August 16, 30, and September 23, 1780, printed in Moore's *Songs*, pp. 299–314; reprinted with continuity in Bruce Ingham Granger, *Political Satire . . .* , pp. 215–217. "Irving" is Brigadier General William Irvine, and "Lee" is Major Henry ("Lighthorse Harry") Lee. Parodist John André employing "Chevy Chase" has burlesqued an episode from the earlier bloody warfare between England and Scotland by deriding Wayne's efforts to storm the British blockhouse at Bull's Ferry four miles below Fort Lee on the Hudson and to gather up the neighborhood's cattle in the bargain.

ANONYMOUS

Benedict Arnold

ARNOLD! thy name, as heretofore,
Shall now be Benedict no more;
Since, instigated by the devil,
Thy ways are turn'd from good to evil.

'Tis fit we brand thee with a name,
To suit thy infamy and shame;
And since of treason thou'rt convicted,
Thy name should now be maledicted.

Unless by way of contradiction,
We style thee Britain's Benediction;
Such blessings she, with liberal hand,
Confers on this devoted land.

"Benedict Arnold," *Pennsylvania Packet*, October 24, 1781; reprinted in Bruce Ingham Granger, *Political Satire* . . . p. 268.

PHILIP FRENEAU
[Robert Slender]
(1752-1832)

A Prophecy

When a certain great king, whose initial is G,
Shall force stamps upon paper, and folks to drink tea;
When these folks burn his tea, and stampt paper, like stub-
ble,
You may guess that this king is then coming to trouble.
But when a petition he treads under his feet,
And sends over the ocean an army and fleet;
When that army, half-starved, and frantic with rage,
Shall be coop'd up with a leader whose name rhymes to
cage,
When that leader goes home, dejected and sad,
You may then be assur'd the king's prospects are bad:
But when B and C with their armies are taken,
This king will do well if he saves his own bacon.
In the year seventeen hundred and eighty and two,
A stroke he shall get that will make him look blue;
In the years eighty-three, eighty-four, eighty-five,

You hardly shall know that the king is alive;
In the year eighty-six the affair will be over,
And he shall eat turnips that grow in Hanover.
The face of the lion then shall become pale,
He shall yield fifteen teeth, and be sheer'd of his tail.
O king, my dear king, you shall be very sore,
The Stars and the Lilly shall run you on shore,
And your lion shall growl, but never bite more.

Letter XXIV,
Oyez!!!

Robert Slender, to the aristocrat, the democrat, the would-be-noble, ex-noble, the snug farmer, the lowly plebian, the bishops and clergy, reverend and right reverend, doctors and V. D. M's. little men or title men, gentlemen and simple men, laymen and draymen, and all other men, except hangmen, to whom he hath an aversion, throughout this great and flourishing STATE, sendeth greeting:

Whereas, a great and important day draweth near, in which ye are to exercise a great right, no less than to choose, elect, set apart, solemnly dedicate, appoint, and highly honour, either Thomas M'Kean, chief judge of Pennsylvania, or James Ross, practitioner in law, with the high sounding title, power, and authority, of Governor of this State—Having thrown off his apron, laid aside his tools, and neglected for a small time, the honourable

Freeman's Journal, March 27, 1782, and Philip Freneau, *The Poems of . . . ,* Princeton, N. J. (1902), Volume II, pp. 126–127. King George III and his rare illness, General Thomas Gage commanding Great Britain's forces in America on the eve of the Revolution, General John Burgoyne vanquished at Saratoga by the Americans, Lord Cornwallis defeated at Yorktown, the British Lion, and France's Bourbon lily are referred to in the lines above.

and ancient employment of shoe-*mending,* he hath, on account of the great division, dissension, and contradiction that exists, the fictions, lies, stories, calumnies, misrepresentations, wrong interpretations, addresses, resolutions, assertions, and confutations, thought proper not to address one of you, but all of you, to call upon you in the most solemn, awful, serious, earnest, and interesting manner, to be upon your guard, to open your ears, and attend even to a mender of shoes.

Ye aristocrats, and great men, whether merchants, doctors, proctors, or lawyers, who sigh for greatness, and long for dominion, whose hearts yearn for the glory of a *Crown,* the splendor of a court, or the sweet marrow bones that are to be pick'd in his Majesty's kitchen—whose eyes ache painfully, once again to see the stars, crosses, crescents, coronets, with all the hieroglyphicals, enigmaticals, emblematicals, and all the other cals, including *rascals,* which adorn the court of kings—give a strong, true, and decided vote for James Ross, who supports, approves, hopes for, longs for, and sighs for all these.

Ye bishops and clergy, adorers of the triple crown, the mitre, the sable, the high seat in civil power, the much longed for, an established church, and the ancient and profligate thing called tythes—unite your forces, set *Christianity* at defiance, and give a firm vote for James Ross.

Ye old tories and refugees, British spies, speculators, guides, and pensioners, approvers of British policy, aimers and designers, who in your hearts wish again to crouch under the protecting paw of the British lion—arrange your forces, and give a fair vote for James Ross, he's your sincere friend.

Ye supporters of the British treaty, alien bill, sedition law, stamp act, excise, standing army, funding system, who believe that public debt is a public blessing, who say that republicanism is any thing or nothing, and maintain that treaties made under the sanction of the CONSTITUTION are superior to it—draw near—be not idle on the day of election, support James Ross, he thinks as ye do, acts as you act, and will follow where ye lead.—

Ye democrats, soldiers of '76, ye supporters of our independence, ye quellers of Great Britain, ye Americans, in heart and in hand, draw near, remember Thomas M'Kean is your brother, the firm freeman, and the real Christian—give him your vote.—

Ye free born Americans, whose hearts beat high for liberty and independence, who fear not the threats, and disdain the frown of all the tyrants on earth, assert your right, make known that ye have not forgotten the late struggle, that the mean devices, and shallow arguments of the X. Y. and Z's. of the present day, are not able to trick you out of your liberties, or make you the tools of a foreign despot—vote for Thomas M'Kean, the constant asserter of your rights and liberties.—

Ye honest, ye independent, ye virtuous farmers, who sincerely wish to support that unequalled and glorious instrument, the *Constitution of the United States,* untarnished and unadulterated, that ye may leave it whole and entire, a sacred deposit to posterity—be not inattentive, your best interest is at stake, join not with that troop, but give an honest vote for Thomas M'Kean, the asserter, supporter, and defender of the invaluable rights of his country.—

Ye honest and industrious mechanics, who daily sweat for the support of your families, who, in the hour of danger, are ever found foremost in the ranks to defend your own and your country's rights—remember the *frame* law of the city of Philadelphia, and vote for Thomas M'Kean, whom great men cannot make wink at injustice and oppression.—

Let Porcupine growl, Liston pet, the long list of English agents, speculators, approvers of the fate of Jonathan Robbins, tories, and refugees, gnash their teeth in vain; be true to your country, proof against bribery, true to posterity, true to yourselves—arrange ye under the banners of freedom, and ONCE MORE conquer—let the word be, LIBERTY and M'KEAN.

Philip Freneau [Robert Slender], *Letters on Various Interesting and Important Subjects,* Philadelphia (1799) , pp. 138–142. The divisions between Hamiltonians and Jeffersonians were clearly defined, when Freneau began to write his *Letters* early in 1799. In his vehement "Oyez!" letter, the contending ideals are sharply contrasted in the local Pennsylvania election for the governorship contested by "Tory" James Ross and Democrat Thomas McKean.

HUGH HENRY BRACKENRIDGE
(1748-1816)

Selection from *Modern Chivalry*

How shall we account for this eternal babbling in our
public bodies, which delays and confuses business? Can it
be *French influence?* No. I have no idea that Bonaparte
ever expended a single sous for the purpose of inculcating
this tediousness, or loquacity. The French themselves are
far from being a taciturn people; nevertheless I do not find
reason to believe that it is from an imitation of the French
orators, that this prolixity occurs. There was no great
length of time taken up by the member of the constituent,
or national assembly, when he ascended the Tribune.

Some have thought that it was a proof of the hypothesis
of Darwin, that men have been once magpies, and parrots.
I am of opinion that it resolves itself into one of two natural causes, *want of self-denial,* or want of sense. I know
there are babbling schools at the present time, as there
were at a former period; debating societies among the
manufacturers in towns and villages, as there is in Great
Britain. In some of the New-England seminaries, I am
told, debating and discussing questions is made a part of

the academic exercises. Of this I do not approve, if the students are to take, one, one side, and another a contrary, to whet their wits; and to say what ingenuity prompts, without a reference to the truth, and a just decision of the question. It would vary the exercise, at least that, of the class each should propound a question in his turn on the science which makes the subject of his studies; and the one who explains best, and forms the soundest judgment on the question, and with the greatest brevity expressed, should take the prize. I would commend brevity and truth, not the diffuse harangue, with sophism and errors. This would lay a foundation of eloquence for a legislature. Something ought to be done to correct this logomachy, or war of words, and nothing else. The vox, et preterea nihil is at all times abominable. If those of this class will speak, let them pronounce the word whippor-will a reasonable length of time, and that may suffice. Whippor-will; whippor-will; whippor-will; imitating the sound of that bird, for a quarter of an hour, might pass for a speech. O, how I have wished for a gag or a muzzle, when I have seen four or five columns of a newspaper taken up with verbosity. I would take it off only on condition of giving a good instead of these. The fact is, an amendment of the constitution would be the reducing the ratio of the representation; fewer to speak, there would be less said. Many hands make light work; but this applies to bodily labour only, where a certain object is to be accomplished; such as the removing a fence, or cutting down a wood. Fewer members would do more in a short time; and perhaps would do it better; for though in a multitude of counsellors there is safety; yet if all speak there is delay. Could we not give a power to the chairman, or president of a deliberative body, to knock down a member, when he had seemed to trespass on the patience of the house. At any rate, he might be permitted to give him a wink, or a nod, which it should be understood as a hint to have done. But there is great difficulty in breaking bad habits; and there are some whose tongues, according to the expression of the poet, speaking of a stream,

"Which runs, and runs, and ever will run on."

Things have come to such a pass, that I generally take it for granted, that the man who gives his vote, and says nothing, is the man of sense. Adonizabee, in the scripture, "had three score and ten kings, having their thumbs cut off." Why did he cut off their thumbs? It must have been to keep them from writing out their speeches. At least I have been led to think that it would be a gain to our republic if Adonizabee had *our members of Congress in hands a while.*

Hugh Henry Brackenridge, *Modern Chivalry.* Edited by Claude M. Newlin. New York (1937). Vol. IV, Ch. 16, pp. 801–802.